"America's leading source of self-h
information." ★★★★
—YAHOO!

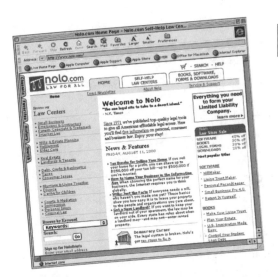

LEGAL INFORMATION ONLINE ANYTIME

24 hours a day

www.nolo.com

AT THE NOLO.COM SELF-HELP LAW CENTER, YOU'LL FIND

- **Nolo's comprehensive Legal Encyclopedia** filled with plain-English information on a variety of legal topics
- **Nolo's Law Dictionary**—legal terms <u>without</u> the legalese
- **Auntie Nolo**—if you've got questions, Auntie's got answers
- **The Law Store**—over 200 self-help legal products including Downloadable Software, Books, Form Kits and eGuides
- **Legal and product updates**
- **Frequently Asked Questions**
- **NoloBriefs,** our free monthly email newsletter
- **Legal Research Center,** for access to state and federal statutes
- **Our ever-popular lawyer jokes**

Quality LAW BOOKS & SOFTWARE FOR EVERYONE

Nolo's user-friendly products are consistently first-rate. Here's why:

- A dozen in-house legal editors, working with highly skilled authors, ensure that our products are accurate, up-to-date and easy to use
- We continually update every book and software program to keep up with changes in the law
- Our commitment to a more democratic legal system informs all of our work
- We appreciate & listen to your feedback. Please fill out and return the card at the back of this book.

OUR "NO-HASSLE" GUARANTEE

Return anything you buy directly from Nolo for any reason and we'll cheerfully refund your purchase price. No ifs, ands or buts.

Read This First

The information in this book is as up-to-date and accurate as we can make it. But it's important to realize that the law changes frequently, as do fees, forms and procedures. If you handle your own legal matters, it's up to you to be sure that all information you use—including the information in this book—is accurate. Here are some suggestions to help you:

First, make sure you've got the most recent edition of this book. To learn whether a later edition is available, check the edition number on the book's spine and then go to Nolo's online Law Store at www.nolo.com or call Nolo's Customer Service Department at 800-728-3555.

Next, even if you have a current edition, you need to be sure it's fully up to date. The law can change overnight. At *www.nolo.com*, we post notices of major legal and practical changes that affect the latest edition of a book. To check for updates, find your book in the Law Store on Nolo's website (you can use the "A to Z Product List" and click the book's title). If you see an "Updates" link on the left side of the page, click it. If you don't see a link, that means we haven't posted any updates. (But check back regularly.)

Finally, we believe accurate and current legal information should help you solve many of your own legal problems on a cost-efficient basis. But this text is not a substitute for personalized advice from a knowledgeable lawyer. If you want the help of a trained professional, consult an attorney licensed to practice in your state.

1st edition

Create Your Own Employee Handbook

A Legal and Practical Guide

by Attorneys Lisa Guerin & Amy DelPo

NOLO

First Edition	APRIL 2003
Editor	ILONA BRAY
Cover Design	TONI IHARA
Book Design	TERRI HEARSH
CD-ROM Preparation	JENYA CHERNOFF
	ANDRÉ ZIVKOVICH
Index	SUSAN CORNELL
Proofreading	ROBERT WELLS
Printing	ARVATO SERVICES, INC.

Guerin, Lisa, 1964-
    Create your own employee handbook : a legal & practical guide / by Lisa Guerin & Amy DelPo
       p. cm.
    Includes index.
    ISBN 0-87337-916-0
    1. Employee orientation. 2. Employees--Training of. I. DelPo, Amy, 1967- II. Title.
    HF5549.5.I53D45 2003
    658.3'01--dc21

                 2003042107

For information on bulk purchases or corporate premium sales, please contact the Special Sales Department. For academic sales or textbook adoptions, ask for Academic Sales. Call 800-955-4775 or write to Nolo at 950 Parker Street, Berkeley, CA 94710.

Acknowledgments

The authors would like to thank the following people who helped to make this book possible:

- Our editor, Ilona Bray, whose good humor and easy nature made the editing process fun—and whose words and insights never failed to improve upon what we gave her
- Mary Randolph, for helping us in the beginning to mold and formulate our vision of this book
- Nolo jack-of-all-trades Stan Jacobson, who tirelessly haunted libraries throughout the Bay Area to meet our research needs
- Andre Zivkovich and Jenya Chernoff, who managed to take our printed pages and turn them into a CD-ROM that people could use on their computers
- Terri Hearsh, for working with us on a wonderful book design, and
- Robert Wells, for his meticulous proofing.

In addition, Amy would like to dedicate her work on this book to her daughter, Sophia, whose early birth delayed this book by almost half a year. She is everything and more.

About the Authors

Lisa Guerin worked for Nolo as a research and editorial assistant during her years as a law student at Boalt Hall School of Law. After a stint as a staff attorney at the U.S. Court of Appeals for the Ninth Circuit, Lisa worked primarily in the field of employment law, in both government and private practice. Lisa has litigated on behalf of her clients in all levels of state and federal courts and in agency proceedings. Lisa recently returned to Nolo as an editor, where she specializes in employment law and civil litigation.

Amy DelPo practiced law for six years before leaving the day-to-day grind of lawsuits to join Nolo's editorial staff in 2000. As an attorney, she specialized in employment law and general civil litigation, representing her clients in all levels of state and federal courts. At Nolo, she continues her work in the field of employment law, authoring and editing a number of books on the subject, including the best-selling *The Employer's Legal Handbook*, by Fred Steingold. She also added retirement planning and independent contractor law to her fields of expertise, editing a number of books on these subjects.

Together, the authors have written *Dealing with Problem Employees, Everyday Employment Law: The Basics* and Federal *Employment Laws: A Desk Reference*, all published by Nolo.

Table of Contents

8 Employee Benefits

9 Use of Company Property

10 Leave and Time Off

16 Employee Records

17 Drugs and Alcohol

18 Trade Secrets and Conflicts of Interest

19 Discrimination and Harassment

20 Complaint Policies

21 Ending Employment

Appendix

A How to Use the CD-ROM

B Model Handbook

C Where to Go for Further Information

Index

Introduction

If you're like most employers, you (or people who work for you) probably devote a good part of every day to employee relations. You may find yourself making decisions or relaying information about everything from benefits to vacation time to disciplinary problems. Sometimes, you may know the answer right away ("You get ten vacation days"); other times, you may have to think a bit or come up with something new ("What *is* our policy on paternity leave?").

In such situations, a good employee handbook is as essential as any real live member of your management team. It knows all the answers—and it communicates them clearly to your employees. Indeed, an employee handbook can do a lot for you, such as:

- save you time by cutting down on the number of questions employees ask every day
- ensure that you treat your employees consistently, and
- give you legal protection when an employment relationship goes sour.

We talk more about these benefits in Section A, below; we explain how this book can help you create an effective handbook in Section B.

A. What an Employee Handbook Can Do for Your Business

Simply defined, an employee handbook is a written document describing the benefits and responsibilities of the employment relationship. In reality, however, the handbook's role is much more complex and powerful. While it sits quietly on the shelf, the employee handbook can actually help you manage and control your relationship with your employees.

1. The Purposes of an Employee Handbook

An employee handbook is an indispensable workplace tool, because it can help you communicate with your employees, manage your workforce (and your managers), streamline your organization and protect your business from lawsuits. We cover each of these benefits in detail below.

a. Communication

Your handbook tells your employees what your company expects from them and what they can expect from the company. "What time do I have to be at work?" "Does my employer provide health insurance?" "How do I complain about my supervisor's sexual advances?" A well-drafted handbook will answer all of these questions and many more.

In addition to relaying basic information about benefits, hours and pay, your employee handbook imparts your company's culture, values and history. When was your company founded? Why do you think it is successful? What attitude do you want your employees to take towards their jobs and customers?

As you take our standard policies and modify them to suit your workplace, remember this most basic and obvious aspect of employee handbooks: Through the written policies, you are talking to your employees. Make sure you are saying what you want to say in the way you want to say it.

b. Management

Workers are not mind readers. Although you may know what your practices and policies are, without a handbook, employees, managers and supervisors have no place to turn for this information. This creates an environment ripe for trouble, both legal and practical. Employee morale will drop if some employees are treated differently from others, and you might find yourself involved in a discrimination lawsuit if employees think that this inconsistent treatment is based on race, gender or some other protected characteristic.

Handbooks promote positive employee relations by ensuring that all of your employees get treated consistently and fairly. They prevent misunderstandings, confusion and complaints by giving everyone in your workplace the same resource for learning your personnel practices. If there is ever any doubt or dispute about a particular policy, you can simply open the book and take a look. You don't need to have long, agonizing discussions or try to reinvent the wheel.

c. Planning

The process of creating your handbook will force you to think about every aspect of your relationship with your employees. Rather than doing things just because that's the way they've always been done, you can reflect on how you have been treating your employees and decide whether any changes are in order. For each policy, ask yourself: Do I really want to continue doing things this way? If so, why?

Creating an employee handbook necessarily requires you to communicate with, and get feedback from, supervisors and employees about your current personnel practices. In this way, you learn what works and what doesn't, what is enhancing employee morale and what is dampening it.

d. Legal Protection

Just having a handbook on your shelf can help you comply with the law and cut your risk of lawsuits:

- Some laws require employers to communicate certain information to their employees. The handbook provides you with a convenient place to put this information.
- Even when you aren't required to give information to your employees, there are times when you can protect yourself by providing it. For example, no law requires you to tell your employees how to complain about sexual harassment, but if you do, you can use the complaint policy as a defense should someone ever sue you. (You can find a sexual harassment policy in Chapter 19.)
- Your policies can affirm your commitment to equal employment opportunity laws. This is one step toward creating a tolerant and discrimination-free workplace—something that most employers are legally obligated to do. (You can find standard equal employment opportunity policies in Chapter 3.)

- In certain situations, your company will be responsible for the actions of its employees and supervisors who violate the law, even if the company did not condone or even know about the illegal conduct. Cut down the risk of unlawful behavior by providing guidance and prohibitions in your handbook.

Perhaps the most important reason to have an employee handbook is to protect your legal right to terminate employees at will. In theory, you already have this right. Unless you have entered into a contract with an employee promising something else, your relationship with that employee is automatically at will—meaning you can terminate the employment relationship at any time for any reason that is not illegal, and the employee can do the same.

However, the absence of a written contract doesn't fully protect you. You can inadvertently destroy your right to terminate at will by creating an *implied* contract with your employees, promising not to fire them unless you have a legitimate business reason. Some employers with badly written handbooks have gotten burned over this issue. Courts have found that certain statements in their handbooks—including that employees will only be fired for certain reasons, that employees won't be fired if they are doing a good job or that employees are considered "permanent"—created implied contracts that limited the employers' right to fire at will. (For more on at-will employment and implied contracts, see Chapter 2.)

In this book, we help you avoid this trap by providing you with standard policies that steer clear of any promises of continued employment and by providing disclaimers that specifically state that employment relationships at your company are at will.

2. What an Employee Handbook Is Not

Your handbook can do a lot, but it can't do everything, nor should it. As we explain more fully in this section, a handbook is just one piece of your employee relations picture. It's up to you, your managers and supervisors to provide the other pieces.

a. Your Handbook Is No Substitute for You

Although your handbook is an important communication tool, it cannot take the place of one-on-one personal interaction between you and the people who work for you. If you want good employee relations—that is, if you want your employees to trust you and feel loyal to you—your employee handbook can help, but it can't do the job on its own. Your employees need a human face behind the policies. They need to see and hear from you and to feel that you are interested in them and the job they are doing.

b. Your Handbook Is No Substitute for Good Practices

No matter how many policies you write, they won't do you any good unless you follow them. In fact, they might actually do some harm.

From a practical standpoint, personnel practices that are inconsistent with written policies can damage employee relations. Employees who read one thing but experience another won't trust—or feel loyal to—their employer.

From a legal standpoint, you are courting trouble if you don't deliver what you promise in your handbook. Even though you will have disclaimers in your handbook telling employees that the handbook is not a contract (see Chapter 1 for these disclaimers), you can't predict when a judge or jury will think differently and try to hold you to your words—or at least make you pay for not following them. For these reasons, you should include in your handbook only those policies that you are prepared to follow.

c. Your Handbook Is Not a Personnel Policy Manual

Employee handbooks are written in general terms, for use by employees. A policy or procedures manual, on the other hand, is a detailed guide that sets out very specifically how supervisors and managers are to do their jobs in your company. Usually, employees are not allowed access to these manuals.

You may wonder why you can't just have one book for both audiences. There are a number of reasons:

- There might be sensitive information (on pay scales, for example) that you don't necessarily want to reveal to your employees.
- Employees don't need to know every little detail of how things are done. If you throw too much information at your employees—some of it irrelevant to their day-to-day work—they might get overwhelmed and not read the handbook at all.
- The details of how you implement policies are more likely to change than the general policies themselves. If you put these details in your handbook, you limit your ability to change how things are done.

B. Who Can Use This Book

This book is for business owners, managers, supervisors and human resource professionals in any size company, from a small outfit with only a handful of employees to a large corporation. It is also appropriate for virtually every industry, from manufacturing to sales to service provision.

There are two types of workplaces for which this book won't work: public workplaces (that is, workplaces with federal, state or local government employees) and unionized workplaces.

C. Icons Used in This Book

To aid you in using this book, we use the following icons:

 The caution icon warns you of potential problems.

 This icon indicates that the information is a useful tip.

 This icon refers you to helpful books or other resources.

 This icon indicates when you should consider consulting an attorney or other expert.

 This icon refers you to a further discussion of the topic somewhere else in this book.

■

How to Use This Book

If you're eager to be the proud owner of an employee handbook, we should warn you that there is a catch. Well, two catches: Handbooks don't write themselves, and there is no such thing as a "one size fits all" handbook. You can't simply purchase a generic handbook, slap your company's name on the cover and distribute it to your employees. If you want an effective handbook for your workplace, you are going to have to sit down and actually create it, with policies and language that reflect your company's culture, values and personnel practices.

Don't despair, however. We've designed this book to make the process easy and straightforward, taking you step by step through planning, writing and distributing a handbook. Using this book, you can create an employee handbook that's tailored to your company's needs, with minimal time and headaches.

In this chapter, we:

- explain what you'll find in the different parts of this book (Section A)
- advise you on what information you'll need to obtain from other sources (Section B), and
- instruct you on each phase of the handbook creation process, from gathering the information you'd like to include in your handbook to picking a distribution method once your handbook is complete (Section C).

Don't jump right to the CD-ROM. The CD-ROM contains all of the standard policies and modifications discussed in this book. However, you cannot simply print out those policies verbatim and distribute them to your employees. If you do that, you will have wasted your money, for you will end up with a handbook that doesn't accurately reflect your workplace. Read the discussions that accompany each handbook section in this book first, then cut and paste what you need.

A. What You'll Find in This Book

This book is both a workbook and a guidebook. The heart of the book (Chapters 1 through 21) contains a combination of important material. First, it contains prewritten personnel policies that you'll be able to cut and paste (and modify, if necessary), policy by policy, into the handbook you're creating. Along with these prewritten policies, however, these chapters provides valuable explanatory material, including:

- background information
- guidance to help you decide whether you want to include that policy in your handbook
- standard language that you can cut and paste into your handbook (or, if there is no standard way to word a policy, an example of what such policies look like and detailed guidance on writing your own from scratch)
- instructions on completing the standard policy with information specific to your workplace
- when appropriate, modifications that you can use to change the standard policy to suit your needs
- information on potential trouble spots, both practical and legal, and
- advice on when to consult an attorney for more assistance.

When you're ready to start compiling your handbook, you'll find the prewritten portions on the CD-ROM at the back of this book. Instructions for using the CD-ROM are in Appendix A.

To see an example of what all the prewritten policies look like once they're pulled together, see the model handbook in Appendix B.

Finally, Appendix C gives you information on where to go for more assistance.

B. What You Won't Find in This Book

This book is not a treatise on employment law. To keep it trim and to the point, we assume that our readers already have personnel practices in place. This book helps you communicate those practices to your employees; it does not help you choose those practices in the first place. For example, we provide you with a policy that warns employees that they might have to take a drug test, but we don't go into detail on when to conduct drug tests or how to conduct them so that they comply with your state's laws.

Thus, before you start creating a handbook from this book, you need to know—or find out—your legal obligations as an employer in your state. If you need help understanding employment law and how you should treat your employees, other books will meet that need, including the following two from Nolo:

- *The Employer's Legal Handbook,* by Attorney Fred Steingold.
- *Everyday Employment Law: The Basics,* by Attorneys Amy DelPo & Lisa Guerin.

C. The Creation Process

By now, you've probably gotten our message that creating a handbook requires more than simply stringing together a bunch of boilerplate paragraphs. It takes planning and research. Don't worry, however. It doesn't have to be a time-consuming or arduous task. With a little investigation, you can put together your handbook in no time. Let's talk about how to start the process (Section 1), your formatting options (Section 2), revising and updating the handbook (Section 3) and distributing the handbook to your employees (Section 4).

1. In the Beginning

The very first thing you must do is to put someone in charge of creating your handbook. If you own a small business, that someone will be one or two people—perhaps you, perhaps an office manager. In larger companies, it might make sense to assign this task to a group of people. Whomever you choose should be familiar with your employment practices and should have the power to decide what to include in the handbook. From here on, when we refer to "you," we are referring to the person or people creating the handbook.

We suggest the following three-step process for creating your handbook:

- investigate
- compile and write, and
- review and revise.

Now let's look at each step in detail.

Step 1: Investigate

Before you can communicate your policies to your employees, you must know precisely what those policies are. This is often more complex than it sounds. Policy is really just a word for how you treat your employees, and how you treat your employees is often determined informally and inconsistently—especially in a small business. Let's say, for example, that your secretary, whom you think the world of, was in a car accident last year and you paid her salary for the two months it took her to rehabilitate. Does this mean that everyone in your company is entitled to two months of paid sick leave? Or only people who are in car accidents? Or only people whom you like?

The situation can be even worse in large companies, where supervisors are in charge of employees' day-to-day work lives. Different supervisors do things differently, so you may have as many variations of a policy as you have supervisors.

Of course, once you have a handbook in place, these inconsistencies won't be a problem. For now, however, you must put on your Perry Mason hat and figure out how personnel matters are being handled. We suggest the following:

- interview managers and supervisors
- distribute a questionnaire to managers and supervisors
- consult your current personnel policies manual (if you have one)
- consult old handbooks and policy manuals (if they exist)
- obtain handbooks from competitors in your area
- distribute a questionnaire to employees
- talk to people in your human resources department and your payroll department
- consult with your benefits administrator and office manager, and
- review bulletin board notices, memos, newsletters and employee complaints.

The chapters and headings in this book can help you structure your interviews or questionnaires. We recommend scanning them to remind yourself of the various categories that you need to inquire into, from work hours to benefits to complaints procedures.

Step 2: Compile and Write

When you sit down to actually create the policies, you will start with the standard policies and modifications that we provide here. By reading our explanatory text, you'll be able to decide whether to include that policy in your handbook—and what the policy should include. For the most part, this will be a straightforward cut and paste job. However, when you need to modify policies or write them from scratch, keep these rules in mind:

- use simple vocabulary
- use short sentences
- don't use legalese or jargon
- keep paragraphs short
- be clear and concise
- use language that reflects the culture of your company (for example, formal or informal)
- write to the education and sophistication level of your employees
- use terms consistently

- emphasize the positive aspects of any policy, and
- where appropriate, briefly explain the rationale behind the policy.

Step 3: Review and Revise

All managers and supervisors should read the initial draft of the handbook and give feedback. After all, they are the ones on the front lines, dealing with the employees every day—and they are the ones who are going to have to actually enforce the policies you've chosen. They can alert you to inconsistencies or to policies that won't work in the real world. They can also tell you when your writing is unclear or misleading. And they might be able to recommend new or different policies.

2. Formatting the Handbook

Once you have a final draft of your handbook, the next step is deciding how it should look. We suggest grouping your policies into chapters by topic (for example, your handbook might have a benefits chapter and a payroll chapter). This book presents the standard policies in chapters by topic. You can use our organization or come up with your own. Here are some other formatting tips:

- **Include a table of contents at the beginning of your handbook.** Since your handbook's most common use will probably be to answer employees' specific question, a table of contents helps assure that they'll find the answers.
- **Include an index at the end.** This is also helpful for employees who can't find what they're looking for.
- **Start each policy on a new page.** This enables employees to insert updates and remove old policies without disturbing the surrounding policies.
- **Double space the text of policies.** This makes them easier to read.
- **Give each policy its own bold-faced heading.**
- **Don't use page numbers.** Instead, number your policies by chapter (for example, a policy numbered "1:3" is the third policy in the first chapter). You'll notice that we number our policies in this way as well. This method enables employees to remove old policies and insert new ones without ruining the handbook's pagination. If you want to insert a policy where there wasn't one before, you can use letters (for example, "1:3a").

- **Put the policies in a three-ring binder.** This allows employees to insert new policies or replace old policies when instructed to do so. Not only does this method make it easy to revise policies, it saves you money, because you invest in the binder only once.

3. Revising and Updating

You have the right to revise and update your handbook at any time. We recommend reviewing it once a year to determine which policies need to be revised or updated. Usually, policies must be revised for one of two reasons: (1) because your personnel practices have changed, or (2) because the law has changed.

If only one or two policies need to be revised, it's easy enough to distribute the new policy to employees, with instructions to remove the old policy and insert the new one in its place. Require employees to return the old policy to you. That way, you know that they actually updated the book and didn't simply drop the new policy in the recycling bin.

Over time, you will see that more and more of the policies in your book are revised policies and not the original ones. You may also notice that the language or tone of the original policies has become outdated or stale. When this happens, it's time to consider revising the entire handbook and handing out a new edition to your employees.

4. Distributing Your Handbook

Once your employee handbook is complete, it's time to distribute it to your workforce. The best way to do this—particularly if your company has never had a handbook or hasn't had one for a long time—is to hold a meeting.

Call all of your employees together (or, if this is impossible, hold a series of meetings and require each of your employees to attend one). At the meeting, explain that the company has a new employee handbook to set forth the company's policies. Let your employees know that you expect each of them to read the handbook and abide by its contents. And tell everyone that you want them to sign a form acknowledging that they have received the handbook (this important form is contained in Chapter 2).

Once you distribute the handbooks, stick around for a while to answer any employee questions. And make sure to pass out the

Handbook Acknowledgment Forms and ask employees to sign them.

When you hire new employees, give them a copy of the handbook—and ask them to sign the acknowledgment form—during their orientation meeting or when they fill out their other first-day paperwork. ■

1

Handbook Introduction

Your handbook's introductory statements will be the first policies your employees read, so they will set the tone for everything else to come. For this reason, they should be friendly and non-threatening, easing employees into the drier—and sometimes less pleasant—information that will follow. Envision the handbook as a pleasant tour leader, personally guiding employees through your company. Employees will be more receptive to—and pay more attention to—a handbook that that they perceive as warm and friendly than one that feels impersonal and cold.

Start by introducing your employees to your company, its history, products and goals. You'd be surprised how many long-term employees—let alone employees whom you've just hired—don't know this basic information. Your handbook can be an effective way of indoctrinating your employees into your company's culture and values. This knowledge can inform everything the employees do at your company—from choosing how to deal with customers and vendors to deciding what standard of quality to apply to their own work.

Depending on the type of company, some employers might want to make the policies in this chapter more formal, and some might want to make them more casual. Regardless of the level of formality you choose, however, try to make the tone as pleasant and friendly as possible.

The following are the policies that we address in this chapter:

1:1   Welcoming Statement

Though it's not a legal requirement, we recommend you begin your handbook by welcoming employees to your company. After all, the vast majority of your employees will only read the handbook from cover to cover at the beginning of their employment with you. Thereafter, they will only look at it in bits and pieces, finding the information that they need and nothing more.

A hearty welcome can quickly and effectively establish the friendly tone that you want to convey. An effective welcoming statement is positive and upbeat, and it begins the process of selling your company to your employees.

Standard Policy

Welcome to Our Company!

It's our pleasure to welcome you to _____[Company name]_____. We're an energetic and creative bunch, dedicated to high standards of excellence and quality. We value each one of our employees, and we hope that you find your work here rewarding and satisfying.

This section introduces you to our Company's history, purpose and goals. Please read it carefully so that you can better understand who we are and what we do. We think we are a special place—made all the more so by the hard work and dedication of our employees.

Optional Modification to Add Company-Specific Information

This welcome will be even more effective if you add some concrete information about your company. Although some of this information will overlap with information you include in your introduction and history sections (see Policies 1.2 and 1.3, below), it doesn't hurt to give employees a preview here. Consider mentioning:

- How long your company has been in existence. For example: *We're an energetic and creative bunch, dedicated to high standards of excellence since 1902 when the Martinez family first opened this company's doors at 311 Main Street.*

- The services or products that your company provides. For example: *Our company has dedicated itself to providing superior printing services since 1902.*
- A description of your company's culture. For example: *As a family-owned company, we run a casual operation where people feel free to decorate their workspaces and wear clothes that reflect their personality. Don't let the informality fool you, however. We demand excellence from ourselves and our employees, and we consider ourselves to be the premier printing company in the Tri-State Area.*

If you do add company-specific information to this welcome statement, keep it brief. Your employees will be getting more detailed information from the policies that follow.

⚠ Don't make big promises in your handbook. Assuming you choose to include a welcoming statement, be careful not to say anything that could create an implied contract with your employees promising to terminate them only for cause. (See Chapter 2 for more about implied contracts and termination for cause.) Avoid statements that promise employees a long future at the company or that describe your company as a "family."

1:2   Introduction to the Company

The beginning pages of your handbook are a great place to briefly introduce employees to your company's background, history and culture. (You will delve into your company's history in more detail later. See Policy 1:3, below.) In your Introduction, you can speak directly to your employees and present your company as you want it presented.

During employees' day-to-day existence at your company, information about your company's values and goals will trickle down to them from supervisors, managers, coworkers and customers. Unfortunately, this means that sometimes employees will hear things about your company that aren't true or that are distorted by the prejudices and personalities of the people around them. If these are an employee's first impressions of your company, they will be hard for you to undo. The Introduction is your opportunity to get in the first word about your company—to make a good first impression.

Unfortunately, there is no standard policy language that we can provide to you, because each company is unique. Here is an example of what a typical Introduction looks like:

SAMPLE POLICY LANGUAGE: Juanita Jones founded this company in 1978 on a very basic principle: Customers will pay for exceptional service and knowledge. Using that principle as her beacon, she took a small independent book store and created a chain of 300 stores serving customers throughout the Western United States.

Here at J&J Books, we continue to believe that a knowledgeable and courteous staff can sell more books than discount prices can. For this reason, we encourage our employees to read the publishing and literary magazines that you will find in the break room, to use your employee discount to buy and read as many books as possible and to take advantage of our tuition reimbursement program to take literature and writing classes at local colleges. When our customers come to you with questions, we want you to be able to answer them—with a smile.

We know that only happy and relaxed employees can give the quality and good-natured service that our customers demand. So take all of the breaks you are scheduled for, alert your manager to any problems in your work area and communicate any ideas you might have for making this a better place to work.

At J&J Books, we want our employees to put the customer first. That's why we, in management, put our employees first. We know that we are only as good as you are.

Drafting Your Own Policy

All sorts of information can go into your Introduction, from a heart-felt description of your company's values to an inventory of the products you produce. When you write this policy, imagine sitting across from a single employee. What do you want this person to know about your company? What do you think the essence of your company is? What sort of attitude do you want this employee to have toward customers and clients? What information about your company would be useful to this employee in doing the job?

Consider including the following information in this policy:

- The values that you think are most important to your company's success—for example, customer service, product quality, high-speed productivity. Be as concrete as possible. Do you always do what the customer wants, no matter how much time and effort it takes? Do you try to fill all orders within one day? Do you always redo orders, no questions asked, if a customer complains?
- An explanation of why each of the values you've set out are important to your company's success.
- Any goals you have for your company—for example, doubling sales in the next decade or lowering operating costs.
- A description of the values and goals that you want each employee to have—for example, perhaps it's more important that employees develop friendly relationships with customers than that they pressure customers into making purchases they don't really need.
- A description of your company culture.
- A description of the products your company produces or the services it provides.
- An organizational chart for your company.

1:3   History of the Company

The more pride your employees take in your company as a whole, the more pride they will take in their performance as individual employees. Telling the history of your company is one way to instill this pride. It can make employees feel like they are part of something special.

In addition, knowing this history can make employees more effective in their jobs. Anecdotes about your company's noble beginnings can help your employees sell your company to customers and clients. Funny stories from your company's past can make the company seem more human and friendly.

Although you may have previewed this information in the Introduction and Company Culture (see Policies 1.1 and 1.2, above), now is the time to go into more detail.

Unfortunately, there is no standard policy language that we can provide to you, because each company is unique. Here is an example of what this kind of policy might look like:

SAMPLE POLICY LANGUAGE: In 1855, Dante DeMarco opened this newspaper's doors at 111 Main Street—right between City Hall and the county courthouse. It was a fitting geographic location for Dante, who always kept both eyes peeled for scandal and corruption among the city's power elite. While he ran this newspaper, he lived and breathed the journalist's creed: "Afflict the comfortable and comfort the afflicted." He often said his proudest moment was the day Mayor Lou Mixon was forced to resign because of the great Black and Tan Scandal of 1925, a scandal uncovered and publicized by "DeMarco's Moles," as the reporters were then called. "I would have gotten away with it if it hadn't been for that meddling paper," Mixon was heard to say on his way up the jailhouse steps.

Here at the Daily Conscience and News, we still believe in the ideals that won this newspaper three Pulitzer Prizes (the first for the Black and Tan Scandal). As Dante said, we must be the conscience of the city. We want reporters with suspicious and inquisitive minds and editors who won't breath easy until a story is just right. We are committed to hiring the highest quality staff. We will provide whatever resources our employees need to keep their work at the highest level. We will never bow to pressure from advertisers or civic leaders. In short, we will continue to be the daily conscience of Cedar Falls.

Drafting Your Own Policy

Try to entertain your employees; tell them a good story. Get them hooked on your company—its past and its future. Be as specific as possible. Use concrete details like names, dates and amounts. If you have pictures from the early days, include them.

In writing your history, don't forget the values and goals that you laid out in the Introduction to the Company section (see Policy 1:2, above). If you can, use the history to illustrate those values—to show where they came from.

1:4   Handbook Purpose

Every employer should include a purpose statement in the hand-book. After all, what's the use of a handbook if the employees don't read it? From the beginning, you must make it clear to your employees that you expect them to read the whole handbook—and to incorporate the information they read into their work.

There is also a legal reason to have this policy. As we explained in the Introduction to this book, one of the biggest risks of using an employee handbook is that a judge or jury might view it as a contract and hold you to what it says. One way to minimize this risk is to plainly state that the handbook is not a contract and to emphasize to employees that the policies can change at any time, for any reason and without warning.

Standard Policy

The Purpose of This Handbook

We think that employees are happier and more valuable if they know what they can expect from our Company and what our Company expects from them. In the preceding sections, we introduced you to our Company's history, values, culture and goals. We expect you to incorporate that information into your day-to-day job performance, striving to meet our Company's values in everything you do.

The remainder of this Handbook will familiarize you with the privileges, benefits and responsibilities of being an employee at _____[Company name]_____ . Please understand that this Handbook can only highlight and summarize our Company's policies and practices. For detailed information, you will have to talk to your supervisor or _____.

In this Company, as in the rest of the world, circumstances are constantly changing. As a result, we may have to revise, rescind or supplement these policies from time to time. Nothing in this Handbook is a contract or a promise. The policies can change at any time, for any reason, without warning.

We are always looking for ways to improve communications with our employees. If you have suggestions for ways to improve this Handbook in particular or employee relations in general, please feel free to bring them to _____.

How to Complete This Policy

Of course, no handbook can anticipate all of the questions and concerns that your employees might have. For this reason, you must designate people at your company to whom your employees can go for more information. If you have a very small company, there might be only one member of management: You. In larger companies, there might be several levels of management to choose from. Adjust this policy to reflect the situation at your company. If possible, name two people to whom employees can turn (for example, a supervisor and a human resources director). That way, employees have a choice: If they are uncomfortable with one of their options, they can pick the other. Of course, if you have a small company, there may only be one appropriate person. That's fine, too.

Because it is so important that your employees read the handbook, we also suggest that you require them to sign a Handbook Acknowledgment Form. You can find a copy of that form and a related discussion in Chapter 2.

⚠ **Monitoring the bulletin board.** If you allow employees to post information on your bulletin board, you open yourself up to complaints and legal entanglements over what you allow, and do not allow, employees to post. For example, the federal National Labor Relations Act requires you to allow employees to post information about union activities if you also allow them to post information about other things. If you don't want to have union information in your workplace, then you should not allow employees any access to your bulletin boards at all. In other words, if you open the door for information you like, then you will have to open it for some information you don't like, as well.

On the other hand, you have a duty to keep employees from posting offensive, harassing and discriminating things on the bulletin board. If problematic material slips through, you will be liable for it because it is on your official board. Only allow employees access to the board if you feel up to the task of monitoring postings for this type of material.

1:5 Bulletin Board

Many employers use a company bulletin board to communicate with their employees about various events, laws and rules—and to inform employees about changes to information in the handbook. Typical bulletin board postings include legally required notices about equal employment opportunity laws and wage laws, flyers about special company events and an organizational chart.

If you have a company bulletin board, include in the introductory section of your handbook a policy that alerts employees to the board's existence, instructs employees to periodically read the board and identifies who is allowed to put things on the board.

Standard Policy

Be Sure to Check Out Our Bulletin Board

You can find important information about this Company and your employment posted on the bulletin board located at _____. This is also the place where we post important information regarding your legal rights, including information about equal employment opportunity laws and wage and hour laws. We expect all employees to periodically read the information on the bulletin board.

Because this bulletin board is our way of communicating with employees, we do not allow anyone but managers and Company officials to post information there.

Optional Modification to Allow Employee Postings

Some companies like to allow their employees to post information on company bulletin boards. If you would like to do so, substitute the following modification for the last paragraph of the standard policy, above:

Modification

If you would like to communicate information to your coworkers, consider using the Company bulletin board. To post something, you must first give it to _____ for approval. Employee notices may only stay on the bulletin board for 90 days. After that period, they will be removed.

At-Will Protections

One of the first—and probably the most important—policies to include in your handbook is an at-will statement. This policy confirms that your employees work at will: that is, you can fire them at any time and for any reason that is not illegal and they can quit at any time they like. This policy gives you some very important legal protection against lawsuits. If an employee sues you, claiming that your handbook, your unwritten personnel practices or statements by your company managers constituted a promise that he or she would not be fired except for good cause, an at-will policy in your handbook will be your best defense.

The law generally presumes that your employees work at will unless they can prove otherwise. As evidence, they'll need to show that they entered into an employment contract with you that changed the at-will relationship. If you enter into a *written* employment contract that limits your right to fire an employee—such as a contract that the employee will work for you for a specified period of time, or a contract stating that the employee may only be fired for specified reasons (misconduct, criminal behavior or good cause are common examples)—that employee no longer works at will. These written contracts won't be affected by the sample at-will policy we provide—and you don't want them to be. In those relatively rare situations when you really need an employee to come on board (or stay there) for a set period of time, offering an employment contract that limits your right to fire will help you seal the deal.

If an at-will policy sounds harsh to you, remember that it will help you preserve your managerial prerogatives over the rest of your workforce. Even if employees don't have written contracts of employment, they can still argue that you promised, either outright or by implication, not to fire them without good cause. These employees will point to conversations with managers ("He said I would always have a position with the company, as long as my sales numbers were strong"), your personnel practices ("The

Need more information on at-will employment and employment contracts? You can find it in *Dealing with Problem Employees*, by Amy DelPo & Lisa Guerin (Nolo), which explains at-will employment in detail. It also covers employment contracts, including the kinds of evidence an employee might use to try to prove that you made an implied contract (and tips on how to avoid creating this evidence in the first place). The book also contains a sample at-will offer letter that you can modify for use in your own company.

company has never fired someone without a good reason") or official company statements ("At ABC company, we believe that our employees are our greatest asset—and we treat them accordingly") to argue that they had an unwritten contract of employment that limits your right to fire at will.

Throughout this book, we show you how to write policies that will not undermine your at-will rights. But legal claims could still arise—"oral contract" claims if the employee argues that you made an explicit promise limiting your right to fire, or "implied contract" claims if the employees argues that your statements and actions indicated that you had limited your right to fire. To defeat these claims, you will need something more than an at-will policy. You'll also need a form for your employees to sign agreeing to their at-will status. You'll find both in this chapter, where, we cover:

2:1   At-Will Policy

Your at-will policy should clearly state that you retain the right to fire employees at will and that nothing in your handbook constitutes a contract or promise to the contrary. You should also designate someone (or more than one person) who is solely authorized to make employment contracts on behalf of the company—this will allow you to relinquish your at-will rights if you need or want to for a particular employee.

Standard Policy

Employment Is At Will

We are happy to welcome you to [*Company name*]. We sincerely hope that your employment here will be a positive and rewarding experience. However, we cannot make any guarantees about your continued employment at [*Company name*]. Your employment here is at will. This means that you are free to quit at any time, for any reason, just as we are free to terminate your employment at any time, for any reason—with or without notice, with or without cause.

No employee or company representative, other than _____ _____, has the authority to change the at-will employment relationship or to contract with any employee for different terms of employment. Furthermore, _____ may change the at-will employment relationship only in a written contract, signed by _____ and the employee. Nothing in this Handbook constitutes a contract or promise of continued employment.

Who Needs This Policy

Some employers, particularly small businesses, "mom and pop" enterprises and companies with trusted, long-term employees, wonder if they want an at-will policy. After all, they are not planning to fire workers without a good reason, so why adopt a policy that says they can? The reason is simply to hedge your bets. Even if you never plan to act without good cause, your safest course of action is to adopt an at-will policy that preserves your right to do so, just in case. If a worker you fire decides to challenge your decision in a lawsuit, you won't have to prove that you had good cause for your actions—you can simply point to your at-will policy. Most judges will be easily convinced to throw out the worker's contract claim very early on in the lawsuit, saving you from spending a lot of time and money justifying your decisions.

And the truth is, employers cannot know ahead of time that they will never have to rely on an at-will policy. Sometimes, an employee just doesn't work out, for reasons that you can't quite put your finger on or couldn't prove conclusively in court. If you have a clear at-will policy, you can simply fire that worker and move on. If you don't, your safest legal bet might be to keep the worker on, gathering evidence and documenting problems until you're sure that you can prove good cause to fire. For as long as it takes, the worker will keep on mucking up the works, while you spend some of your time building a legal case—instead of running your business.

Despite the benefits of an at-will policy, some employers choose not to adopt one. And there are a few advantages to foregoing an at-will policy, with improved employee relations topping the list. Workers are generally not happy to open an employee handbook and read that they can be fired at any time, for any reason. If you promise to give your workers a fair shake, you might reap some rewards—like improved loyalty and more positive attitudes towards your company.

Only you can decide whether you want to assert your at-will rights in your handbook. Given the clear benefits of having such a policy—and the real dangers of leaving one out—we strongly recommend that all employers adopt an at-will policy, whether they plan to rely on it or not. There are plenty of other ways to show your employees that you value their work.

How to Complete This Policy

The sample policy above provides a space where you should name a company officer who can modify the at-will relationship. This provision gives you the discretion to enter into employment contracts that limit your right to fire, while at the same time protecting your at-will rights over the rest of your workforce.

Most companies will want to designate the highest company officer—for example, the president, CEO or owner of the company. Take care to select someone at the highest echelons of company management—you want the company to have complete control over who gets an employment contract and who doesn't. And designate this person by position (for example, *the president of the company*) rather than by name. Although you may not anticipate any changes in your company ladder, you never know what the future might bring. By omitting any names from this policy, you ensure that the policy won't require any changes if your company has a personnel shake-up.

Some companies designate more than one person who can make contracts. This is fine as long as you authorize only a few people, at most. The more people who have the right to make contracts, the higher the likelihood that there will be contracts that you don't know about.

Form A: Handbook Acknowledgment Form

If you decide to have an at-will policy (see discussion above), you should also ask employees to sign an at-will acknowledgment form. To anyone who isn't a lawyer, it probably seems like overkill to have both a policy and a form that essentially restates that policy. But in the legal world, redundancy is not only encouraged, it is sometimes required. In this case, using both a policy and an acknowledgment form gives you more protection against future lawsuits.

Using an acknowledgment form offers you two important benefits. First, it will prevent your employees from arguing that they didn't know about or read the at-will policy in your handbook. While some courts might listen to such an argument—especially if that policy was buried deep in a thousand-page manual—all courts presume that people read a written agreement before signing it. Second, a signed, written agreement legally trumps agreements in less reliable forms—like an oral agreement or an implied contract. While a written policy helps your argument, it is not a contract—it will weight the scales strongly in your favor, but might not deliver the knockout blow. But a signed written agreement is generally conclusive. Courts are not interested in hearing people argue "well yes, I signed it, but I thought it didn't apply to me." If an employee tells a court that you entered into an oral or implied agreement not to fire him without good cause, the signed acknowledgment form should put a stop to that claim.

Your handbook acknowledgment form should explain the importance of the handbook, state that the handbook can be changed at any time and does not constitute a contract of continued employment, and explain the at-will policy again—this time, so your workers can sign the form to acknowledge their understanding of the policy.

Handbook Acknowledgment Form

By signing this form, I acknowledge that I have received a copy of the Company's Employee Handbook. I understand that it contains important information about the Company's policies, that I am expected to read the Handbook and familiarize myself with its contents and that the policies in the Handbook apply to me. I understand that nothing in the Handbook constitutes a contract or promise of continued employment and that the Company may change the policies in the Handbook at any time.

By signing this form, I acknowledge that my employment is at will. I understand that I have the right to end the employment relationship at any time and for any reason, with or without notice, with or without cause, and that the Company has the same right. I acknowledge that neither the Company nor I has entered into an employment agreement for a specified period of time, that only _____ may make any agreement contrary to the at-will policy, and that any such agreement must be in writing, signed by myself and _____.

_____   _____
Employee's Signature   Date

_____
Employee's Name (Print)

How to Complete This Form

In the spaces provided, insert the position of the person whom you have chosen to enter into contracts on behalf of the company. This language should track the language of your at-will policy, above.

Reality Check: Don't Ask Employees to Acknowledge That They've Read the Whole Handbook

Many employers ask employees to agree, in the acknowledgment form, that they have already read the handbook. This is not realistic —nor is it sensible. You want your employees to sign the at-will acknowledgment right away, preferably as part of the first-day paperwork. This lets employees know where they stand right from the start, so they don't feel like you waited to spring an unpleasant surprise on them. It also gives employees less time to have the kinds of conversations and interactions with others that can lead to implied or oral contract claims. In short, the sooner this form is signed, the better.

On the other hand, most employees are not going to take an hour or more out of their first day of work to read the employee handbook from cover to cover. While we hope the sample policies we provide in this book are down to earth and easy to understand, let's face it—an employee handbook just isn't thrilling reading material. Your employees are more likely to skim through the handbook early on in their employment, then read particular policies in detail as the need arises. By asking the employee to acknowledge only that the handbook is important and that you expect it to be read, you create a form that employees can sign honestly on their first day of work.

3

Hiring

You may wonder why you should discuss hiring in an employee handbook. After all, by the time people read the handbook, they've already been hired, right? While this is true, your current employees do need to know a few things about your hiring practices, both for themselves if they choose to apply for another job within your company and for friends and colleagues whom they might try to recruit to come work for you. In addition, communicating how you hire is yet another way to inform employees about your company culture and values.

In this chapter, we include the following policies:

3:1   Equal Opportunity

It's nice to start your handbook's hiring section with an Equal Opportunity Policy that acknowledges the existence of anti-discrimination laws and affirms your commitment to them, especially in the hiring process. (For more information about anti-discrimination laws, see Chapter 19.)

Standard Policy

Commitment to Equal Opportunity

____[Company name]____ believes that all people are entitled to equal employment opportunity. We follow state and federal laws prohibiting discrimination in hiring and employment. We do not discriminate against employees or applicants in violation of those laws.

Who Needs This Policy

Although neither state nor federal law requires it, all employers who are covered by any combination of state or federal anti-discrimination laws should begin the hiring section of their handbook with a statement acknowledging these laws. The statement should also include a promise to follow the laws throughout the hiring process. Not only will your employees appreciate hearing this from you, the handbook language can be a handy piece of evidence should a disgruntled applicant ever file a lawsuit against you alleging discriminatory hiring practices.

Optional Modification to Specify Protected Characteristics

If you know which state and federal laws cover your workplace, and if you know which characteristics these laws protect (for example, race, color, religion, national origin, gender, age, disability and veteran status, among others), you can be more specific in this policy and actually list for your employees the characteristics that are protected. To do so, replace the last sentence of the Standard Policy above with the following:

Modification

> We do not discriminate against employees or applicants on the basis of [*list characteristics protected by the state and federal laws covering your workplace*]or any other characteristic protected by state or federal law.

If you don't know which anti-discrimination laws cover your workplace, then you need to find out—and fast. These laws cover every aspect of your relationship with your employees, and ignorance of them leaves you vulnerable to costly and embarrassing accusations and lawsuits. See Chapter 19 for help in finding out which laws cover your workplace.

3:2   Recruitment

If you want current employees to help you in your recruitment efforts, then you should ask for their help in the hiring section of your handbook. The following policy explains where and how you will look for new employees. It also encourages current employees to help you generate ideas about how to find talented people who will fit into your workplace.

Standard Policy

Recruitment

We know that we are only as good as our employees, so we search as widely as possible for talented and motivated individuals to fill vacant positions in our Company. Our recruitment methods include [*list the methods you use—for example, advertising, employment agencies and referrals*].

Although these methods have served us well in the past, we know that the marketplace is ever changing and that finding high quality people is an evolving process. We encourage our employees to share with us their ideas as to what more we can do to find and recruit talented and motivated individuals.

We conduct all recruiting in a fair and nondiscriminatory manner.

Optional Modifications

To Encourage Current Employees to Apply

If you would like to encourage current employees to apply for transfer or promotion to vacant positions (see 3:3, below, for more on this), add the following paragraph to the end of the standard policy:

Modification

In addition to looking outside the Company for new hires, we also look within. After all, we already know the value and quality of our current employees. We post all internal job openings on [*give the location where you will post job openings*]. If you see a posting for a job that interests you, we encourage you to apply for it by following our Internal Application Procedures (see below).

Promote from within, but don't tie your hands. Some commentators suggest that employers promise to give priority for vacant positions to current employees. We recommend against limiting your options in this way, however. Sometimes, you'll want to look outside your workplace for a new hire, even if there is someone currently on staff who would be perfect for the position.

If You Have a Referral Bonus Program

If you give bonuses to employees who refer new hires to you (see 3:4, below, for more on this), add the following sentence to the end of the second paragraph of the standard policy:

Modification

We also encourage employees to recruit and refer external applicants for open positions. If you refer someone whom we eventually hire, we will thank you for your efforts with a referral bonus. See Employee Referral Bonus Program, below, for details.

3:3   Internal Application Process

If you'd like to encourage your current employees to apply for open positions, a good place to start is in your handbook. Allowing good employees to change jobs within your company (as opposed to looking for better jobs outside your company), is a win-win situation: It means that you get to retain good employees, while your employees get to keep fresh and motivated by taking jobs that interest them rather than staying in a job that has grown stale.

The following standard policy gives employees permission to apply for vacancies and it tells them how to do so.

Standard Policy

Internal Application Procedures

Sometimes, the best person for a job is right under our Company's nose. As a result, we encourage current employees to apply for vacant positions that interest them.

We post all internal job openings on [*give location*]. To apply for a position, give a cover letter, current resumé and copy of the job posting to _____.

3:4   Employee Referral Bonus Program

Sometimes, your employees are the ones best situated to find and recruit new talent on your behalf. Although some employees will do this out of dedication to your company (and their job-seeking friends), others need a little more motivation. Many employers like to sweeten the pot by promising bonuses to employees who find successful applicants for open positions.

The following policy promises a bonus to employees who successfully refer a potential employee to fill a vacant position.

Standard Policy

Refer a New Hire; Get a Bonus!

Our employees know our needs and Company culture better than anyone else and are often the best situated to find and recruit new employees to fill open positions within our ranks.

To encourage employees to act as recruiters on our behalf, and to reward employees who help make a successful match, we operate an Employee Referral Bonus Program. We will give [*specify the bonus that you are offering*] to any employee who refers an individual whom we hire.

To find out more about the program, or to refer a potential applicant for an open position, contact _____.

How to Complete This Policy

You will have to decide what kind of bonus to give to employees. In part, this will depend upon your company culture and finances, and in part it will depend upon the standards in your industry. For example:
- many non-profits give one or two paid days off as a bonus
- small businesses give anything from $500 to $1,000, and
- corporate law firms give as much as $10,000.

Optional Modifications

To Offer Different Bonuses for Different Positions

Some companies would pay a king's ransom to find a top-notch professional, such as a design engineer or a chief financial officer, but wouldn't pay peanuts to locate a rank-and-file employee, such as an assembly line worker or a sales clerk.

If there are positions in your company that you value more highly than others, you can create a policy that pays a different bonus depending on the position. For example, if you operate a law firm, you might offer a bonus of $5,000 for lawyers, $2,500 for paralegals, $1,000 for secretaries and $500 for file clerks.

You can either name the positions (as in the previous example) or you can give a category of positions (for example, professional, support staff and so on).

If you would like to create a tiered bonus system, substitute the following paragraph for the second paragraph of the sample policy above:

Modification

To encourage employees to act as recruiters on our behalf, and to reward employees who help make a successful match, we operate an Employee Referral Bonus Program. The amount of the bonus depends on the position that you have helped to fill:

- Position: _____ Bonus: _____
- Position: _____ Bonus: _____
- Position: _____ Bonus: _____
- Position: _____ Bonus: _____

To Exclude Some From the Policy

If you have people in your company whose job it is to find new employees for you, their paycheck is reward enough for accomplishing the task—you don't need to add a bonus on top of that. These people usually include officers in the company (the president, the chief executive officer and the chief financial officer), members of the human resources department and on-staff recruiters.

If you would like to exclude some people from your bonus program, add the following paragraph to the sample policy above:

Modification

The following people may not participate in the Employee Referral
Bonus Program: _____
_____.

3:5   Nepotism

Many employers like to think of their company as a family. However, when actual family members of your employees start filling your ranks, complications can arise. How do you feel about a husband supervising a group of employees that includes his wife? What about the CEO's son taking a part-time job in the mailroom? Or siblings working side by side on the assembly line?

Even if you don't have any concerns about these things, your other employees might. For example, it could be a little awkward for the mailroom manager to supervise and discipline his boss's son. Or downright impossible for an employee to complain to a supervisor about the behavior of the supervisor's spouse. Not to mention the troubles that can arise for coworkers when family members don't get along.

Many employers choose to allow family members to work for the same company, so long as they don't work together—or at least don't supervise each other. Other employers have a strict policy against nepotism, preferring to play it safe and keep clear of any potential conflicts or favoritism that could crop up.

The standard policy allows employment of relatives. To prohibit employment of relatives, use the modifications that follow the standard policy.

Standard Policy

Employment of Relatives

Usually, this Company will not refuse to hire someone simply because he or she is related to one of our current employees. If you have a relative who you think would be perfect to fill an open position in our Company, please don't hesitate to refer this person to us.

There are times, however, when employing relatives is inappropriate and has the potential to affect the morale of other employees and to create conflicts of interest for the relatives involved.

Therefore, we will not hire relatives of current employees where one relative will have to supervise the other.

If two employees become related while working for this Company, and if one of them is in a position of supervision over the other, only one of the employees will be allowed to keep his or her current position. The other will either have to transfer to another position or leave the Company.

Under this policy, the term "relatives" encompasses husbands, wives, live-in partners, parents, children, siblings, in-laws, cousins, aunts and uncles. This policy covers biological relationships, marriage relationships and step relationships.

Optional Modifications

To Prohibit Employment of Relatives

If you want to prohibit employment of relatives, then use the following policy instead of the standard policy.

Modification

Employment of Relatives

Although we value all of our employees and, by extension, their families, we do not allow family members of current employees to take jobs with our Company. We believe the risk of morale problems, security problems and conflict of interest problems is too great.

Under this policy, the term "relatives" encompasses husbands, wives, live-in partners, parents, children, siblings, in-laws, cousins, aunts and uncles. This policy covers biological relationships, marriage relationships and step relationships.

If you operate your business in a state that prohibits discrimination based on marriage or family status, check with a lawyer for assistance in creating and administering your nepotism policy. Some of these states (for example, Montana) view transferring, terminating or refusing to hire someone because they are married or related to a coworker as discrimination—and these states allow lawsuits against employers who do it. Other states view a nepotism policy as an acceptable exception to the anti-discrimination law. You'll need a lawyer's assistance to find out where your state stands on the issue. To find out if you live in a state that prohibits discrimination based on marriage or family status, see the chart at the end of Chapter 19.

To Deal With Current Employees Who Become Related

Sometimes, current employees become related through marriage. In such a situation, an employer with a strict anti-nepotism policy (see the first modification, above) will have to decide whether it will make an exception for those employees, or whether it will force one of the employees to quit.

Doing the latter is certainly the most consistent approach, but it has two significant drawbacks:

- it punishes employees for marrying each other rather than just dating, and
- it forces an otherwise valuable employee to leave your ranks.

Only you can decide the way you want to go on this issue. If you would like to allow current employees to marry, add the following paragraph to the first modification, above:

Modification

If two employees become related while working for this Company, they will both be allowed to remain with the Company. However, if one of them supervises the other, only one of the employees will be allowed to keep his or her current position. The other will either have to transfer to another position or leave the Company.

4

New Employee Information

Although your entire handbook will include information for new employees and long-term employees alike, there are a couple of policies exclusively for new employees. In this section, you can tell your new employees what to expect during their initial weeks of employment—and advise them about information you will be collecting for the government regarding their immigration status and any outstanding child support obligations.

In this chapter, we cover:

Don't forget the Handbook Acknowledgment Form. In addition to the policies in this chapter, make sure your new employees sign the "Handbook Acknowledgment Form" included in Chapter 2. The at-will policy and acknowledgment form explained in that chapter provide essential information for new employees. Because the legal doctrine of at-will employment is so important, we have given that information its own stand-alone chapter—but the acknowledgment form should be part of your first-day paperwork with all of your new employees.

4:1   New Employee Orientation

Some employers schedule an orientation meeting or program for new employees. This meeting can take many forms. Large employers who routinely hire many employees at a time might schedule a group gathering in a conference room, while smaller employers might simply set up a time for a new hire to get together with a benefits administrator or human resources employee. No matter what type of orientation you use, its purpose is three-fold: to explain your procedures (about payroll, scheduling vacations and signing up for health insurance benefits, for example) to new employees, to take care of all of that pesky first-day paperwork and to answer any questions new employees might have.

Standard Policy

New Employee Orientation

Within a day or two of starting work, you will be scheduled for a new employee orientation meeting. During this meeting, you will receive important information about our Company's policies and procedures. You will also be asked to complete paperwork and forms relating to your employment, such as tax withholding forms, emergency contact forms and benefits paperwork.

Please feel free to ask any questions you might have about the Company during the orientation meeting. If additional questions come up after the meeting, you can ask your supervisor or

_____.

How to Complete This Policy

In the blank, insert the title or position of the person who conducts the new employee orientation meetings (for example, *human resources manager*, *benefits administrator* or *office manager*).

4:2 Orientation Period

Many employers use an orientation period for their new employees. During this time, the employee can learn how to do the job and what the company expects, and the company can offer the employee some extra supervision and make sure that the employee is going to make the grade. Sensible as such policies may be, they can also create a legal risk for employers. Orientation policies must be carefully drafted with an eye towards preserving the at-will employment relationship (for more on at-will employment, see Chapter 2).

Employers get in trouble with orientation policies when they state or imply that completion of the orientation period guarantees the worker a job, makes the worker a "permanent employee" or otherwise limits the employer's right to fire the worker at will. The orientation period is a trial run of sorts: it gives both employer and employee a chance to make sure that there's a good fit between the worker and the job. But emphasizing this too strongly in an orientation policy can lead workers to expect that completing their orientation means they've "made the cut" and thereafter will be fired only for good cause. The sample policy we provide clearly states that employment is at will both during and after the orientation period, to avoid this potential legal pitfall.

Standard Policy

Orientation Period

The first _____ days of your employment are an orientation period. During this time, your supervisor will work with you to help you learn how to do your job successfully and what the Company expects of you. This period also provides both you and the Company with an opportunity to decide whether you are suited for the position for which you were hired.

When your employment begins, you will meet with _____ _____, who will explain our benefits and payroll procedures and assist you in completing your employment paperwork. (For our Company's benefits policies, see Section _____ of this Handbook.) You will also meet with your supervisor to go over your job goals and performance requirements. During the orientation period, your supervisor will give you feedback on your performance and will be available to answer any questions you might have.

Employees are not eligible for the following benefits unless and until they complete the orientation period: _____

_____

_____.

Although we hope that you will be successful here, the Company may terminate your employment at any time, either during the orientation period or afterwards, with or without cause and with or without notice. You are also free to quit at any time and for any reason, either during the orientation period or afterwards, with or without notice. Successful completion of your orientation period does not guarantee you a job for any period of time or in any way change the at-will employment relationship. (For an explanation of at-will employment, see Section_____ of this Handbook.)

Who Needs This Policy

Employers are not required to use or offer an orientation policy, or to make any special arrangements to bring new employees up to speed. If you choose to simply treat new employees like everyone else, you don't need this policy.

However, many employers do use a probationary, orientation or "new employee" period. If you are one of them, using this policy will help you make sure that you don't inadvertently jeopardize your right to fire employees at will.

This orientation policy offers other benefits as well. It lets new workers know where to go with questions or concerns, and allows you to create a waiting period before employee benefits go into effect (see "How to Complete This Policy," below).

How to Complete This Policy

Our sample policy leaves you a space to indicate how long the orientation period will be. Ninety days is a fairly standard length for an orientation period. It's long enough to give employees a chance to learn the ropes and show what they can do, but not so long that you'll be stuck mentoring new workers forever. However, some employers use a 60-day period or some other time frame that better fits their business model. For example, if your workers have quarterly sales goals or change assignments every two months, you might want to use these time periods instead.

We also leave you space to list the benefits that won't be available during the orientation period. For example, many employers impose a waiting period for health insurance coverage or employer contributions to a retirement fund. Some employers do not allow their employees to use sick or vacation time during the orientation period. If you plan to impose a waiting period, list the benefits that will not be available to new employees here.

We also leave you space to designate the person who will explain benefits, payroll procedures and other administrative matters to new employees. If you have a human resources function, you can insert *someone from the human resources department* here. If not, designate the position that handles these matters (for example, *the payroll administrator* or *our benefits coordinator*).

Optional Modification to Extend Orientation Period

Some orientation policies provide that the orientation period can be extended at the employer's discretion. The purpose of such an addition is to give you some extra time to evaluate a worker, if necessary. For example, if the worker doesn't seem to be getting the hang of things or unusual circumstances during the orientation period prevented you from giving the worker sufficient training and feedback, the option of a longer period might be helpful. If you wish to include this provision, add this language to the end of the first paragraph:

New employees have legal rights, too. Although you can require new employees to work for a certain period of time before they are eligible for fringe benefits—benefits of the job that you are not legally required to provide, such as insurance coverage or a company car—you must follow the law in your dealings with new employees. Wage and hour laws, anti-discrimination laws, occupational safety laws and the many other laws governing your workplace apply to your workers from their very first day of employment. While you can condition discretionary benefits on tenure at the company, you cannot place your new employees' legal rights on hold while they complete an orientation period.

Modification

Your orientation period may be extended if the Company decides that such an extension is appropriate.

4:3   Work Eligibility

For a policy explaining where you will store employees' I-9 Forms, see Chapter 16.

A federal law called the Immigration Reform and Control Act (IRCA) requires all employers to verify, within the first three days of employment, that a new hire is legally eligible to work in the United States. You must require each new employee to complete an I-9 form, show identification and present you with proof of employment eligibility.

Your work eligibility policy should tell employees that they will have to present certain documents and complete the I-9 Form, and tell them where they can go for more information.

Standard Policy

Proof of Work Eligibility

Within three business days of your first day of work, you must complete federal Form I-9 and show us documentation proving your identity and your eligibility to work in the United States. The federal government requires us to do this.

If you have worked for this Company previously, you need only provide this information if it has been more than three years since you last completed an I-9 Form for us or if your current I-9 Form is no longer valid.

_____ will give you an I-9 Form and tell you what documentation you must present to us.

How to Complete This Policy

You should designate someone to be responsible for completing and answering questions about the I-9 Form. Typically, that person is the human resources manager or office manager. The same person who deals with new employees' tax forms and insurance forms can also handle this form.

For a comprehensive discussion of your duties under IRCA, see *Federal Employment Laws: A Desk Reference*, by Amy DelPo & Lisa Guerin (Nolo). You can also obtain free information about the law from the federal Bureau of Citizenship and Immigration Service ("BCIS," formerly known as the "INS"). You can find the BCIS in the federal listings of your local phone book, or on the Web at www.bcis.gov.

Optional Modification for Companies With New Hire Interviews

If you adopt the first policy in this chapter, you'll hold a new hire interview or orientation meeting at which someone from the company gives new employees all of the forms they'll need to complete as part of joining the company. This stack of forms often includes a Handbook Acknowledgment Form (see Chapter 2), an IRS W-4 Form and a Form I-9. If you adopt this type of process for new employees, substitute the following modification for the final paragraph of the standard policy, above.

Modification

At your [*give title of meeting—for example, "new hire interview" or "orientation"*], you should have received a blank Form I-9 and instructions on completing it. If you did not, contact _____ _____ immediately.

Reality Check: Citizenship and Employment Eligibility Are Two Different Things

Asking for proof of employment eligibility is not the same thing as asking whether an employee is a citizen of the United States. You are legally required to verify that an employee is authorized to work in the U.S., but you are legally prohibited from asking whether an employee or applicant for employment is a citizen of this country. Discrimination on the basis of citizenship status is illegal.

Non-citizens are eligible to work in this county as long as they have proper authorization from the government. For example, lawful permanent resident aliens, aliens granted asylum in the U.S. and aliens allowed into the U.S. as refugees are all entitled to work here, as long as they have documents proving their identity and eligibility to do so.

4:4   Child Support Reporting Requirements

All employers are required to report information on new employees to a state agency, the State Directory of New Hires. Once the state receives this information, it checks to see whether any of these new employees appear on its list of parents who owe child support. If the government finds a match, it will send the employer a withholding order, requiring that a certain amount of that employee's income be withheld and paid to the other parent.

Every state requires you to provide at least the employee's name, address and Social Security number, and the employer's name, address and employer identification number. Some states require additional information, such as the employee's birth date or the date of the employee's first day of work. Some states allow you to simply submit a copy of the employee's W-4 form; others require you to use a different format. To find out more about your state's requirements, and to see if your state has a preprinted form you can use, contact your state's Directory of New Hires. You can find contact information through the website of the Department of Health and Human Services, at the address listed above.

For more information on these reporting requirements, see *Federal Employment Laws: A Desk Reference*, by Amy DelPo & Lisa Guerin (Nolo). You'll also find several helpful resources on these requirements at the website of the Administration for Children and Families, a subdivision of the federal government's Department of Health and Human Services, at www.acf.dhhs.gov/programs/cse.

Standard Policy

Child Support Reporting Requirements

Federal and state laws require us to report basic information about new employees, including your name, address and Social Security number, to a state agency called the State Directory of New Hires. The state collects this information to enforce child support orders. If the state determines that you owe child support, it will send us an order requiring us to withhold money from your paycheck to pay your child support obligations.

Who Needs This Policy

You don't have to tell your employees about this requirement; many employers simply gather the information and send it off, without ever mentioning it to their employees. However, an explicit policy explaining the requirement to your employees can save you a few hassles down the road. If one of your new hires owes child support and you have to withhold money from his paycheck, you will have to explain the situation to your employee—including how the state found the employee in the first place. By explaining up front that you are legally required to provide this information and obey withholding orders, you let your employees know that you aren't singling anyone out or going out of your way to cause problems for anyone. You also pave the way for easier conversations about any withholding orders you have to follow in the future.

We recommend that employers include a brief policy in their handbook explaining this requirement. You can also include a form for employees to fill out, giving the information your state requires. ■

5

Employee Classifications

In any given workplace, there might be five, ten, 30 or more classifications of employees—from regular to temporary to on call to per diem and so on. The list is as endless as the employer's imagination.

Employers like to group workers into classifications for a wide variety of reasons, most having to do with identifying which employees are entitled to which wages, benefits and privileges. For example, an employer who doesn't want to provide benefits to employees who are scheduled to work fewer than 40 hours a week will likely classify employees as part time or full time and will have a policy that allows only full-time employees to receive benefits.

For the most part, the law does not dictate how you classify employees. For example, you can decide how many hours per week employees have to work to be considered full-time employees.

The more complicated your workplace, the more employee classifications you might have. We cannot cover all of the various categories into which different employers group their employees. Instead, we tackle the most common ones. The classifications below will meet the needs of the vast majority of small- to mid-sized businesses. They are:

It is important to understand that these categories are not mutually exclusive. They divide employees up according to different criteria, so you could use all (or none) of these classifications depending on your needs. For example, an employee easily could be both full time and exempt. This would mean that the employee is scheduled to work at least 40 hours per week (full time) and is not entitled to receive overtime under state or federal law (exempt). We will talk more about these possibilities in the descriptions of the various employee classifications below.

5:1   Temporary Employees

Most businesses experience times when they need a little extra help. Perhaps you run a toy shop and tend to hire more salespeople during the holiday season, or maybe you operate an accounting firm and must hire additional clerical help during tax season.

Whatever your reasons for hiring someone on a temporary basis, it's important that you distinguish that employee from the ones who are with you day in and day out, 365 days a year. Most employers choose not to extend optional benefits (such as health insurance and life insurance) or leave accrual to temporary employees, and they reserve their right to terminate the employee once the need for his or her services ends.

The following Temporary Employee policy distinguishes those employees who are working for you on a temporary basis from those whose jobs with you are more long-term. It also explains that temporary employees are not entitled to the same benefits and privileges as are regular employees.

Standard Policy

Temporary Employees

Periodically, it becomes necessary for us to hire individuals to perform a job or to work on a project that has a limited duration. Typically, this happens in the event of a special project, special time of year, abnormal workload or emergency.

Individuals whom we hire for such work are temporary employees. They are not eligible to participate in any of our Company benefit programs, nor can they earn or accrue any leave, such as vacation leave or sick leave.

Of course, we will provide to temporary employees any and all benefits mandated by law.

Temporary employees cannot change from temporary status to any other employment status by such informal means as remaining in our employ for a long period of time or through oral promises made to them by coworkers, members of management or supervisors. The only way a temporary employee's status can change is through a written notification signed by _____.

Like all employees who work for this Company, temporary employees work on an at-will basis. This means that both they and this Company are free to terminate their employment at any time for any reason that is not illegal—even if they have not completed the temporary project for which they have been hired.

How to Complete This Policy

Sometimes, temporary employees will begin to feel that they are regular employees simply by virtue of the length of time that they have spent with your company. And sometimes, they will think that their status has changed because of something you or a manager or supervisor has said to them.

It is important that you don't allow the status of temporary employees to change through these informal methods. Otherwise, you may find yourself obligated to provide benefits and leave to individuals whom you never wanted to hire in the first place.

Of course, you may on occasion find that you do want to hire temporary employees on a more regular basis, so you'll need some method by which you can change the status of temporary employees.

The fourth paragraph of the sample policy, above, warns temporary employees that their status cannot change informally or by implication. It does, however, give you the ability to change their status through a written notification signed by someone within your company. Choose a person who is likely to be involved in all of the hiring decisions at your company or who oversees employee benefit or leave programs. A human resources manager or an office manager is often a good choice.

 For information about at-will employment, including a standard policy, see Chapter 2.

Depending on your state law, you might have to extend some legally mandated benefits to your temporary employees. These benefits might include workers' compensation coverage and state disability insurance. Contact your state labor department for details. (See Appendix for contact information.)

Are those temporary employees really independent contractors? An individual who works for you on a temporary basis may really be an independent contractor, not a temporary employee. If possible, it will usually be to your advantage to classify a worker as an independent contractor, because independent contractors tend to be less expensive than temporary employees. (For example, you don't have to provide workers' compensation insurance for them, nor do you have to withhold any taxes from their compensation.) To learn more about independent contractors, see *Hiring Independent Contractors,* by Stephen Fishman (Nolo).

This standard policy does not explain which benefits part-time employees are and are not entitled to. We deal with that issue in Chapters 8 and 10.

Under some circumstances, state or federal law will govern whether you can deny certain benefits to part-time workers. Understanding these benefits laws can be quite difficult, and determining which workers must be allowed to participate can require some complex calculations. Talk to your benefits administrator, accountant or financial advisor before denying benefits to part-time employees.

5:2   Part-Time and Full-Time Employees

If you have any employees who are scheduled to work for you for fewer than 40 hours per week, you may want to treat them differently from your other employees in terms of benefits and other non-monetary perks. To do this, it is helpful to classify employees as either part-time or full-time, depending on how many hours they are scheduled to work each week.

Standard Policy

Part-Time and Full-Time Employees

Depending on the number of hours per week you are regularly scheduled to work, you are either a part-time or a full-time employee. It is necessary that you understand which of these classifications you fit into, because it will be important in determining whether you are entitled to benefits and leave. (See Section ___ of this Handbook for information about who is entitled to benefits and leave.)

Part-time employees: Employees who are regularly scheduled to work fewer than ___ hours per week are part-time employees.

Full-time employees: Employees who are regularly scheduled to work at least ___ hours per week are full-time employees.

How to Complete This Policy

It is up to you to decide how many hours per week you will require of employees to entitle them to benefits and leave. Many employers require 40 hours; others require 32, and still others require only 24. No matter which number you choose, remember that you have the option of prorating benefits and leave. For example, you may call an employee who works 32 hours per week a full-time employee, thereby guaranteeing him some amount of benefits and leave, but still prorate the amount of vacation that person is entitled to based on the number of hours in a 40-hour work week the employee is regularly scheduled to work. Under such a system, an employee who works 40 hours per week would earn five vacation days per year, and an employee who works 32 hours per week would only earn four.

5:3   Exempt and Non-Exempt Employees

Depending on the type of work employees do, they may be entitled to overtime pay for any work they do in excess of 40 hours in a week (or, in some states, in excess of eight hours in a day). Classifying workers as exempt or non-exempt is not a matter of choice for you; it is a matter of state and federal law. Most likely, you have already determined for payroll purposes which workers fall into which category.

This policy explains to employees that their right to overtime compensation depends on whether they are classified as exempt or non-exempt—and it explains to them the difference between the two classifications.

Standard Policy

Exempt and Non-Exempt Employees

Your entitlement to earn overtime pay depends on whether you are classified as an exempt or a non-exempt employee.

Exempt employees are those who do not earn overtime because they are exempt from the overtime provisions of the federal Fair Labor Standards Act and applicable state laws.

Non-exempt employees are those who meet the criteria for being covered by the overtime provisions of the federal Fair Labor Standards Act and applicable state laws.

If you are uncertain about which category you fall into, speak to _____.

6

Hours

Employers generally want to be able to dictate when their employees will be working: what time they will start and finish work, when they will take breaks and how much—if any—overtime they will work. The policies in this chapter can help you accomplish this. Although some state and federal laws impose restrictions on work hours—requiring you to pay certain employees an overtime premium if they work more than a prescribed number of hours in a day or week, or mandating that employees receive certain breaks during their shifts, for example—you are generally free to tell your employees when they must work.

In this chapter, we cover:

6:1   Hours of Work

Your policy on work hours should tell your employees when the company is open for business and when you expect them to be at work. This policy will set the stage for your policies on absenteeism and punctuality (see Chapter 12).

Standard Policy

Hours of Work

Our Company's regular hours of business are from *[start time]* to *[end time]*, *[days of operation—for example, "Monday through Friday" or "seven days a week"]*.

   Your supervisor will let you know your work schedule, including the time when you will be expected to start and finish work each day.

Optional Modifications

To Specify Hours for All Employees

In some companies, all employees work the same hours. For example, if you run a business with limited hours (such as a convenience store that caters to office workers or an after-hours nightclub), you may need all of your employees to show up at the same time and clock out at the same time. You can use this modification to set the schedule for all of your workers. Simply delete the second paragraph of the sample policy, above, and replace it with the following:

Modification

All employees are expected to be here, ready to start work, when we open. Unless you make other arrangements with your supervisor, you are expected to work until closing time.

To Include Shift Schedules

A variety of businesses, from restaurants and stores to manufacturers and hospitals, operate in shifts. If your company assigns workers to shifts with set schedules, you should modify your work hours policy to let employees know when each shift starts and ends. This will not only tell your workers when you expect them to work, but will also let them know what other shifts might be available, if they need or want to change their work schedules.

Our modification also advises that any shift changes, whether temporary or permanent, must be approved by a supervisor. This will put employees on notice that they may not simply swap shifts with a coworker whenever they wish, which will give you more control over work schedules.

If you want to include a shift schedule in your policy, replace the second paragraph in our sample policy, above, with the language that follows. In the blanks, fill in the number of shifts you use and the start and end time of each shift. Our modification includes space for three shifts; if you have more or fewer shifts, you will have to modify this accordingly.

Modification

Our Company operates in _____ shifts: from _____ to _____, from _____ to _____ and from _____ to _____. Your supervisor will let you know your shift assignment.

If you wish to change shifts permanently, talk to your supervisor. Although the Company will consider all requests to change shifts, we cannot guarantee that any particular request will be granted.

You may exchange shifts with another employee (that is, switch shifts on a one-time basis) only with the prior approval of your supervisor.

6:2   Flexible Scheduling ("Flextime")

Many companies offer their employees some form of flexible scheduling, often to accommodate the busy lives of working parents, employees who are attending school or those who have other pressing needs off the job.

You can reap many benefits from allowing your employees to work a flexible schedule. Employees who have sufficient time off work to deal with their outside concerns, be they family commitments, health problems, volunteer work or school responsibilities, will be better able to concentrate and perform well when they are on the job. Showing that you are concerned about your employees' lives outside the workplace also goes a long way towards instilling respect and commitment to the company. And some workers simply do a better job—they are more efficient or productive—during certain times of the day. If you have a lot of "morning people" on the payroll, for example, allowing them to start work earlier could boost your bottom line.

If you choose to allow flexible scheduling, your policy should tell workers how to request a flexible schedule and what kinds of schedules might be allowed.

Standard Policy

Flexible Scheduling

We understand that many employees have to balance the demands of their job with the needs of their families and other outside commitments. Therefore, we offer our employees the opportunity to work a flexible schedule.

If you would like to change your work schedule—for example, to come in and leave a couple of hours earlier or to work more hours on some days and fewer on others—please talk to your supervisor. The Company will try to accommodate your request, to the extent practical. Because not all jobs are suitable to flexible scheduling, and because we must ensure that our staffing needs are met, we cannot guarantee that the Company will grant your request.

Reality Check: Deciding Who Gets to Flex

Flexible scheduling can be a tremendous boon to employer and employee alike. However, employers who choose to offer this opportunity must make sure that they dole out the benefits fairly.

Any time you offer a benefit that is discretionary—that is, a benefit that you may grant for some employees but not for others—you must be very careful to have solid business reasons for your decisions. Otherwise, you may face legal claims of discrimination. For example, if you routinely allow working mothers to alter their schedules to meet child care needs but don't always extend the same benefit to working fathers, you could get into trouble. Consider each claim for flexible scheduling on its own merits: can the company accommodate the request without substantial disruption? Does the employee's job lend itself to flexibility? Has the employee demonstrated the responsibility and self-motivation to work outside usual work hours?

6:3   Meal and Rest Breaks

Most employers offer their employees some breaks during the day. The laws of seven states require employers to provide paid breaks; other states require breaks, but don't insist that employers pay employees for this time. You can find out what your state requires by consulting the "State Meal and Rest Break Laws" chart, at the end of this Chapter.

Even if your state doesn't require any breaks, you should adopt a break policy if you generally allow your employees to take breaks. Having a written policy will reduce confusion over how much time can be taken and whether it will be paid or unpaid.

Your policy on meal and rest breaks should let employees know when they get breaks, how long they can take and whether those breaks are paid. If you require employees to schedule their breaks or take them at a particular time, your policy should include this information as well.

Standard Policy

Meal and Rest Breaks

Employees are allowed a _____-minute break every _____ hours. These breaks will be *[paid or unpaid]*. In addition, all employees who work at least _____ hours in a day are entitled to take a _____-minute meal break. Meal breaks are generally unpaid. However, employees who are required to work or remain at their stations during the meal break will be paid for that time.

How to Complete This Policy

Federal law doesn't require you to offer employees breaks of any length during the workday. However, federal law does require you to pay employees for any breaks of 20 minutes or less that you choose to provide. Seven states currently require paid breaks during the workday: five (California, Colorado, Kentucky, Nevada and Washington) require a paid ten-minute break every four hours, one (Oregon) requires a paid 15-minute break every four hours and one (Minnesota) requires a paid "adequate" break period, to allow employees to use the restroom. State laws are summarized in the "State Meal and Rest Break Laws" chart, at the end of this chapter.

To complete this policy, fill in the blanks with the length and frequency of the break your state requires—or the length of the break you plan to offer, as long as it meets or exceeds your state's legal requirements. Also, indicate whether rest breaks will be paid or unpaid. Because no state explicitly requires paid meal breaks, our policy provides that such breaks will be unpaid.

6:4   Overtime

If you ever anticipate asking any of your employees to work overtime, you should have an overtime policy. An overtime policy offers a number of benefits. For starters, it lets your workers know, up front, that you expect them to work overtime when necessary. This will go a long way towards eliminating later complaints when you have to actually ask employees to stay beyond their scheduled shifts. An overtime policy also protects you from having to pay workers for unnecessary overtime—or overtime work made necessary only by the employee's poor planning or faulty time management. Our sample policy requires workers to get advance authorization before working any overtime hours, which should prevent these abuses. And the policy explains how overtime is calculated, including which hours count towards the overtime threshold. Placing this information in the policy will save you the time it would otherwise take to explain the system to each worker who puts in extra time at the job.

Standard Policy

Overtime

On occasion, we may ask employees to work beyond their regular scheduled hours. We expect employees to work a reasonable amount of overtime—this is a job requirement.

We will try to give employees advance notice when overtime work is necessary; however, it will not always be possible to notify workers in advance.

Exempt employees will not be paid for working beyond their regular scheduled hours. Non-exempt employees are entitled to payment for overtime, according to the rules set forth below. (For information on which employees are exempt and which are non-exempt, see Section ____ of this Handbook.)

- All overtime work must be approved in writing, in advance, by the employee's supervisor. Working overtime without permission violates Company policy and may result in disciplinary action.
- For purposes of calculating how many hours an employee has worked in a day or week, our workweek begins at 12:01 a.m. on Monday and ends at midnight on Sunday. Our workday begins at 12:01 a.m. and ends at midnight each day.

- Only time actually spent working counts as hours worked. Vacation time, sick days, holidays or any other paid time during which an employee did not actually work will not count as hours worked.

- Non-exempt employees will be paid 1½ times their regularly hourly rate of pay for every hour worked in excess of _____
_____.

Reality Check:
Calculating a Worker's Regular Rate of Pay

Federal law requires you to pay overtime based on the employee's regular rate of pay—the total amount the employee generally earns per hour. However, this may add up to more than just the employee's hourly rate. You must include other compensation the employee regularly receives in the regular rate of pay, unless that compensation is discretionary. For example, say an employee regularly receives $10 per hour, but works one eight-hour swing shift per week, for which he receives an additional shift differential of $2 per hour. That employee's regular rate of pay would not be $10 per hour, but would instead be his total pay for a 40-hour week ($10 x 32 hours = $320, plus $12 x 8 hours =$96, for a total of $416) divided by forty hours ($416 divided by 40), or $10.40.

You must include any non-discretionary pay—such as regular bonuses or shift differentials—in the employee's regular rate of pay, but you do not have to count discretionary pay. For example, if you reward your best performers with a bonus, you don't have to include that money in a worker's regular rate of pay.

How to Complete This Policy

In the blank, insert the overtime standard—state or federal—that you have to follow. Federal law requires you to pay overtime to any non-exempt worker who works more than 40 hours in a seven-day week. However, a few states (including California) have a daily overtime standard, which requires employers to pay overtime to covered workers who put in more than a specified number of hours in a single work day. Check the "State Overtime Rules" chart at the end of this chapter for information on your state's

California employers take note. California offers employees more extensive wage and hour protections than most other states. In California, not only are workers entitled to time and a half for any hours worked beyond eight in a day or 40 in a week, but they are also entitled to double time—that is, twice their regular hourly wage—for hours worked beyond 12 in a day or for working more than eight hours on a seventh consecutive work day (see "State Overtime Rules" chart for details). And California law defines the categories of workers who are entitled to overtime more broadly than federal law. If you do business in California, you should consult with an employment lawyer to make sure that you are in compliance with these rules.

rules. Then complete the policy as follows: if federal law is more protective, or as protective, of workers as your state's law, insert *forty hours in a work week* in the blank. If your state has a daily overtime standard, insert that standard in the blank. For example, California employers should insert *eight hours in a work day or forty hours in a work week*.

Optional Modifications

To Count Paid Time Off As Time Worked

Most employers will want to pay overtime only when they are legally required to do so. Under federal law, paid hours that are not worked—such as vacation days, sick time or holidays—do not count towards the overtime threshold of 40 hours a week, as we have provided in our policy.

However, employers are free to count paid hours as hours worked, and some choose to do so. An employer might adopt this more generous policy to recognize the value of paid time off—such time is supposed to be a true break from the job. The therapeutic value of paid days off diminishes if an employee has to work extra hours as a result.

If you wish to treat some or all paid time off as hours worked, simply delete the third bullet in the sample policy, above, and replace it with the following modifications. In the blank, insert the types of paid time off you wish to count as hours worked, for example, *paid vacation days* or *paid sick days*. If you wish to count all paid time off, insert *all days off for which the employee is paid*.

Modification

Hours worked means all time spent actually working, plus
_____.

To Pay a Premium for Holiday Work

Federal law does not require employers to pay extra for hours worked on a holiday, unless those hours push the employee's weekly total above 40 hours. Nonetheless, some employers want to reward their employees for working unpopular shifts. Any employer who has tried to staff shifts on Thanksgiving or New Year's Day knows that a little incentive helps fill the ranks.

If you want to pay employees more to work on holidays, add the following modification to the overtime policy. In the first blank, list the holidays for which you will pay a premium (for example, *New Year's Eve and New Year's Day*). In the second blank, insert the premium you will pay (such as 1½ or 2 times the employee's regular hourly wage).

Modification

The Company will pay employees a premium for working on the following holidays: _____
_____.

Employees who agree to work on these days will receive
_____.

To Choose Employees for Overtime

In certain industries and businesses, employees jump at the chance to earn the extra money that overtime work provides. Other companies might find that no one ever wants to work overtime. In either situation, you may want to adopt a policy that explains how you choose employees for overtime work. Such a policy will assure employees in companies where overtime is popular that you are doling out the opportunity to work overtime fairly. And in companies where no one wants to work overtime, it will let workers know that they will have to put in their time when their turn comes.

Modification

Please let your supervisor know if you want to work overtime. Your supervisor will add your name to the overtime list. When overtime is available, it will be offered first to employees on the list, in the order in which their names appear.

If overtime work is necessary and no employees on the list are available, employees who are eligible to perform the work—that is, employees who do the same type of work during their regular work hours—will be asked to work overtime, in alphabetical order. Once an employee, on the list or off, has worked overtime, the next employee on the list or in alphabetical order will be asked to work overtime when it next becomes available, and so on.

State Meal and Rest Break Laws

Note: The states of Alabama, Alaska, Arizona, Arkansas, District of Columbia, Florida, Idaho, Indiana, Iowa, Louisiana, Maryland, Michigan, Mississippi, Missouri, Montana, New Jersey, New Mexico, North Carolina, Ohio, Oklahoma, Pennsylvania, South Carolina, South Dakota, Texas, Utah, Virginia and Wyoming are not listed in this chart because they do not have laws or regulations on rest and meal breaks for adults employed in the private sector. Check with your state department of labor if you need more information (see Appendix C for contact list.)

California

Cal. Code Regs. tit. 8, §§ 11010, 11160; Cal. Lab. Code §§ 512, 1030

Applies to: Employers in most industries.

Exceptions: Motion picture, agricultural & household occupations.

Meal Break: 30 minutes, after 5 hours, except when workday will be completed in 6 hours or less and employer and employee consent to waive meal break. Employee cannot work more than 10 hours a day without a second 30-minute break; except, if workday is no more than 12 hours, second meal break may be waived as long as first meal break was not waived.

On-duty meal period counted as time worked and permitted only when nature of work prevents relief from all duties and there is written agreement between parties.

Rest Break: Paid 10-minute rest period for each 4 hours worked or major fraction thereof; as practicable, in the middle of the work period. Not required for employees whose total daily work time is less than $3\frac{1}{2}$ hours.

Breastfeeding: Reasonable time to breastfeed infant or to express breast milk; paid if taken concurrent with other break time; otherwise, unpaid.

Colorado

Colo. Code Regs. § 1103-1

Applies to: Retail and service, food and beverage, commercial support service, food and beverage.

Exceptions: Excludes certain occupations, such as teacher, nurse and other medical professionals.

Meal Break: 30 uninterrupted minutes after 5 hours of work. On-duty paid meal period permitted when nature of work prevents break from all duties and there is a written agreement between all parties.

Rest Break: Paid 10-minute rest period for each 4-hour or major fraction period worked; if practical in the middle of the work period.

Connecticut

Conn. Gen. Stat. Ann. §§ 31-51ii, 31-40w

Applies to: All employers, except as noted.

Exceptions: Does not apply to employers who provide 30 or more minutes of paid or meal break within each $7\frac{1}{2}$-hour work period.

Does not apply if collective bargaining agreement or written agreement between employer and employee provides for different breaks.

Exemptions may be allowed where breaks would adversely affect public safety; duties can be performed only by one employee or in continuous operations; there are less than 5 employees on a shift and the exemption applies only to employees on that shift.

Meal Break: 30 minutes (to be taken after first 2 hours of work and before last 2 hours) for employees who work $7\frac{1}{2}$ or more consecutive hours.

Breastfeeding: Employee may use meal or rest break for breastfeeding or expressing breast milk.

Delaware

Del. Code Ann. tit. 19, § 707

Applies to: All employers, except as noted.

Exceptions: Excludes teachers and workplaces covered by a collective bargaining agreement or other written employer/employee agreement providing otherwise.

Exemptions may be allowed where breaks would adversely affect public safety; only one employee can perform the duties of a position; an employer has fewer than five employees on a shift where the continuous nature of an employer's operations requires employees to respond to urgent or unusual conditions at all times. Employees must be paid for their meal break periods.

Meal Break: 30 minutes after first 2 hours and before the last 2 hours, for employees who work $7\frac{1}{2}$ consecutive hours or more.

Georgia

Ga. Code Ann. § 34-1-6

Applies to: All employers.

Breastfeeding: Reasonable unpaid break time to breastfeed infant or to express breast milk.

Hawaii

Haw. Rev. Stat. § 378-2

Applies to: All employers.

State Meal and Rest Break Laws (continued)

Breastfeeding: Reasonable unpaid break time to breastfeed infant or to express breast milk.

Illinois

820 Ill. Comp. Stat. § 140/3; 850 Ill. Comp. Stat. § 260/10

Applies to: All employers.

Exceptions: Employees whose meal periods are established by collective bargaining agreement.

Employees who monitor individuals with developmental disabilities or mental illness, or both, and who are required to be on-call during an entire 8-hour work period; these employees must be allowed to eat a meal while working.

Meal Break: 20 minutes, no later than 5 hours after the beginning of the shift, for employees who work 7½ or more continuous hours.

Breastfeeding: Reasonable unpaid time to breastfeed infant or express breast milk.

Kansas

Kan. Admin. Reg. 49-30-3

Applies to: Employees not covered under FLSA.

Meal Break: Not required, but if less than 30 minutes is given, break must be paid.

Kentucky

Ky. Rev. Stat. Ann. §§ 337.355, 337.365

Applies to: All employers, except as noted.

Exceptions: Excludes employers subject to Federal Railway Labor Act.

Meal Break: Reasonable off-duty period close to the middle of the shift; can't be required to take it before the 3rd or after the 5th hour of work.

A collective bargaining agreement or written agreement between employer and employee may provide for a different meal period.

Rest Break: Paid 10-minute rest period for each 4-hour work period.

Rest period must be in addition to regularly scheduled meal period.

Maine

Me. Rev. Stat. Ann. tit. 26, § 601

Applies to: Most employers.

Exceptions: Small businesses with under 3 employees where the nature of their work allows them to take frequent breaks during the workday. Collective bargaining or other written agreement between employer and employee may provide for different breaks.

Meal Break: 30 minutes after 6 consecutive hours of work, except in cases of emergency.

Massachusetts

Mass. Gen. Laws ch. 149, §§ 100, 101

Applies to: All employers, except as noted.

Exceptions: Excludes iron works, glass works, paper mills, letterpresses, print works and bleaching or dyeing works. Attorney general may exempt businesses that require continuous operation if it won't affect worker safety. Collective bargaining agreement may also provide for different breaks.

Meal Break: 30 minutes, if work is for more than 6 hours.

Minnesota

Minn. Stat. Ann. §§ 177.253, 177.254, 181.939

Applies to: All employers.

Exceptions: Excludes certain agricultural and seasonal employees.

A collective bargaining agreement may provide for different rest and meal breaks.

Meal Break: Sufficient unpaid time for employees who work 8 consecutive hours or more.

Rest Break: Paid adequate rest period within each 4 consecutive hours of work, to utilize nearest convenient restroom.

Breastfeeding: Reasonable unpaid time to breastfeed infant or express milk.

Nebraska

Neb. Rev. Stat. § 48-212

Applies to: Assembly plant, workshop or mechanical establishment, unless it operates three 8-hour shifts daily.

Meal Break: 30 minutes off premises, between 12 noon and 1 p.m. or at other suitable lunch time.

Nevada

Nev. Rev. Stat. Ann. § 608.019

Applies to: Employers of two or more employees.

Exceptions: Employees covered by collective bargaining agreement.

Meal Break: 30 minutes, if work is for 8 continuous hours.

Rest Break: Paid 10-minute rest period for each 4 hours or major fraction worked; as practicable, in middle of the

State Meal and Rest Break Laws (continued)

work period. Not required for employees whose total daily work time is less than 3½ hours.

New Hampshire

N.H. Rev. Stat. Ann. § 275:30-a

Applies to: All employers.

Meal Break: 30 minutes after 5 consecutive hours, unless the employer allows the employee to eat while working and it is feasible for the employee to do so.

New York

N.Y. Lab. Law § 162

Applies to: Factories, workshops, manufacturing facilities, mercantile (retail and wholesale) establishments.

Meal Break: Factory employees, 60 minutes between 11 a.m. and 2 p.m.; mercantile employees, 30 minutes between 11 a.m. and 2 p.m. If a shift starts before 11 a.m. and ends after 7 p.m., every employee gets an additional 20 minutes between 5 and 7 p.m. If a shift starts between 1 p.m. and 6 a.m., a factory employee gets 60 minutes, and a mercantile employee gets 45 minutes, in the middle of the shift. Labor commissioner may permit a shorter meal break; the permit must be in writing and posted conspicuously in the main entrance of the workplace.

North Dakota

N.D. Admin. Code § 46-02-07-02 (5)

Applies to: Applicable when two or more employees are on duty.

Exceptions: Collective bargaining agreement takes precedence over meal period requirement.

Meal Break: 30-minutes for each shift over 5 hours. Unpaid as long as employee is completely relieved of duties. Employee may waive right to meal break in an agreement with employer.

Oregon

Or. Admin. R. § 839-020-0050

Applies to: All employers except as noted.

Exceptions: Agricultural workers and employees covered by a collective bargaining agreement.

Meal Break: 30-minute break for each work period of 6 to 8 hours, between 2nd and 5th hour for work period of 7 hours or less and between 3rd and 6th hour for work period over 7 hours; a 20-minute paid break, if employer can show that it is industry practice or custom; or a paid meal break while on duty for each period of 6 to 8 hours,

if employer can show that nature of work prevents taking a break from all duties.

Rest Break: Paid 15-minute rest period for each 4 hours or major fraction worked; if practical in the middle of the work period.

Rest period must be in addition to usual meal break and taken separately; can't be added to meal period or deducted from beginning or end of shift to reduce length of total work period.

Rest period is not required for employees age 18 or older who work alone in a retail or service establishment serving the general public, and who work less than 5 hours in a period of 16 continuous hours; however employee must be allowed to leave to use rest room.

Rhode Island

R.I. Gen. Laws § 28-3-14

Applies to: Factory, workshop and mechanical or mercantile establishments.

Exceptions: Nighttime switchboard operators who are not working continuously and can sleep during shift.

Meal Break: 20 minutes after 6 hours of work.

Employees are not entitled to a break if shift lasts for 6½ hours or less and ends by 1 p.m.; or if shift lasts for 7½ hours or less and ends by 2 p.m., and employee has enough time to eat during work.

Tennessee

Tenn. Code Ann. §§ 50-2-103(d), 50-1-305

Applies to: Employers with 5 or more employees.

Meal Break: 30 minutes for employees scheduled to work 6 consecutive hours or more unless work is such that there is ample time for breaks throughout the day.

Breastfeeding: Reasonable unpaid break time to breastfeed infant or express breast milk.

Vermont

Vt. Stat. Ann. tit. 21, § 304

Applies to: All employers.

Meal Break: Employees must be given reasonable opportunities to eat and use toilet facilities during work periods.

Washington

Wash. Admin. Code 296-126-092, 286-131-020

Applies to: All employers except as noted.

State Meal and Rest Break Laws (continued)

Exceptions: Newspaper vendor or carrier, domestic or casual labor around private residence, sheltered workshop. Separate provisions for agricultural labor.

Meal Break: 30-minute break, if work period is more than 5 consecutive hours, not less than 2 hours nor more than 5 hours from beginning of shift. Employees who work 3 or more hours longer than regular workday are entitled to an additional ½ hour, before or during overtime. Agricultural employees: 30 minutes if working more than 5 hours; additional 30 minutes if working 11 or more hours in a day.

Rest Break: Paid 10-minute rest break for each 4-hour work period, scheduled as near as possible to midpoint of each work period. Employee cannot be required to work more than 3 hours without a rest break.

Scheduled rest breaks not required where nature of work allows employee to take intermittent rest breaks equivalent to required standard.

Agricultural employees: 10-minute paid rest break for each 4 hours worked.

West Virginia

W.Va. Code § 21-3-10a; W.Va. Code St. R. § 42-5-2(2.6)

Applies to: All employers.

Meal Break: 20-minute break for each 6 consecutive hours worked, where employees are not allowed to take breaks as needed and/or permitted to eat lunch while working.

Rest Break: Rest breaks of 20 minutes or less must be counted as paid work time.

Wisconsin

Wis. Admin. Code § DWD 274.02

Applies to: All employers.

Meal Break: Recommended but not required: 30 minutes close to usual meal time or near middle of shift. Shifts of more than six hours without a meal break should be avoided. If employee is not free to leave the workplace, meal period is considered paid time.

Current as of February 2003

State Overtime Rules

This chart covers private sector employment only. The overtime rules summarized are not applicable to all employers or all employees. Occupations that generally are not subject to overtime laws include: healthcare and attendant care, emergency medical personnel, seasonal workers, agricultural labor, camp counselors, nonprofits exempt under FLSA, salespeople working on a commission, transit drivers, baby-sitters and many others. For more information contact your state's department of labor and be sure to check its website, where most states have posted their overtime rules. (See Appendix for contact details.)

Alabama

No overtime provisions.

Alaska

Alaska Stat. §§ 23.10.055 and following

Hours per DAY after which time and a half is paid: 8

Hours per WEEK after which time and a half is paid: 40

Employment overtime laws apply to: Employers of 4 or more employees; commerce or manufacturing businesses.

Employment excluded from overtime laws: Occupations not subject to minimum laws. Agriculture, cab drivers, caretaker, domestic work, emergency medical personnel, fishing, janitors, watchmen.

Notes: Voluntary flexible work hour plan of 10-hour day, 40-hour week, with premium pay after 10 hours is permitted.

Arizona

No overtime limits for private sector employers.

Arkansas

Ark. Code Ann. §§ 11-4-211; 11-4-203

Hours per WEEK after which time and a half is paid: 40

Employment overtime laws apply to: Employers of 4 or more employees.

Employment excluded from overtime laws: Employment that is subject to the FLSA.

California

Cal. Lab. Code §§ 510 and following; Cal. Code Regs. tit. 8, § 11010 and following

Hours per DAY after which time and a half is paid: 8; after 12 hours, double time.

Hours per WEEK after which time and a half is paid: 40. 7th day: time and a half for the first 8 hours; after 8 hours, double time.

Employment excluded from overtime laws: Computer software employees who design, develop, create, analyze, test or modify programs using independent judgment or who are paid at least $43.58/hour.

Notes: Alternative four 10-hour-day workweek is permitted, if established prior to 7/1/99.

7th day premium pay not required when employee works no more than 30 hours per week or 6 hours per day.

Colorado

Colo. Rev. Stat. §§ 8-13-101; 8-12-101; 7 Colo. Code Regs. § 1103-1(4)

Hours per DAY after which time and a half is paid: 12

Hours per WEEK after which time and a half is paid: 40

Employment overtime laws apply to: Employees in retail and service, commercial support service, food and beverage, health and medical industries.

Connecticut

Conn. Gen. Stat. Ann. §§ 31-58; 31-76b(E),(F),(G); Conn. Agencies Regs. § 31-60-1

Hours per DAY after which time and a half is paid: 8

Hours per WEEK after which time and a half is paid: 40; premium pay on weekends, holidays or 6th or 7th consecutive day.

Employment excluded from overtime laws: Camps and resorts run by nonprofits among other seasonal occupations.

Notes: In restaurants, time and a half pay required for the 7th consecutive day of work.

Delaware

No overtime provisions.

District of Columbia

D.C. Code Ann. § 32-1003(c); D.C. Mun. Regs. tit. 7, § 906

Hours per WEEK after which time and a half is paid: 40

Notes: Split shift work: one hour extra pay per day.

Florida

No overtime provisions.

Georgia

No overtime provisions.

State Overtime Rules (continued)

Hawaii

Haw. Rev. Stat. § 387-3

Hours per WEEK after which time and a half is paid: 40. Dairy, sugarcane and seasonal agricultural work: 48 hours per week.

Employment excluded from overtime laws: Employees earning guaranteed compensation of $2,000 or more per month.

Notes: Split shifts permitted only if they fall within a period of 14 consecutive hours per 24 hours.

Idaho

No state overtime rules that differ from FLSA.

Illinois

820 Ill. Comp. Stat. § 105/4a

Hours per WEEK after which time and a half is paid: 40

Employment overtime laws apply to: Applicable to employers of 4 or more employees.

Indiana

Ind. Code Ann. § 22-2-2-4(j)

Hours per WEEK after which time and a half is paid: 40

Employment excluded from overtime laws: Employment that is subject to the FLSA, movie theaters, seasonal camps or amusement parks, FLSA-exempt nonprofits.

Notes: Collective bargaining agreements ratified by the NLRB may have different overtime provisions. Domestic service work is not excluded from overtime laws.

Iowa

No state overtime limits.

Kansas

Kan. Stat. Ann. § 44-1204

Hours per WEEK after which time and a half is paid: 46

Employment excluded from overtime laws: Not applicable to employment that is subject to the FLSA.

Kentucky

Ky. Rev. Stat. Ann. §§ 337.050; 337.285

Hours per WEEK after which time and a half is paid: 40

Notes: 7th day, time and a half if employee worked 40 hours in the previous 6 days.

Louisiana

No overtime provisions.

Maine

Me. Rev. Stat. Ann. tit. 26, § 664(3)

Hours per WEEK after which time and a half is paid: 40

Employment excluded from overtime laws: Auto mechanics, parts clerks and salespersons; hotels, motels & restaurants; canning, freezing, packing and shipping produce and perishable foods.

Maryland

Md. Code Ann., [Lab. & Empl.] § 3-420

Hours per WEEK after which time and a half is paid: 40. 48 hours: bowling alleys; residential employees caring for the sick, aged or mentally ill in institutions other than hospitals. 60 hours: agricultural work.

Notes: Craft or trade employees at concerts, shows, music festivals and pavilions are not excluded from overtime laws.

Massachusetts

Mass. Gen. Laws ch. 151, § 1A

Hours per WEEK after which time and a half is paid: 40

Michigan

Mich. Comp. Laws §§ 408.382 and following

Hours per WEEK after which time and a half is paid: 40

Employment overtime laws apply to: Employers of 2 or more employees.

Employment excluded from overtime laws: Employees not subject to state minimum wage laws.

Notes: Employee may elect up to 240 hours comp time a year at time and a half rate. Only allowed if: choice is voluntary, all employees get at least 10 days leave with pay per year and provision is part of a collective bargaining or other work agreement. Employee must submit express written request.

Minnesota

Minn. Stat. Ann. § 177.25

Hours per WEEK after which time and a half is paid: 48

Mississippi

No overtime provisions.

Missouri

Mo. Rev. Stat. §§ 290.500 and following

Hours per WEEK after which time and a half is paid: 40. 52 hours: seasonal amusement or recreation businesses.

State Overtime Rules (continued)

Employment excluded from overtime laws: Employment that is subject to the FLSA. Retail or service business with gross annual sales or contracts of less than $500,000.

Montana

Mont. Code Ann. §§ 39-3-405 and following

Hours per WEEK after which time and a half is paid: 40. 48 hours: students working seasonal jobs at amusement or recreational areas.

Employment excluded from overtime laws: Many exclusions including agricultural, livestock and forestry workers; auto mechanics, parts and salespersons; retail personnel who earn 50% more than minimum wage.

Nebraska

No overtime provisions.

Nevada

Nev. Rev. Stat. Ann. § 608.018

Hours per DAY after which time and a half is paid: 8

Hours per WEEK after which time and a half is paid: 40

Employment excluded from overtime laws: Businesses with a gross annual sales volume of less than $250,000.

Notes: Employer and employee may agree to flex-time schedule of four 10-hour days.

New Hampshire

N.H. Rev. Stat. Ann. § 279:21(VIII)

Hours per WEEK after which time and a half is paid: 40

Employment excluded from overtime laws: Employees covered by FLSA.

New Jersey

N.J. Stat. Ann. §§ 34:11-56a4 and following

Hours per WEEK after which time and a half is paid: 40

Employment excluded from overtime laws: June to September: summer camps; conferences and retreats operated by nonprofit or religious groups.

New Mexico

N.M. Stat. Ann. § 50-4-22(C)

Hours per WEEK after which time and a half is paid: 40

New York

N.Y. Lab. Law §§ 160(3), 161; N.Y. Comp. Codes R. & Regs. tit. 12, § 142-2.2

Hours per WEEK after which time and a half is paid: 40 for non-residential workers; 44 for residential workers.

Employment excluded from overtime laws: Same exemptions as FLSA.

Notes: Standard workday is 8 hours; 24 consecutive hours rest per 7 days is mandatory in most professions.

North Carolina

N.C. Gen. Stat. §§ 95-25.14; 95-25.4

Hours per WEEK after which time and a half is paid: 40. 45 hours a week in seasonal amusement or recreational establishments.

Employment excluded from overtime laws: Employment that is subject to the FLSA.

North Dakota

N.D. Admin. Code § 46-02-07-02(4)

Hours per WEEK after which time and a half is paid: 40. 50 hours per week, cab drivers,

Employment excluded from overtime laws: Computer professionals who design, develop, create, analyze, test or modify programs using independent judgment or who are paid at least $27.63/hour.

Notes: Private sector employees can't be given comp time instead of premium pay.

Hospital or residential care workers may agree to 80 hours per 14-day work period.

Ohio

Ohio Rev. Code Ann. § 4111.03

Hours per WEEK after which time and a half is paid: 40

Employment overtime laws apply to: Employers who gross more than $150,000 a year.

Notes: Follows FLSA guidelines.

Oklahoma

No state overtime provisions.

Oregon

Or. Rev. Stat. §§ 653.261; 653.265

Hours per WEEK after which time and a half is paid: 40

Notes: Time and a half required after 10 hours a day in canneries, driers or packing plants, unless they are a single farm operation.

Pennsylvania

43 Pa. Cons. Stat. Ann. § 333.104(c); 34 Pa. Code § 231.41

Hours per WEEK after which time and a half is paid: 40

State Overtime Rules (continued)

Rhode Island

R.I. Gen. Laws §§ 28-12-4.1 and following; 5-23-2(h)

Hours per WEEK after which time and a half is paid: 40

Notes: Time and a half for Sunday and holiday work is required for most retail businesses except bakeries and pharmacies (hours not included in calculating weekly overtime).

South Carolina

No overtime provisions.

South Dakota

No overtime provisions.

Tennessee

No overtime provisions.

Texas

No overtime provisions.

Utah

No overtime provisions.

Vermont

Vt. Stat. Ann. tit. 21, §§ 382, 384(b); Vt. Code R. 24 090 001

Hours per WEEK after which time and a half is paid: 40

Employment overtime laws apply to: Employers of two or more employees.

Employment excluded from overtime laws: Retail and service businesses if 75% of annual sales not for resale; seasonal amusement and recreation establishments; hotels, motels, restaurants; transportation workers exempt under FLSA.

Virginia

Va. Code Ann. §§ 40.1-28.1 and following

Notes: No state overtime provisions. Every employer must allow at least 24 consecutive hours rest per 7 days worked.

Employee entitled to choose Sunday as day of rest, or Saturday if observed as Sabbath.

Washington

Wash. Rev. Code Ann. § 49.46.130

Hours per WEEK after which time and a half is paid: 40

Employment excluded from overtime laws: Most agricultural workers.

Notes: Employee may choose comp time instead of paid overtime.

West Virginia

W.Va. Code § 21-5c-3

Hours per WEEK after which time and a half is paid: 40

Employment overtime laws apply to: Employers of 6 or more employees at one location.

Employment excluded from overtime laws: Employees that are subject to the FLSA.

Notes: Employment contract or collective bargaining agreement may set a longer work week for employees whose jobs require irregular hours.

Wisconsin

Wis. Stat. Ann. §§ 103.01; 103.03; Wis. Admin. Code DWD 274.01 and following

Hours per WEEK after which time and a half is paid: 40

Employment overtime laws apply to: Manufacturing, mechanical or retail businesses; beauty parlors, laundries, restaurants, hotels; telephone, express, shipping and transportation companies.

Employment excluded from overtime laws: Farming, domestic service.

Wyoming

No overtime provisions.

Current as of February 2003

7

Pay Policies

Let's face it—no matter how wonderful you are to work for and no matter how much you encourage camaraderie, creativity and teamwork on the job, your employees don't show up every day for the sheer joy of spending time with you. They want to get paid.

The basic exchange of the work relationship—labor for money—is easy enough to understand. But the laws regulating when, how and how much you pay your workers can get pretty complicated. One of the reasons for this complexity is that every level of government gets involved in legislating pay. The federal government has one set of rules, state governments have another and sometimes even local or municipal governments get into the act. And employers have to follow whichever law gives workers the most rights in any particular situation—which means you have to piece together a crazy quilt of laws from a variety of sources.

In this chapter, we'll show you how to put together compensation policies that tell your workers what they need to know: when they get paid, what kinds of work might entitle them to extra pay and the reasons why you might have to withhold money from their paychecks. We'll cover:

For information and policies on overtime and compensatory time, see Chapter 6.

7:1   Payday

The title pretty much says it all: your payday policy should tell employees when they will get paid. It should also let employees know when they will get their paychecks if payday falls on a holiday.

How often you pay your employees is governed by state law (the federal law doesn't require employers to follow any particular pay schedule). You can get information on your state's wage laws by contacting your state labor department (see Appendix C for contact information). For information on payday requirements, you can also check the U.S. Department of Labor's website—it has a chart of state payday laws at www.dol.gov/dol/esa/public/programs/whd/state/payday.htm.

Standard Policy

Payday

Employees are paid _____. You will receive your paycheck _____. If payday falls on a holiday, you will receive your paycheck on the last workday immediately before payday.

How to Complete This Policy

To complete this policy, you will need to decide how often you will pay your employees, and on what day of the week or month. Many states require employers to pay workers no less frequently than a certain interval—for example, weekly, biweekly, twice a month or once a month. You may pay your workers more often, but you may not make them wait longer than the law allows to receive their paychecks.

Some states, including Connecticut, Michigan, New Hampshire, New York, Rhode Island and Vermont, require some employers to pay workers on a weekly basis. You can find out more about these laws by visiting the U.S. Department of Labor's website, at the URL listed above. Some of these laws only apply to certain kinds of workers (for example, manual laborers). If you do business in one of these states, you could adopt a dual payday policy, one for the workers whom you must pay every week and one for the rest of your workforce.

Other than the handful of states that require at least some workers to be paid weekly, state law usually allows you to pay your workers every other week. However, some states allow you to pay your workers less frequently—for example, twice a month or even monthly.

Once you figure out how often you have to pay your employees—and how often you want to pay them, if you are considering more frequent paychecks—you can fill in the blanks in our sample policy. If you do business in a state that requires weekly paychecks, insert *every week* in the first blank and the day of the week (usually Friday) on which you will pay workers in the second. For biweekly paychecks, insert *every other week* in the first blank and the day when the paychecks will arrive in the second. For paydays that fall twice a month, insert *twice a month* in the first blank and the days of the month (often the 1st and the 15th of every month) when employees will be paid. Finally, for monthly paychecks, insert *monthly* in the first blank and the day of the month (usually the 1st or last day of the month) when you will distribute paychecks.

Who Needs This Policy

Your state's law may require employers to give employees written notice of when they will be paid, in certain circumstances. For example, Vermont requires workers to be paid weekly, but allows employers to pay workers less frequently if they give their workers written notice of the pay schedule. If you do business in one of these states, adopting a written payday policy may be not only a good idea, but also a legal requirement.

Even if state law doesn't require you to put your pay schedule in writing, doing so is generally a good idea. Workers take an active interest in when they will be paid, for understandable reasons. If you adopt a written policy, you can avoid having to answer a lot of anxious questions about when paychecks will arrive.

Reality Check: Pay Your Employees Before a Holiday

Our sample policy provides that paychecks will be distributed on the last working day before payday, if the designated payday falls on a holiday. The purpose of this language is to make sure that you meet your state's time limits: if your state requires workers to be paid every week or two, or provides (as a few do) that no more than a specified number of days may elapse between paychecks, you have to hit that mark, no matter what the calendar says. If you pay workers late because the designated payday came on a holiday or weekend, you will be in violation of the law.

Optional Modification to Require Submission of Time Cards

If you require your workers to turn in a written record of hours worked each pay period, specify that in your payday policy. For example, some employers require workers to hand in time cards, time sheets or other records. Here is a modification you can add to our sample policy if you require such records—note that you may have to tinker with our modification if you use some other form of timekeeping. The blank space allows you to tell your workers how many days in advance they must submit their records—most employers require workers to turn in their hours at least two or three days before payday.

Modification

Employees must submit their time cards or time sheets to their supervisor [*number of days*] before payday.

7:2   Advances

Advances (loans made against an employee's coming paycheck) can be the bane of a payroll administrator's existence. They create additional recordkeeping hassles and exceptions to the usual procedures. And there are some employees who are happy to take advantage of an employer's liberal policy by requesting frequent advances, rather than spending the time (and using the willpower) to balance their personal budgets more carefully.

Because of these potential problems, many employers choose not to offer advances at all, or to offer advances on a discretionary basis only, for situations that legitimately qualify as emergencies. Employers who allow advances often limit how often an employee can request them and how much money the employee can receive. To allow you to choose the policy that best meets your needs, we offer alternative sample policies. Policy A prohibits advances; Policy B allows advances only at the company's discretion.

No law requires you to give your employees pay advances—or to let them know what your policy is, one way or the other. However, regardless of how you decide to handle pay advances, you will save time and misunderstandings by adopting a policy setting out your rules. Some employees may assume you will give an advance; if you routinely deny all such requests, these employees will be in for an unpleasant surprise. And if you do offer advances, you should let employees know how and when advances must be paid back—and that you reserve the right not to grant an advance request.

Standard Policy A

No Advances

Our Company does not allow employees to receive pay advances for any reason.

Standard Policy B

Advance Policy

Please submit requests for pay advances to _____ ; requests will be granted or denied at the sole discretion of the Company.

   If we grant your request for an advance, you may receive no more than _____. All advances must be repaid within _____ days. Your request for an additional advance will be denied automatically if you have not yet repaid a previous advance.

How to Complete This Policy

Sample Policy B includes three blanks for you to fill in: the person to whom advance requests must be submitted, the amount of money an employee can receive and the length of time an employee has to pay back the advance.

- **Who receives advance requests:** Designate someone with a substantial amount of authority, such as the Chief Financial Officer, President or Director of Human Resources. You should choose the person who will ultimately decide whether advances will be granted, to minimize the paper shuffling. And it doesn't hurt to choose someone whose gravitas will cut back on the number of frivolous advance requests.

- **How much money can be advanced:** Here, you can use either a dollar figure (such as $200, $500 or $1,000) or a percentage of the employee's pay (25% or 50% of the employee's regular earnings, for example). Make sure to set a reasonable limit, based on what your workers generally earn—otherwise, it could prove hard for the employee to pay you back.

- **Time limits for repayment:** The time limit should be based, in part, on how large an advance you allow. If you offer only limited advances, 30 days should be sufficient. If the advance is substantial, it might take workers more than a month to pay you back—perhaps 60 days.

Optional Modifications

To Allow Advances for Vacations

Even employers who don't allow any advances may be willing to give early paychecks to employees who will be on vacation or on other paid leave when payday comes around. Although this is an advance of sorts, it's much easier for the employer to manage because the employee is simply getting paid a bit early, rather than borrowing money that will have to be paid back later. Your payroll administrator won't have to change the size of the employee's paychecks, just the timing.

If you want to allow these advances, you can add the following language to the end of either of the policies above:

Modification

An employee who will be on vacation or other paid leave on payday may request an early paycheck. Please submit these requests to the payroll administrator. Although we cannot guarantee that every request will be granted, we will do our best to accommodate your request.

To Allow Payroll Deductions to Pay Back Advances

Some employers adopt advance policies that allow them to deduct money from an employee's paycheck to repay an advance. These policies are eminently sensible—after all, it is much easier to get your money back if the employee never lays hands on it. However, state laws may restrict your right to withhold money to repay an advance—and federal law puts some limits on how much you can deduct.

Under federal law, you are allowed to deduct money from an employee's paycheck to repay an advance, but only if the money the employee actually receives, after your deduction, is at least equal to the minimum wage (currently $5.15 an hour, under federal law). Many states are more restrictive: some do not allow employers to deduct money from an employee's paycheck to repay an advance or other employer loan, while others allow such deductions only if the employee agrees to them, in writing.

Contact your state labor department to find out your state's requirements (you can find contact information in Appendix C). If you are allowed to take these deductions, with or without written consent, you can replace the second sentence of the last paragraph of Standard Policy B with the language below. Fill in the blank with the number of days you will give employees to repay advances. If written consent is required, use Form B (below) to obtain your employee's authorization for the deduction.

Modification

All advances must be paid back, through payroll deductions, within _____ days.

Form B: Payroll Deduction Authorization Form

If you plan to require employees to repay an advance through payroll deductions, ask them to sign the Payroll Deduction Authorization Form before they receive their money. The amount of the advance, what your employee earns and your state's law on payroll deductions will dictate how you fill in the blanks. Once you figure out how much you are legally entitled to withhold from each paycheck, calculate how many paychecks it will take for the employee to pay you back. Do this by dividing the total amount of the advance by the amount you can withhold from each paycheck. Then fill in the blanks accordingly.

Payroll Deduction Authorization Form

I have requested an advance from the Company. This advance is a loan, which I am fully obligated to repay. In consideration of the Company's decision to grant this request, I agree to repay the Company through payroll deductions. I hereby authorize the Company to withhold $_____ from my paycheck in _____ equal installments to repay the advance. The total amount deducted from my pay shall be equal to the amount of the advance.

If my employment is terminated or I quit before this advance is repaid, I hereby authorize the Company to deduct the full amount I still owe the Company from my final paycheck, if allowed by law.

_____   _____

Employee's Signature   Date

_____

Employee's Name (Print)

7:3   Tip Credits

If your employees earn tips from customers, you may be entitled to pay them a salary that is less than the minimum wage, as long as that salary plus the tips they actually earn adds up to at least the minimum wage per hour worked. If you follow this procedure (legally referred to as a "tip credit", you are legally required to adopt a policy explaining it to employees. Laying your intentions on the table will also let your workers know what to expect, so they won't be surprised when they get that first paycheck.

Not all states allow you to take a tip credit. Consult the chart, "State Minimum Wage Laws for Tipped and Regular Employees," at the end of this chapter, to find out whether your state allows you to take a tip credit—and how much of a credit you can take. The chart also indicates each state's minimum wage, how much you must pay your workers per hour if you take a tip credit and which workers qualify for a tip credit.

Standard Policy

Tip Credit

Employees who hold certain positions in our Company receive some of their compensation in the form of tips from customers. If you receive tips, the Company will pay you an hourly wage of at least $_____. However, if that wage plus the tips you actually earn during any pay period does not add up to at least the minimum wage for every hour you work, the Company will pay you the difference.

Who Needs This Policy

Only those employers who employ workers who receive tips *and* pay those workers less than the minimum wage need this policy. In other words, you don't necessarily need this policy just because your workers receive tips: If you pay your workers an hourly wage that meets or exceeds the minimum wage, this policy is inapplicable.

7:4   Tip Pooling

Tip pooling (also known as "tipping out") is a source of much anxiety and frustration in the tipped workforce. Some employees—particularly those who have to deal most with the customers, such as wait staff or bell persons—deeply resent having to share their tips with employees who have less customer contact. Adopting a policy explaining exactly who is required to share how much of their tips can help ease this problem. If everyone knows, ahead of time, how the pool will work, there is less likelihood of irritation and resentment.

Standard Policy

Tip Pooling

Employees in the following positions are required to pool tips: _____. If you hold one of these positions, you must contribute _____% of your tips to the pool at the end of each work day. The pool will be divided equally among all employees who worked that day and hold one of the positions listed above.

How to Complete This Policy

Your tip pooling policy must meet certain legal requirements. First, you can only require tip pooling among employees who customarily receive tips, such as wait staff, bussers, bartenders, bellhops and counter clerks. You may not include any workers in the pool who do not receive tips of their own—such as dishwashers, cooks, chefs and janitors. Keeping these rules in mind, fill in the first blank, above, with the titles of all of the positions that will be required to contribute to the tip pool.

The law also limits how much workers can be required to contribute to a pool. Only tips in excess of tips used for the tip credit may be taken for a pool—in other words, your employees must be allowed to keep enough of their own tips to earn the minimum wage, when those tips are combined with the employees' hourly wage. In addition, tipped employees cannot be required to contribute a greater percentage of their tips than is customary and reason-

⚠ **Don't take a dip in the tip pool.** All of the money in the tip pool must be shared among the workers who contribute to it—and only those workers. You cannot take any portion of the pooled tips for yourself, under any circumstances. If you violate this basic rule, the Department of Labor will find your tip pooling arrangement invalid, disallow any tip credit you are taking and require you to pay back the money you took from your workers, with interest and penalties.

able. This amount varies depending on your industry and location—check with a local trade organization to find out what percentage is usual. Once you do, insert that percentage in the second blank, above.

Who Needs This Policy

Only employers who employ workers who receive tips *and* require those employees to share their tips with other workers need this policy.

7:5   Shift Premiums

A shift premium policy should tell employees whether they'll be paid extra for working certain shifts, if applicable.

Employers in industries that work in shifts often find it difficult to staff those shifts that fall outside of the regular 9 to 5 workday. Some employers find that offering workers higher pay to work night shifts, swing shifts or split shifts solves this problem. If you choose to offer a shift premium, you should adopt a policy explaining the premium in your handbook. After all, the incentive only works if your employees know about it.

Standard Policy

Shift Premiums

Employees who work the _____ shift will be paid a premium for each shift. This premium will be _____.

How to Complete This Policy

In the first blank, insert the shifts for which you plan to adopt a premium (for example, *night shift*, *graveyard shift* or *3 p.m. to 11 p.m. shift*). In the second blank, insert the premium amount. If all of your workers make the same wage, you can simply insert the dollar amount you plan to pay these shift workers per hour. If your workers earn varying rates, you can insert the dollar amount or percentage by which you will increase their pay for agreeing to work the tough-to-fill shift (for example, *two dollars more per hour in addition to their regular hourly pay* or *an additional 20% of their regular hourly pay*).

Some states (including California) require employers to pay their workers a certain premium for working a split shift—that is, for working one shift, then coming back to work another one after a relatively short break. Contact your state labor department (you can find contact details in Appendix C) to find out if your state imposes this type of requirement. If so, you must pay split shift workers this premium—and you should set the premium in your policy to at least meet this minimum required amount.

7:6   Payroll Deductions

Your payroll deduction policy should explain the mandatory deductions you take from employees' paychecks, as well as the deductions an employee can request. Although all the information is usually right there on the pay stub, a policy can help clarify the reasons why deductions are taken (and why that paycheck is always so much smaller than the worker thinks it will be).

Standard Policy

Payroll Deductions

Your paycheck reflects your total earnings for the pay period, as well as any mandatory or voluntary deductions from your paycheck. Mandatory deductions are deductions that we are legally required to take. Such deductions include federal income tax, Social Security tax (FICA) and any applicable state taxes. Voluntary deductions are deductions that you have authorized. Such deductions might include _____.

If you have any questions about your deductions, or wish to change your federal withholding form (Form W-4), contact _____.

How to Complete This Policy

In the space for voluntary deductions, list any contributions you allow employees to make through payroll withholding, such as:
- insurance premiums
- flexible spending accounts
- contributions to pensions, 401(k)s or other retirement accounts
- union dues
- charitable contributions, or
- contributions to credit unions or savings accounts.

In the second blank, insert the name of the person or position that handles payroll matters. This might be the payroll administrator, human resources department, benefits coordinator, or whoever makes sure that paychecks go out on time or reports employee compensation to the IRS.

7:7 Wage Garnishments

Any employer can be required, by a court order, the IRS or another government agency, to garnish an employee's wages. Most employers dislike these orders. Wage garnishments are a payroll hassle. If you receive one, you will have to deduct the prescribed amount from the employee's wages—for a limited time in some cases (when the employee owes a specified amount of money in unpaid taxes or student loans, for example) or indefinitely (for garnishments relating to child or spousal support, for example).

But no matter how much you dislike having to deal with a wage garnishment order, you can rest assured that at least one person is even more put out by the order: the employee whose wages you have to garnish. Adopting a policy lets employees know that you have no choice but to comply with these orders—and that you intend to. Your employees will know that there's not much point asking you to reduce, forgive or postpone the garnishment—it's out of your hands. And hopefully, employees who are upset about a garnishment will take their complaints to the responsible person or agency, rather than complaining to someone who can't change the situation (you).

Your wage garnishment policy should tell employees what a wage garnishment is and the reasons why their wages might be garnished—and let employees know that you must comply with orders to garnish wages.

 Need more information on wage garnishments? The Department of Labor offers a helpful fact sheet on the federal law governing wage garnishments, including how much of an employee's wages can be garnished. You can download this fact sheet from the agency's website, at www.dol.gov/asp/programs/handbook/garnish.htm.

Standard Policy

Wage Garnishments

A wage garnishment is an order from a court or a government agency directing us to withhold a certain amount of money from an employee's paycheck and send it to a person or agency. Wages can be garnished to pay child support, spousal support or alimony, tax debts, outstanding student loans or money owed as a result of a judgment in a civil lawsuit.

If we are instructed by a court or agency to garnish an employee's wages, the employee will be notified of the garnishment at once. Please note that we are legally required to comply with these orders. If you dispute or have concerns about the amount of a garnishment, you must contact the court or agency that issued the order.

7:8   Expense Reimbursement

Expenses often become a source of conflict between workers and management. Workers don't want to incur work-related expenses that the company refuses to pay—they want to know, ahead of time, what they will be reimbursed for, what they need to do to get reimbursed and when they can expect repayment. Just as understandably, employers don't want to get hit with requests for reimbursement for extravagant, fraudulent or unnecessary expenses—and they want some proof that the worker actually incurred the expenses claimed. An expense reimbursement policy can help you set things straight before any expenses are incurred.

Your expense reimbursement policy should tell employees which expenses will be reimbursed, how to get authorization to incur expenses and the procedures for requesting reimbursement.

Standard Policy

Expense Reimbursement

From time to time, employees may incur expenses on behalf of _____[Company name]__. We will reimburse you for the actual work-related expenses you incur, as long as those expenses are reasonable. You must follow these procedures to get reimbursed:

- Get permission from your supervisor before incurring an expense.
- Spend the Company's money wisely—make an effort to save money and use approved vendors if possible.
- Keep a receipt or some other proof of payment for every expense.
- Submit your receipts, along with an expense report, to your supervisor for approval within 30 days of incurring an expense.
- Your supervisor is responsible for submitting your expense report to _____. If your report is approved, you will receive your reimbursement _____.

Remember that you are spending the Company's money when you pay for business-related expenses. We expect you to save money wherever possible. Your supervisor can assist you in deciding whether an expense is appropriate.

Reality Check: An Expense by Any Other Name

Sometimes, state law dictates whether you or your employee has to pay for a particular expense. For example, some states require employers to pay the cost of everything an employee needs in order to do the job—including uniforms and tools. Other states don't have such strict requirements—they allow employers to pass these costs on to their employees (or to refuse to reimburse these expenses, as the case may be). Contact your state labor department (you'll find contact information in Appendix C) to find out what your state requires.

How to Complete This Policy

In the first blank, insert the position or department responsible for payroll matters (for example, *the payroll department*, *the accounting department* or *human resources*). In the second blank, indicate when and how employees will receive their reimbursements (for example, *with your next paycheck* or *within fourteen days*).

Optional Modifications

To Require Employees to Use Particular Vendors

If your company has business accounts with particular vendors, such as messengers, caterers or suppliers, you may want to modify our standard policy to require your employees to do business with those vendors, if possible. This will save time and money—you'll know you're getting a good deal, and your workers won't have to shop around. To modify the policy, add this language between the second and third bullets in our sample policy. Fill in the blank with the name of the position or department that handles payroll.

Modification

- The Company maintains a list of preferred vendors for various work-related items and services. You must use these vendors, if possible. You can get a current copy of the list from _____ _____.

To Include More Detail on Travel Expenses

The sample policy above is sufficient to handle very occasional employee travel. However, if the nature of your business requires your employees to travel frequently, you may need a more detailed travel expense policy. Your employees need to know what expenses will be reimbursed—are you going to pay for them to fly first class? To stay in a four-star hotel? You can modify the basic expense reimbursement policy above by simply adding this language at the end.

In the blank, insert the total amount you will pay employees per day for meals and other incidentals. To get an idea of how much other employers in your field are offering as a per diem, contact a local industry organization or professional association—or ask at your local Chamber of Commerce.

Modification

Procedures for Travel Expenses

If employees are required to travel for work, the Company will reimburse you for your travel expenses, including:

- The cost of travel to and from the airport or train station, including parking expenses and tolls.
- The cost of airline or train tickets—such tickets must be coach class if possible.
- The cost of an economy class rental car, if necessary.
- A mileage reimbursement, for those employees who prefer to use their own cars for company travel.
- The cost of lodging. Employees should select moderately priced lodging if possible.
- The cost of meals and other incidental expenses, up to a per diem of $_____ per day.

You must request advance approval of all travel expenses from your supervisor and follow the procedures above to have your expenses reimbursed.

To Allow Mileage Reimbursement

If your employees use their own cars for company business, you should modify our standard policy to include a mileage reimbursement. You must also require your employees to have a valid driver's license and adequate insurance coverage.

Fill in the blanks as follows: in the first blank, insert the rate of reimbursement. Most employers pay a per-mile rate based on IRS standards (currently 36.5 cents per mile). In the second blank, include the name of the department or position that handles payroll—this should be identical to what you inserted in the main sample policy, above.

Modification

Mileage Reimbursement

Employees who use their own vehicle for Company business will be reimbursed at the rate of _____. Employees are not entitled to separate reimbursement for gas, maintenance, insurance or other vehicle-related expenses—the reimbursement rate, above, is intended to encompass all of these expenses.

Before using a personal vehicle for work-related purposes, employees must demonstrate that they have a valid driver's license and adequate insurance coverage.

The Company does not reimburse employees for their commute to and from the workplace.

To claim mileage reimbursement, you must follow these procedures:

- Keep a written record of your business-related travel, including the total mileage of each business trip, the date of travel, the location to which you traveled and the purpose of your trip.
- If you anticipate having to travel an unusually long distance, get your supervisor's approval before making the trip.
- Submit your record to your supervisor for approval on the last day of the month.
- Your supervisor is responsible for submitting your record to _____. If your record is approved, you will receive your reimbursement payment with your next paycheck.

Form C: Expense Reimbursement Form

If your employees will incur expenses, you should provide them with an expense form. A preprinted form will remind your employees of what they have to submit along with their expense request—and streamline your paperwork.

Expense Reimbursement Form

Date of Expense	Item or Service Purchased	Reason for Expense	Cost	Receipt Attached

_____   _____
Employee's Signature   Date Submitted

_____
Employee's Name (Print)

_____   _____
Supervisor's Signature   Date Approved

_____
Supervisor's Name (Print)

State Minimum Wage Laws for Tipped and Regular Employees

The chart below gives the basic state minimum wage laws. Depending on the occupation, the size of the employer's business or the conditions of employment, the minimum wage may vary from the one listed here. Minimum wage rates in a number of states change from year to year; to be sure of your state's current minimum, contact your state department of labor or check its website, where most states have posted the minimum wage requirements. (See Appendix for contact information.)

"Maximum Tip Credit" is based on tips the employee actually receives, and is the highest amount of tips that an employer can subtract from the employee's hourly wage. The employee's wages plus the tip credit cannot be less than the state minimum wage. If an employee's tips exceed the maximum tip credit, the employee gets to keep the extra amount.

"Minimum Cash Wage" is the lowest hourly wage that an employer can pay a tipped employee.

State and Statute	Notes	Basic Minimum Hourly Rate (*=Tied to Federal rate)	Maximum Tip Credit (tips only, not food & lodging unless noted)	Minimum Cash Wage for Tipped Employee	Minimum Tips to Qualify As a Tipped Employee (monthly unless noted otherwise)
United States 29 U.S.C. § 206		$5.15	$3.02	$2.13	More than $30.
Alabama	No minimum wage law.				
Alaska Alaska Stat. § 23.10.065; Alaska Admin. Code Tit. 8, § 15.120	Adjusted annually on 9/30. Wage is current minimum plus 100% CPI inflation rate, or $1 more than FLSA, whichever is greater.	$7.15	$0	$7.15	N/A
Arizona	No minimum wage law.				
Arkansas Ark. Code Ann. §§ 11-4-210 to -213	Applies to employers with 4 or more employees.	$5.15	50%	$2.575	Not specified.
California Cal. Code Regs. tit. 8, § 11000		$6.75	$0	$6.75	
Colorado Colo. Rev. Stat. §§ 8-6-108.5 to -109; 7 Colo. Code Regs. § 1103-1	Minimum wage applies to these industries: retail and service, commercial support service, food and beverage and health and medical.	$5.15	$3.02	$2.13	More than $30.
Connecticut Conn. Gen. Stat. Ann. § 31-58(j)	Effective 1/1/04: $7.10 or 0.5% more than FLSA minimum, if higher.	$6.90 or 0.5% more than FLSA minimum, if higher.	Generally, $0.35	$6.35	Not specified.
Delaware Del. Code Ann. tit. 19, § 902(a)		$6.15 or FLSA rate if higher.	$3.02	$2.13	More than $30.
District of Columbia D.C. Code Ann. §§ 32-1003 to -1004		$6.15* $1 above FLSA rate.	55%	$2.77	Not specified.
Florida	No minimum wage law.				
Georgia Ga. Code Ann. § 34-4-3	Applies to employers with 6 or more employees and over $40,000 per year in sales.	$5.15	Minimum wage does not apply to tipped employees.	N/A	

State Minimum Wage Laws for Tipped and Regular Employees					
State and Statute	Notes	Basic Minimum Hourly Rate (*=Tied to Federal rate)	Maximum Tip Credit (tips only, not food & lodging unless noted)	Minimum Cash Wage for Tipped Employee	Minimum Tips to Qualify As a Tipped Employee (monthly unless noted otherwise)
Hawaii Haw. Rev. Stat. §§ 387-1 to 387-2		$6.25	$0.25	$6.00	More than $20; employee's cash wage plus tips must be at least $.50 higher than the minimum wage.
Idaho Idaho Code § 44-1502		$5.15	35%	$3.35	More than $30.
Illinois 820 Ill. Comp. Stat. § 105/4; Ill. Admin. Code tit. 56, § 210.110	Applies to employers with 4 or more employees.	$5.15*	40%	$3.09	$20
Indiana Ind. Code Ann. § 22-2-2-4	Applies to employers with 2 or more employees.	$5.15	$3.02	$2.13	Not specified.
Iowa Iowa Code § 91D.1	Minimum wage does not apply to first 90 calendar days of employment.	$5.15*	40%	$3.09	More than $30.
Kansas Kan. Stat. Ann. § 44-1203	Applies to employers not covered by the FLSA.	$2.65	40%	$1.59	Not specified.
Kentucky Ky. Rev. Stat. Ann. § 337.275		$5.15*	$3.02	$2.13	More than $30.
Louisiana	No minimum wage law.				
Maine Me. Rev. Stat. Ann. tit. 26, § 664		$6.25, or FLSA rate if higher.	50%	$3.13	More than $20.
Maryland Md. Code Ann., [Lab. & Empl.] §§ 3-413, 3-419		$5.15*	$2.77	$2.38	More than $30.
Massachusetts Mass. Gen. Laws ch. 151, § 1; Mass. Regs. Code tit. 455, §§ 2.02 & following		$6.75, or $0.10 above FLSA rate if higher.	$4.12	$2.63	More than $20.
Michigan Mich. Comp. Laws §§ 408.382 to 408.387a	Applies to employers with 2 or more employees. Excludes all employers subject to FLSA, unless state minimum wage is higher than federal.	$5.15	$2.50	$2.65	Not specified.
Minnesota Minn. Stat. Ann. § 177.24	$4.90, for small employer (business with annual receipts of less than $500,000).	$5.15	None	$5.15	
Mississippi	No minimum wage law.				
Missouri Mo. Rev. Stat. §§ 290.502, 290.512		$5.15*	Up to 50%	$2.575	

State Minimum Wage Laws for Tipped and Regular Employees					
State and Statute	Notes	Basic Minimum Hourly Rate (*=Tied to Federal rate)	Maximum Tip Credit (tips only, not food & lodging unless noted)	Minimum Cash Wage for Tipped Employee	Minimum Tips to Qualify As a Tipped Employee (monthly unless noted otherwise)
Montana Mont. Code Ann. §§ 39-3-404, 39-3-409; Mont. Admin. R. 24.16.1508 & following	$4.00, for businesses with gross annual sales of $110,000 or less.	$5.15*	None	$5.15*	
Nebraska Neb. Rev. Stat. § 48-1203	Applies to employers with 4 or more employees.	$5.15	$3.02	$2.13	Not specified.
Nevada Nev. Rev. Stat. Ann. §§ 608.160, 608.250		$5.15*	None	$5.15	
New Hampshire N.H. Rev. Stat. Ann. § 279:21		$5.15*	$2.57	$2.38 or 45% of minimum wage, if higher.	More than $20.
New Jersey N.J. Stat. Ann. §§ 34: 11-56a4; N.J. Admin. Code tit. 12, §§ 56-3.1 & following, 56-14.4	Minimum wage varies depending on occupation.	$5.15*	$2.13	$3.02	Not specified.
New Mexico N.M. Stat. Ann. § 50-4-22		$4.25	50% minimum wage	$2.125	More than $30.
New York N.Y. Lab. Law § 652; N.Y. Comp. Codes R. & Regs. tit. 12, § 137-1.4		$5.15*	$0.95, if tips per hour are under $1.35; $1.35, if tips per hour are $1.35 or more		Receives at least $0.95 per hour in tips.
North Carolina N.C. Gen. Stat. §§ 95-25.2(14), 95-25.3		$5.15*	$3.02	$2.13	More than $20.
North Dakota N.D. Cent. Code § 34-06-03; N.D. Admin. Code R. 46-02-07-01(17) to -03		$5.15	33%	$3.45	More than $30.
Ohio Ohio Rev. Code Ann. § 4111.02	$3.35, for employers with gross annual sales of $150,000 to $500,000. $2.80, for employers with gross annual sales of less than $150,000.	$5.15	50%	$3.075; $2.01, for employers with sales under $500,000.	More than $30.
Oklahoma Okla. Stat. Ann. tit. 40, §§ 197.2, 197.4, 197.16	Applies to employers with 10 or more full-time employees OR gross annual sales over $100,000. $2.00, for all other employers who are not subject to FLSA.	$5.15*	50% For tips, food and lodging combined.	$2.58	Not specified.

State Minimum Wage Laws for Tipped and Regular Employees					
State and Statute	Notes	Basic Minimum Hourly Rate (*=Tied to Federal rate)	Maximum Tip Credit (tips only, not food & lodging unless noted)	Minimum Cash Wage for Tipped Employee	Minimum Tips to Qualify As a Tipped Employee (monthly unless noted otherwise)
Oregon Or. Rev. Stat. §§ 653.025, 653.035(3)		$6.50	None	$6.50	
Pennsylvania 43 Pa. Cons. Stat. Ann. §§ 333.104 & following; 34 Pa. Code § 231.1		$5.15*	45%	$2.83	More than $30.
Rhode Island R.I. Gen. Laws §§ 28-12-3 & following		$6.15	$3.26	$2.89	Not specified.
South Carolina	No minimum wage law.				
South Dakota S.D. Codified Laws Ann. §§ 60-11-3 to -3.1		$5.15	$3.02	$2.13	More than $35.
Tennessee	No minimum wage law.				
Texas Tex. Lab. Code Ann. §§ 62.051 & following	Applies to employers not covered by FLSA.	$5.15*	$3.02	$2.13	More than $20.
Utah Utah Code Ann. §§ 34-40-102 to -103; Utah Admin. R. 610-1	Applies to employers not covered by FLSA.	$5.15*	$3.02	$2.13	More than $30.
Vermont Vt. Stat. Ann. tit. 21, § 384(a); Vt. Code R. 24 090 001 & following	Applies to employers with 2 or more employees.	$6.25, or FLSA rate if higher.	45%	$3.44	More than $30.
Virginia Va. Code Ann. §§ 40.1-28.9(D) to 28.10	Applies to employers with 4 or more employees	5.15*	Actual amount received.		Not specified.
Washington Wash. Rev. Code Ann. § 49.46.020; Wash. Admin. Code 296-126-022	Adjusted annually for inflation. Posted at: www.lni.wa.gov	$7.01 in 2003.	None	$6.90	
West Virginia W.Va. Code §§ 21-5C-2, 21-5C-4	Applies to employers with 6 or more employees at one location who are not covered by the FLSA.	$5.15	20%	$4.12	Not specified.
Wisconsin Wis. Stat. Ann. § 104.02		$5.15	$2.42	$2.33	Not specified.
Wyoming Wyo. Stat. § 27-4-202; Wis. Admin. Code DWD 272.001 & following		$5.15	$3.02	$2.13	More than $30.

Current as of February 2003

CHAPTER

8

Employee Benefits

Most employers spend a significant amount of their labor budget on benefits for their employees. Indeed, about 40% of an average employee's compensation package goes toward benefits. Employers do this with good reason. Generous employee benefits can help you entice high quality workers, retain valuable employees and improve labor relations. In addition, good benefits can actually assist your employees in being more productive and effective. An employee with health insurance is less likely to miss work due to an untreated illness than an employee who's worried about racking up doctor bills, for example.

Of course, you can only reap these rewards if your employees actually know about—and take advantage of—the benefit programs that you offer. Too often, employers pay for benefit programs that their employees don't even use, because the employees either don't know about the program or don't understand it. Your employee handbook is the ideal place to acquaint your employees with their benefits.

The handbook is not, however, the ideal place to educate your employees about every last detail of each benefit program. This is because benefit programs, unlike employee handbooks, tend to change, even if only slightly, every year. If you put too much information in your handbook, you'll have to rewrite it every time you need to change and adjust your benefit programs. Or if you leave out-of-date information in your handbook, you risk having your employees rely on that information, unaware that the benefit no longer exists or that it has changed significantly. This could damage labor relations (the opposite of what you want) and even leave you vulnerable to a claim from the employee that you breached a contract (in the form of handbook language) over the benefits that you would offer.

As a result, most employers choose to make their handbook descriptions of benefits quite general, leaving the details to separate handouts and brochures that they can distribute to employees whenever the need arises. The standard and sample policies in this chapter follow that model. They allow you to toot your own horn, as it were, and announce how wonderful your benefits are without binding you to the details.

The benefits that employers provide usually fall into one of two groups: those that the employer provides voluntarily and those that are mandated by law. Voluntary benefit programs include health insurance, dental insurance, on-site childcare, life insurance and retirement coverage (for example, a pension plan or a 401(k) plan). Legally mandated benefit programs include workers' compensation coverage and unemployment insurance. To find out what sorts of benefits are legally mandated in your state, contact your state labor department. (See Appendix C for contact details.)

Your handbook should contain policies for every kind of benefit program you offer, regardless of whether the program is voluntary or legally mandated. In this chapter, we provide you with the following policies:

8:1   Employee Benefits: Introductory Statement

As we explained above, you don't want to pack too many details into your benefits section because you want to maintain flexibility: You want to be able to change the benefits at any time and you want to avoid making promises in your handbook that you won't be able to keep.

This standard language maintains your flexibility to change benefits, explains the significance of official plan documents and tells employees where to go for more information.

Standard Policy

Employee Benefit Plans

As part of our commitment to our employees and their well-being, __[Company Name]__ provides employees with a variety of benefit plans: _____ *[List all of the voluntary and legally mandated benefit plans that you provide—for example, health insurance, retirement benefits, stock options, unemployment compensation, workers' compensation]*.

Although we introduce you to those plans in this section, we cannot provide the details of each plan here. You should receive official plan documents for each of the benefit plans that we offer. Those documents (along with any updates that we give to you) should be your primary resource for information about your benefit plans. If you see any conflict between those documents and the information in this Handbook, the official plan documents are what you should rely upon.

The benefits we provide are meant to help employees maintain a high quality of life—both professionally and personally. We sincerely hope that each employee will take full advantage of these benefits. If you don't understand information in the plan documents or if you have any questions about the benefits we offer, please talk to

_____.

How to Complete This Policy

In addition to listing all of the benefits that you offer, you will have to choose someone to whom employees can go for more information about the various benefit plans. Try to pick someone in your company—for example, an office manager or a human resources worker—who is willing and able to get up to speed on these matters. Don't simply instruct employees to call the customer service numbers at the various providers of your benefits plans. If employees are to make the most of the benefits that you offer—and if you are to get your money's worth in terms of improved labor relations—you need to have someone on site who can help employees wade through the often confusing maze of benefits rules.

Reality Check: Don't Forget ERISA

The word ERISA often strikes fear into the hearts of employers, because it is the acronym for one of the most dense and confusing federal laws on the books: The Employee Retirement Income Security Act.

Although it has the word "retirement" in its title, ERISA does not limit itself to retirement plans alone. In fact, the law governs the operation of virtually all employee benefit plans and most likely covers every benefit plan that you offer to your employees.

Among ERISA's many rules are ones regarding the information that employees must receive about their benefit plans. This information includes a summary plan description, notification of any changes to the plan and information about how to appeal any adverse decisions made by the plan.

If you pay someone to administer a plan for you (for example, if a health insurance company provides the healthcare coverage for your employees), then that plan administrator will usually take care of complying with ERISA's requirements. Talk to your plan administrator and make sure that ERISA is being followed to the letter.

If you administer your own plan, however, that burden will fall on you. Unless you are incredibly sophisticated and experienced in ERISA matters, complying with ERISA is not something you can do on your own. Seek out professional help. To learn more about ERISA and other federal employment laws, see *Federal Employment Laws: A Desk Reference,* by Amy DelPo & Lisa Guerin (Nolo.)

8:2   Domestic Partner Coverage

In the past few decades, our concept of family has changed dramatically. In 1998, only 25% of U.S. households were living in traditional family units—husband, wife and children. What was everyone else doing? Well, 5.9 million people were living with a domestic partner (and 28% of those partnerships were same-sex partnerships).

Just as our concept of family is evolving, so too is our concept of who should be covered by an employee's benefits. Everyone expects a spouse and child to be eligible for coverage, but what about the non-employee partner in a committed relationship who either chooses to forego marriage or is legally prohibited from marriage?

To keep up with this evolving set of norms, employers are increasingly providing coverage for domestic partners. Deciding whether to include domestic partner coverage is a very complicated task, one that involves research into your state and local laws. Some localities require domestic partners to be covered, others prohibit it. Therefore, this is not something you can decide to do— or not to do—based solely on your gut instinct or sense of morality. Make this decision only after consulting with your benefits administrator and/or your lawyer.

The wording of your domestic partner policy will depend on many things, including your state and local laws and the preferences

For a comprehensive guide to domestic partner coverage, including information on state and local laws and advice on how to decide whether to offer such coverage in your own workplace, see *Domestic Partner Benefits: An Employer's Guide*, by Joseph Adams & Todd Solomon (Thompson Publishing Group).

of your benefits administrator. The following is just an example of what such a policy might look like.

SAMPLE POLICY LANGUAGE:

At J&J Books, we recognize that some of our employees are members of families that do not meet the traditional definition of the word—that is, a husband, wife and, perhaps, children. For those employees who are not married but who are in a committed relationship with another adult, we provide domestic partnership coverage.

To be eligible for benefits, the employee and the employee's partner must meet all of the following criteria:

1. *They must have lived together in an exclusive committed relationship for at least 12 months.*
2. *They must be at least 18 years of age.*
3. *They must live together in the same residence.*
4. *They cannot be legally married to—or in a registered domestic partnership with—anyone else.*
5. *They must not be related by blood more closely than would be allowed under the marriage laws of this state.*
6. *They must complete and sign a Domestic Partnership Affidavit.*

8:3   Healthcare Benefits

The healthcare coverage that you offer to your employees is the flagship of your employee benefits program. No matter what other benefits you offer (tuition reimbursement, employee assistance programs and the like) the most important one to your employees will be your healthcare program. Healthcare benefits include more than simply medical coverage. They also include any vision, dental or similar benefits that you provide.

Because healthcare benefits have so many permutations and options, we cannot provide you with a standard policy to place in your handbook. We do, however, provide an example of a healthcare policy, followed by detailed guidance on how to write one of your own.

SAMPLE POLICY LANGUAGE:

Because your health is of great importance to us, we provide you with the following healthcare benefits: medical, dental, vision and alternative (including acupuncture and massage). If you have not already received detailed plan documents about each of these benefits, contact Myrtle Means in the Human Resources Department. She can provide you with all of the information that you need to start enjoying your healthcare benefits package right away. Even if you have received plan documents, Myrtle can answer any questions you might have.

Eligibility to receive healthcare benefits depends on your employee classification. (See Section D of this Handbook for information about employee classifications.) If you are a regular full-time or regular part-time employee, you are eligible to receive full healthcare benefits, and we will pay 100 percent of the premium for you.

And don't worry. We haven't forgotten about your loved ones. We will pay 100 percent of the premium for eligible dependents (including domestic partners).

You and your dependents become eligible for benefits 30 days after the day you start work.

As with all of the policies in this Handbook, our healthcare coverage may change at any time. For the most up-to-date information about your healthcare benefits, refer to the plan documents or contact Myrtle.

What to Include in This Policy

When writing your healthcare benefits policy, it's important to keep in mind the advice we gave at the beginning of this chapter:

- keep the information in the handbook general and non-specific, and
- refer employees to official plan documents for details.

That being said, there are some details that you should include in your policy language. These details are not about the benefit itself, but are about who is eligible for the benefit and who will pay for it. Include the following information in your medical benefits policy:

- The classification(s) of employees who are eligible for the benefit (for example, regular full-time employees). (See Chapter 5 for policy language about employee classifications.)
- The classification(s) of employees who are not eligible for the benefit (for example, temporary employees).
- The amount of the premium that you will pay.
- The amount of the premium that the employee must pay.
- Whether dependents and/or domestic partners will be covered.

8:4   Disability

Most states require employers to withhold a portion of an employee's paycheck to pay for disability insurance. When employees suffer non-work injuries that prevent them from doing their jobs, they can receive disability benefits.

Even though money is taken out of their paychecks to pay for this benefit, many employees do not know about or understand it. This policy explains in general terms who is eligible for state disability benefits and alerts employees to the difference between disability coverage and workers' compensation.

Standard Policy

State Disability Insurance

Sometimes, an employee suffers an illness or injury outside of the workplace that prevents the employee from working and earning income. If this happens to you, the state disability insurance may provide you with a percentage of your salary while you are unable to work. All employees are eligible for this coverage and pay for it through deductions from their paychecks.

To find out more about state disability insurance, contact _____.

If you suffer from an illness or injury that is work-related, then you may be eligible for workers' compensation insurance instead of state disability insurance. See the Workers' Compensation policy, below, or contact _____ for more information.

Who Needs This Policy

If your state requires you to withhold a percentage of your employees' wages to fund a state disability insurance program, you should have this policy in your handbook. Your payroll department should know whether you are withholding disability money—or you can contact your state department of labor (see Appendix C for contact information).

8:5   Workers' Compensation

Most employers must carry workers' compensation insurance to cover them when an employee suffers a work-related injury. This policy explains what workers' compensation insurance is, and it instructs employees to notify the company immediately if they are injured or become ill. This is a very important requirement, for it will help you prevent harm to other employees.

Standard Policy

Workers' Compensation Insurance

If you suffer from an illness or injury that is related to your work, you may be eligible for workers' compensation benefits. Workers' compensation will pay for medical care and lost wages resulting from job-related illnesses or injuries.

If you are injured or become ill through work, please inform your supervisor immediately regardless of how minor the injury or illness might be.

To find out more about workers' compensation coverage, contact _____.

If you are unable to work because of an illness or injury that is not related to work, then you might be eligible for state disability insurance instead of workers' compensation. See the Disability Insurance policy, above, or contact _____ for more information.

Who Needs This Policy

All employers who are required by state law to provide workers' compensation coverage must have this policy in their handbooks. Contact your state workers' compensation office to find out about requirements in your state. (See Appendix C for contact details.)

8:6   Unemployment Insurance

Unemployment insurance is another state-mandated benefit. Usually, employers withhold a portion of each employee's paycheck to fund this insurance program, which pays benefits to employees who suddenly find themselves out of work.

The ins and outs of who is eligible for unemployment insurance can be rather complicated. As a result, this policy simply notifies employees that this benefit exists, and it instructs them on whom to contact for more information.

Standard Policy

Unemployment Insurance

If your employment with our Company ends, you may be eligible for unemployment benefits. These benefits provide you with a percentage of your wages while you are unemployed and looking for work. To find out more, contact _____ _____.

Who Needs This Policy

All employers who are required by state law to provide unemployment coverage must have this policy in their handbooks. Contact your state labor department to find out about requirements in your state. (See Appendix C for contact details.) ■

9

Use of Company Property

In virtually every workplace, employees must use company equipment and property to do their jobs. This includes everything from the $2 stapler to the $2,000 computer. Because you invest so much money in your equipment, it makes sense to say something about it in your handbook. There are a lot of issues to address, from personal use to proper maintenance and safety.

In this chapter, we cover the following policies:

For policies on personal use of the telephone and voicemail system, see Chapter 14. For policies on personal use of computers, software and the Internet, see Chapter 15. For policies on confidentiality and intellectual property, see Chapter 18.

9:1   Use of Company Property: In General

Regardless of the type of property or equipment, you probably want your employees to take good care of it and use it only for company business. Anything less would affect your pocketbook as replacement and repair costs piled up.

The following general use policy explains to employees what you mean by proper use, what you expect of them and why all this matters in the first place.

Standard Policy

Company Property

We have invested a great deal of money in the property and equipment that you use to perform your job. It is a senseless and avoidable drain on this Company's bottom line when people abuse Company property, misuse it or wear it out prematurely by using it for personal business.

We ask all employees to take care of Company property and to report any problems to _____. If a piece of equipment or property is unsafe for use, please report it immediately.

Please use property only in the manner intended and as instructed.

We do not allow personal use of Company property unless specifically authorized in this Handbook.

Failure to use Company property appropriately, and failure to report problems or unsafe conditions, may result in disciplinary action, up to and including termination.

For information on use of the voicemail system, see Section ___ of this Handbook.

For information on use of computers, the Internet and software, see Section ___ of this Handbook.

How to Complete This Policy

Choose an individual to whom employees can report problems. At some companies, this will simply be the employee's supervisor. Other companies appoint a property manager.

9:2   Company Car

If you provide cars for employees to drive, then you should explain in your handbook the rules for their use. You must address a variety of issues, from maintenance to personal use.

Standard Policy

Company Cars

We have invested in Company vehicles so that our employees can use them on Company business in place of their own vehicle. This saves wear and tear on personal vehicles and eliminates the need for keeping track of mileage.

We need your help in keeping Company cars in the best condition possible. Please keep them clean, and please remove any trash or personal items when you are finished using the vehicles.

Please immediately report any accidents, mechanical problems or other problems to _____. We will try to have Company vehicles repaired or serviced as soon as possible.

Only authorized employees may use Company cars, and they may do so only on Company business.

You may not use Company vehicles while under the influence of drugs or alcohol or while otherwise impaired.

You must have a valid driver's license to use Company cars, and we expect that you will drive in a safe and courteous manner. If you receive any tickets for parking violations or moving violations, you are responsible for taking care of them.

Violating this policy in any way may result in disciplinary action, up to and including termination.

Optional Modification for Employees With Assigned Cars

At some workplaces, the company car is not simply a vehicle that the employee checks out for a few hours while attending some event off site. In these workplaces (often in places where employees are salespeople who are almost constantly on the road), employees are assigned a company car on a more or less permanent basis. For as long as the employee works for the company, the employee is in possession of the car and uses it for all business.

In such a situation, employers often place on the employee's shoulders the responsibility for maintaining the car. If you are in such a workplace, make the following modification the second to the last paragraph of the standard policy, above.

Modification

If you have been assigned a Company car, it is your responsibility to keep the car in good condition and repair. At a minimum, this means keeping the car clean, bringing it in for scheduled maintenance by an authorized service department and checking and changing the oil on schedule. Periodically, we may inform you of other ways in which you must care for the car. We will, of course, reimburse you for any ordinary expenses associated with maintaining the vehicle.

9:3   Telephones

It's a good idea to let employees know that you expect them to use work phones for company business only, except in case of emergencies or quick calls. It isn't reasonable to prohibit all personal calls, as long as they are brief and infrequent—certainly you can allow an employee to tell a spouse that she'll be home late or to make sure that his kids made it home from school. But without a policy limiting personal calls, some employees will inevitably take advantage.

Standard Policy

Telephone System

The Company's telephone system is for business use only. Employees are expected to keep personal calls to a minimum. If you must make or receive a personal call, please keep your conversation brief. Extensive personal use of Company phones is grounds for discipline.

See Section ___ of this Handbook for information on privacy and telephones.

9:4   Return of Company Property

No employment relationship lasts forever, and when an employee leaves—whether through termination, layoff or resignation—one of the loose ends to tie up is company property.

Standard Policy

Return of Company Property

When your employment with this Company ends, we expect you to return Company property—and to return it clean and in good repair. This includes this Employee Handbook, all manuals and guides, documents, phones, computers, equipment, keys and tools.

We reserve the right to take any lawful action to recover or protect our property.

Optional Modification to Garnish Final Paycheck

Some states allow for employers to garnish an employee's final paycheck to pay for lost, stolen or damaged company property. Other states expressly do not allow employers to do this. To find out whether your state allows garnishment, contact your state labor department. (See Appendix C for contact details.)

If you live in a state that allows garnishment, consider substituting the following paragraph for the last paragraph in the standard policy, above:

Modification

If you do not return a piece of property, we will withhold from your final paycheck the cost of replacing that piece of property. If you return a piece of property in disrepair, we will withhold from your final paycheck the cost of repair. We also reserve the right to take any other lawful action necessary to recover or protect our property.

Leave and Time Off

We can all agree that a little time off is a good thing. Your workers get a chance to have fun, deal with personal, civic and family obligations and recharge their batteries. And your company benefits, too—your business will be more productive if your employees are healthy, rested and focused on their jobs.

Although many employers believe otherwise, no law requires you to offer your employees paid vacation or sick leave (although California recently passed a law to require paid sick leave in certain circumstances, which will go into effect in July, 2004). By now, however, it's a nationwide standard. And you may be legally required to let your employees take unpaid leave, in certain circumstances. No matter what type of leave program you decide to adopt, the policies in this chapter will help you set rules that are consistent, sensible and easy to follow.

In this chapter, we cover the following policies:

10:1   Vacation

Most employers offer paid vacation benefits to at least some of their employees, even though they aren't legally required to do so. Paid vacation has become a standard business practice in this country—employers who don't offer some paid days off for rest and relaxation will almost certainly have trouble attracting and retaining good employees.

Your vacation policy should explain who is eligible for vacation, how vacation time accrues and how the employee can schedule time off.

Standard Policy

Vacation

Our Company recognizes that our employees need to take time off occasionally, to rest and relax, to enjoy a vacation or to attend to personal matters. That's why we offer a paid vacation program. _____ employees are eligible to participate in the paid vacation program.

Eligible employees accrue vacation time according to the following schedule:

_____ *[insert schedule here]* _____

Employees must schedule their vacations in advance, with their supervisor. We will try to grant every employee's vacation request for the days off of their choice. However, we must have enough workers to meet our day-to-day needs—which means we might not be able to grant every vacation request, especially during holiday periods.

How to Complete This Policy

In the first blank space, indicate which employees will be eligible to participate in the vacation program. Some employers limit these benefits to full-time employees or require employees to complete a waiting period before they can accrue or use benefits. For information and policies on these employee classifications, see Chapter 5.

In the second blank, write in the schedule by which employees will accrue benefits. Many employers provide increases in benefits to employees who stay with the company over time. For example, a worker might accrue ten days of vacation during the first year or two of employment, then move up to 15 the next year, then 20. Once you figure out how many days of vacation employees will accrue, divide that number by 12 to figure out how many days of vacation they accrue each month.

SAMPLE POLICY LANGUAGE: Here is an accrual schedule that allows employees to accrue ten days of vacation during their first and second years of employment, 15 the third and fourth years and 20 thereafter:

Years of Employment	_Vacation Accrual_
0-2	10 days per year, at the rate of $5/6$ of a day per month
2-4	15 days per year, at the rate of $1^1/4$ days per month
4 or more	20 days per year, at the rate of $1^2/3$ days per month

Optional Modifications

To Cap Accrual of Vacation Time

You can encourage your employees to use their vacation regularly—and avoid having employees out for months of collected vacation at a time—by capping how much vacation time your employees can accrue. Employees who reach this limit won't earn any more vacation time until they take some vacation and bring themselves back down below the cap. To cap how much vacation time an employee can accrue, add this modification immediately following the accrual schedule. In the blank space, insert the cap—how many hours or days of vacation time an employee will be allowed to accrue.

Use it or lose it policies are illegal in some states. An employer is legally entitled to cap how much vacation time an employee can accrue. However, some states forbid "use it or lose it" policies, by which an employee would have to forfeit accrued but unused vacation time over a certain limit or past a certain date. Because these states view earned vacation time as a form of compensation, which must be cashed out when the employee quits or is fired, a policy that takes vacation time away is seen as an illegal form of failing to pay employees money that they have already earned. Although the difference may seem merely technical, an accrual cap is legal in these states because it prohibits the employee from earning vacation time in the first place, rather than taking away vacation time after the employee has earned it. Contact your state labor department to find out about your state's rules (see Appendix C for contact information).

Modification

Employees may not accrue more than _____ of vacation time. Once an employee's vacation balance reaches this limit, an employee may accrue more vacation only by taking some vacation time to bring the employee's balance back below the limit.

To Pay Unused Vacation at Termination

Some states require employers to cash out unused, accrued vacation time when an employee quits or is fired. You can find out your state's rule by checking the chart "State Laws That Control Final Paychecks," at the end of Chapter 21. If you do business in a state that requires you to pay unused vacation, you might consider modifying the policy to inform employees that they will receive payment for unused vacation. To do so, simply add the modification below as the final paragraph of the policy:

Modification

Employees will be paid for any accrued and unused vacation when their employment terminates.

10:2 Holidays

Most companies offer their employees paid time off on certain holidays, such as New Year's Day, Independence Day and Thanksgiving. Your holiday policy should tell employees what holidays the company observes and what happens when a holiday falls on a weekend.

Standard Policy

Holidays

Our Company observes the following holidays each year:

*[list]*_____

_____

_____.

   If a holiday falls on a weekend, the Company will inform you when the holiday will be observed. Ordinarily, holidays falling on a Saturday will be observed the preceding Friday; holidays falling on a Sunday will be observed the following Monday.

How to Complete This Policy

In the blank space, list the holidays your company will observe. The days you choose will, of course, depend on when your business is open. Most employers offer some combination of the following: New Year's Day, Martin Luther King Day, President's Day, Good Friday, Memorial Day, Independence Day, Labor Day, Columbus Day, Veterans' Day, Thanksgiving, the Friday following Thanksgiving, Christmas Eve, Christmas Day and New Year's Eve.

Optional Modification to Allow Floating Holidays

Some of your employees may not observe the religious holidays you choose to offer—for example, Christmas or Good Friday—and may wish to take a holiday on a day of significance to their own religion. You are legally obligated to accommodate your workers' religious observations, which in some cases may require you to give these workers time off for important religious holidays. Rather than requiring your workers to come to you with these requests, you can make floating holidays available to all of your workers, to allow them to participate in religious activities or attend to other personal matters.

Some employers offer only one or two floating holidays per year; others offer more floating holidays, but trim the list of company-recognized holidays accordingly. If you wish to offer floating holidays, add the modification below as the second paragraph of the policy, immediately after the list of holidays your company observes. In the blank, insert the number of floating holidays you will allow your employees to take each year.

Modification

Eligible employees are also entitled to take _____ floating holidays each year. These holidays may be used to observe a religious holiday, to celebrate your birthday or simply to take a day off for personal reasons. You must schedule your floating holidays with your supervisor in advance. If you do not use your floating holidays during the year, you may not carry them over to the next year.

10:3   Sick Leave

Although employers are not legally required to provide paid sick days, it's common practice to do so. And there are sound reasons to offer paid days off for workers who are ill—it will help your workers who live paycheck to paycheck make ends meet, it will create fewer payroll hassles and, perhaps most importantly, it will encourage sick workers to stay home rather than coming to work to infect the rest of your workforce or perform at a substandard level.

Your sick leave policy should explain who is eligible for leave, how much leave employees can take and any notice requirements you wish to impose.

Standard Policy

Sick Leave

Our Company provides paid sick days to _____ _____. (For information on employee classifications, see Section ____ of this Handbook.) Eligible employees accrue _____ sick days per year at the rate of _____ per month. The Company will not pay employees for sick days that have accrued but have not been used when employment ends.

Employees may use sick leave when they are unable to work due to illness or injury. Sick leave is not to be used as extra vacation time, personal days or "mental health" days. Any employee who abuses sick leave may be subject to discipline.

You must report to your supervisor if you will need to take sick leave. We ask that employees call in as soon as they realize that they will be unable to work, before the regular start of their work day. You must report to your supervisor by phone each day you are out on leave.

How to Complete This Policy

In the first blank, indicate who is eligible for paid sick leave. Some employers only provide sick days to certain employees—for example, only full-time employees, only full-time employees and part-timers who work at least a minimum number of hours per week or only employees who have been employed for at least a certain period of time. See Chapter 5 for more information and policies on these employee classifications.

In the second and third blank, indicate the rate at which sick leave will accrue. For example, many employers provide that employees will accrue 12 paid sick days per year, at a rate of one per month. Others allow employees to accrue ten or six sick days per year, at a fractional rate.

Optional Modifications

To Prohibit or Limit Carry Over

The policy above is silent on the issue of carry over—whether employees can simply keep accruing unused sick leave month after month, year after year. However, many employers either set a cap on how much sick leave an employee can accrue or don't allow employees to carry over sick leave from one year to the next at all. The problem with a flat "no carry over" policy is that an employee might get sick at the beginning of the year, before enough sick leave hours have accrued to cover the absence. And policies that zero out sick leave at the end of the year tend to encourage employees to take that leave before it disappears, whether they're sick or not—resulting in numerous cases of "holiday flu."

In most cases, the better approach is simply to cap how many hours or days of sick leave an employee can accrue—for example, once an employee has 24 unused sick days, that employee accrues no more sick leave until some of the accrued time is used.

If you wish to prohibit carry over of sick leave from year to year, use Modification A. If you wish to limit sick leave accrual, use Modification B. In the blank space, insert the cap—the maximum number of sick days or hours that an employee may accrue. In either case, insert the modification at the end of the first paragraph.

Modification A: Modification to Prohibit Carry Over of Sick Leave

Employees may not carry over unused sick leave from one year to the next.

Modification B: Modification to Cap Accrual of Sick Leave

Employees may accrue a maximum of _____ of sick leave. Once an employee has reached this limit, no more sick leave will accrue until the employee uses sick leave to reduce the accrued total below the maximum.

To Address Additional Uses for Sick Leave

Our policy indicates that employees can use sick leave when they are too injured or ill to work. However, many employers make sick leave available for other purposes—for example, to go to appointments with a doctor or dentist, to care for a sick family member or to take a family member for medical care. And some state laws require employers to make sick leave available for particular purposes—usually, to care for a sick family member. These laws are summarized in the chart, "State Family and Medical Leave Laws," at the end of this chapter.

If your state requires you to make sick leave available for additional purposes, or if you want to allow your employees to use sick leave for additional reasons, add this modification immediately after the first sentence in the second paragraph. In the blank, indicate the additional uses of sick leave you wish to offer (for example, *care for a sick family member* or *attend necessary medical and dental appointments*).

Modification

Employees may also use sick leave to _____ _____.

10:4   Paid Time Off

Rather than adopting separate policies on vacation, sick leave, floating holidays or other types of leave, many employers now adopt a single policy to give employees a certain number of paid days off per year, which the employees can use as they wish. Using a unified paid time off ("PTO") policy can benefit your company by reducing paperwork and recordkeeping hassles and reducing the oversight you need to exercise over your employees, particularly regarding their use of sick leave. Because employees are entitled to take PTO for any reason, you won't need to make sure they are really sick—and they won't feel compelled to prove it to you ("(cough), I really caught a *bad* cold (sniffle)").

However, adopting a unified PTO policy can have significant drawbacks in some states. Because PTO is legally considered vacation time and sick leave, any state laws that regulate these issues apply to an employee's entire allotment of PTO. For example, some states require you to pay an employee for accrued, unused vacation time when the employee quits or is fired—if you have a PTO policy, you will have to pay out the entire unused allotment of PTO. If you do business in one of these states, you should think twice—and perhaps consult with a lawyer—before adopting a PTO policy.

If you adopt a PTO policy, remember that the policy takes the place of vacation, sick leave and floating holiday policies—you should adopt one or the other, not both. Your PTO policy should explain which employees are eligible for PTO, how many days of PTO will be granted per year and any procedures employees must follow to take PTO.

Standard Policy

Paid Time Off

Instead of offering separate vacation, sick leave and personal days or floating holidays, [*Company name*] offers a paid time off ("PTO") program that combines all of these benefits. We believe this program will give employees the flexibility to manage their time off as they see fit. Employees may use PTO for sickness, vacation, to attend a child's school activities, to care for elderly or ill family members, to take care of personal errands or business or simply to take a day off work.

You are eligible to participate in the PTO program if you

_____

_____

_____ .

(For information on employee classifications, see Section _____ of this Handbook.)

PTO accrues according to the following schedule:
*[insert schedule here]*_____

Employees must schedule time off in advance with their supervisors. We will try to grant every employee's PTO request for the days off they choose. However, we must have enough workers to meet our day-to-day needs—which means we might not be able to grant every PTO request, especially during holiday periods.

If circumstances, such as a medical or family emergency, prevent advance scheduling, you must inform your supervisor as soon as possible that you are taking paid time off.

Because PTO encompasses vacation and sick leave, employees must manage their PTO responsibly to ensure that they have time available for emergencies, such as personal or family illness. An employee who needs time off but has no accrued PTO may be eligible to take unpaid leave. The company will decide these requests on a case-by-case basis.

How to Complete This Policy

In the first space, indicate which employees will be eligible to participate in the PTO program. Some employers limit these benefits to full-time employees or full-time employees and part-time employees who work a minimum number of hours per week, or institute a waiting period before employees may accrue or use benefits. For information and policies on these employee classifications, see Chapter 5.

In the second blank, write in the schedule by which employees will accrue benefits. Many employers provide higher benefits to employees who have been with the company longer. For example, a worker might accrue 20 days of PTO during the first year or two of employment, then move up to 25, then 30. Once you figure out how many days of PTO employees will accrue, divide that number by 12 to figure out how many days of PTO employees accrue each month.

> **SAMPLE POLICY LANGUAGE:** Here is a PTO accrual schedule that allows employees to accrue 20 days of PTO during their first year of employment, 25 the second year and 30 thereafter:
>
> | Years of Employment | PTO Accrual |
> | --- | --- |
> | 0-1 | 20 days per year, at the rate of $1^2/_3$ days per month |
> | 1-2 | 25 days per year, at the rate of $2^1/_{12}$ days per month |
> | 2 or more | 30 days per year, at the rate of $2^1/_2$ days per month |

Optional Modifications

To Cap Accrual of PTO

Some employers place an upper limit on the amount of PTO an employee can accrue. An employee who reaches this limit does not accrue any more PTO until he or she takes some time off. Imposing this type of cap can prevent employees from going months, or even years, without taking enough time off to prevent burnout. It can also help you guard against having an employee gone for months at a time. If you wish to place a cap on PTO accrual, add this modification as the third paragraph of the policy, immediately following the accrual schedule. In the blank, insert the maximum number of PTO days or hours an employee can accrue.

Modification

Employees may not accrue more than _____ of PTO. Once an employee's PTO balance reaches this limit, an employee may accrue more PTO only by taking some PTO to bring the employee's balance back below the limit.

To Pay Unused PTO at Termination

In those states that require employers to cash out unused accrued vacation time when an employee quits or is fired (see Section 10:1, above), you will generally have to pay an employee for unused accrued PTO on termination. If you do business in one of these states, consider modifying the policy to inform employees that they will receive payment for unused PTO. To do so, simply add the modification below as the final paragraph of the policy.

Modification

Employees will be paid for any accrued and unused PTO when their employment ends.

If your state requires employers to cash out vacation pay, you might be better off with separate policies on vacation, sick leave and floating holidays. Talk to a local lawyer who knows about your state's employment laws to find out the best choice for your business.

Many states have passed laws similar to the FMLA—and some of these laws apply to employers with fewer than 50 employees. Some state laws require employers to provide leave for a wider variety of circumstances than the FMLA—for example, to attend parent-teacher conferences and other school activities related to the employee's child, to take a child or parent to necessary medical and dental appointments or to donate bone marrow. And some of these laws provide for more than 12 weeks of leave each year. These state laws are summarized in the "State Family and Medical Leave Laws" chart at the end of this chapter.

10:5   Family and Medical Leave

Working people have always had a tough time balancing the demands of a job with personal and family needs. And today, with large numbers of women in the workforce and many workers having to care for young children *and* aging parents, the stresses created by this juggling act have become more acute than ever.

In response to this problem, Congress passed the Family and Medical Leave Act ("FMLA"), a federal law that requires employers who have at least 50 employees to allow eligible workers to take up to 12 weeks of unpaid leave per year in the following circumstances:

- for the arrival of a new child—through birth, adoption or foster care
- to care for a family member who is suffering from a serious health condition, or
- when the employee suffers from a serious health condition that makes it impossible to work.

Because of these potential overlaps, an employer might find itself in one of four situations, any of which may require a different policy:

1. The employer has fewer than 50 employees, and either does not do business in a state with a family and medical leave law or does not have to comply with that law (because the employer is too small). These employers are free to offer family and medical leave, but are not legally required to do so.
2. The employer has fewer than 50 employees and does business in a state with a family and medical leave law that applies to it. These employers must follow their state's law, but not the FMLA.
3. The employer has at least 50 employees, but does not do business in a state with a family and medical leave law. These employers must comply only with the FMLA.
4. The employer has at least 50 employees and does business in a state with a family and medical leave law. These employers must comply with both the FMLA and their state's law.

Because of the intricacies of state family and medical leave laws—and the sometimes complicated ways they interact with the FMLA—we cannot address the needs of employers who find themselves in groups 2 or 4 here. If the chart at the end of this chapter indicates that you have to follow a state family and medical leave law, either alone or in conjunction with the FMLA, consult a lawyer who can help you work out a family and medical leave policy that meets your state's requirements.

We offer two alternative policies below. The first is for employers who have to comply with the FMLA only. The second is for smaller employers—those who, because they have fewer than 50 employees, do not have to comply with the FMLA—who wish to adopt a family and medical leave policy.

Policy A: For Employers Who Must Comply With the FMLA

Family and Medical Leave

Employees who have worked for our Company for at least a full year, and have worked an average of at least 25 hours per week during that time, are eligible to take unpaid family and medical leave for one or more of these purposes:

- because the employee's own serious health condition makes the employee unable to work
- to care for a spouse, child or parent who has a serious health condition, or
- to care for a newborn, newly adopted child or recently placed foster child.

Leave Available

Eligible employees may take up to 12 weeks of unpaid leave per calendar year for any of the above purposes. For purposes of calculating available family and medical leave, the year starts on

_____.

A parent who takes leave to care for a newborn, newly adopted child or recently placed foster child must begin this leave within a year after the birth, adoption or placement.

Notice Requirements

Employees are required to give notice at least 30 days in advance of their need for a family and medical leave, if their need for leave is foreseeable. In emergencies and unexpected situations, employees must give as much notice as is practicable under the circumstances.

Reinstatement Rights

When you return from an approved family and medical leave, you have the right to return to your former position or an equivalent position, except:

- You have no greater right to reinstatement than you would have had if you had not been on leave. If your position is eliminated for reasons unrelated to your leave, for example, you have no right to reinstatement.

- The Company is not obligated to reinstate you if you are a key employee—that is, you are among the highest-paid 10% of our workforce and holding your job open during your leave would cause the Company substantial economic harm. If the Company classifies you as a key employee under this definition, you will be notified when you request leave.

Substitution of Paid Leave

An employee who has accrued paid time off [*must or may*] use these benefits to receive pay for all or a portion of family and medical leave.

Medical Certification

The Company may ask employees who take leave for their own serious health condition or to care for a spouse, parent or child with a serious health condition to provide a doctor's form certifying the need for leave. The Company is also entitled to seek a second opinion and periodic recertifications. In some cases, the Company may ask employees who take leave because of their own serious health condition to provide a fitness for duty report from their doctors before they return to work.

Intermittent Leave

If you will need to take family and medical leave on an intermittent basis—that is, a day or two at a time rather than all at once—for your own serious health condition or to take care of a family member with a serious health condition, you will be allowed to do so. However, the Company may temporarily reassign you to a different position with equivalent pay and benefits to accommodate the intermittent schedule.

The Company will consider requests for intermittent leave to care for a new child on a case-by-case basis.

How to Complete This Policy

The FMLA allows eligible employees to take up to 12 weeks of unpaid leave per 12-month period. In the blank space, indicate how you will measure this 12-month period. You have four choices:
- the calendar year (insert *January 1*)
- a fiscal year or a year that starts on an employee's anniversary date (insert the date your fiscal year begins or the date when the employee started work)

- a year that begins on the date the employee first takes FMLA leave (insert *on the date an employee first takes FMLA leave*), or
- a year measured backward from the date the employee uses any FMLA leave (insert *one year before an employee uses any FMLA leave*).

In the second blank, insert either *may* or *must*. The FMLA allows employers to require employees to use any paid time off—such as vacation leave, personal days or sick leave—during their FMLA leave. This prevents employees from taking 12 weeks of unpaid leave, then tacking on available vacation or sick days. If you choose this option, insert *must*. Even if an employer does not require employees to use paid time off, the FMLA always gives employees this option—so if you don't require your employees to use paid time off, insert *may*.

Optional Modification to Continue Health Insurance

The FMLA requires employers who provide a health insurance benefit to continue that benefit while employees are on leave. Employers must continue to pay whatever portion of the premium the employer would pay if the employee were not on leave. However, if the employee does not return from leave, the employer can require the employee to pay back the employer—unless the employee doesn't return for reasons beyond the employee's control (for example, a serious health condition that does not improve sufficiently to allow the employee to return to the job).

If you offer health insurance, add the following modification to the policy, immediately following the "Substitution of Paid Leave" section:

Modification

Health Insurance During Leave

Your health insurance benefits will continue during leave. You will be responsible for paying any portion of the premium that you ordinarily pay while you are working, and you must make arrangements to make these payments while you are out. Employees who do not return from family and medical leave may be required to reimburse the Company for any premiums paid on the employee's behalf during the leave.

Policy B: For Employers Who Don't Have to Comply With the FMLA

Family and Medical Leave

Because of our small size, our Company is not required to comply with the federal Family and Medical Leave Act (FMLA). However, we recognize that our employees may occasionally need to take unpaid leave to care for a new child, to care for a seriously ill family member or to handle an employee's own medical issues.

If you anticipate that you might need time off to deal with family and medical issues, please talk to your supervisor. We can't guarantee that we'll grant every request, but we will seriously consider every request on a case-by-case basis. Among other things, we may consider our staffing needs, your position at the Company, the reason why you need leave and how long you expect your leave to last.

10:6   Bereavement Leave

Many employers offer their employees a few days off when a family member dies. These policies recognize that an employee who has experienced the death of a loved one will likely have issues both practical and personal that require attention. No law requires employers to offer bereavement leave, and some employers choose to let their employees take sick or vacation leave for this purpose. By offering bereavement leave, however, an employer communicates sensitivity and concern for its employees' well-being.

Your bereavement policy should explain who is eligible for leave, how many days of leave will be granted and whether that leave will be paid or unpaid.

Standard Policy

Bereavement Leave

If you suffer the death of an immediate family member, you are entitled to take up to _____ days off work. This leave will be [*paid or unpaid*].

   Immediate family members include _____

_____ .

   The Company will consider, on a case-by-case basis, requests for bereavement leave for the death of someone who does not qualify as an immediate family member under this policy.

How to Complete This Policy

In the first blank space, insert the number of days you will offer employees for bereavement leave. Many employers offer three days, although you are free to offer more or fewer, as you prefer.

In the second blank, indicate whether bereavement leave will be paid or unpaid.

In the third blank, list those who qualify as immediate family members. Some employers limit bereavement leave, particularly if it is paid, to parents, children, siblings and spouses. A number of employers also make bereavement leave available to those who have lost their domestic partners, grandparents, aunts, uncles or in-laws. You can also include *any family member who lives with the employee*.

For more on USERRA, see *Federal Employment Laws: A Desk Reference*, by Amy DelPo & Lisa Guerin (Nolo). You'll also find lots of helpful materials at the U.S. Department of Labor's website (www.dol.gov) and at the website of the National Committee of Employer Support for the Guard and Reserve (www.esgr.org).

10:7   Military Leave

The federal Uniformed Services Employment and Reemployment Rights Act of 1994 ("USERRA") requires all employers (regardless of size) to reinstate employees who take time off work to serve in the U.S. armed forces. USERRA protects employees who give proper notice before taking leave, spend no more than five years on leave, are released or discharged from service under honorable conditions and report back or apply for reinstatement within specified time limits (which depend on the length of the employee's service). When employees return from military leave, you must reinstate them to the same position they would have held had they been continuously employed throughout their leave, as long as they are otherwise qualified for the job—including any pay raises, promotions or additional job responsibilities they would have received had they never taken a leave.

Almost every state has a law prohibiting discrimination against those in the state's militia or National Guard—and many of these laws also require employers to grant leave for certain types of military service. These state laws are summarized in the "State Laws on Military Leave" chart at the end of this chapter.

Your policy on military leave should include an explanation of eligibility and notice requirements and a description of employees' reinstatement rights when their military service ends.

Standard Policy

Military Leave

Our Company supports those who serve in the armed forces to protect our country. In keeping with this commitment, and in accordance with state and federal law, employees who must be absent from work for military service are entitled to take a military leave of absence. This leave will be [*paid or unpaid*].

When an employee's military leave ends, that employee will be reinstated to the position he or she formerly held, or to a comparable position, as long as the employee meets the requirements of federal and state law.

Employees who are called to military service must tell their supervisors as soon as possible that they will need to take military leave. An employee whose military service has ended must return to work or inform the Company that he or she wants to be reinstated in accordance with these guidelines:

- For a leave of 30 or fewer days, the employee must report back to work on the first regularly scheduled workday after completing military service, allowing for travel time.
- For a leave of 31 to 180 days, the employee must request reinstatement within 14 days after military service ends.
- For a leave of 181 days or more, the employee must request reinstatement within 90 days after military service ends.

How to Complete This Policy

In the blank, indicate whether military leave will be paid or unpaid. USERRA requires employers to offer only unpaid leave; however, you are free to offer paid leave if you wish. Because some military commitments can be lengthy, many employers who offer paid leave do so only for a limited number of days—two or three weeks, for example. If you decide to offer a limited amount of paid leave, insert *paid for _____ days, and unpaid after that.*

Optional Modifications

For Employers Who Offer Paid Time Off

If you, like most employers, offer any type of paid time off—such as vacation and/or personal days—you should modify this policy to allow employees to use this paid time during their military leaves, unless you have chosen to pay employees for all military leaves. If you offer paid time off, and you have decided that military leave will be unpaid or paid only for a limited number of days, add this sentence to the end of the first paragraph:

Modification

During this unpaid leave, employees are entitled to use applicable paid time off (vacation time or personal days) during their leave.

For Employers Who Offer Health Benefits

If you make health insurance available to your employees as a benefit (see Chapter 8), you should modify this policy to inform your workers of the circumstances in which these benefits will continue during their military leave. USERRA requires employers to continue to offer health insurance to employees on leave for military service. Employees who return to work after an absence of 30 or fewer days are entitled to insurance continuation at the same cost, if any, paid by employees not on leave. Employees who are absent for more than 30 days must be offered the chance to continue their coverage, but they can be required to pay the full premium. If you offer health insurance, modify the policy by adding this language to the end of the second paragraph:

Modification

The Company will continue your health insurance benefits during your leave, under these circumstances:
- If you are absent for 30 or fewer days, you will be treated as any employee not on leave. The Company will continue to pay its share of the insurance premium, and you must continue to pay your usual share.
- If your leave lasts longer than 30 days, you will have to pay the entire premium to continue your benefits.

10:8 Time Off to Vote

The laws of almost every state take the responsibilities of citizenship very seriously. Most states prohibit employers from firing or disciplining employees for taking some time off work to cast their ballots, especially if their work schedules or commute make it difficult to vote outside of work hours. Some states require employers to pay employees for this time, and some states allow employers to require advanced notice or proof that the employee voted. These state laws are summarized in the "State Laws on Taking Time Off to Vote" chart at the end of this chapter.

Your policy on voting leave should explain how many hours employees can take off to vote, state whether employees will be paid for these hours and describe any notice or other requirements employees have to meet to qualify for leave.

Standard Policy

Voting

Our Company encourages employees to exercise their right to vote. If your work schedule and the location of your polling place will make it difficult for you to get to the polls before they close, you are entitled to take up to [*number*] hours off work, at the beginning or end of your shift, to cast your ballot. This time will be [*insert "paid" or "unpaid"*].

Employees who will need to take time off work to vote must inform their supervisors at least [*number*] day(s) in advance. Employees are expected to work with their supervisors to ensure that their absence doesn't negatively impact Company operations.

How to Complete This Policy

There are three spaces for you to fill in, based on your state's legal requirements and your preferences. In the first space, insert the number of hours you will allow employees to take off work in order to vote. Consult the chart at the end of this chapter to find out what your state requires; most states that mandate time off to vote require employers to provide two hours, although a few require more. If your state doesn't impose a requirement, you can decide how many hours you will allow.

In the second space, indicate whether this time off will be paid or unpaid. As you can see from the chart, some states require paid leave. If you do business in one of these states, insert *paid* in the blank. If your state does not require you to pay employees for the time they take off work to vote, you can say that time off will be paid or unpaid, as you choose.

In the final space, insert the number of days' notice you will require employees to give before taking time off to vote. The chart indicates whether your state requires employees to give notice. If you do business in a state with a notice requirement, simply insert the number of days your state mandates (some states require only one day's notice). If your state has no rules about notice, you can decide for yourself how much notice to require, if any.

Optional Modification to Require Proof of Voting

A few states, including Hawaii and Maryland, allow employers to require employees to supply proof that they actually voted in order to claim leave time. If you do business in one of these states, you can modify our policy to require such proof.

Your state may require employees to supply a certain type of proof—for example, a receipt or a state elections form. The modification, below, gives your supervisors the authority to tell employees what types of proof are acceptable.

To inform employees of this proof requirement, simply add the following sentences to the end of the policy:

Modification

Employees who take time off to vote must supply their supervisor with proof that they actually voted. Your supervisor can tell you what types of proof of voting are acceptable.

10:9   Jury Duty

Almost every state prohibits employers from firing or disciplining employees for jury service. Generally, employers must allow employees to take time off for this purpose—and some states require employers to provide at least some pay for this time off. Check the chart, "State Laws on Jury Duty," at the end of this chapter, to find out what your state requires.

Your policy on jury duty should let employees know whether jury service will be paid or unpaid, explain any notice requirements for employees called to jury duty and clearly state that employees will not face discipline or retaliation for serving on a jury.

Standard Policy

Jury Duty

If you are called for jury duty, you are entitled to take time off, as necessary, to fulfill your jury obligations. This leave will be *[paid or unpaid]*. No employee will face discipline or retaliation for jury service.

You must immediately inform your supervisor when you receive your jury duty summons. If you are chosen to sit on a jury, you must inform your supervisor how long the trial is expected to last. You must also check in with your supervisor periodically during your jury service, so the Company knows when to expect you back at work.

How to Complete This Policy

In the blank, indicate whether leave to serve on a jury will be paid or unpaid. Check the chart, "State Laws on Jury Duty," to find out whether your state requires paid leave for any employees. Even if your state doesn't require paid leave, you are free to provide it.

You will see that some states require paid leave only for full-time employees. If you do business in one of these states, you can limit your policy accordingly by filling in the blank as follows: *paid for full-time employees only; part-time employees will not be paid for time taken off for jury service.* If your state requires employers to pay only a certain number of days of jury duty leave, you can modify your policy to reflect this limit—see Modification, below.

Optional Modifications

To Limit Number of Paid Days of Leave

Some states that require paid leave for jury duty allow employers to pay for only a certain number of days off. If you do business in one of these states, or if you have decided to offer paid leave even though your state law doesn't require it, you may want to limit how much paid leave an employee can take. If so, add the following sentence immediately after the second sentence of the standard policy. In the blank, indicate how many days of paid leave you will offer.

Modification

You will be paid for up to _____ days of jury service; if your service extends beyond this period, the remainder of your leave will be unpaid.

Reality Check: Juror Fees Don't Pay the Bills

Many states pay jurors a fixed amount per day for serving on a jury. However, these stipends are usually meager—in some states, your employees probably give their children a larger allowance than the court will pay for serving on a jury. In light of this sad state of affairs, many employers voluntarily take on the responsibility of paying their employees for time spent on jury duty.

But what if your employee gets called for the next "trial of the century" and is out of work for months? That's where the modification to limit how much paid leave you'll provide comes in. If you do choose to compensate your employees for jury duty, you can put some outside limit on your obligation. Employers commonly adopt a policy limiting paid jury duty leave to ten to 20 workdays per year.

To Require Employees to Report Back to Work

Some employers require employees to call in on any day when jury service ends before the end of the work day, so that the employee can be asked to report back to work for the remainder of the day, if desired. If you want to impose this requirement, add the sentence below to the end of the standard policy. If you offer unpaid leave, remember that your employees are entitled to be paid for any time they actually spend working.

Modification

On any day when your jury service ends before the end of your usual work day, you must check in with your supervisor to find out whether you need to return to work for that day.

State Family and Medical Leave Laws

This chart covers some basic aspects of state family and medical leave laws. The federal FMLA applies to all covered employers in every state. However, an employer must follow those portions of the state or federal law that provide the most protection for employees.

We don't address every aspect of these laws (such as notice requirements, medical certifications or reinstatement rules). For more information contact your state's department of labor and be sure to check its website, where most states have posted their family leave rules. (See Appendix for contact details.)

States that are not listed below do not have laws that apply to private employers or have laws that offer less protection than the FMLA.

California

Cal. Gov't. Code § 12945; Cal. Lab. Code §§ 230 and following

Employers Covered: Employers with 5 or more employees must offer pregnancy leave; with 25 or more employees must offer leave for victims of domestic violence or sexual assault and school activity leave.

Eligible Employees: All employees.

Pregnancy/Maternity: Up to 4 months for disability related to pregnancy.

Family Member's or Employee's Serious Health Condition: Family member includes registered domestic partner.

School Activities: 40 hours per year.

Other: Reasonable time for issues dealing with domestic violence or sexual assault, including health, counselling and safety measures.

Colorado

Colo. Rev. Stat. § 19-5-211

Employers Covered: All employers who offer leave for birth of a child.

Eligible Employees: All employees.

Adoption: Employee must be given same leave for adoption as allowed for childbirth.

Connecticut

Conn. Gen. Stat. Ann. §§ 31-51kk to -51qq; 46a-51(10); 46a-60(7)

Employers Covered: Employers with 75 employees must offer childbirth, adoption and serious health condition leave; with 3 employees, must offer maternity disability.

Eligible Employees: Any employee with one year and at least 1,000 hours of service in last 12 months.

Childbirth: 16 weeks per any 24-month period.

Adoption: 16 weeks per any 24-month period.

Pregnancy/Maternity: "Reasonable" amount of maternity disability leave.

Family Member's or Employee's Serious Health Condition: Family member includes parents-in-law. 16 weeks per any 24-month period.

District of Columbia

D.C. Code Ann. §§ 32-501 and following; 32-1202

Employers Covered: Employers with at least 20 employees.

Eligible Employees: Employees who have worked at company for at least one year and at least 1,000 hours during the previous 12 months.

Childbirth: 16 weeks per any 24-month period.

Adoption: 16 weeks per any 24-month period.

Pregnancy/Maternity: 16 weeks per any 24-month period.

Family Member's or Employee's Serious Health Condition: 16 weeks per any 24-month period. Family member includes persons sharing employee's residence and with whom employee has a committed relationship.

School Activities: Up to 24 hours of leave per year.

Hawaii

Haw. Rev. Stat. §§ 398-1 to 398-11; 378-1

Employers Covered: Employers with at least 100 employees must offer childbirth, adoption and serious health condition leave; all employers must offer pregnancy leave.

Eligible Employees: Employees with 6 months of service are eligible for childbirth, adoption and serious health condition benefits; all employees are eligible for pregnancy and maternity leave.

Childbirth: 4 weeks per calendar year.

Adoption: 4 weeks per calendar year.

Pregnancy/Maternity: "Reasonable period" required by discrimination statute and case law.

Family Member's or Employee's Serious Health Condition: 4 weeks per calendar year. Family member includes parents-in-law, grandparents, grandparents-in-law, stepparents. Hawaii's leave law does not include employee's own serious health condition.

Illinois

820 Ill. Comp. Stat. §§ 147/1 and following

Employers Covered: All.

State Family and Medical Leave Laws (continued)

Eligible Employees: Employees who have worked at least half-time for 6 months.

School Activities: 8 hours per year, but no more than 4 hours per day.

Iowa

Iowa Code § 216.6

Employers Covered: Employers with 4 or more employees.

Eligible Employees: All.

Pregnancy/Maternity: Up to 8 weeks for disability due to pregnancy, childbirth or legal abortion.

Kentucky

Ky. Rev. Stat. Ann. § 337.015

Employers Covered: All.

Eligible Employees: All.

Adoption: Up to 6 weeks for adoption of a child under 7 years old.

Louisiana

La. Rev. Stat. Ann. §§ 23:341 to :342; 23:1015 and following; 40:1299.124

Employers Covered: Employers with at least 25 employees must offer pregnancy/maternity leave; with at least 20 employees must comply with bone marrow donation provisions; all employers must offer leave for school activities.

Eligible Employees: All employees are eligible for pregnancy/maternity or school activities leave; employees who work 20 or more hours per week are eligible for leave to donate bone marrow.

Pregnancy/Maternity: "Reasonable period of time" not to exceed four months, if necessary for pregnancy or related medical condition.

School Activities: 16 hours per year.

Other: Bone marrow donation, up to 40 hours paid leave per year.

Maine

Me. Rev. Stat. Ann. tit. 26, §§ 843 and following

Employers Covered: Employers with 15 or more employees at one Maine location.

Eligible Employees: Employees with at least one year of service.

Childbirth: 10 weeks in any two-year period.

Adoption: 10 weeks in any two-year period (for child age 16 or younger).

Family Member's or Employee's Serious Health Condition: 10 weeks in any two-year period.

Maryland

Md. Code Ann., [Lab. & Empl.] § 3-802

Employers Covered: Employers that allow workers to take leave for the birth of a child.

Eligible Employees: All employees.

Adoption: Employee must be given same leave for adoption as allowed for childbirth.

Massachusetts

Mass. Gen. Laws ch. 149, §§ 52D, 105D; ch. 151B, § 1(5)

Employers Covered: Employers with 6 or more employees must provide maternity and adoption leave; all employers must offer leave for school activities.

Eligible Employees: Full-time female employees who have completed probationary period, or 3 months of service if no set probationary period, are eligible for maternity and adoption leave. Employees who are eligible under FMLA are eligible for all other leave.

Childbirth/Maternity: 8 weeks.

Adoption: 8 weeks for child under 18, or under 23 if disabled.

School Activities: 24 hours per year total (combined with medical care under "other").

Other: 24 hours per year for events directly related to medical or dental care of a minor child or elderly relative age 60 or over. (24 hours total when combined with school activities.)

Minnesota

Minn. Stat. Ann. §§ 181.940 and following

Employers Covered: Employers with at least 21 employees at one site must provide maternity leave; with at least 20 employees must allow leave to donate bone marrow; all employers must provide leave for school activities.

Eligible Employees: Employees who have worked at least half-time for one year are eligible for maternity leave; at least 20 hours per week are eligible for leave to donate bone marrow; at least one year are eligible for school activities.

Childbirth/Maternity: 6 weeks.

Adoption: 6 weeks.

Family Member's or Employee's Serious Health Condition: Can use accrued sick leave to care for sick or injured child.

State Family and Medical Leave Laws (continued)

School Activities: 16 hours in 12-month period. Includes activities related to childcare, preschool or special education.

Other: Bone marrow donation, up to 40 hours paid leave per year.

Montana

Mont. Code Ann. §§ 49-2-310, 49-2-311

Employers Covered: All.

Eligible Employees: All.

Childbirth: "Reasonable leave of absence."

Pregnancy/Maternity: "Reasonable leave of absence."

Nebraska

Neb. Rev. Stat. § 48-234

Employers Covered: Employers that allow workers to take leave for the birth of a child.

Eligible Employees: All employees.

Adoption: Employee must be given same leave as allowed for childbirth to adopt a child under 9 years old or a special needs child under 19. Does not apply to stepparent or foster parent adoptions.

Nevada

Nev. Rev. Stat. Ann. §§ 392.490, 613.335

Employers Covered: All.

Eligible Employees: Parent, guardian or custodian of a child.

Childbirth: Same sick or disability leave policies that apply to other medical conditions must be extended to childbirth.

Pregnancy/Maternity: Same sick or disability leave policies that apply to other medical conditions must be extended to pregnancy or miscarriage.

School Activities: Employers may not fire or threaten to fire a parent, guardian or custodian for attending a school conference or responding to a child's emergency.

New Hampshire

N.H. Rev. Stat. Ann. § 354-A:7(VI)

Employers Covered: Employers with at least 6 employees.

Eligible Employees: All.

Childbirth: Temporary disability leave for childbirth or related medical condition.

Pregnancy/Maternity: Temporary disability leave for childbirth or related medical condition.

New Jersey

N.J. Stat. Ann. §§ 34:11B-1 to 34B:16

Employers Covered: Employers with at least 50 employees.

Eligible Employees: Employees who have worked for at least one year and at least 1,000 hours in previous 12 months.

Childbirth: 12 weeks (or 24 weeks reduced leave schedule) in any 24-month period.

Adoption: 12 weeks (or 24 weeks reduced leave schedule) in any 24-month period.

Pregnancy/Maternity: 12 weeks (or 24 weeks reduced leave schedule) in any 24-month period.

Family Member's or Employee's Serious Health Condition: Family member includes parents-in-law. Child includes legal ward. Parent includes someone with visitation rights.

New York

N.Y. Lab. Law §§ 201-c; 202-a

Employers Covered: Employers that allow workers to take leave for the birth of a child must allow adoption leave; employers with at least 20 employees at one site must allow leave to donate bone marrow.

Eligible Employees: All employees are eligible for adoption leave; employees who work at least 20 hours per week are eligible for leave to donate bone marrow.

Adoption: Employees must be given same leave as allowed for childbirth to adopt a child of preschool age or younger, or no older than 18 if disabled.

Other: Bone marrow donation, up to 24 hours of leave.

North Carolina

N.C. Gen. Stat. § 95-28.3

Employers Covered: All employers.

Eligible Employees: All employees.

School Activities: Parents and guardians of school-aged children must be given up to 4 hours of leave per year.

Oregon

Or. Rev. Stat. §§ 659A.150 and following; 659A.312; Or. Admin. R. §§ 839-009-0200 and following

Employers Covered: Employers of 25 or more employees (for at least 20 weeks for the year before or for the same year that leave is taken) must provide childbirth, adoption and serious health condition leave; all employers must allow leave to donate bone marrow.

Eligible Employees: Employees who have worked 25 or more hours per week for at least 180 days are eligible for childbirth, adoption and serious health condition leave;

State Family and Medical Leave Laws (continued)

employees who work an average of 20 or more hours per week are eligible for leave to donate bone marrow.

Childbirth: 12 weeks per year.

Adoption: 12 weeks per year.

Pregnancy/Maternity: 12 weeks per year.

Family Member's or Employee's Serious Health Condition: 12 weeks per year. Family member includes parents-in-law, same-sex domestic partner and domestic partner's parent or child.

Other: In addition to 12 weeks for sickness of family member or own serious health condition, employee may take 12 weeks for illness, injury or condition related to pregnancy or childbirth. Parents who have taken 12 weeks maternity or adoption leave may take an additional 12 weeks to care for sick child.

Bone marrow donation, up to 40 hours or amount of accrued paid leave (whichever is less).

Pennsylvania

18 Pa. Cons. Stat. Ann. § 4957

Employers Covered: All.

Eligible Employees: All.

Other: Victims or witnesses of crimes, or family member of victim or witness, must be allowed time off and may not be penalized or threatened for attending court.

Rhode Island

R.I. Gen. Laws §§ 28-48-1 and following

Employers Covered: Employers with 50 or more employees.

Eligible Employees: Employees who have worked an average of 30 or more hours a week for at least 12 consecutive months.

Childbirth: Up to 13 weeks in any two calendar years.

Adoption: For adoption of child up to 16 years old, up to 13 weeks in any two calendar years.

Family Member's or Employee's Serious Health Condition: Up to 13 weeks in any two calendar years. Family member includes parents-in-law.

South Carolina

S.C. Code Ann. § 44-43-80

Employers Covered: Employers with 20 or more workers at one site in South Carolina.

Eligible Employees: Employees who work an average of at least 20 hours per week.

Other: Bone marrow donation, up to 40 hours paid leave per year.

Tennessee

Tenn. Code Ann. § 4-21-408

Employers Covered: Employers with at least 100 employees.

Eligible Employees: All female employees who have worked 12 consecutive months.

Childbirth: Up to four months of unpaid leave (includes nursing).

Pregnancy/Maternity: Up to four months of unpaid leave (includes nursing). Employee must give 3 months notice unless a medical emergency requires the leave to begin sooner.

Other: Provisions must be included in employee handbook.

Vermont

Vt. Stat. Ann. tit. 21, §§ 471 and following

Employers Covered: Employers with at least 10 employees must provide parental leave for childbirth and adoption; with at least 15 employees must provide family medical leave to care for a seriously ill family member or to take a family member to medical appointments.

Eligible Employees: Employees who have worked an average of 30 or more hours per week for at least one year.

Childbirth: 12 weeks per year.

Adoption: 12 weeks per year to adopt a child age 16 or younger.

Family Member's or Employee's Serious Health Condition: 12 weeks per year. Family member includes parents-in-law. Serious illness is one that poses imminent danger of death and requires inpatient care in a hospital or extended home care under the direction of a physician.

School Activities: Up to 4 hours of unpaid leave in a 30-day period (but not more than 24 hours per year) to participate in child's school activities.

Other: Combined with school activities leave, up to 4 hours of unpaid leave in a 30-day period (but not more than 24 hours per year) to take a family member to a medical, dental or professional well-care appointment or to respond to a family member's medical emergency.

State Family and Medical Leave Laws (continued)

Washington

Wash. Rev. Code Ann. §§ 49.78.010 and following; 49.12.265 and following; 49.12.350 to .370; Wash. Admin. Code 296-130-010 and following; 162-30-020

Employers Covered: All employers must provide family care leave. Employers with 8 or more employees must provide pregnancy and post partum disability leave. Employers with 100 or more employees must provide parental leave.

Eligible Employees: All employees are eligible for family care leave. Employees who have worked at least 35 hours per week for the previous year are eligible for parental leave.

Childbirth: Family care leave—employee may use any paid leave to care for spouse or child before, during and after childbirth. Pregnancy/post partum disability leave—employee entitled to same leave as for sickness or other temporary disability, in addition to 12 weeks allowed under FMLA. Parental leave—12 weeks during any 24-month period to care for a newborn or an adopted child under 6.

Adoption: Employers that allow workers to take leave for the birth of a child must provide the same leave to adoptive parents of children under the age of six.

Pregnancy/Maternity: Family care leave—employee may use any paid leave to care for spouse or child before, during and after childbirth. Pregnancy/post partum disability leave—same amount as for sickness or other temporary disability, in addition to 12 weeks allowed under FMLA.

Family Member's or Employee's Serious Health Condition: Family member includes parents-in-law, grandparents and stepparents. 12 weeks during any 24-month period to care for a terminally ill child under 18. All employees can use any paid leave to care for sick family member.

Wisconsin

Wis. Stat. Ann. § 103.10

Employers Covered: Employers of 50 or more employees in at least six of the preceding 12 months.

Eligible Employees: Employees who have worked at least one year and 1,000 hours in the preceding 12 months.

Childbirth: 6 weeks per 12-month period.

Adoption: 6 weeks per 12-month period.

Pregnancy/Maternity: 6 weeks per 12-month period.

Family Member's or Employee's Serious Health Condition: 2 weeks per 12-month period. (8 weeks total leave per year when combined with maternity or adoption leave.)

Other: Employee may substitute accrued paid or unpaid leave.

Current as of February 2003

State Laws on Military Leave

Note: The District of Columbia and the states of Delaware and North Dakota are not listed in this chart because they do not have laws or regulations on military leave that govern private employers. Remember that all employers are still subject to federal military leave laws (USERRA). Check with your state department of labor if you need more information (see Appendix C for contact list.)

Alabama

Alabama Stat. § 31-12-1 and following

Employees covered: State national guard members called to active duty for at least 30 consecutive days or for federally funded duty for homeland security are entitled to the same benefits USERRA provides.

Alaska

Alaska Stat. § 26.05.075

Employees covered: Employees called to active service in the state militia.

Amount of leave: Unlimited unpaid leave.

Reinstatement: To former or comparable position at same pay, seniority and benefits as before military service.

Return to work: Next workday after the time required to travel from service site.

Disability due to service: If disability leaves employee unable to perform job duties, must be offered another position with similar pay and benefits. Employee must request reemployment within 30 days of being released to return to work.

Arizona

Ariz. Rev. Stat. §§ 26-167, 26-168

Employees covered: Members of state military forces or national guard members called up by state for training or duty have same leave and reinstatement rights and benefits as members of the U.S. uniformed services.

Amount of leave: Unlimited unpaid leave. Does not affect vacation rights that already exist, but is not considered work for purpose of accruing vacation benefits and pay.

Reinstatement: To former or comparable position at same pay, seniority and benefits as before military service.

Benefits and rights: Employer may not dissuade employees from enlisting in state or national military forces by threatening economic reprisal.

Employer penalties: Discrimination or opposing service is a class 2 misdemeanor, which carries a fine of up to $750 or imprisonment of up to 4 months, or both. Violating leave provisions is a class 3 misdemeanor, which carries a fine of up to $500 or imprisonment of up to 30 days, or both.

Arkansas

Ark. Code Ann. § 12-62-413

Employees covered: Employees called by the governor to active duty in the Arkansas National Guard or the state militia have the same leave and reinstatement rights and benefits as members of the U.S. uniformed services.

California

Cal. Mil. & Vet. Code §§ 394, 394.5

Employees covered: Employees who are called into service or training in the state military or naval forces have the same leave and reinstatement rights and benefits as members of the U.S. uniformed services called to active federal duty.

Amount of leave: Employees who are in the U.S. armed forces, national guard or naval militia reserves entitled to 17 days unpaid leave per year for training or special exercises.

Benefits and rights: Employer may not discriminate in hiring or dissuade employee from enlisting. May not terminate employee or limit any benefits or seniority because a of temporary disability (52 weeks or less).

Colorado

Colo. Rev. Stat. § 28-3-609

Employees covered: Permanent employees who are members of Colorado National Guard or U.S. armed forces reserves.

Amount of leave: 15 days unpaid leave per year for training.

Reinstatement: Same or similar position with same status, pay and seniority.

Connecticut

Conn. Gen. Stat. Ann. §§ 27-33, 27-33a

Employees covered: Employees who are active or reserve members of the state militia or national guard.

Amount of leave: Sufficient leave of absence to attend meetings or drills that take place during regular working hours.

Benefits and rights: No loss or reduction of vacation or holiday benefits; no discrimination in terms of promotion or continued employment.

State Laws on Military Leave (continued)

Florida

Fla. Stat. Ann. §§ 250.482; 627.6692(h) to (j)

Employees covered: Employees who are members of the Florida National Guard and are called into active duty by the governor have the same leave and reinstatement rights as members of the U.S. uniformed services.

Benefits and rights: Employees not covered by COBRA whose employment is terminated while on active duty are entitled to a new 18-month benefit period beginning when active duty or job ends, whichever is later.

Employer penalties: Employee who has worked at least 1 year may sue employer who violates law for actual damages or $500, whichever is greater.

Georgia

Ga. Code Ann. § 38-2-280

Employees covered: Members of U.S. armed forces or Georgia National Guard called into active federal or state service.

Amount of leave: Unlimited unpaid leave for active service. Up to 6 months leave for service school or annual training, but no more than 6 months total during any 4-year period.

Reinstatement: Reinstatement with full benefits unless employer's circumstances have changed and reemployment is impossible or unreasonable. Employee must apply within 90 days of discharge from active duty or within 10 days of completing school or training.

Employer penalties: Employer who does not reinstate employee with full benefits is liable to employee for lost wages and benefits; upon request, employee may be represented by the state attorney general.

Hawaii

Haw. Rev. Stat. § 121-43

Employees covered: Employees serving in the state national guard are entitled to the same protections as those called into active duty in U.S. uniformed services.

Idaho

Idaho Code §§ 46-224, 46-225

Employees covered: Members of national guard and armed forces reserves.

Amount of leave: 15 days unpaid (or paid at employer's discretion) leave per year for training. Leave does not affect vacation, sick leave, bonus or promotion rights. Employee must give 90 days' notice of training dates.

Reinstatement: Entitled to same position with no loss of seniority or benefits.

Illinois

20 Ill. Comp. Stat. §§ 1805/30.1 to 1805/30.20, 1805/ 100, 1815/79; 225 Ill. Comp. Stat. §§ 60/21, 80/16, 115/ 15, 415/17, 441/5-16, 450/17.1, 458/5-25; 730 Ill. Comp. Stat. § 5/5-9-1

Employees covered: Members of Illinois State Guard and members of U.S. uniformed services. Employees who are called into state active duty in the Illinois National Guard have the same leave and reinstatement rights and benefits as members called into active federal duty.

Benefits and rights: Employer may not in any way discriminate against employees who are members of the military, obstruct their employment or dissuade them from enlisting. Many occupations including veterinary technician, court reporter, real estate appraiser, home inspector, optometrist and accountant may renew licenses that expired during military service or training without paying late fees or fulfilling continuing education requirements.

Employer penalties: Discrimination is a petty offense, punishable by a fine of up to $1,000.

Indiana

Ind. Code Ann. §§ 10-5-9-1, 10-5-9-2

Employees covered: Members of U.S. armed services reserves.

Amount of leave: 15 days unpaid (or paid at employer's discretion) leave per year for training. Leave does not affect vacation, sick leave, bonus or promotion rights.

Reinstatement: Entitled to same or similar position with no loss of seniority or benefits.

Iowa

Iowa Code § 29A.43

Employees covered: Members of state military forces called into temporary duty have same protections as members of U.S. uniformed services called into active duty.

Kansas

Kan. Stat. Ann. §§ 48-517, 48-222

Employees covered: Members of state military forces called into active duty by the state entitled to same protections as members of U.S. uniformed services.

Amount of leave: In addition to unlimited leave for active duty, 5 to 10 days leave each year to attend state national guard training camp.

State Laws on Military Leave (continued)

Return to work: Must report to work within 72 hours of release from duty or recovery from service-related injury or illness.

Employer penalties: Failure to excuse employee for training or duty: $5 to $50 fine for each offense. Failure to fully reinstate employee: liable for lost wages or benefits or double that amount if failure is willful.

Kentucky

Ky. Rev. Stat. Ann. §§ 38.238, 38.460

Employees covered: Members of Kentucky National Guard or Kentucky active militia.

Amount of leave: Unlimited unpaid leave for training.

Reinstatement: To former position with no loss of seniority, pay or benefits.

Benefits and rights: Employer may not in any way discriminate against employee or threaten to prevent employee from enlisting in the Kentucky National Guard or active militia.

Louisiana

La. Rev. Stat. Ann. §§ 29:38, 29:38.1, 29:410

Employees covered: Employees called into active duty in any branch of the state military forces have the same leave and reinstatement rights and benefits as members of the U.S. uniformed services.

Return to work: Must report to work within 72 hours of release from state military duty or recovery from state service-related injury or illness.

Employer penalties: Employer who fails to comply liable for lost wages and benefits; upon request employee may be represented by the parish district attorney.

Maine

Me. Rev. Stat. Ann. tit. 37-B, § 342(5); tit. 17-A, §§ 1252, 1301

Employees covered: Members of state military forces.

Benefits and rights: Employer may not discriminate against employee for membership or service in state military forces.

Employer penalties: Employer who discriminates is guilty of a Class E crime, punishable by up to 6 months in the county jail or a fine of up to $1,000.

Maryland

Md. Code 1957 Art. 65, § 32A

Employees covered: Members of the organized militia called to active duty or training by the governor are entitled to the same leave and reinstatement rights and benefits as members of the U.S. uniformed services.

Reinstatement: Must apply for reemployment within 30 days of release from duty or training.

Employer penalties: Liable for lost wages and benefits.

Massachusetts

Mass. Gen. Laws ch. 33, § 13; ch. 149, §§ 52A to 52A 1/2

Employees covered: Employees who are members of U.S. armed forces reserves or who are members or connected with the state armed forces.

Amount of leave: 17 days per year for training in the U.S. armed forces reserves. Leave does not affect vacation, sick leave, bonus or promotion rights. Veterans who want to participate in a Veterans Day or Memorial Day exercise, parade or service must be given leave.

Reinstatement: Employee who is still qualified must be reinstated in former or similar position with no loss of status, pay or seniority.

Benefits and rights: Employer may not in any way discriminate against employee or threaten to prevent employee from enlisting in the state armed forces.

Employer penalties: Employers who violate law protecting members of state armed forces are subject to a fine of up to $500, or up to 6 months imprisonment, or both.

Michigan

Mich. Comp. Laws §§ 32.271 to 32.274

Employees covered: Members of state or U.S. uniformed services called into active state or federal duty.

Amount of leave: Unpaid leave authorized for taking a physical, enlisting, being inducted, attending encampment or drill or instruction.

Reinstatement: Employee has 15 days of release or rejection from service to apply for reemployment. Must be reinstated to former position with no loss of seniority, benefits or pay for up to 90 days. After 90 days employee may have to take a lesser position, if no longer qualified and employer cannot retrain with reasonable efforts.

Benefits and rights: Employer may not in any way discriminate against employee or threaten to prevent employee from enlisting in the state armed forces.

Employer penalties: Violations of the law are a misdemeanor.

State Laws on Military Leave (continued)

Minnesota

Minn. Stat. Ann. §§ 192.34; 609.03

Employees covered: Employees who are members of the U.S., Minnesota or any other state military or naval forces.

Benefits and rights: Employer may not discharge employee or interfere with military service or dissuade employee from enlisting by threatening employee's job.

Employer penalties: Employer who violates law is guilty of a gross misdemeanor and is subject to a fine of up to $3,000, or up to one year imprisonment, or both.

Mississippi

Miss. Code Ann. § 33-1-19

Employees covered: Members of U.S. uniformed services and Mississippi armed forces.

Amount of leave: Unpaid leave for active state duty or state training duty.

Reinstatement: If still qualified to perform job duties, employee entitled to previous or similar position with no loss of seniority, status or pay.

Missouri

Mo. Rev. Stat. §§ 41.730; 557.021; 558.011; 560.016

Employees covered: Members of the state organized militia.

Benefits and rights: Employer may not discharge employee or interfere with employee's military service or threaten to dissuade employee from enlisting.

Employer penalties: Violations of the law are a class A misdemeanor punishable by a fine of up to $1,000 or by up to one year imprisonment.

Montana

Mont. Code Ann. § 10-1-603

Employees covered: Members of the state organized militia called to active service during a state-declared disaster or emergency.

Amount of leave: Unpaid leave for duration of service. Leave may not be deducted from sick leave or vacation or other leave, although employee may voluntarily use that leave.

Reinstatement: To same or similar position.

Benefits and rights: Employer may not in any way discriminate against employee or dissuade employee from enlisting by threatening employee's job.

Nebraska

Neb. Rev. Stat. §§ 28-106; 55-161 to 55-166

Employees covered: Employees who are members of the Nebraska National Guard and are called into active state duty have the same leave and reinstatement rights and benefits as members of the U.S. uniformed services called to active federal duty.

Employer penalties: Employer who discharges employee or denies rights and benefits is guilty of a Class IV misdemeanor, punishable by a fine of $100 to $500. In addition, liable to employee for damages.

Nevada

Nev. Rev. Stat. Ann. §§ 193.150; 412.139, 412.606; 683A.261

Employees covered: Members of Nevada National Guard called into active service by the governor.

Benefits and rights: Employers may not discriminate against members of the Nevada National Guard and may not discharge any employee who is called into active service. Insurance brokers given extended time to renew license and fines and examinations waived.

Employer penalties: Employer who violates the law is guilty of a misdemeanor punishable by a fine of up to $1,000, or up to 6 months in the county jail, or both.

New Hampshire

N.H. Rev. Stat. Ann. §§ 110-B:65(II); 625:9; 651:1

Employees covered: Members of the state national guard.

Benefits and rights: Employer may not discriminate against employee because of connection or service with national guard; may not dissuade employee from enlisting by threatening job.

Employer penalties: Violation of the law is a misdemeanor which carries a fine of up to $1,000 and up to 1 year in prison.

New Jersey

N.J. Stat. Ann. § 38A:14-4

Employees covered: Members of the state organized militia.

Benefits and rights: Employer may not discharge employee or interfere with military service or dissuade employee from enlisting by threatening employee's job.

Employer penalties: Violation of the law is a misdemeanor.

New Mexico

N.M. Stat. Ann. §§ 20-4-6; 28-15-1 to 28-15-3; 31-19-1

Employees covered: Members of the state national guard.

State Laws on Military Leave (continued)

Reinstatement: Employee who is still qualified must be reinstated in former or similar position with no loss of status, pay or seniority for up to one year from end of service. Must apply for reemployment within 90 days.

Benefits and rights: Employer may not discriminate against or discharge employee because of membership in the national guard; may not prevent employee from performing military service.

Employer penalties: Employer who willfully violates law is guilty of a misdemeanor and subject to a fine of up to $1,000, imprisonment of up to 1 year, or both.

New York

N.Y. Mil. Law §§ 317, 318

Employees covered: Members of the state military forces called up by governor and members of U.S. uniformed services.

Amount of leave: Unpaid leave available for: active service; reserve drills or annual training; service school; initial full-time or active duty training.

Reinstatement: Employee entitled to previous position, or to one with the same seniority, status and pay, unless the employer's circumstances have changed and reemployment is impossible or unreasonable. Employee must apply within: 90 days of discharge from active service; 10 days of completion of annual training or school; 60 days of completion of initial training.

Benefits and rights: It is state policy not to discriminate against employees who are subject to state or federal military service. Employee who is fired or suspended and who applies for reemployment within 10 days of termination must be fully reinstated (does not apply to routine R.O.T.C. training).

Employer penalties: Employer may be liable to employee for lost wages and benefits; upon request state attorney general may appear and act on employee's behalf.

North Carolina

N.C. Gen. Stat. §§ 127A-201 and following; 127B-14

Employees covered: Members of the North Carolina National Guard called to active duty by the governor.

Reinstatement: Must make written application for reemployment within 5 days of release from state duty or recovery from service-related injury or illness. If still qualified, employee must be restored to previous position or one of comparable seniority, status and salary; if no longer quali-

fied, employee must be placed in another position with appropriate seniority, status and salary, unless the employer's circumstances now make reinstatement unreasonable.

Benefits and rights: It is state policy to protect an individual's right to serve in the state national guard without fear of employment discrimination or reprisal. Employer may not deny employment, promotion or any benefit because employee is a member, enlists or serves in the state national guard; employer may not discharge employee called up for emergency military service.

Ohio

Ohio Rev. Code Ann. §§ 5903.01, 5903.02, 5903.99

Employees covered: Employees who are members of the Ohio militia called for active duty or training, members of the commissioned public health service corps or any other uniformed service called up in time of war or emergency, have same leave and reinstatement rights and benefits as members of the U.S. uniformed services.

Employer penalties: Employer who violates employee's rights to reinstatement and benefits may be fined up to $1,000 or imprisoned for up to 6 months, or both.

Oklahoma

Okla. Stat. Ann. tit. 44, §§ 71, 208, 208.1

Employees covered: Members of state military forces. Employees called to state active duty in the Oklahoma National Guard have the same leave and reinstatement rights and benefits guaranteed under USERRA.

Benefits and rights: Employer may not fire employee or hinder or prevent employee from performing military service.

Employer penalties: Firing employee or preventing employee from performing service: fine of up to $100 or up to 30 days in the county jail, or both. Refusing to permit employee to attend state national guard drill, ceremony or exercise: fine of $50 to $100 or 10 to 60 days in the county jail, or both.

Oregon

Or. Rev. Stat. § 399.230

Employees covered: Members of state organized militia called into active duty by the governor.

Amount of leave: Unpaid leave for term of service.

Reinstatement: Full reinstatement with no loss of seniority or benefits including sick leave, vacation or service credits under a pension plan.

State Laws on Military Leave (continued)

Pennsylvania

51 Pa. Cons. Stat. Ann. §§ 7302, 7309

Employees covered: Members of national guard or U.S. armed forces reserves called into active or emergency state duty by the governor.

Amount of leave: Employee who enlists or is drafted during a time of war or emergency called by the president or governor is entitled to unpaid military leave along with reservists called into active duty.

Reinstatement: Employee must be restored to same or similar position with same status, seniority and pay.

Benefits and rights: Employers may not discharge or discriminate against any employee because of membership or service in the military. Employees called to active duty are entitled to 30 days health insurance continuation benefits at no cost.

Disability due to service: If disability leaves employee unable to perform job duties, must be restored to another position with similar pay and benefits.

Rhode Island

R.I. Gen. Laws §§ 11-1-2; 30-11-2 to 30-11-6; 30-21-1

Employees covered: Members of state military forces and national guard members on state active duty are entitled to the same rights and protections as members of U.S. uniformed services on active federal duty.

Amount of leave: Unpaid leave of absence for state active duty.

Reinstatement: If still qualified to perform duties, employee must be restored to same or similar position with no loss of status, seniority or pay. Employee who enlists in U.S. army, navy or air force entitled to reinstatement in former or similar position if: employee makes request within 40 days of discharge; employee is still qualified to do job; employer's circumstances have not changed so that reemployment is impossible or unreasonable.

Benefits and rights: Employer may not discharge employee because of membership in the military, or interfere with employee's military service or dissuade employee from enlisting by threatening employee's job.

Employer penalties: Employer who discriminates is guilty of a misdemeanor which carries a fine of up to $1,000, up to 1 year imprisonment, or both; employer who does not reinstate an enlisted veteran is subject to a fine of $50 to $500.

South Carolina

S.C. Code Ann. §§ 25-1-2310 to 25-1-2340

Employees covered: Members of the South Carolina National Guard and State Guard called to state duty by the governor.

Reinstatement: If still qualified, employee must be restored to previous position or one with same seniority, status and salary; if no longer qualified, must be given another position, unless employer's circumstances make reinstatement unreasonable. Employee must apply in writing within 5 days of discharge from service or from related hospitalization.

South Dakota

S.D. Codified Laws Ann. § 33-17-15.1

Employees covered: Members of the South Dakota National Guard ordered to active duty by the governor or president entitled to same protections as members of U.S. uniformed services on active federal duty.

Tennessee

Tenn. Code Ann. § 58-1-604

Employees covered: Members of the Tennessee National Guard.

Benefits and rights: Employer may not refuse to hire or terminate an employee because of national guard membership or because employee is absent for a required drill or annual training.

Employer penalties: Violation of law is a class E felony which is subject to a prison term of 1 to 2 years and a possible fine of up to $3,000.

Texas

Tex. Gov't. Code Ann. § 431.006

Employees covered: Members of the state military forces called to active duty or training.

Reinstatement: Employee is entitled to return to the same position with no loss of time, efficiency rating, vacation or benefits unless employer's circumstances have changed so that reemployment is impossible or unreasonable. Employee must apply in writing as soon as practical after release.

Benefits and rights: Employer may not terminate an employee because of active military duty or training.

Employer penalties: Employer may be liable for up to 6 months' compensation and attorney fees.

State Laws on Military Leave (continued)

Utah

Utah Code Ann. §§ 39-1-36; 76-3-204, 76-3-301

Employees covered: Members of U.S. armed forces reserves who are called to active duty, active duty for training, inactive duty training or state active duty.

Amount of leave: Up to 5 years leave.

Reinstatement: Upon release from duty, training or related hospitalization, employee is entitled to return to previous employment with same seniority, status, pay and vacation rights.

Benefits and rights: Employer may not discriminate against an employee based on membership in armed forces reserves.

Employer penalties: Employer who willfully discriminates, discharges or refuses to rehire an employee is guilty of a class B misdemeanor which carries a fine of up to $1,000 or up to 6 months imprisonment.

Vermont

Vt. Stat. Ann. tit. 21, § 491

Employees covered: Permanent employees who are members of an organized unit of the national guard or the ready reserves and are called to active state duty or training with the U.S. military.

Amount of leave: Leave of absence with or without pay. Employee must give 30 days' notice for U.S. training and as much notice as is practical for state duty.

Reinstatement: If still qualified, employee must be reinstated to former position with the same status, pay and seniority, including any seniority that accrued during the leave of absence.

Benefits and rights: Employer may not discriminate against an employee who is a member or an applicant for membership in the state or federal national guard.

Virginia

Va. Code Ann. §§ 44-93.2 to 44-93.5; 44-98

Employees covered: Member of the Virginia National Guard, Virginia State Defense Force or naval militia called to active state duty by the governor.

Amount of leave: Leave of absence with or without pay. May not be required to use vacation or any other accrued leave unless employee wants to.

Reinstatement: Employee must be restored to previous position or one with same seniority, status and pay. If position no longer exists, then to a comparable position, unless employer's circumstances would make reemploy-

ment unreasonable. Must apply in writing within 5 days of release or from related hospitalization.

Benefits and rights: Employees may not be discriminated against in hiring, retention, promotion or benefits.

Employer penalties: Employer who discriminates against employee or who violates leave provisions may be liable for any loss of wages or benefits. Any employer who tries to hinder or dissuade an employee from serving in the state military is guilty of a misdemeanor and is subject to a fine of up to $500 or up to 30 days in jail, or both.

Washington

Wash. Rev. Code Ann. §§ 73.16.032 to 73.16.035

Employees covered: Permanent employees who are Washington residents or employed within the state and who volunteer or are called to serve in the uniformed services have the same leave and reinstatement rights and benefits as members of the U.S. uniformed services called to active federal duty.

Reinstatement: If still qualified, employee must be restored to previous position or one with same seniority, status and salary; if no longer qualified, must be given another position, unless employer's circumstances make reinstatement unreasonable.

Return to work: After completing service, employee must observe time limits set by federal law when applying for reemployment. For less than 31 days of service, report to work at beginning of next work week; 31 to 180 days of service, apply in writing within 14 days; over 180 days of service, apply within 90 days.

West Virginia

W.Va. Code § 15-1F-8

Employees covered: Employees who are members of the organized militia in active state service have the same reemployment rights as members of the U.S. uniformed services under USERRA.

Wisconsin

Wis. Stat. Ann. §§ 45.50; 21.72

Employees covered: Permanent employees who enlist, are inducted or called to serve in the uniformed services; civilians requested to perform national defense work during an officially proclaimed emergency.

Amount of leave: Up to 4 years leave for military service and/or training unless period of service is extended by law.

State Laws on Military Leave (continued)

Reinstatement: Employee is entitled to previous position, or to one with the same seniority, benefits and pay, unless the employee is no longer qualified or the employer's circumstances have changed and reemployment is impossible or unreasonable.

Return to work: Employee must apply for reemployment and resume work within 90 days of release from service or within 6 months of release from service-related hospitalization.

Benefits and rights: A member of the uniformed services on active federal or state duty after 9/11/2001 may renew any license that expired during that period within 90 days after discharge.

Employer penalties: Employer who refuses to reinstate employee may be sued for lost wages and benefits.

Wyoming

Wyo. Stat. §§ 19-11-101 to 19-11-123

Employees covered: Employees who are members or who apply for membership in the uniformed services; employees who report for active duty, training or a qualifying physical exam or who are called to state duty by the governor.

Amount of leave: Up to 4 years leave of absence. Employee may use vacation or any other accrued leave but is not required to do so.

Reinstatement: Within 10 days of making application, employee is entitled to reemployment with the same seniority, rights and benefits, plus any additional seniority and benefits that employee would have earned if there had been no absence. Does not apply if employer's circumstances have changed so that reemployment is impossible or unreasonable or would impose an undue hardship.

Return to work: Employee is entitled to complete any training program that would have been available to employee's former position during period of absence. Employee may not be terminated without cause for one year after returning to work.

Benefits and rights: Employers may not discriminate in hiring, reemployment, retention, promotion or any benefit because of an employee's membership, service or enlistment in the uniformed services.

Employer penalties: Employer will be liable for reasonable costs and attorney's fees in any action to make employer comply with these laws.

Current as of February 2003

State Laws on Jury Duty

Alabama

Ala. Code §§ 12-16-8 to 12-16-8.1

Paid leave: Full-time employees are entitled to usual pay minus any fees received from the court.

Notice employee must give: Must show supervisor jury summons the next working day; must return to work the next scheduled hour after discharge from jury duty.

Employer penalty for firing or penalizing employee: Liable for actual and punitive damages.

Alaska

Alaska Stat. § 09.20.037

Unpaid leave: Yes

Additional employee protections: Employee may not be threatened, coerced or penalized.

Employer penalty for firing or penalizing employee: Liable for lost wages and damages; must reinstate employee.

Arizona

Ariz. Rev. Stat. § 21-236

Unpaid leave: Yes

Additional employee protections: Employee may not lose vacation rights, seniority or precedence.

Employer penalty for firing or penalizing employee: Class 3 misdemeanor, punishable by a fine of up to $500 or up to 30 days' imprisonment.

Arkansas

Ark. Code Ann. § 16-31-106

Unpaid leave: Yes

Additional employee protections: Absence may not affect sick leave and vacation rights.

Employer penalty for firing or penalizing employee: Class A misdemeanor, punishable by a fine of up to $1,000 or up to one year imprisonment.

California

Cal. Lab. Code §§ 230, 230.1

Unpaid leave: Employee may use vacation, personal leave or comp time.

Additional employee protections: Victims of crime, domestic violence or sexual assault are protected against discharge, discrimination or retaliation for attending a court proceeding or seeking judicial relief.

Notice employee must give: Reasonable notice.

Employer penalty for firing or penalizing employee: Employer must reinstate employee with back pay and lost wages and benefits. Willful violation is a misdemeanor.

Colorado

Colo. Rev. Stat. §§ 13-71-126, 13-71-134

Paid leave: All employees (including part-time and temporary who were scheduled to work for the 3 months preceding jury service): regular wages up to $50 per day for first 3 days of jury duty. Must pay within 30 days of jury service.

Additional employee protections: Employer may not make any demands on employee which will interfere with effective performance of jury duty.

Employer penalty for firing or penalizing employee: Class 2 misdemeanor, punishable by a fine of $250 to $1,000 or 3 to 12 months' imprisonment, or both. May be liable to employee for triple damages and attorney fees.

Connecticut

Conn. Gen. Stat. Ann. §§ 51-247 to 51-247c

Paid leave: Full-time employees: regular wages for the first 5 days of jury duty; after 5 days, state pays up to $50 per day.

Employer penalty for firing or penalizing employee: Criminal contempt: punishable by a fine of up to $500 or up to 30 days' imprisonment, or both. Liable for up to 10 weeks' lost wages for discharging employee.

Delaware

Del. Code Ann. tit. 10, § 4515

Unpaid leave: Yes

Employer penalty for firing or penalizing employee: Criminal contempt: punishable by a fine of up to $500 or up to 6 months' imprisonment, or both. Liable to discharged employee for lost wages and attorney fees.

District of Columbia

D.C. Code Ann. §§ 11-1913; 15-718

Paid leave: Full-time employees: regular wages for the first 5 days of jury duty.

Employer penalty for firing or penalizing employee: Criminal contempt: punishable by a fine of up to $300 or up to 30 days imprisonment, or both, for a first offense; up to $5,000 or up to 180 days imprisonment, or both, for any subsequent offense. Liable to discharged employee for lost wages and attorney fees.

State Laws on Jury Duty (continued)

Florida

Fla. Stat. Ann. § 40.271

Unpaid leave: Yes

Additional employee protections: Employee may not be threatened with dismissal.

Employer penalty for firing or penalizing employee: Threatening employee is contempt of court. May be liable to discharged employee for compensatory and punitive damages and attorney fees.

Georgia

Ga. Code Ann. § 34-1-3

Unpaid leave: Yes

Additional employee protections: Employee may not be discharged or penalized or threatened with discharge or penalty for responding to a subpoena or making a required court appearance.

Notice employee must give: Reasonable notice.

Employer penalty for firing or penalizing employee: Liable for actual damages and reasonable attorney fees.

Hawaii

Haw. Rev. Stat. § 612-25

Unpaid leave: Yes

Employer penalty for firing or penalizing employee: Petty misdemeanor: punishable by a fine of up to $1,000. May be liable to discharged employee for up to 6 weeks' lost wages.

Idaho

Idaho Code § 2-218

Unpaid leave: Yes

Employer penalty for firing or penalizing employee: Criminal contempt: punishable by a fine of up to $300. Liable to discharged employee for triple lost wages.

Illinois

705 Ill. Comp. Stat. § 310/10.1

Unpaid leave: Yes

Additional employee protections: A regular night shift employee may not be required to work if serving on a jury during the day. May not lose any seniority or benefits.

Employer penalty for firing or penalizing employee: Employer will be charged with civil or criminal contempt, or both; liable to employee for lost wages and benefits.

Indiana

Ind. Code Ann. § 35-44-3-10

Unpaid leave: Yes

Additional employee protections: Employee may not be deprived of benefits or threatened with the loss of them.

Employer penalty for firing or penalizing employee: Class B misdemeanor: punishable by up to 180 days imprisonment; may also be fined up to $1,000. Liable to discharged employee for lost wages and attorney fees.

Iowa

Iowa Code § 607A.45

Unpaid leave: Yes

Employer penalty for firing or penalizing employee: Contempt of court. Liable to discharged employee for up to 6 weeks' lost wages and attorney fees.

Kansas

Kan. Stat. Ann. § 43-173

Unpaid leave: Yes

Additional employee protections: May not lose seniority or benefits. (Basic and additional protections are not available to temporary employees.)

Employer penalty for firing or penalizing employee: Liable for lost wages and benefits, damages and attorney fees.

Kentucky

Ky. Rev. Stat. Ann. § 29A.160

Unpaid leave: Yes

Employer penalty for firing or penalizing employee: Class B misdemeanor: punishable by up to 90 days imprisonment or fine of up to $250, or both. Liable to discharged employee for lost wages and attorney fees. Must reinstate employee with full seniority and benefits.

Louisiana

La. Rev. Stat. Ann. § 23:965

Paid leave: Regular employee entitled to one day full compensation for jury service. May not lose any sick, vacation or personal leave or other benefit.

Additional employee protections: Employer may not create any policy or rule that would discharge employee for jury service.

Employer penalty for firing or penalizing employee: For each discharged employee: fine of $100 to $1,000; must

State Laws on Jury Duty (continued)

reinstate employee with full benefits. For not granting paid leave: fine of $100 to $500; must pay full day's lost wages.

Maine

Me. Rev. Stat. Ann. tit. 14, § 1218

Unpaid leave: Yes

Additional employee protections: May not lose or be threatened with loss of health insurance coverage.

Employer penalty for firing or penalizing employee: Class E crime: punishable by up to 6 months in the county jail or a fine of up to $1,000. Liable for up to 6 weeks' lost wages, benefits and attorney fees.

Maryland

Md. Code Ann., [Cts. & Jud. Proc.] § 8-105

Unpaid leave: Yes

Massachusetts

Mass. Gen. Laws ch. 234A, §§ 48 and following

Paid leave: All employees (including part-time and temporary who were scheduled to work for the 3 months preceding jury service): regular wages for first 3 days of jury duty. If paid leave is an "extreme financial hardship" for employer, state will pay. After first 3 days state will pay $50 per day.

Michigan

Mich. Comp. Laws § 600.1348

Unpaid leave: Yes

Additional employee protections: Employee may not be threatened or disciplined; may not be required to work in addition to jury service, if extra hours would mean working overtime or beyond normal quitting time.

Employer penalty for firing or penalizing employee: Misdemeanor, punishable by a fine of up to $500 or up to 90 days in the county jail, or both. Employer may also be punished for contempt of court, with a fine of up to $250 or up to 30 days' imprisonment, or both.

Minnesota

Minn. Stat. Ann. § 593.50

Unpaid leave: Yes

Employer penalty for firing or penalizing employee: Criminal contempt: punishable by a fine of up to $700 or up to 6 months' imprisonment, or both. Also liable to employee for up to 6 weeks' lost wages and attorney fees.

Mississippi

Miss. Code Ann. § 13-5-23

Unpaid leave: Yes

Additional employee protections: Employer may not threaten or intimidate, persuade or attempt to persuade employee to avoid jury service.

Employer penalty for firing or penalizing employee: If found guilty of interference with the administration of justice, at least one month in the county jail or up to 2 years in the state penitentiary, or a fine of up to $500, or both. May also be found guilty of contempt of court, punishable by a fine of up to $1,000 or up to 6 months' imprisonment, or both.

Missouri

Mo. Rev. Stat. § 494.460

Unpaid leave: Yes

Additional employee protections: Employer may not take or threaten to take any adverse action.

Employer penalty for firing or penalizing employee: Employer may be liable for lost wages, damages and attorney fees and ordered to reinstate employee.

Montana

Mont. Admin. R. 24.16.2520

Paid leave: No laws regarding private employers.

Nebraska

Neb. Rev. Stat. § 25-1640

Paid leave: Normal wages minus any compensation (other than expenses) from the court.

Additional employee protections: Employee may not lose pay, sick leave, vacation or be penalized in any way; may not be required to work evening or night shift.

Notice employee must give: Reasonable notice.

Employer penalty for firing or penalizing employee: Class IV misdemeanor, punishable by a fine of $100 to $500.

Nevada

Nev. Rev. Stat. Ann. § 6.190

Unpaid leave: Yes

Additional employee protections: Employer may not recommend or threaten termination; may not dissuade or attempt to dissuade employee from serving as a juror.

Notice employee must give: At least one day's notice.

Employer penalty for firing or penalizing employee: Terminating or threatening to terminate is a gross misdemeanor, punishable by a fine of up to $2,000 or up to one year imprisonment, or both; in addition employer may be

State Laws on Jury Duty (continued)

liable for lost wages, damages equal to lost wages, punitive damages to $50,000 and must reinstate employee. Dissuading or attempting to dissuade is a misdemeanor, punishable by a fine of up to $1,000 or up to 6 months in the county jail, or both.

New Hampshire

N.H. Rev. Stat. Ann. § 500-A:14

Unpaid leave: Yes

Employer penalty for firing or penalizing employee: Employer will be found guilty of contempt of court; also liable to employee for lost wages and attorney fees and must reinstate employee.

New Jersey

N.J. Stat. Ann. § 2B:20-17

Unpaid leave: Yes

Employer penalty for firing or penalizing employee: Employer may be found guilty of a disorderly persons offense, punishable by a fine of up to $1,000 or up to 6 months' imprisonment, or both. May also be liable to employee for economic damages and attorney's fees, and may be ordered to reinstate employee

New Mexico

N.M. Stat. Ann. §§ 38-5-18 to 38-5-9

Unpaid leave: Yes

Employer penalty for firing or penalizing employee: Petty misdemeanor, punishable by a fine of up to $500 or up to 6 months in the county jail, or both.

New York

N.Y. Jud. Ct. Acts Law § 519

Unpaid leave: Yes

Paid leave: Employers with more than 10 employees must pay first $40 of wages for the first 3 days of jury duty.

Notice employee must give: Must notify employer prior to beginning jury duty.

Employer penalty for firing or penalizing employee: May be found guilty of criminal contempt of court, punishable by a fine of up to $1,000 or up to 6 months in the county jail, or both.

North Carolina

N.C. Gen. Stat. § 9-32

Unpaid leave: Yes

Additional employee protections: Employee may not be demoted.

Employer penalty for firing or penalizing employee: Liable to discharged employee for reasonable damages; must reinstate employee to former position.

North Dakota

N.D. Cent. Code § 27-09.1-17

Unpaid leave: Yes

Additional employee protections: Employee may not be laid off, penalized or coerced because of jury duty, responding to a summons or subpoena or serving as a witness or testifying in court.

Employer penalty for firing or penalizing employee: Class B misdemeanor, punishable by a fine of up to $1,000 or up to 30 days' imprisonment, or both. Liable to employee for up to 6 weeks' lost wages and attorney fees and must reinstate employee.

Ohio

Ohio Rev. Code Ann. § 2313.18

Unpaid leave: Yes

Notice employee must give: Reasonable notice. Absence must be for actual jury service.

Employer penalty for firing or penalizing employee: May be found guilty of contempt of court, punishable by a fine of up to $250 or 30 days imprisonment, or both, for first offense; a fine of up to $500 or 60 days imprisonment, or both, for second offense; a fine of up to $1,000 or 90 days imprisonment, or both, for third offense.

Oklahoma

Okla. Stat. Ann. tit. 38, §§ 34, 35

Unpaid leave: Yes

Additional employee protections: Employee can't be required to use sick leave or vacation; may choose to take paid or unpaid leave.

Employer penalty for firing or penalizing employee: Misdemeanor, punishable by a fine of up to $5,000. Liable to discharged employee for actual and exemplary damages; actual damages include past and future lost wages, mental anguish and costs of finding suitable employment.

Oregon

Or. Rev. Stat. § 10.090

Unpaid leave: Yes (or according to employer's policy)

Employer penalty for firing or penalizing employee: Employer must reinstate discharged employee with back pay.

State Laws on Jury Duty (continued)

Pennsylvania

42 Pa. Cons. Stat. Ann. § 4563; 18 Pa. Cons. Stat. Ann. § 4957

Unpaid leave: Yes (applies to retail or service industry employers with 15 or more employees and to manufacturers with 40 or more employees).

Additional employee protections: Employee may not lose seniority or benefits. (Any employee who would not be eligible for unpaid leave will be automatically excused from jury duty.) Employee who must appear in court as a victim or witness or as a family member of a victim or witness must also be given unpaid leave.

Employer penalty for firing or penalizing employee: Liable to employee for lost benefits, wages and attorney fees; must reinstate employee.

Rhode Island

R.I. Gen. Laws § 9-9-28

Unpaid leave: Yes

Additional employee protections: Employee may not lose wage increases, promotions, length of service or other benefit.

Employer penalty for firing or penalizing employee: Misdemeanor punishable by a fine of up to $1,000 up to one year imprisonment, or both.

South Carolina

S.C. Code Ann. § 41-1-70

Unpaid leave: Yes

Additional employee protections: Employee may not be demoted.

Employer penalty for firing or penalizing employee: For discharging employee, liable for one year's salary; for demoting employee, liable for one year's difference between former and lower salary.

South Dakota

S.D. Codified Laws Ann. §§ 16-13-41.1, 16-13-41.2

Unpaid leave: Yes

Additional employee protections: Employee may not lose job status, pay or seniority.

Employer penalty for firing or penalizing employee: Class 2 misdemeanor, punishable by a fine of up to $200 or up to 30 days in the county jail, or both.

Tennessee

Tenn. Code Ann. § 22-4-108

Paid leave: Regular wages minus jury fees (does not apply to employers with fewer than 5 employees or to temporary employees who have worked less than 6 months).

Additional employee protections: Night shift employees are excused from shift work during and for the night before the first day of jury service.

Notice employee must give: Employee must show summons to supervisor the day after receiving it.

Employer penalty for firing or penalizing employee: Violating employee rights or any provisions of this law is a Class A misdemeanor, punishable by up to 11 months, 29 days imprisonment or a fine up to $2,500, or both. Liable to employee for lost wages and benefits and must reinstate employee.

Texas

Tex. Civ. Prac. & Rem. Code Ann. §§ 122.001, 122.002

Unpaid leave: Yes

Notice employee must give: Employee must notify employer of intent to return after completion of jury service.

Employer penalty for firing or penalizing employee: Liable to employee for not less than one year nor more than 5 years' compensation and attorney fees. Must reinstate employee.

Utah

Utah Code Ann. § 78-46-21

Unpaid leave: Yes

Additional employee protections: Employee may not be threatened or coerced.

Employer penalty for firing or penalizing employee: May be found guilty of criminal contempt, punishable by a fine of up to $500 or up to 6 months' imprisonment, or both. Liable to employee for up to 6 weeks' lost wages and attorney fees.

Vermont

Vt. Stat. Ann. tit. 21, § 499

Unpaid leave: Yes

Additional employee protections: Employee may not be penalized or lose any benefit available to other employees; may not lose seniority, vacation credit or any fringe benefits. Protections also apply to an employee appearing as a witness in court or testifying before a board, commission or tribunal.

Employer penalty for firing or penalizing employee: Fine of up to $200.

State Laws on Jury Duty (continued)

Virginia

Va. Code Ann. § 18.2-465.1

Unpaid leave: Yes

Additional employee protections: Employee may not be subject to any adverse personnel action; may not be forced to use sick leave or vacation. If employee has to attend any future hearings, the same protections apply.

Notice employee must give: Reasonable notice.

Employer penalty for firing or penalizing employee: Class 4 misdemeanor, punishable by a fine of up to $250.

Washington

Wash. Rev. Code Ann. § 2.36.165

Unpaid leave: Yes

Additional employee protections: Employee may not be threatened, coerced, harassed or denied promotion.

Employer penalty for firing or penalizing employee: Intentional violation is a misdemeanor, punishable by a fine of up to $1,000 or up to 90 days' imprisonment, or both; also liable to employee for damages and attorney fees and must reinstate employees.

West Virginia

W.Va. Code § 52-3-1

Unpaid leave: Yes

Additional employee protections: Employee may not be threatened or discriminated against; regular pay cannot be cut.

Employer penalty for firing or penalizing employee: May be found guilty of civil contempt, punishable by a fine of $100 to $500. Must reinstate employee. May be liable for back pay and for attorney fees.

Wisconsin

Wis. Stat. Ann. § 756.255

Unpaid leave: Yes

Additional employee protections: Employee may not lose seniority or pay raises; may not be disciplined.

Employer penalty for firing or penalizing employee: Fine of up to $200. Must reinstate employee with back pay.

Wyoming

Wyo. Stat. § 1-11-401

Unpaid leave: Yes

Additional employee protections: Employee may not be threatened, intimidated or coerced.

Employer penalty for firing or penalizing employee: Liable to employee for up to $1,000 damages, costs and attorney fees. Must reinstate employee with no loss of seniority.

Current as of February 2003

State Laws on Taking Time Off to Vote

Note: The states of Connecticut, Delaware, District of Columbia, Florida, Idaho, Indiana, Louisiana, Maine, Michigan, Mississippi, Montana, New Hampshire, New Jersey, Oregon, Pennsylvania, Rhode Island, South Carolina, Vermont and Virginia are not listed in this chart because they do not have laws or regulations on time off to vote that govern private employers. Check with your state department of labor if you need more information (see Appendix C for contact list).

Alabama

Ala. Code § 17-6-17

Time off work for voting: Employers with 25 or more employees must allow appointed election officials time off to work at precinct on election day.

Time off is paid: No

Employee must request leave in advance: 7 days before election; employee must also show proof of appointment.

Alaska

Alaska Stat. § 15.56.100

Time off work for voting: Not specified.

Time off not required if: Employee has 2 consecutive non-work hours at beginning or end of shift when polls are open.

Time off is paid: Yes

Arizona

Ariz. Rev. Stat. § 16-402

Time off work for voting: As much time as will add up to 3 hours when combined with non-work time. Employer may decide when hours are taken.

Time off not required if: Employee has 3 consecutive non-work hours at beginning or end of shift when polls are open.

Time off is paid: Yes

Employee must request leave in advance: One day before election.

Arkansas

Ark. Code Ann. § 7-1-102

Time off work for voting: Employer must schedule work hours so employee has time to vote.

Time off is paid: No

California

Cal. Elec. Code § 14000

Time off work for voting: Up to 2 hours at beginning or end of shift, whichever gives employee most time to vote and takes least time off work.

Time off not required if: Employee has sufficient time to vote during non-work time.

Time off is paid: Yes (up to 2 hours)

Employee must request leave in advance: 2 working days before election.

Colorado

Colo. Rev. Stat. § 1-7-102

Time off work for voting: Up to 2 hours. Employer may decide when hours are taken, but employer must permit employee to take time at beginning or end of shift, if employee requests it.

Time off not required if: Employee has 3 non-work hours when polls are open.

Time off is paid: Yes (up to 2 hours)

Georgia

Ga. Code Ann. § 21-2-404

Time off work for voting: As much as is necessary up to 2 hours. Employer may decide when hours are taken.

Time off not required if: Employee has 2 non-work hours when polls are open.

Time off is paid: No

Employee must request leave in advance: "Reasonable notice."

Hawaii

Haw. Rev. Stat. § 11-95

Time off work for voting: 2 consecutive hours excluding meal or rest breaks. Employer may not change employee's regular work schedule.

Time off not required if: Employee has 2 consecutive non-work hours when polls are open.

Time off is paid: Yes

Employee required to show proof of voting: Yes (voter's receipt). If employer verifies that employee did not vote, hours off will be deducted from pay.

Illinois

10 Ill. Comp. Stat. §§ 5/7-42; 5/17-15

Time off work for voting: 2 hours. Employer may decide when hours are taken.

State Laws on Taking Time Off to Vote (continued)

Time off is paid: No

Employee must request leave in advance: One day in advance (for general or state election). Employer must give consent (for primary).

Iowa

Iowa Code § 49.109

Time off work for voting: As much time as will add up to 3 hours when combined with non-work time. Employer may decide when hours are taken.

Time off not required if: Employee has 3 consecutive non-work hours when polls are open.

Time off is paid: Yes

Employee must request leave in advance: In writing "prior to the election."

Kansas

Kan. Stat. Ann. § 25-418

Time off work for voting: Up to 2 hours or as much time as will add up to 2 hours when combined with non-work time. Employer may decide when hours are taken, but may not be during a regular meal break.

Time off not required if: Employee has 2 consecutive non-work hours when polls are open.

Time off is paid: Yes

Kentucky

Ky. Rev. Stat. Ann. § 118.035

Time off work for voting: "Reasonable time," but not less than 4 hours. Employer may decide when hours are taken.

Time off is paid: No

Employee must request leave in advance: One day.

Employee required to show proof of voting: No proof specified, but employee who takes time off and does not vote may be subject to disciplinary action.

Maryland

Md. Code Ann. [Elec.] § 10-315

Time off work for voting: 2 hours.

Time off not required if: Employee has 2 continuous non-work hours when polls are open.

Time off is paid: Yes

Employee required to show proof of voting: Yes (must use state board of elections form).

Massachusetts

Mass. Gen. Laws ch. 149, § 178

Time off work for voting: First 2 hours that polls are open. (Applies to workers in manufacturing, mechanical or retail industries.)

Time off is paid: No

Employee must request leave in advance: Must apply for leave of absence (no time specified).

Minnesota

Minn. Stat. Ann. § 204C.04

Time off work for voting: May be absent during the morning of election day.

Time off is paid: Yes

Missouri

Mo. Rev. Stat. § 115.639

Time off work for voting: 3 hours. Employer may decide when hours are taken.

Time off not required if: Employee has 3 consecutive non-work hours when polls are open.

Time off is paid: Yes (if employee votes).

Employee must request leave in advance: "Prior to the day of election."

Employee required to show proof of voting: None specified, but pay contingent on employee actually voting.

Nebraska

Neb. Rev. Stat. § 32-922

Time off work for voting: As much time as will add up to 2 consecutive hours when combined with non-work time. Employer may decide when hours are taken.

Time off not required if: Employee has 2 consecutive non-work hours when polls are open.

Time off is paid: Yes

Employee must request leave in advance: Prior to or on election day.

Nevada

Nev. Rev. Stat. Ann. § 293.463

Time off work for voting: If it is impracticable to vote before or after work: employee who lives less than 2 miles from polling place may take 1 hour; 2 to 10 miles, 2 hours; over 10 miles, 3 hours.

Time off not required if: Employee has sufficient non-work time when polls are open.

Time off is paid: Yes

State Laws on Taking Time Off to Vote (continued)

Employee must request leave in advance: Prior to election day.

New Mexico

N.M. Stat. Ann. § 1-12-42

Time off work for voting: 2 hours. (Includes Indian nation, tribal and pueblo elections.)

Time off not required if: Employee's workday begins more than 2 hours after polls open or ends more than 3 hours before polls close.

Time off is paid: Yes

New York

N.Y. Elec. Law § 3-110

Time off work for voting: As many hours at beginning or end of shift as will give employee enough time to vote when combined with non-work time. Employer may decide hours.

Time off not required if: Employee has 4 consecutive non-work hours at beginning or end of shift when polls are open.

Time off is paid: Yes (up to 2 hours)

Employee must request leave in advance: Not more than 10 or less than 2 working days before election.

North Carolina

N.C. Gen. Stat. § 163-41.2

Time off work for voting: Appointed precinct officials may take time off to work on election day or canvass day.

Time off is paid: No

Advance notice to employer required: 30 days written notice.

North Dakota

N.D. Cent. Code § 16.1-01-02.1

Time off work for voting: Employers encouraged to give employees time off to vote when regular work schedule conflicts with times polls are open.

Time off is paid: No

Ohio

Ohio Rev. Code Ann. § 3599.06

Time off work for voting: "Reasonable time."

Time off is paid: Yes

Oklahoma

Okla. Stat. Ann. tit. 26, § 7-101

Time off work for voting: 2 hours, unless employee lives so far from polling place that more time is needed. Employer may decide when hours are taken or may change employee's schedule to give employee non-work time to vote.

Time off not required if: Employee's workday begins at least 3 hours after polls open or ends at least 3 hours before polls close.

Time off is paid: Yes

Employee must request leave in advance: Orally or in writing one day before election.

Employee required to show proof of voting: Yes

South Dakota

S.D. Codified Laws Ann. § 12-3-5

Time off work for voting: 2 consecutive hours. Employer may decide when hours are taken.

Time off not required if: Employee has 2 consecutive non-work hours when polls are open.

Time off is paid: Yes

Tennessee

Tenn. Code Ann. § 2-1-106

Time off work for voting: "Reasonable time" up to 3 hours.

Time off not required if: Employee's workday begins at least 3 hours after polls open or ends at least 3 hours before polls close.

Time off is paid: Yes

Employee must request leave in advance: Before noon on election day.

Texas

Tex. Elec. Code Ann. § 276.004

Time off work for voting: Employer may not refuse to allow employee to take time off, but no time limit specified.

Time off not required if: Employee has 2 consecutive non-work hours when polls are open.

Time off is paid: Yes

Utah

Utah Code Ann. § 20A-3-103

Time off work for voting: 2 hours at beginning or end of shift. Employer may decide when hours are taken.

Time off not required if: Employee has at least 3 non-work hours when polls are open.

Time off is paid: Yes

State Laws on Taking Time Off to Vote (continued)

Employee must request leave in advance: "Before election day."

Washington

Wash. Rev. Code Ann. § 49.28.120

Time off work for voting: Employer must either arrange work schedule so employee has enough non-work time (not including meal or rest breaks) to vote, or allow employee to take off work for a "reasonable time," up to 2 hours.

Time off not required if: Employee has 2 non-work hours when polls are open or enough time to get an absentee ballot.

Time off is paid: Yes

West Virginia

W.Va. Code § 3-1-42

Time off work for voting: Up to 3 hours. (Employers in health, transportation, communication, production and processing facilities may change employee's schedule so that time off doesn't impair essential operations, but must allow employee sufficient and convenient time to vote.)

Time off not required if: Employee has at least 3 non-work hours when polls are open.

Time off is paid: Yes (if employee votes).

Employee must request leave in advance: Written request at least 3 days before election.

Employee required to show proof of voting: None specified, but time off will be deducted from pay if employee does not vote.

Wisconsin

Wis. Stat. Ann. § 6.76

Time off work for voting: Up to 3 consecutive hours. Employer may decide when hours are taken.

Time off is paid: No

Employee must request leave in advance: "Before election day."

Wyoming

Wyo. Stat. § 22-2-111

Time off work for voting: One hour, other than a meal break.

Time off not required if: Employee has at least 3 consecutive non-work hours when polls are open.

Time off is paid: Yes (if employee votes).

Employee required to show proof of voting: None specified, but pay contingent on employee voting.

Current as of February 2003

Performance

As the saying goes, your company is only as good as your employees or, more to the point, as your employees' performance. After all, you hired them and pay them to do a job and to do it well.

It makes sense, then, for you to say something about performance in your employee handbook. Your employees need to see, in writing, that you expect a certain level of performance from them and that you will accept no less. They also need to understand that how they perform affects everyone else at your company.

Of course, with all of the people doing the various jobs within your company, it's hard for one handbook policy to tell each one what you expect. That is the stuff of performance evaluations. The policies in this chapter will let you establish a benchmark of excellence for employees to strive for, then refer employees to your performance evaluation system (if you have one) for more details.

This chapter contains the following policies:

If you would like to institute a performance evaluation system in your workplace, but aren't sure how, refer to *Dealing With Problem Employees: A Legal Guide*, by Amy DelPo & Lisa Guerin (Nolo). It tells you everything you need to know to put a good system in place.

11:1   Job Performance Expectations

Although it should be self-evident that you want your employees to perform well, this policy reminds your employees that you have this expectation. It also warns them that if they don't perform well, you may discipline or even terminate them. This tells your employees that you take their performance seriously, and that you expect them to do so as well. It also points out to employees that their performance doesn't only affect your or other members of management. It also affects them and their coworkers, for as the fortunes of your company go, so go the fortunes of your employees.

Standard Policy

Your Job Performance

Each and every employee at ___*[Company name]*___ contributes to the success or failure of our Company. If one employee allows his or her performance to slip, then all of us suffer. We expect everyone to perform to the highest level possible.

Poor job performance can lead to discipline, up to and including termination.

Optional Modification to Specify Performance Standards

Depending on the products or services your company provides, you may want to give more information about the type of performance you expect from your employees. For example, a software company might want to encourage innovation and "thinking outside the box," while a manufacturer might want to stress adherence to workplace rules.

If you would like to say more about your expectations, insert an additional paragraph after the first paragraph of the standard policy, above. Although we can't give you a standard modification to use, the following is an example of what you might write:

SAMPLE POLICY LANGUAGE:

We believe our connection to our customers is of the utmost importance to our success. Therefore, every employee at Better Bread Bakery, from the accountant on up to the head baker, must make customer service a top priority. Excellent performance includes excellent customer service.

⚠️ **Include this language only if you do, in fact, have a performance evaluation system that you intend to use to evaluate each and every employee.** If you use this language, but fail to evaluate your employees, you risk being accused of making a promise that you haven't kept—something that could complicate matters if you fire an employee or fail to promote an employee because of performance issues. That employee could cry foul over the fact that you never reviewed her as promised in your handbook. This could lead to a disgruntled workforce or, even worse, a lawsuit.

11:2   Job Performance Reviews

Rather than rely on casual feedback to keep their employees' performance on track, many companies have structured performance evaluation systems by which supervisors formally evaluate each employee's performance every so often (usually every six months or year).

If you have such a system, then you should mention it in your handbook. To keep your flexibility, however, the following standard policy doesn't give a detailed description of how the system works. It simply alerts employees to the fact that you have a system, and it states that you require employees to participate in it. You can give employees the details in other forms of communication, such as memoranda and company meetings.

Standard Policy

Performance Reviews

Because our employees' performance is vital to our success, we conduct periodic reviews of individual employee performance. We hope that, through these reviews, our employees will learn what we expect of them and we will learn what they expect of us.

We require all employees to participate in the review process. Failure to participate could lead to discipline, up to and including termination.

To learn more about our performance review system, contact

_____.

Workplace Behavior

The Workplace Behavior section of your handbook is something of a grab bag of policies that define the minimum standards of conduct that you expect from your employees. Other sections of your handbook will give more details about the various rules that your employees must follow, but this section is where you set out the basics of how your employees must behave while at work. It is also where you set out your discipline policy, if you have one. In this chapter, we include the following policies:

12:1   Professional Conduct

Although you may not have articulated it before, you probably expect from your employees something more than mere work product. After all, they come into your workplace every day and interact with your other employees, your clients and your vendors. How they conduct themselves during these interactions is important to the smooth operation—indeed, to the success—of your business.

The following Professional Conduct policy tells employees that you expect them to behave in a professional manner. It provides an explanation of what professional conduct is and informs employees that acting unprofessionally can be grounds for discipline.

Standard Policy

Please Act Professionally

People who work together have an impact on each other's performance, productivity and personal satisfaction in their jobs. In addition, how our employees act toward customers and vendors will influence whether those relationships are successful for our Company.

Because your conduct affects many more people than just yourself, we expect you to act in a professional manner whenever you are on Company property, conducting Company business or representing the Company at business or social functions.

Although it is impossible to give an exhaustive list of everything that professional conduct means, it does, at a minimum, include the following:

- following all of the rules in this Handbook that apply to you
- refraining from rude, offensive or outrageous behavior
- refraining from ridicule and hostile jokes
- treating coworkers, customers and vendors with patience, respect and consideration
- being courteous and helpful to others, and
- communicating openly with supervisors, managers and co-workers.

Individuals who act unprofessionally will face discipline, up to and including termination.

Who Needs This Policy

Depending on the nature of your business, you may have more or less interest in how your employees behave. Nonetheless, a professional conduct policy can do no harm to your business, and it might even do it a lot of good. It encourages your employees to Play Nice, and it gives you additional leeway in disciplining employees who behave unpleasantly, but who don't violate a specific rule or let their performance or productivity drop.

Optional Modification Regarding Treatment of Customers

If your employees have a great deal of customer contact, you might want to emphasize in this policy how you expect your employees to treat your customers. Do you have a The Customer Is Always Right approach to customer relations? Do you expect your employees to do whatever it takes to make customers happy? Or are there limits to what you expect your employees to do for your customers?

If you would like to include specific information about customer relations in this policy, add the following paragraph to the standard policy, above. The best place to add this paragraph is just before the last paragraph regarding disciplinary action.

Modification

The success of this Company depends in great part on the loyalty and good will of our customers. As a result, we expect our employees to behave in the following manner when interacting with customers:

- to treat all customers with courtesy and respect
- to always be helpful and cheerful toward customers
- to _____
- to _____, and
- to _____.

This policy does not police employee conduct outside of work. Some employers believe that how employees act at all times—including during their private time—reflects on the company. Or maybe they want only employees of a certain moral character working for them so they allow employees' off-work conduct to have an impact on their decisions about the employee.

If you are an employer who is concerned about your employees' off-work conduct, tread carefully—and consult with a lawyer. Many states have laws that protect employees from the prying eyes of their employer when they are not at work. These include laws protecting employees' right to privacy, laws prohibiting discrimination based on lawful conduct, laws prohibiting discrimination based on political activity and laws prohibiting discrimination based on marital or family status.

12:2   Punctuality and Attendance

You may think that it goes without saying that you expect your employees to show up to work consistently and on time. In these days of flex time and telecommuting, however, prudent employers who care about punctuality and attendance specifically demand it. Otherwise, employees may think that it doesn't really matter what time they show up, as long as they get their work done. This policy makes it clear that it does matter—and that you will discipline employees who take a lax attitude. It also sets out a process that employees can follow if they are unable to be at work or if they are going to be late.

Standard Policy

Punctuality and Attendance

You are important to the effective operation of this business. When you are not here at expected times or on expected days, someone else must do your job or delay doing his own job while he waits for you to arrive. If you work with customers or vendors, they may grow frustrated if they can't reach you during your scheduled work times.

As a result, we expect you to keep regular attendance and to be on time and ready to work at the beginning of each scheduled workday. (In Section ___ of this Handbook, you can find a description of this Company's work hours, timekeeping and scheduling policies.)

Of course, things will sometimes happen that will prevent you from showing up to work on time. For example, you may be delayed by weather, a sick child or car trouble. If you are going to be more than ___ minutes late, please call _____. If you cannot reach this person, please _____ _____ _____. Please give this notice as far in advance as possible.

If you must miss a full day of work for reasons other than vacation, sick leave or other approved leave (such as leave to serve on a jury or for a death in a family), you must notify _____ as far in advance as possible. If you cannot reach this person, _____ _____. (You can find information about this Company's vacation and leave policies in Handbook Section ___.)

If you are late for work or fail to appear without calling in as required by this policy or by other policies in this Handbook, you will face disciplinary action, up to and including termination.

How to Complete This Policy

To complete the standard policy, above, you must decide three things:

- How much leeway will you give employees in terms of punctuality? That is, how many minutes late must they be before you require them to call in? This is something that you must decide based on the needs of your business. Typical periods range from 15 minutes to two hours.

- Whom do your employees have to call if they are going to be late or miss work? Typically, this person is the employee's supervisor, but in some businesses this person might be the human resources manager or the office manager—whoever will be responsible for making sure the employee's duties are covered while the employee is out of the office.

- What should your employees do if they can't reach the designated person? You might instruct employees to simply leave a voicemail for the individual, or you might require them to leave a message for that person with someone who holds a position that is always staffed—the office receptionist, for example.

12:3   Dress, Grooming and Personal Hygiene

Workplace dress standards vary. Some employers ask only that their employees be clean and neat. Other employers have more specific policies—requiring a certain mode of dress or a uniform, for example.

The standard policy below simply requires a clean and neat appearance from employees. It is very general and nonspecific. This allows you flexibility to set standards department by department, if you wish, through memos and instructions from supervisors. It also informs employees that you will accommodate the needs of people with disabilities or people with specific religious or ethnic practices.

We also provide instructions on how to modify the policy if you want to require a uniform or if you want to require your employees to dress professionally.

Standard Policy

Employee Appearance and Dress

We ask all employees to use common sense when they dress for work. Please dress appropriately for your position and job duties, and please make sure you are neat and clean at all times.

If you have any questions about the proper attire for your position, please contact _____. We will try to reasonably accommodate an employee's special dress or grooming needs that are the result of religion, ethnicity, race or disability.

Who Needs This Policy

Whether you need this policy will depend on your company culture and image and on the amount of contact that your employees have with outsiders. The more formal or professional a culture you have, and the more that your employees interact with people outside the company, the more you will need a policy governing dress and appearance.

Optional Modifications

If Your Employees Must Wear Uniforms

If you require your employees to wear uniforms, replace the standard policy, above, with the following policy:

Modification

Employees must wear a uniform during work hours. Please make sure you are neat and clean at all times, and please keep your uniform clean and in good condition.

   If you have any questions about your uniform or about our appearance standards, please contact _____.

Most states have rules regarding who must pay for a work uniform—the employer or the employee. States also have rules as to who must pay for cleaning and repairing the uniform. If you require your employees to wear uniforms, be sure to check out your state's laws on these issues. Once you do that, you can add that information to the policy. A good place to start your research is at your state labor department. (See Appendix C for contact information.)

If Your Employees Must Dress Professionally

Some businesses like to cultivate a professional culture and image through their employees' appearance and dress. If you would like your employees to dress professionally, substitute the following in the place of the first paragraph of the standard policy, above.

Modification

We believe that a professional image enhances our work product and makes us more competitive in the marketplace. In part, we convey that image through the appearance of our employees. We ask all employees to use their common sense when dressing for work and to wear attire that is professional and appropriate. We also ask our employees to maintain a neat and clean appearance at all times.

If You Allow Casual Dress on Fridays

Many employers allow professional employees to "dress down" on Fridays. For some, this means that employees still have to dress up, but that they can forego the suit and tie. For others, it means T-shirts and blue jeans. If you require professional dress during the week but would like to allow your employees to relax more on Fridays, add the following paragraph to the professional dress modification paragraph, above.

Modification

> Although we do require professional attire Monday through Thursday, we celebrate Fridays here by allowing employees to dress casually. Acceptable casual clothing includes [*List the types of clothing that you find acceptable, for example, slacks, collared shirts, jeans, T-shirts, dress shorts, sandals*]. Unacceptable casual clothing includes [*List the types of clothing that you don't find acceptable, even on Fridays—for example, T-shirts, tank tops, shorts above the knee, athletic shorts, torn clothing, sheer or see-through clothing*]. Even on Fridays, however, we ask employees to use good judgment and to maintain a neat and clean appearance.

If You Have Safety Concerns

In some workplaces, employees cannot wear certain clothing or wear their hair in a certain style because of safety concerns. For example, most food service companies require employees to wear hair nets, and many companies in the manufacturing industry prohibit loose-fitting clothes and jewelry, which could get caught in machinery.

If there are health and safety reasons for your dress and grooming standards, you should detail those either in the health and safety chapter of your handbook or through memos and instructions from supervisors. In this policy, you can simply refer employees to those rules by making the following paragraph the second paragraph of the standard policy, above:

WORKPLACE BEHAVIOR   12/9

Modification

We place specific restrictions on the dress and appearance of some employees for safety reasons. To learn about those restrictions, refer to _____.

Anti-discrimination laws don't mean that you can't require certain modes of dress; they just mean you must have a really good reason for doing so. If you would like to impose a grooming or dress standard that might raise discrimination issues, consult a lawyer for help.

Reality Check: Avoid Discriminatory Dress Codes

For the most part, the law will allow you to govern how your employees appear when they work for you. Be careful, however, that you don't bump up against anti-discrimination laws when demanding certain modes of dress or appearance. Particular areas to watch out for include the following:

- **Sexual harassment:** If you require employees of a certain gender to dress in a sexually provocative way (for example, requiring female employees to wear tight, low-cut tops or short skirts), you may be accused of harassing those employees or of encouraging other people to harass them.
- **Sex discrimination:** Demanding different modes of dress for your female and male employees leaves you vulnerable to claims of gender discrimination. In addition, some states specifically prohibit employers from requiring female employees to wear skirts.
- **Race discrimination:** Some grooming policies disproportionately affect members of one race. For example, requiring that all men be clean-shaven can have a negative impact on African-American men, many of whom have a physical sensitivity to shaving.
- **Religious discrimination:** Some religions impose certain dress and grooming requirements on their members. For example, some Native Americans can't cut their hair; some Muslims must wear long beards and certain garments. If your grooming or dress policies force people to violate the tenets of their religion, you may be guilty of religious discrimination.

12:4   Pranks and Practical Jokes

Most employers understand that employees who enjoy their work tend to be better and more productive performers. In some workplaces, however, employees carry enjoyment too far and play pranks and practical jokes on each other. Although this may seem harmless at first blush, pranks and practical jokes can lead to real trouble.

For example, some pranks that employees think are harmless have racial or sexual undertones. For the victim of the prank, this may feel more like harassment or discrimination than innocent fun—and the employee may take up the issue with an attorney.

Even if the prank or joke doesn't cross the legal line, it may have the effect of disrupting your workplace and lowering the morale of the individual who was on the receiving end of the so-called humor.

This policy prohibits all pranks and practical jokes. It warns employees that they might face disciplinary action if they engage in such behavior.

Standard Policy

Pranks and Practical Jokes

Although we want our employees to enjoy their jobs and have fun working together, we cannot allow employees to play practical jokes or pranks on each other. At best, these actions disrupt the workplace and dampen the morale of some; at worst, they lead to complaints of discrimination, harassment or assault.

If you have any questions about this policy, contact

_____.

Employees who play pranks or practical jokes will face disciplinary action, up to and including termination.

Who Needs This Policy

Although this type of conduct occurs in all types of workplaces—from corporate law firms to longshoring operations—it does tend to be more prevalent in male-dominated and blue-collar industries. If you operate a business in these industries, or if your company has had problems with pranks and practical jokes in the past, you should consider having a policy explicitly prohibiting such activity.

On the other hand, if your employees do not tend to engage in such behavior, you can probably forego this policy. Your policies regarding professional conduct, discrimination and harassment should help you deal with any situations that arise.

12:5   Threatening, Abusive or Vulgar Language

Despite the old playground taunt, words *can* hurt you. They can lead to harassment and discrimination lawsuits, lower the morale and productivity of your employees and destroy the congenial atmosphere of your workplace.

In addition, employee violence is often preceded by threatening and abusive language. If you have an employee who makes threats or says abusive things, don't treat the situation lightly simply because the incident involves only words. Not only could you be held legally liable if the employee later becomes violent (under a theory of law called negligent retention), you or one of your employees could be injured or worse. Having a policy against this sort of language is a good first step in protecting your workplace from potential violence—and it can lay the groundwork for nipping a bad situation in the bud.

Standard Policy

Threatening, Abusive or Vulgar Language

We expect our employees to treat everyone they meet through their jobs with courtesy and respect. Threatening, abusive and vulgar language has no place in our workplace. It destroys morale and relationships, and it impedes the effective and efficient operation of our business.

As a result, we will not tolerate threatening, abusive or vulgar language from employees while they are on the worksite, conducting Company business or attending Company-related business or social functions.

If you have any questions about this policy, contact _____ _____.

Employees who violate this policy will face disciplinary action, up to and including termination.

12:6   Horseplay

Horseplay is boisterous physical interaction that disrupts the ordinary operation of a workplace. It usually begins innocently enough, arising from the more juvenile and playful impulses of your employees. Initially, it does not involve malice, ill will or anger—it's just a matter of employees goofing off.

That being said, such aggressive playful conduct can often get out of hand, and what started out as innocent, yet loud, fun can turn into a fight or a brawl. Depending on the circumstances, it can also turn into discrimination, harassment or assault. It is also a safety hazard.

Because horseplay is disruptive and can often lead to trouble, many employers ban it outright.

Standard Policy

Horseplay

Although we want our employees to have fun while they work, we don't allow employees to engage in horseplay—which is fun that has gotten loud and boisterous and out of control. Horseplay disrupts the work environment and can get out of hand, leading to fighting, hurt feelings, safety hazards or worse.

Employees who engage in horseplay will face disciplinary action, up to and including termination.

12:7   Fighting

Fights among employees not only injure the people involved, they damage collegiality among workers, disrupt the workplace and, sometimes, lead to more violence, physical and emotional injuries and lawsuits. This policy prohibits fighting among employees and promises disciplinary action to those who engage in it. Verbal fighting can be just as damaging as physical fighting and is therefore encompassed by this policy.

Standard Policy

Fighting

Verbal or physical fighting among employees is absolutely prohibited. Employees shall not engage in, provoke or encourage a fight. Those who violate this policy will be disciplined, up to and including termination.

12:8   Sleeping on the Job

Depending on the type of business you run, employees who sleep on the job can create anything from a nuisance to a safety hazard. Most employers ban sleeping on the worksite outright, but some employers who schedule employees for exceptionally long shifts (for example, 24 hours) will expressly allow employees to sleep during designated times.

The following standard policy prohibits sleeping entirely and is designed for a business in which sleeping employees do not pose a safety hazard. If you would like to allow employees to sleep at designated times, or if you would like to emphasize the unsafe nature of sleeping, see the modifications that follow the standard policy.

Standard Policy

Sleeping on the Job

When our employees arrive at work, we expect them to be physically prepared to work through their day. Employees who sleep on the job dampen morale and productivity and deprive us of their work and companionship.

As a result, we do not allow any employees to sleep while at work. Employees who feel sick or unable to finish the day because of weariness should talk to _____ about using sick leave to take the rest of the day off. (See Section ___ of this Handbook for information about our sick leave policy.)

Optional Modifications

To Allow Employees to Sleep Sometimes
If you would like to allow your employees to sleep at certain times, add the following to the bottom of the sample policy, above:

Modification

We make an exception to this policy for certain employees who _____. To find out if you fit within this exception, contact _____.

To Emphasize the Safety Hazard of Sleeping

If employees who sleep on the job pose a safety risk (either to themselves or to others), make the following paragraph the second paragraph of the sample policy, above:

Modification

For certain employees, sleeping on the job creates a safety hazard. Employees who work in [*describe—either by department or job title—which employees pose a safety hazard when they sleep*] create unacceptable risks to their own safety and the safety of others when they fail to be attentive and alert while working. For these employees, sleeping on the job violates both this policy and our safety policies. (See Section __ of this Handbook for information about our safety program.)

12:9   Insubordination

Employee insubordination comes in two forms: (1) refusing to obey direct orders or instructions and (2) undermining authority through words and conduct. Insubordination is a particularly destructive force in the workplace, because it interferes with one of your most basic rights as an employer: to operate your business as you see fit. This means telling your employees what jobs need to be done and how—and expecting them to obey. It also means directing and controlling your company's business and culture.

Of course, not every time an employee refuses to follow an order is insubordination. Under federal law and the laws of most states, employees have a right to refuse to work in unsafe conditions. Similarly, they also have a right to refuse to do anything illegal.

And these legal issues aren't the only reason to have an insubordination policy with some flexibility in it: Sometimes, your employees might have ideas about how jobs can be done better and more efficiently. You don't want to completely squelch employee opinion and innovation by turning your workers into robots who unthinkingly follow your orders.

The following standard policy prohibits insubordination, but it also explains to employees how to disobey orders in an acceptable way if circumstances warrant.

Standard Policy

Insubordination

This workplace operates on a system of mutual respect between supervisors and employees. Supervisors must treat their employees with dignity and understanding, and employees must show due regard for their supervisors' authority.

Insubordination occurs when employees unreasonably refuse to obey the orders or follow the instructions of their supervisors. It also occurs when employees, through their actions or words, show disrespect toward their supervisors.

Insubordinate employees will face discipline, up to and including termination.

We understand, however, that there will be times when employees have valid reasons for refusing to do as their supervisor says. Perhaps the employee fears for his safety or the safety of others, believes that following instructions will violate the law or pose some other problem for this Company. Or maybe the employee thinks that there is a better way to accomplish a goal or perform a task. When these issues arise, we do not ask that employees blindly follow orders. Instead, we ask that employees explain the situation to their supervisor. If, after hearing the employee's side, the supervisor continues to give the same order or rule, the employee must either obey or use the complaint procedures described in Section ___ of this Handbook.

12:10 Progressive Discipline

In a progressive discipline system, employers use a range of disciplinary actions and counseling sessions to motivate employees to improve their conduct. In such a system, the goal of the discipline is not punitive, but rather is communicative. A progressive discipline system can be a valuable tool in improving employee performance and productivity. It can also protect you from lawsuits by ensuring that you are fair to employees and by forcing you to document employee misconduct and your responses to it.

If you have a progressive discipline system at your workplace, you should explain it to employees in general terms in your handbook.

Progressive discipline systems vary greatly from workplace to workplace. As a result, we cannot provide standard policy language. An example of what a progressive discipline policy might look like the one on the next page.

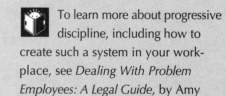 To learn more about progressive discipline, including how to create such a system in your workplace, see *Dealing With Problem Employees: A Legal Guide,* by Amy DelPo & Lisa Guerin (Nolo).

Reality Check: Follow Your Disciplinary Policy

If you put a written progressive discipline policy in your handbook, you must follow it—even when you don't want to. From an employee relations standpoint, your failure to follow your own policies will only make you look arbitrary and unfair. In addition, you might have trouble convincing employees to follow rules when you fail to do so.

From a legal standpoint, failing to follow your own progressive discipline policy leaves you vulnerable to lawsuits. Even if you have a good reason for firing someone, you'll have trouble proving it if you didn't follow your own policy. In addition, some courts might view a written policy as a type of contract between you and your employees. In such a situation, the court might view your failure to follow the policy as a breach of contract.

SAMPLE POLICY LANGUAGE:

Any employee conduct that, in the opinion of the Company, interferes with or adversely affects our business is sufficient grounds for disciplinary action.

Disciplinary action can range from oral warnings to immediate discharge. Our general policy is to take disciplinary steps in the following order:

- *oral warning(s)*
- *written reprimand(s)*
- *suspension, and*
- *termination.*

However, we reserve the right to alter the order described above, to skip disciplinary steps, to eliminate disciplinary steps or to create new and/or additional disciplinary steps.

In choosing the appropriate disciplinary action, we may consider any number of the following things:

- *the seriousness of your conduct*
- *your history of misconduct*
- *your employment record*
- *your length of employment with this Company*
- *the strength of the evidence against you*
- *your ability to correct the conduct*
- *your attitude about the conduct*
- *actions we have taken for similar conduct by other employees*
- *how your conduct affects this Company, its customers and your coworkers, and*
- *any other circumstances related to the nature of the misconduct, to your employment with this Company and to the affect of the misconduct on the business of this Company.*

We will give those considerations whatever weight we deem appropriate. Depending on the circumstances, we may give some considerations more weight than other considerations—or no weight at all.

Some conduct may result in immediate termination. Here are some examples:

- *theft of company property*
- *excessive tardiness or absenteeism*
- *arguing or fighting with customers, coworkers, managers or supervisors*
- *brandishing a weapon at work*

- *threatening the physical safety of customers, coworkers, managers or supervisors*
- *physically or verbally assaulting someone at work*
- *any illegal conduct at work*
- *using or possessing alcohol or illegal drugs at work*
- *working under the influence of alcohol or illegal drugs*
- *failing to carry out reasonable job assignments*
- *insubordination*
- *making false statements on a job application*
- *violating Company rules and regulations, and*
- *unlawful discrimination and harassment.*

Of course, it is impossible to compile an exhaustive list of the types of conduct that will result in immediate termination. The ones listed above are merely illustrations.

You should remember that your employment is at the mutual consent of you and this Company. This policy does not change this fact. This means that you or this Company can terminate our employment relationship at will, at any time, with or without cause, and with or without advance notice.

As a result, this Company reserves its right to terminate your employment at any time, for any lawful reason, including reasons not listed above. You also have the right to end your employment at any time.

■

Health and Safety

Workplace safety is of paramount concern to savvy employers—and for good reason. Dangerous situations, accidents, violence or breaches of security can have disastrous workplace consequences, including lost productivity, raised insurance premiums, stolen or damaged equipment, employee injuries or even deaths.

What's more, the government regulates workplace safety issues very heavily. Both federal and state laws require you to provide a workplace free of hazards that could cause serious harm to your employees. These laws also require you to investigate and report workplace accidents, provide employees with safety training for their jobs and keep records on workplace safety. Depending on the type of business you run, virtually every aspect of your operations may be subject to detailed safety rules.

Although you can never guarantee that your workplace will be accident-free, policies that promote workplace safety are a good start. This chapter includes policies on:

⚠️ **Some states require particular policy language.** The federal law that regulates health and safety on the job is called the Occupational Safety and Health Act or OSHA (29 U.S.C. §§ 651 and following). In addition, almost half the states have adopted their own workplace safety laws that are at least as strict as OSHA. Although OSHA doesn't require employers to adopt a written workplace safety policy, some of these state laws do. For example, employers in California must adopt a written "injury and illness prevention program." To find out what your state requires, contact your state labor department (see Appendix C for contact details)—or consult with an experienced employment attorney.

13:1   Workplace Safety

A basic safety policy is a must for every employer, no matter what type of business you run. Federal and state laws require employers to keep their workplace free of hazards, investigate accidents quickly and keep proper safety records. You can't meet these legal requirements unless your employees follow safe work habits and report workplace accidents and injuries—as our sample policy directs them to do.

Your workplace safety policy should tell employees that safety is a top concern for your company, let employees know about your safety rules and explain how to report accidents or injuries.

Standard Policy

Safety Policy

Our Company takes employee safety very seriously. In order to provide a safe workplace for everyone, every employee must follow our safety rules:

- Horseplay, roughhousing and other physical acts that may endanger employees or cause accidents are prohibited.
- Employees must follow their supervisors' safety instructions.
- Employees in certain positions may be required to wear protective equipment, such as hair nets, hard hats, safety glasses, work boots, ear plugs or masks. Your supervisor will let you know if your position requires protective gear.
- Employees in certain positions may be prohibited from wearing dangling jewelry or apparel, or may be required to pull back or cover their hair, for safety purposes. Your supervisor will tell you if you fall into one of these categories.
- All equipment and machinery must be used properly. This means all guards, restraints and other safety devices must be used at all times. Do not use equipment for other than its intended purpose.
- All employees must immediately report any workplace condition that they believe to be unsafe to their supervisor. The Company will look into the matter promptly.
- All employees must immediately report any workplace accident or injury to _____.

Optional Modification to Give Specific Safety Instructions

Every type of industry has its own unique safety hazards. Our basic standard policy can be modified to include safety rules particular to yours. For example, you might want to include rules on the proper use of certain types of equipment and machinery, proper techniques for physical labor, such as lifting and carrying heavy objects, or ergonomic rules for those who operate computers or cash registers or perform other types of repetitive motions.

For more information on federal and state health and safety laws, go to the website of the Occupational Safety and Health Administration (OSHA), at www.osha.gov. This federal agency administers workplace health and safety rules. At its website, you can find a number of helpful publications describing your obligations as an employer. You will also find a list of parallel state agencies.

 For policies on workplace behavior, see Chapter 12.

13:2   Workplace Security

A workplace security policy explains what measures you expect your employees to take to keep your premises and property safe from intruders. Clearly, what you include in your policy will depend on the nature of your workplace: An office building in a bustling metropolis will have different security concerns than a farming operation. However, any security policy should include rules on securing the premises (locking up, closing gates, shutting off machinery or securing tools, for example), rules on after-hours access to the workplace and rules on workplace visitors.

Standard Policy

Workplace Security

It is every employee's responsibility to help keep our workplace secure from unauthorized intruders. Every employee must comply with these security precautions.

When you leave work for the day, please do all of the following:

_____

_____

_____ .

After-hours access to the workplace is limited to those employees who need to work late. If you are going to be working past our usual closing time, please let your supervisor know.

Employees are allowed to have an occasional visitor in the workplace, but workplace visits should be the exception rather than the rule. If you are anticipating a visitor, please let _____ _____ know. When your visitor arrives, you will be notified.

How to Complete This Policy

In the first blank space, list all of the things you expect employees to do before they leave for the day. For example, you might want employees to shut off their computers, turn off equipment, turn off lights, close and lock office windows, store and secure tools, lock and garage company vehicles or lock any area that won't be used any more that day.

In the second blank space, list the position of the person who will greet visitors to your company. This might be the receptionist, security guard or front desk attendant.

Optional Modifications

To Require Escorts or Badges for Visitors

Our sample policy allows employees to have visitors, but asks them to keep visitors to a minimum. Some businesses, particularly large companies and companies that have industrial operations, put more restrictions on visitors in the workplace. Visitors might be required to wear a badge or other identification, or the employee who invited the visitor might be required to accompany the visitor at all times on company premises—including escorting the visitor to and from the entrance. If you wish to adopt either of these policies, simply add one or both of the modifications below to the policy paragraph on visitors.

Modification

Visitors must wear an identification badge at all times when they are in our workplace. Visitors can get a badge at _____. They must return the badge when they leave Company premises.

Modification

Do not leave your visitor unattended in the workplace. If you have a visitor, you must accompany your visitor at all times. This includes escorting your visitor to and from the entrance to our Company.

To Give Instructions to Employees Who Are the Last to Leave the Workplace

In many companies, supervisors, managers or the owner are always the last to leave the workplace. And some workplaces (such as 24-hour convenience stores or factories that operate round-the-clock) never close. However, if your employees are sometimes the last ones at work, you'll have to modify this policy to let them know how to secure the premises. Insert the sample modification, below, after the paragraph on working late, filling in the blank to tell employees what you expect of them. For example, you might direct employees to lock the building or security gates, set an alarm, make sure all windows are closed and locked or turn off all equipment and lights.

Modification

If you are the last to leave the workplace for the evening, you are responsible for doing all of the following:

_____

_____

_____.

    If you have questions about any of these responsibilities, please talk to your supervisor.

13:3   What to Do in an Emergency

Every business should have a written policy letting employees
know what to do in case of emergency. Employees should be
familiar with evacuation routes and procedures, in order to ensure
their safety should disaster strike. Employees should also be told
where to congregate once they have left the workplace. This will
help you—and rescue workers—figure out whether anyone is
missing and may need assistance getting out of the workplace.
In this policy, you can describe evacuation plans, any emergency
equipment (such as first-aid supplies or fire extinguishers) you
keep on site and where employees should go if they are forced to
leave the workplace.

Standard Policy

What to Do in an Emergency

In case of an emergency, such as a fire, earthquake or accident,
your first priority should be your own safety. In the event of an
emergency causing serious injuries, *IMMEDIATELY DIAL 9-1-1* to
alert police and rescue workers of the situation.

If you hear a fire alarm or in case of an emergency that requires
evacuation, please proceed quickly and calmly to the fire exits. The
Company will hold periodic fire drills to familiarize everyone with
the routes they should take. Remember that every second may
count—don't return to the workplace to retrieve personal belongings or work-related items. Once you have exited the building,
head towards the _____.

(For our Company's policy on workplace violence, see Section
___ of this Handbook)

Reality Check: Fire Drills Are Not Just for Kids

All of us probably remember the fire drills of grade school, but when was the last time you held a fire drill in your workplace? Emergency drills are vitally important for every business. They help your workers learn emergency evacuation procedures, so they'll know what to do if a real disaster strikes. Of course these drills disrupt business and may take 15 or 20 minutes to conduct. But if your advance planning later saves lives or prevents serious injuries, that inconvenience will seem a very small price to pay.

Optional Modification to Direct Workers to Emergency Supplies

Many businesses keep a store of emergency supplies in the workplace. If your company takes this very sensible precaution, you should modify your policy to let employees know where the supplies are kept. You can add the modification below, filling in the blanks to indicate the location of the supplies. If you keep additional types of supplies that are not listed below, add them on at the end.

Modification

[Company name] keeps emergency supplies on hand. First aid kits are located _____.
Fire extinguishers can be found _____.
Earthquake preparedness kits are kept _____.
We also keep a supply of flashlights in _____.

13:4   Smoking

Few workplace issues are so divisive as smoking. Smokers want the freedom to enjoy a cigarette without having to stand outside in the cold; nonsmokers want to work comfortably, without smoke irritating their eyes and throats. And it's your unfortunate job to decide how to balance these interests.

There are a few legal guidelines that can help you. Most states *allow* employers to ban smoking in the workplace—so if you'd prefer that your employees not light up, you're probably within your rights to tell them so. However, if you want to allow smoking, or allow it in certain areas, you will have to check your state and local laws to find out whether you can. These laws are summarized in the "State Laws on Smoking in the Workplace" chart, at the end of this chapter. Some states require you to ban smoking, at least in certain kinds of businesses. For example, California bans smoking in the workplace, public or private. And other states prohibit smoking in certain kinds of business establishments, such as hospitals or restaurants.

Because of these variations, we offer you two sample policies to choose from. Policy A bans smoking altogether, Policy B allows smoking in designated areas.

Standard Policy A

Smoking Is Prohibited

For the health, comfort and safety of our employees, smoking is not allowed on Company property.

Standard Policy B

Smoking Policy

To accommodate employees who smoke as well as those who do not, the Company has created smoking and nonsmoking areas. Smoking is allowed only in _____.
The Company has posted signs designating smoking and non-smoking areas. Employees who smoke are required to observe these signs and to smoke in designated areas only.

Reality Check: Special Rules for Smoking Areas

States that allow smoking on the job often impose strict rules to prevent smoke from spreading to the rest of the workplace. Some require that any workplace smoking area have a separate ventilation system, so the smoky air does not recirculate to the rest of the office. Others require physical barriers—such as walls or partitions—to separate smoking and nonsmoking areas.

Even if your state does not impose these requirements, however, it's a good idea to keep smoking areas separate from the rest of the workplace. Nonsmokers who are physically troubled by smoke can complain to the Occupational Safety and Health Administration (OSHA) and may even have a legal claim under the Americans with Disabilities Act (ADA). There's no need to invite this kind of trouble—if you decide to allow smoking, keep the air clean for nonsmokers by designating a smoking area that won't allow smoke to enter the rest of the workplace.

Who Needs This Policy

This is one of the few policies that is mandatory, at least in some states. If you plan to allow smoking anywhere in the workplace, certain states—including Delaware, Florida and New York—require employers to adopt a written smoking policy. In states that require a smoking policy, the rules vary as to what the policy must include. Check the "State Laws on Smoking in the Workplace" chart at the end of this chapter to see what your state requires.

Optional Modifications

To Regulate When Employees May Smoke

"Smoking breaks" are a major source of workplace tension. Nonsmokers wonder why their smoking coworkers feel they have a right to take ten minutes off every hour or so to light up—and employers notice the lost work time (and resulting lost productivity). To combat this problem, some employers add language to their smoking policies reminding employees that they may smoke during scheduled or authorized breaks only. The modification below can be added to Policy A—you should add it to Policy B only if employees are required to smoke somewhere other than their workspaces (otherwise, they can smoke while working and need not take a break).

Modification

You may smoke during meal or rest breaks only. Employees may not take "smoking breaks" in addition to the regular breaks provided to every employee under our policies.

(For our Company's policy on work and rest breaks, see Section ___ of this Handbook.)

To Help Employees Kick the Habit

It's no secret that employees who smoke tend to cost employers more money, on average, than nonsmokers. Smokers tend to have higher rates of absenteeism and higher healthcare costs. At the same time, we all know that smoking is a tough habit to give up—especially for those who try to quit on their own, without any support or encouragement.

Some employers offer to help their employees quit smoking by referring employees to, or paying for, smoking cessation programs. If you offer your employees health insurance and your provider offers such a program, you can refer employees to that program by adding Modification A, below, to the end of your policy. If not, you may want to offer financial and other support to employees who want to enroll in such a program—you can do so by adding Modification B, below, to the end of your policy.

Modification A

Our Company encourages those who wish to quit smoking. Our health insurance provider offers a program to help employees stop smoking. If you are interested in this program, ask [*the human resources department or benefits administrator*] for more details. Or you can contact our insurance carrier directly.

(For information on health insurance, see Section ___ of this Handbook).

Modification B

> Our Company encourages those who wish to quit smoking. If you are interested in participating in getting help to stop smoking, the [*human resources department, benefits administrator*] can direct you to local smoking cessation programs. If you complete one of the programs on the Company's approved list, we will pay the cost of your participation.

To Prohibit Discrimination Against Smokers

Many states prohibit employment discrimination against smokers. Some of these laws apply only to smoking, while others protect any lawful activity in which the employee chooses to engage outside of work hours. Either way, in these states, you may not make employment decisions based on the fact that an employee or applicant smokes. Check the "State Laws on Smoking in the Workplace" chart at the end of this chapter to see whether you have to comply with this type of law.

If your state prohibits this kind of discrimination, you might want to add the following modification to your smoking policy letting employees know that you will comply with the law.

Modification

> We recognize that smoking tobacco products is legal and that employees have the right to smoke outside of work hours. [*Company name*] will not discriminate against any applicant or employee based on that person's choice to smoke.

13:5   Violence

Few employment topics are so frightening as violence in the workplace. Media reports are full of stories about former employees, disgruntled clients or customers or abusive spouses storming into a business, injuring or killing all who cross their paths. Of course, no policy can eliminate the risk that your company might face a violent incident. But a commonsense policy to prohibit violence—and to let employees know what to do if they fear or experience a violent incident—can go a long way towards making your workplace safer.

Standard Policy

Violence Is Prohibited

We will not tolerate violence in the workplace. Violence includes physical altercations, coercion, pushing or shoving, horseplay, intimidation, stalking and threats of violence. Any comments about violence will be taken seriously—and may result in your termination. Please do not joke or make offhand remarks about violence.

No Weapons

No weapons are allowed in our workplace. Weapons include firearms, knives, brass knuckles, martial arts equipment, clubs or bats and explosives. If your work requires you to use an item that might qualify as a weapon, you must receive authorization from your supervisor to bring that item to work or use it in the workplace. Any employee found with an unauthorized weapon in the workplace will be subject to discipline, up to and including termination.

What to Do in Case of Violence

If you observe an incident or threat of violence that is immediate and serious, *IMMEDIATELY DIAL 9-1-1* and report it to the police. If the incident or threat does not appear to require immediate police intervention, please contact _____
and report it as soon as possible, using the Company's complaint procedure. All complaints will be investigated and appropriate action will be taken. You will not face retaliation for making a complaint.

Who Needs This Policy

The benefits of an anti-violence policy are several. First, it lets employees know that you will take all violent incidents seriously— and defines violence in a way that tells employees that jokes about violence, roughhousing or threats will all be considered violent acts. This puts employees on notice that violence is no laughing matter. It should also minimize instances in which an employee alleged to have acted violently comes up with excuses like "I didn't mean it" or "I was only joking."

Second, it lays down the law on weapons in the workplace. And third, it tells employees what to do if a violent incident occurs—to take steps to protect themselves and their co-workers immediately by calling emergency personnel if necessary, and to report less serious incidents to company management. If you aren't made aware of escalating aggressions in the workplace, you won't be able to intervene while the problem is still manageable. Encouraging employees to come forward will go a long way towards helping you prevent more serious incidents.

Reality Check: Pay Attention to the Warning Signs

No one can predict with absolute certainty who will engage in workplace violence and who won't. But experts agree that an employee who commits a violent act often exhibits certain signs of trouble. Some clues that intervention might be necessary include:

- an unexplained rise in absences
- outbursts of anger at coworkers and customers
- verbal abuse or threats towards coworkers
- strained workplace relationships
- overreaction or resistance to even minor changes in work routines or procedures
- lack of attention to personal appearance and hygiene
- comments about firearms or weapons
- signs of paranoia ("everyone's out to get me") or withdrawal, and
- substance abuse problems.

Take this list with a grain of salt, of course. Not every disheveled employee is planning to dispense vigilante justice at the next staff meeting. But training your supervisors and managers to recognize these warning signs—and to talk to the employees who exhibit them, to find out what's going on—can help you nip potential problems in the bud.

Optional Modifications

To Allow Weapons for Certain Employees

Some companies may require their employees to carry weapons. For example, a company that provides security services may require employees to carry a gun or nightstick. Our sample policy contemplates that an employee or two may occasionally need to use a weapon at work. However, if a significant number of your employees will need to carry weapons regularly, you may wish to modify this policy to specify who is authorized to do so and under what circumstances.

Replace the "No Weapons" paragraph with the following modification. In the blank space, list the positions for which workers are required to carry weapons—don't list the names of individual workers, as this will require you to update the policy every time you have a personnel change.

Modification

Weapons in the Workplace

Weapons are generally not allowed in our workplace. Weapons include firearms, knives, brass knuckles, martial arts equipment, clubs or bats and explosives.

However, some of our employees are required to carry weapons in order to perform their jobs. Weapons may be required in the following positions: _____
_____. If you hold one of these positions, ask your supervisor whether you will be required to carry a weapon. If your job requires you to carry a weapon, you must receive authorization from your supervisor to do so. You may be required to complete training courses, pass a safety test and/or get a license in order to be authorized to carry a weapon.

For Companies With Internal Security Staff

Some companies employ their own security personnel or do business in a building that has its own security force. If you run such a company, you may want to ask your employees to contact these security people—who are already on site and are familiar with the layout of the workplace—immediately, rather than dialing 9-1-1. You can use the modification below to accomplish this. Simply use this modification in place of the first sentence under "What to Do in Case of Violence" in the sample policy, above. In the blank, insert the telephone number of the internal security personnel.

Modification

> If you observe an incident or threat of violence that is immediate and serious, call security personnel at _____. If you are unable to reach someone at this number, *IMMEDIATELY DIAL 9-1-1* and report the incident to the police.

Reality Check: Stress Can Lead to Violence

Problems outside the workplace—such as money troubles, relationship problems and drug or alcohol addictions—can lead to violence on the job. Many violent workplace incidents stem from domestic violence, for example. You can take great strides towards minimizing your chances of a violent incident—and improving the lives of your employees—by adopting an Employee Assistance Program (EAP).

EAPs can help employees with a variety of problems inside and outside the workplace. Common offerings include therapy for individuals or couples, help kicking a drug, alcohol or smoking habit, advice on exercise and nutrition, anger management classes, assistance with estate planning and debt management counseling. Talk to your insurance carrier for more information about EAPs—many insurers offer EAP services as part of an overall mental health benefit.

State Laws on Smoking in the Workplace

Note: The states of Alabama, Arizona, Arkansas, Georgia, Kansas, Michigan, New Mexico, Ohio and Texas are not included in this chart because they do not have laws governing smoking in private workplaces. Check with your state department of labor (see Appendix C for contact list) or with your state or local health department if you need more information.

Alaska

Alaska Stat. §§ 18.35.300 & following

Workplaces where laws apply: Any private place of business that posts signs regulating smoking; restaurants serving more than 50.

Where smoking prohibited: Throughout workplace except in designated smoking area. Employer may designate entire site nonsmoking.

Where smoking permitted: Designated smoking area.

Smoking area requirements: Ventilated or separated to protect nonsmokers from active by-products of smoke.

Accommodations for nonsmokers: Reasonable accommodations to protect the health of nonsmokers.

California

Cal. Lab. Code § 6404.5

Workplaces where laws apply: Workplaces with more than 5 employees.

Exceptions: Designated lobby areas; meeting and banquet rooms when food is not being served; warehouses over 100,000 sq. ft. with fewer than 20 employees; truck cabs if no nonsmoking employees are present.

Where smoking prohibited: Employer may not knowingly or intentionally permit smoking in any enclosed workplace; must take reasonable steps to prevent non-employees from smoking. May designate entire site nonsmoking.

Where smoking permitted: Breakrooms designated for smokers.

Smoking area requirements: Breakroom must be in a non-work area. No employee may be required to enter room as part of job (does not apply to custodial work when room is unoccupied). Air must be exhausted directly to the outside with a fan and may not recirculate to other areas of the building.

Accommodations for nonsmokers: If there is a breakroom for smokers, must be enough breakrooms for all nonsmokers.

Accommodations for smokers: None required. However, employers with 5 or fewer employees may permit smoking if:

- all the employees agree;
- no minors are allowed in the smoking area; and
- no employee is required to enter smoking area.

Colorado

Colo. Rev. Stat. §§ 25-14-103; 24-34-402.5

Workplaces where laws apply: Any enclosed indoor workplace.

Exceptions: Offices occupied exclusively by smokers even if visited by nonsmokers. Restaurants.

Accommodations for nonsmokers: Employers encouraged to create physically separate nonsmoking work areas; must make effort to provide separate nonsmoking areas in employee lounges and cafeterias.

Protection from discrimination: Employee may not be fired for lawful conduct offsite during nonwork hours.

Connecticut

Conn. Gen. Stat. Ann. §§ 31-40q, 31-40s

Workplaces where laws apply: Enclosed facilities with 20 or more employees.

Where smoking prohibited: Employer may prohibit smoking throughout the workplace.

Smoking area requirements: Existing ventilation and barriers to minimize effects of smoke.

Accommodations for nonsmokers: Employer must provide one or more work areas for all nonsmoking employees if smoking is permitted anywhere in the building.

Protection from discrimination: Employee may not be discriminated against in hiring, wages, benefits or terms of employment because of smoking outside of work.

Delaware

Del. Code Ann. tit. 16, §§ 2902 to 2908

Workplaces where laws apply: Indoor areas.

Exceptions: Restaurants serving 50 or fewer.

Where smoking prohibited: Any place designated a smoke-free work area.

Smoking area requirements: Walls or other physical barriers that separate area.

Accommodations for nonsmokers: Employer must provide nonsmoking work area for every employee who requests one; must provide sufficient nonsmoking areas in lounges, lunchrooms and cafeterias.

Accommodations for smokers: Employer may provide a smoking work area.

State Laws on Smoking in the Workplace (continued)

Protection from discrimination: Employer may not discriminate or retaliate against employee who files a complaint or testifies in a proceeding about workplace smoking laws.

Employer penalties and liabilities: $1,000 to $5,000 penalty for each discrimination violation.

Employer smoking policy: Must adopt and implement a written policy that outlines accommodations for nonsmokers and smokers.

District of Columbia

D.C. Code Ann. §§ 7-1701 & following; 7-1703.03

Workplaces where laws apply: Any private employer.

Where smoking prohibited: Throughout the workplace except for designated smoking area.

Where smoking permitted: Designated smoking area.

Smoking area requirements: Physical barrier or separate room.

Accommodations for smokers: Employer required to provide smoking area.

Protection from discrimination: Employee may not be fired or discriminated against in hiring, wages, benefits or terms of employment because of being a smoker.

Employer smoking policy: Must have written policy that designates a smoking area; must notify each employee orally and post policy within 3 weeks after adopting it.

Florida

Fla. Stat. Ann. §§ 386.203 to 386.207

Workplaces where laws apply: All enclosed indoor workplaces.

Exceptions: Private office space where public does not have access.

Where smoking prohibited: At least 50% of total square footage of any common enclosed workplace must be nonsmoking.

Where smoking permitted: Designated smoking area; may be an entire work area if all workers routinely assigned there agree.

Smoking area requirements: Existing systems and barriers to minimize smoke. No physical or structural changes necessary.

Accommodations for nonsmokers: Based on proportion of nonsmokers and smokers in workplace.

Accommodations for smokers: Based on proportion of smokers and nonsmokers in workplace.

Employer smoking policy: Must implement and post policy designating smoking and nonsmoking areas.

Hawaii

Haw. Rev. Stat. §§ 328K-11 and following

Workplaces where laws apply: Any private business that receives state grants or subsidies.

Where smoking prohibited: Employer decides based on preferences of nonsmokers and smokers. If decision does not satisfy all employees, workers will vote to prohibit or permit smoking in their work area.

Where smoking permitted: Employer decides based on preferences of smokers and nonsmokers. If decision does not satisfy all employees, workers will vote to permit or prohibit smoking in their work area.

Smoking area requirements: Existing ventilation and partitions. No expenditures or structural changes required.

Accommodations for nonsmokers: If nonsmoker complains about smoke, employer must attempt reasonable accommodation between nonsmokers' and smokers' needs. If nonsmokers are not satisfied, a simple majority may appeal to the director of health for a determination.

Accommodations for smokers: Employer must attempt reasonable accommodation between smokers' and nonsmokers' needs.

Employer smoking policy: Implement and maintain written policy that outlines accommodations for smokers and nonsmokers, procedures for voting and appeal. If employees vote to decide smoking and nonsmoking areas, policy must be announced and posted within 2 weeks after vote.

Idaho

Idaho Code §39-5501

Workplaces where laws apply: Enclosed indoor area used by the general public, including restaurants that seat 30 or more, retail stores and grocery stores.

Exceptions: Bowling alleys, bars.

Where smoking prohibited: Everywhere except designated smoking area.

Where smoking permitted: Employer or proprietor designates.

Accommodations for nonsmokers: "Good faith effort" to minimize effect of smoke on nonsmoking areas.

State Laws on Smoking in the Workplace (continued)

Illinois

410 Ill. Comp. Stat. §§ 80/3 & following; 820 Ill. Comp. Stat. §§ 55/5

Workplaces where laws apply: Any enclosed indoor workplace.

Exceptions: Offices occupied exclusively by smokers even if visited by nonsmokers. Factories, warehouses and other workplaces not visited by the public.

Where smoking prohibited: Entire workplace except for designated smoking area.

Where smoking permitted: Designated smoking area only.

Smoking area requirements: Existing ventilation systems and physical barriers to minimize smoke in nonsmoking areas,

Protection from discrimination: Employee may not be discriminated against for asserting rights under the clean indoor air laws. May not be refused a job, fired or discriminated against in terms of compensation or benefits because of using lawful products outside of work. Different insurance rates or coverage for smokers are not discriminatory if:

- difference is based on cost to employer; and
- employees are given a notice of carriers' rates.

Indiana

Ind. Code Ann. §§ 22-5-4-1 & following

Protection from discrimination: Employer may not: require prospective employee to refrain from using tobacco products outside of work in order to be hired; discriminate against employee who uses them in terms of wages, benefits or conditions of employment.

Iowa

Iowa Code § 142B.1

Workplaces where laws apply: Enclosed indoor area at least 250 sq. ft.; restaurants serving more than 50 people.

Exceptions: Offices occupied exclusively by smokers even if visited by nonsmokers. Factories, warehouses and other workplaces not visited by the public.

Where smoking prohibited: Entire workplace except for designated smoking area.

Where smoking permitted: Designated smoking area only (may not be entire workplace).

Smoking area requirements: Existing physical barriers and ventilation systems to minimize toxic effect of smoke.

Accommodations for nonsmokers: Employee cafeteria in warehouse or factory must have nonsmoking area.

Kentucky

Ky. Rev. Stat. Ann. § 344.040 (3)

Protection from discrimination: As long as employee complies with workplace smoking policy, employer may not:

- discharge employee or discriminate in terms of wages, benefits or conditions of employment because of being a smoker or nonsmoker
- require employee to refrain from using tobacco products outside of work as a condition of employment.

Louisiana

La. Rev. Stat. Ann. §§ 40:1300.21 and following; 23:966

Workplaces where laws apply: Office workplaces of employers with more than 25 employees.

Exceptions: Offices occupied exclusively by smokers even if visited by nonsmokers.

Where smoking prohibited: Employer designates.

Where smoking permitted: Employer designates.

Smoking area requirements: Existing ventilation systems and partitions; no expenditures or structural changes required.

Accommodations for nonsmokers: Law protects the right of nonsmoking workers to breathe smoke-free air in the workplace. If nonsmoker complains about smoke, employer must attempt reasonable accommodation between nonsmokers' and smokers' needs.

Accommodations for smokers: Law does not deny workers the right to smoke. Employer must attempt reasonable accommodation between smokers' and nonsmokers' needs.

Protection from discrimination: Employer may not:

- require prospective employee to refrain from using tobacco products outside of work as a condition of employment;
- discriminate against smokers or nonsmokers regarding termination, layoffs, wages, benefits or other terms of employment.

Employer smoking policy: Implement and maintain written policy that outlines smoking area requirements and procedures for accommodation and complaint. Must be announced and posted within 3 months of being adopted.

Maine

Me. Rev. Stat. Ann. tit. 22, §§ 1580-A & following; tit. 26, § 597

Workplaces where laws apply: Structurally enclosed business facilities.

State Laws on Smoking in the Workplace (continued)

Exceptions: Workplaces where employer and all employees have agreed upon a smoking policy.

Where smoking prohibited: Employer may prohibit throughout entire workplace.

Where smoking permitted: Designated smoking area.

Protection from discrimination: Employer may not discriminate or retaliate against employee for assisting with enforcement of workplace smoking laws. As long as employee follows workplace smoking policy employer may not:

- discriminate in wages, benefits or terms of employment because of use of tobacco products outside of work;
- require employee to refrain from tobacco use as a condition of employment.

Employer penalties and liabilities: Failure to post or supervise implementation of policy, $100 fine.

Employer smoking policy: Written policy concerning smoking and nonsmoking rules. Bureau of Health will assist employees and employers with creating policy.

Maryland

Md. Regs. Code 09.12.23.01 & following

Workplaces where laws apply: Indoor work areas. Employee lounges, restrooms and cafeterias; work vehicle when occupied by more than one employee; conference or meeting room.

Where smoking prohibited: Entire workplace except for designated smoking area.

Where smoking permitted: Designated smoking area. Employer not required to provide one.

Smoking area requirements: May not be in location where any employee required to work (maintenance and cleaning to take place when no one is smoking in area). Must have:

- solid walls and closable door;
- ventilation system that exhausts air outdoors;
- no air recirculating to nonsmoking areas; and
- negative air pressure to prevent smoke migration.

Massachusetts

Mass. Gen. Laws ch. 270 , § 22

Workplaces where laws apply: Colleges, universities, restaurants seating 75 or more, private employers using office space in public buildings.

Exceptions: Completely enclosed private office used by one person.

Where smoking prohibited: Entire workplace except for designated smoking area.

Where smoking permitted: Designated smoking area.

Accommodations for nonsmokers: Employer may designate smoking area only if there is a nonsmoking area large enough for nonsmokers.

Minnesota

Minn. Stat. Ann. §§ 144.411; 181.938

Workplaces where laws apply: Enclosed indoor workplace.

Exceptions: Offices occupied exclusively by smokers even if visited by nonsmokers. Factories, warehouses and other workplaces not visited by the public; however commissioner of health will restrict smoking if smoke pollution affects nonsmokers.

Where smoking prohibited: Entire workplace except for designated smoking area.

Where smoking permitted: Designated smoking area (may not be entire workplace).

Smoking area requirements: Existing barriers and ventilation systems to minimize toxic effects of smoke.

Protection from discrimination: Employer may not refuse to hire, discipline or discharge an employee for using lawful products offsite during nonwork hours; employer may restrict nonwork use if it is a genuine job requirement. It is not discrimination to have an insurance plan with different premiums and coverage for smokers if difference reflects actual cost to employer.

Mississippi

Miss. Code Ann. § 71-7-33

Protection from discrimination: Employer may not make it a condition of employment for prospective or current employee to abstain from smoking during nonwork hours, as long as employee complies with laws or policies that regulate workplace smoking.

Missouri

Mo. Rev. Stat. §§ 191.765 and following; 90.145

Workplaces where laws apply: Enclosed indoor workplaces.

Where smoking prohibited: Entire workplace except for designated smoking area.

Where smoking permitted: Designated smoking area (may not be more than 30% of workplace).

State Laws on Smoking in the Workplace (continued)

Smoking area requirements: Existing physical barriers and ventilation systems that isolate area.

Protection from discrimination: Employer may not refuse to hire, discharge or in any way discriminate against employee for lawful use of tobacco offsite during nonwork hours, unless use interferes with employee's or co-workers' performance or employer's business operations.

Montana

Mont. Code Ann. §§ 50-40-104; 39-2-313

Workplaces where laws apply: Enclosed rooms where more than one person works.

Where smoking prohibited: Employer designates; may designate entire workplace as a nonsmoking area.

Where smoking permitted: Employer designates; may designate entire workplace as a smoking area.

Protection from discrimination: Employer may not discharge, refuse to hire or discriminate against employee in regard to compensation, promotion, benefits or terms of employment because of lawful tobacco use offsite during nonwork hours. Use that affects job performance, other workers' safety or conflicts with a genuine job requirement is not protected. It is not discrimination to have different insurance rates or coverage for smokers if:
- difference is based on cost to employer; and
- employees are given a written statement of carriers' rates.

Nebraska

Neb. Rev. Stat. §§ 71-5702 to 71-5709

Workplaces where laws apply: Any enclosed indoor workplace.

Exceptions: Offices occupied exclusively by smokers even if visited by nonsmokers. Factories, warehouses and other workplaces not visited by the public; however health department will restrict smoking if smoke pollution affects nonsmokers.

Where smoking prohibited: Entire workplace except in designated smoking area.

Where smoking permitted: Designated smoking area (may not be entire workplace).

Smoking area requirements: Existing barriers and ventilation systems to minimize toxic effects of smoke.

Nevada

Nev. Rev. Stat. Ann. § 613.333

Protection from discrimination: Employer may not: fail or refuse to hire, discharge or discriminate in terms of compensation, benefits or conditions of employment, because of employee's lawful use of any product offsite during nonwork hours, unless use adversely affects job performance or the safety of other employees.

Employer penalties and liabilities: Discrimination. Employee may sue for:
- lost wages and benefits;
- reinstatement without loss of position, seniority or benefits;
- an offer of employment; and
- damages equal to lost wages and benefits.

New Hampshire

N.H. Rev. Stat. Ann. §§ 155:64 to 155.77; 275:37-a

Workplaces where laws apply: Enclosed workplaces where 4 or more people work.

Exceptions: Restaurants that seat fewer than 50.

Where smoking prohibited: Throughout the workplace except for designated smoking area. If smoking area cannot be effectively segregated, smoking will be totally prohibited. Employer may declare entire workplace nonsmoking.

Where smoking permitted: Designated smoking area.

Smoking area requirements: Effectively segregated so that smoke does not cause harm or enter nonsmoking area. It must:
- be located as close as possible to exhaust vents;
- have 200 sq. ft. minimum contiguous workspace;
- have (1) a continuous, physical barrier at least 56 in. high or (2) a buffer zone space at least 4 ft. wide separating area from nonsmoking area.

Accommodations for nonsmokers: Special consideration for employees with medically proven conditions adversely affected by smoke, as documented by an occupational physician.

Protection from discrimination: Employer may not require employee or applicant to refrain from using tobacco products outside of work as a condition of employment, as long as employee complies with workplace smoking policy. Employer may not retaliate or discriminate against any employee who exercises rights under smoking laws; however, laws do not give employee right to refuse to perform normal duties, even if duties require entering a smoking area.

Employer penalties and liabilities: Employment discrimination: misdemeanor with a fine of up to $1,000 and up to one year in prison.

State Laws on Smoking in the Workplace (continued)

Employer smoking policy: Written policy outlining either smoking prohibition or areas where smoking permitted. Policy must be handed out or posted; employees must receive policy orientation. If there is a designated smoking area, must be written training procedures for:
- enforcing smoking policy,
- handling complaints and violations, and
- accommodating employees with medical conditions.

New Jersey

N.J. Stat. Ann. §§ 26:3D-23 and following; 34:6B-1

Workplaces where laws apply: Enclosed workspaces with 50 or more employees.

Where smoking prohibited: Entire workplace except for designated smoking area. Employer may designate entire workplace nonsmoking.

Where smoking permitted: Designated smoking area.

Protection from discrimination: Employer may not discharge or discriminate in terms of hiring, compensation, benefits or conditions of employment because employee does or does not smoke, unless smoking or not smoking relates to work and job responsibilities.

Employer smoking policy: Written policy and procedures to protect employees from harmful effects of tobacco smoke: must include designated nonsmoking areas and may include smoking areas. Employees must be given copy upon request.

New York

N.Y. Pub. Health Law §§ 1399-n & following; N.Y. Lab. Law § 201-d(2b),(6)

Workplaces where laws apply: Indoor workspaces not usually open to the public.

Where smoking prohibited: Throughout the workplace except in designated smoking area; copy machine and common equipment areas; company vehicles with more than one occupant and conference and meeting rooms, unless all occupants agree.

Where smoking permitted: Designated smoking area: either a separate room not open to public or a work area where all employees agree to allow smoking.

Smoking area requirements: Must be physically separated from smoke-free area by walls or partitions. Expenditures and structural changes not required, but employer must comply with employee request for a smoke-free work area.

Accommodations for nonsmokers: Employer must designate entire work area smoke-free if there is no other way to accommodate nonsmoking employee's request. Must have sufficient contiguous nonsmoking areas in cafeterias, lunchrooms and lounges; employer may not decide that there is no employee demand for nonsmoking areas.

Protection from discrimination: Employee may not be discharged, refused employment or discriminated against in terms of compensation or benefits because of lawful use of products offsite during nonwork hours when not using employer's equipment or property. It is not discrimination to offer insurance with different rates or coverage for smokers if:
- difference is based on cost to employer; and
- employees are given a written statement of carriers' rates.

Employer penalties and liabilities: Discrimination: fine of $300 for first violation, $500 for each subsequent violation. Employee may sue for relief and damages.

Employer smoking policy: Written policy that:
- provides smoke-free area;
- explains where smoking prohibited and
- explains under what conditions smoking allowed;
- is prominently posted; and
- a written copy given to employee upon request.

North Carolina

N.C. Gen. Stat. § 95-28.2

Workplaces where laws apply: Employers with 3 or more employees (discrimination laws).

Protection from discrimination: Employer may not discharge, refuse to hire or discriminate in regard to compensation, benefits or terms of employment because of employee's use of lawful products offsite during nonwork hours. Use that affects employee's job performance, other workers' safety or conflicts with a genuine job requirement is not protected. It is not discrimination to offer insurance with different rates or coverage for smokers if:
- difference is based on cost to employer;
- employees are given written notice of carriers' rates; and
- employer makes equal contribution for all employees.

Employer penalties and liabilities: Discrimination. Employee may sue for: lost wages and benefits; reinstatement; offer of employment. Employer liable for costs and attorney fees.

North Dakota

N.D. Cent. Code § 14-02.4-03

Protection from discrimination: Employer may not refuse to hire, discharge or discriminate with regard to training,

State Laws on Smoking in the Workplace (continued)

apprenticeship, tenure, promotion, compensation, benefits or conditions of employment because of employee's lawful activity offsite during nonwork hours, unless it is in direct conflict with employer's essential business-related interests.

Oklahoma

Okla. Stat. Ann. tit. 40, §§ 500 to 503

Protection from discrimination: Employer may not:
- discharge or disadvantage employee in terms of compensation, benefits or conditions of employment because of being a nonsmoker or smoking during nonwork hours; or
- require that employee abstain from using tobacco products during nonwork hours as a condition of employment.

Employer may restrict nonwork smoking if it relates to a genuine occupational requirement.

Employer penalties and liabilities: Employee may sue for lost wages and benefits. Employer may be liable for costs and attorney fees.

Oregon

Or. Rev. Stat. §§ 433.835 to 433.875; 659A.315

Workplaces where laws apply: All enclosed areas used by employees.

Where smoking prohibited: Entire workplace unless there are employee lounges designated for smoking.

Where smoking permitted: Employee lounges designated for smoking.

Smoking area requirements: Lounge:
- must be inaccessible to minors;
- must be in a nonwork area;
- air must be exhausted directly to the outside with a fan;
- air may not recirculate to other areas of building. No employee may be required to enter lounge as part of job (does not apply to custodial work when lounge is unoccupied).

Accommodations for nonsmokers: If there is a lounge for smokers, must be enough lounges for nonsmokers.

Protection from discrimination: Employer may not require that employee refrain from lawful use of tobacco products during nonwork hours as a condition of employment, unless there is a genuine occupational requirement.

Employer penalties and liabilities: Discrimination. Employee may sue for employment or reinstatement. May be awarded damages of up to $200.

Pennsylvania

35 Pa. Cons. Stat. Ann. § 1230.1

Workplaces where laws apply: Enclosed indoor workplaces.

Exceptions: Factories, warehouses and other workplaces not visited by the public.

Where smoking prohibited: Employer designates.

Where smoking permitted: Employer designates.

Employer smoking policy: Must have policy that regulates smoking. Must post and provide copy to any employee upon request.

Rhode Island

R.I. Gen. Laws §§ 23-20.7-1 and following; 23-20.7.1-1

Workplaces where laws apply: Enclosed areas used primarily as business, professional and clerical offices. Factories and manufacturing plants.

Exceptions: Public lobbies. Offices occupied exclusively by smokers even if visited by nonsmokers.

Where smoking prohibited: Employer decides; may prohibit smoking throughout workplace.

Where smoking permitted: Employer decides.

Smoking area requirements: Use existing ventilation and partitions to protect nonsmokers.

Accommodations for nonsmokers: If smoking permitted, employer must make reasonable accommodations for nonsmokers, particularly those unduly sensitive to tobacco smoke because of a physical condition. If employee objects to passive smoke, employer must either make physical accommodation or completely prohibit smoking in the area.

Accommodations for smokers: As far as possible employer policy must accommodate needs of smokers and nonsmokers.

Protection from discrimination: Employer may not fire or discriminate against employee who exercises rights under workplace smoking laws. May not: require that employee refrain from smoking outside work as a condition of employment; discriminate against employee who does smoke outside work in terms of compensation, conditions or other benefits.

Employer penalties and liabilities: Discrimination against smoker. Employer liable for treble damages.

State Laws on Smoking in the Workplace (continued)

Employer smoking policy: Must adopt written policy designed to:
- protect nonsmokers' health and air quality;
- ensure a comfortable environment for all employees;
- allow nonsmokers to object to smoke hazards or discomfort.

South Carolina

S.C. Code Ann. § 41-1-85

Protection from discrimination: Employer may not take personnel actions, including hiring, discharge, demotion or promotion, based on use of tobacco outside the workplace.

South Dakota

S.D. Codified Laws Ann. §§ 22-36-2 and following; 60-4-14

Workplaces where laws apply: Any enclosed indoor work area; employee cafeterias, lounges and restrooms; conference and classrooms; hallways.

Where smoking prohibited: It is a petty offense to smoke in the workplace.

Protection from discrimination: Employer may not discharge employee because of using tobacco products offsite during nonwork hours, unless not smoking is a genuine occupational requirement. It is not discrimination to have insurance policies with different rates or coverage for smokers.

Employer penalties and liabilities: Discrimination. Employee may sue for lost wages and benefits.

Tennessee

Tenn. Code Ann. § 50-1-304(e)

Protection from discrimination: Employee may not be fired for use of a lawful product during nonwork hours as long as employee observes workplace policy when at work.

Utah

Utah Code Ann. § 26-38-5

Workplaces where laws apply: Private workplaces.

Where smoking prohibited: Entire workplace except for designated smoking area. Employer may prohibit smoking entirely.

Where smoking permitted: Restricted to designated enclosed smoking area.

Smoking area requirements: Must be enclosed or may be unenclosed, if layout prevents smoke from reaching nonsmokers' work areas and 3/4 of employees agree.

Employer smoking policy: Written policy that either prohibits smoking entirely or restricts to designated areas

(need not be written if there are fewer than 10 full-time employees).

Vermont

Vt. Stat. Ann. tit. 18, §§ 1421 and following

Workplaces where laws apply: Enclosed structures not usually open to the public.

Where smoking prohibited: Throughout workplace except for designated smoking area. Employer may prohibit smoking entirely.

Where smoking permitted: Restricted to designated enclosed smoking area. Up to 30% of employee cafeteria and lounge areas may be designated.

Smoking area requirements: Must be area that nonsmokers are not required to visit on a regular basis. Must be enclosed or may be unenclosed, if layout prevents smoke from irritating nonsmokers and 3/4 of employees agree.

Protection from discrimination: Employer may not discharge, discipline or otherwise discriminate against employee who assists in enforcement of workplace smoking laws.

Employer penalties and liabilities: Discrimination. Employee may sue for reinstatement with back pay.

Employer smoking policy: Written policy that either prohibits smoking entirely or restricts it to designated areas (need be written only if employer has 10 or more employees working more than 15 hours a week).

Virginia

Va. Code Ann. § 15.2-2807

Workplaces where laws apply: No state laws regulate smoking in the workplace. However, if local ordinance permits, employer may:
- regulate smoking, if smoking and nonsmoking areas are designated by written agreement between employer and employees; or
- totally ban smoking, if a majority of the affected employees vote for it.

Washington

Wash. Admin. Code 296-800-240 & following

Workplaces where laws apply: Office environment: indoor or enclosed space used for clerical, administrative or business work. Includes offices in manufacturing, food service, construction and agricultural facilities.

Exceptions: Outdoor structures, gazebos and lean-tos provided for smokers.

State Laws on Smoking in the Workplace (continued)

Where smoking prohibited: Employer must prohibit throughout workplace or restrict to designated enclosed smoking area. Employee cafeterias and lunchrooms, meeting rooms, rest rooms, halls and stairways.

Where smoking permitted: Designated enclosed smoking area.

Smoking area requirements:
- May not be in common areas or places where nonsmokers work or visit;
  - no employee required to enter room when someone is smoking (cleaning and maintenance take place when unoccupied);
  - ventilation at rate of at least 60 cu. ft./min. per smoker;
  - negative air pressure to prevent smoke migration;
  - separate mechanical exhaust system to move air directly outside;
  - no air recirculating into nonsmoking areas;
  - if exhaust system not working room use prohibited until repaired.

Outdoor smoking areas may not be close to doorways, air intakes or other openings that allow airflow into an office.

West Virginia

W.Va. Code § 21-3-19

Protection from discrimination: Employer may not refuse to hire, discharge or penalize an employee with respect to compensation, conditions of employment or other benefits for using tobacco products offsite during nonwork hours. It is not discrimination to have insurance policies with different rates or coverage for smokers if:
- difference is based on cost to employer; and
- employees are given a notice of carriers' rates.

Wisconsin

Wis. Stat. Ann. §§ 101.123; 111.31, 111.35

Workplaces where laws apply: Professional, clerical or administrative services work offices.

Exceptions: Offices occupied exclusively by smokers even if visited by nonsmokers. Manufacturing plants.

Where smoking prohibited: Throughout the workplace except in designated smoking area.

Where smoking permitted: Designated smoking area. Employer may not designate entire building a smoking area.

Smoking area requirements: Existing ventilation systems and physical barriers to minimize smoke in nonsmoking areas; no new construction required.

Accommodations for smokers: Employer must arrange seating to accommodate nonsmokers if they work adjacent to smoking areas.

Protection from discrimination: Employer may not discriminate against employee who uses or does not use lawful products offsite during nonwork hours. Use that impairs employee's ability to perform job or conflicts with a genuine occupational requirement is not protected. It is not discrimination to have insurance policies with different coverage and rates for smokers and nonsmokers if:
- difference is based on cost to employer; and
- each employee is given a written statement of carriers' rates.

Wyoming

Wyo. Stat. § 27-9-105 (a, iv)

Protection from discrimination: Employer may not make use or nonuse of tobacco products outside of work a condition of employment unless nonuse is a genuine occupational qualification. May not discriminate regarding compensation, benefits or terms of employment because of use or nonuse of tobacco products outside of work. It is not discrimination to offer insurance policies with different rates and coverage for smokers and nonsmokers if:
- difference reflects actual cost to employer; and
- employees are given written notice of carriers' rates.

Current as of February 2003

Employee Privacy

Many employers aren't inclined to monitor their employees' every move in the workplace—and this is entirely sensible. There is rarely a need for extensive worker surveillance in most types of businesses. Keeping such close track of your workers can breed resentment and anxiety. And many employers can't afford to spend the time or money it would take to monitor their workers' every phone call or bathroom break, nor do they especially want to.

On the other hand, some employers will, one day, have to take a closer look at what their employees are up to. If you learn or suspect that an employee has brought a weapon to work or stolen company property, for example, you will have to investigate—and this means you may need to conduct a search or keep closer tabs on your employees.

The policies in this chapter protect your ability to search or monitor employees by telling them that their workspaces and workplace communications are not private—and warning them that you reserve the right to search or inspect them at any time. If you conduct searches without policies like these in place, you leave yourself open to lawsuits by angry employees claiming that you violated their right to privacy.

In this chapter, we cover the following policies:

For policies that allow you to monitor employee email and Internet use, see Chapter 15.

Striking a Balance: How Privacy Law Works

In many areas of employment law, the rules are fairly simple: The federal government or state legislature passes laws setting out the rights of employees and employers, then everyone has to do what the law says. Once you enter the realm of privacy law, however, things get a bit more confusing. Although there are a few clear-cut rules, questions of privacy in the workplace are generally resolved on a case-by-case basis. Judges examine the reasons both sides acted as they did: why the employee expected privacy and why the employer searched or monitored. Then they decide whose side of the argument seems more reasonable, in what is aptly called a "balancing test."

Clearly, your goal as an employer is to tip the scales in your favor. Do this by exercising restraint—never search or monitor employees without good reason. At the same time, don't give your employees reason to believe that their communications or work-spaces are private. Adopting the policies in this chapter can help you accomplish this second task, thereby taking some of the weight off the employees' side of the scale. A written policy makes it much harder for employees to later argue that they had a reasonable expectation of privacy.

14:1   Workplace Privacy

Workplace searches are controversial—and carry with them an element of legal risk. You can guess the reason: employees feel a sense of ownership toward their personal workspaces, and they do own their personal possessions. Their assumption will be that no one can snoop into these areas without their permission. Searching calls up images of police and prison, not the enlightened American workplace. For these reasons, many employers don't conduct searches—and don't want to.

However, there may come a time when even the most reluctant employer has to poke around in a desk or locker. For example, if you are told that an employee has brought a gun or pornography collection to work, or has stolen company property, you will need to find out what's going on. And unless the employee volunteers the contraband, you will probably have to search.

Policy A will put your employees on notice that you may search in these worst-case scenarios. You don't have to start conducting random searches or doing a "locker check" every morning if you adopt this policy—you are simply reserving your rights should the unfortunate need to search arise.

Policy B is a more aggressive policy—and it is probably more than most employers need. However, if your company deals in small, valuable items—such as jewelry or electronic components— or handles large amounts of cash, you may want to warn your employees that you reserve your right to find out what they are carrying out of the workplace.

Standard Policy A

Company Property Is Subject to Search

Employees do not have a right to privacy in their workspaces or in any other property belonging to the Company. The Company reserves the right to search Company property at any time, without warning, to ensure compliance with our policies on employee safety, workplace violence, harassment, theft, drug and alcohol use and possession of prohibited items. Company property includes, but is not limited to, lockers, desks, file cabinets, storage areas and workspaces. If you use a lock on any item of Company property (a locker or file cabinet, for example), you must give a copy of the key or combination to _____.

For policies allowing more intrusive searches or surveillance, talk to a lawyer. Some employers want to adopt a search policy that allows them to search an employee's pockets, clothing or body before the employee leaves work. Because we all have a strong expectation of privacy in our own bodies (and the clothing we wear on them), you'll need a carefully drafted search policy before you undertake this type of search (you will also need an *extremely* compelling reason to conduct the search—one that would only arise in a rare and unusual situation). Similarly, some employers want to install security devices—such as hidden cameras or one-way mirrors—to keep an eye on customers and employees. These surveillance devices are highly controversial—and a growing number of states have adopted specific rules that limit an employer's right to use them. If you wish to adopt a surveillance policy or a policy allowing intrusive searches, talk to a lawyer in your state who specializes in employment issues.

Standard Policy B

Company and Personal Property Are Subject to Search

Employees do not have a right to privacy in their workspaces, any other Company property or any personal property they bring to the workplace. The Company reserves the right to search Company premises at any time, without warning, to ensure compliance with our policies on employee safety, workplace violence, harassment, theft, drug and alcohol use and possession of prohibited items. The Company may search Company property, including but not limited to lockers, desks, file cabinets, storage areas and workspaces. If you use a lock on any item of Company property (a locker or file cabinet, for example), you must give a copy of the key or combination to _____. The Company may also search personal property brought onto Company premises, including but not limited to toolboxes, briefcases, backpacks, purses and bags.

14:2 Telephone Monitoring

 For a policy on telephone use generally, see Chapter 9.

If you plan to monitor your employees' telephone calls, you must adopt a policy letting your employees know of your plans. Federal law allows employers to monitor employee phone calls "in the ordinary course of business"—for example, to keep tabs on customer service. However, some states require the consent of at least one party to the conversation for monitoring to be legal. By adopting a policy and requiring your employees to consent, in writing, to monitoring, you will protect yourself from lawsuits claiming invasion of privacy.

Your telephone policy should let employees know whether you plan to monitor calls on work telephones, and under what circumstances.

Standard Policy

Telephone Monitoring

The Company reserves the right to monitor calls made from or received on Company telephones. Therefore, no employee should expect that conversations made on Company telephones will be private.

Optional Modification to Designate Non-Monitored Phones

If you choose to monitor employee phone calls, you may want to designate specified phones—that are not monitored—for employees to use for personal calls. By doing this, you avoid employee claims of invasion of privacy by giving them an opportunity to make personal calls that won't be overheard. Employees who fail to use the designated phones have no cause for complaint if their personal calls from non-designated work phones are monitored.

To use this modification, simply add this language to the end of your telephone policy.

Modification

The Company has designated telephones that employees may use for personal calls. Calls made from these phones will not be monitored. Employees may make personal calls during their breaks; if you must make a personal call during your work hours, you are expected to keep the conversation brief.

Telephones for personal calls are located [*state where the phones are, for example "in the main lobby of the building" or "in the employee lunch room."*]

Reality Check: How to Monitor Telephone Calls

If you plan to monitor employee phone calls, you must make sure not to violate your employees' privacy or the privacy of the person on the other end of the line. Although the law of telephonic monitoring is still in flux, a few clear guidelines have emerged. Following these rules will help you stay on the correct side of the law:

- **Make a monitoring announcement.** We've all called a bank, utility company or other institution and heard that "calls may be monitored for quality assurance." The purpose of this message is simple: to tell the person outside the company that their call may be recorded or overheard. Your company policy will let your own employees know what to expect, but you should also tell the other party to the phone call that the conversation may be monitored. In fact, some states allow eavesdropping only if all parties to the call consent. A monitoring announcement lets everyone on the line know that they may have a silent partner.

- **If the call is personal, get off the line.** Federal law allows monitoring for clear business purposes. However, courts have held that employers no longer have a business purpose to monitor once they realize that they are listening in on a private conversation. You should stop monitoring as soon as you find out that a call is personal.

- **Choose your monitors carefully.** The people who actually listen to employee phone calls must be discreet and professional. Even if you have a solid business reason for monitoring calls, you'll be on shaky legal ground if your monitors blab what they overhear to all who care to listen. Choose monitors who can keep their mouths shut—and use as few monitors as possible.

Computers, Email and the Internet

Computers can be an employer's best friend—or worst nightmare. On the one hand, computers can improve efficiency, allow your employees to communicate with one another across great distances and provide access to the vast ocean of information that is the World Wide Web. On the other hand, computers also give your employees the opportunity to spend their days sending harassing or threatening email, downloading pornographic images or pirated software and shopping online.

So how does a savvy employer get the benefits without the downside? By adopting comprehensive policies that govern how employees may use computer equipment—including email and Internet access. In this chapter, we show you how to create policies that will tell your employees how you expect them to use the company's computer equipment and allow you to read email and monitor Internet traffic, to make sure that your employees follow the rules.

This chapter includes the following policies:

Make sure your employees know that their computer use is not private. Perhaps the most important goal of your computer policies is to reserve your right to monitor employee communications, when necessary. Your policies must tell employees that they should not expect their email or Internet use to be private, as our sample policies do. To learn more about privacy issues, see Chapter 14.

15:1   Email

Any company that makes electronic communications equipment available to employees is asking for trouble if it doesn't have a policy explaining the company's rules for email use and allowing the company to monitor messages sent on that equipment. Even if you have never read employee email and don't plan to set up a regular system of monitoring, you should protect your right to do so. If you are ever faced with a problem involving employee email an employee who sends sexually explicit images, proselytizes other employees to join a religious group, transmits trade secrets to a competitor or gets involved in a "flame war" with a client, for example you will have to read the messages involved to figure out what to do. If you don't have a policy warning employees that you can read their messages at any time, an employee might sue you for violation of privacy.

Your email policy should tell your employees what you consider proper use of your email system, reserve your right to read employee email at any time and establish a schedule for purging the system.

Standard Policy

Email

[*Company name*] provides employees with computer equipment, including an Internet connection and access to an electronic communications system, to enable them to perform their jobs successfully. This policy governs your use of the Company's email system.

Use of the Email System

The email system is intended for official Company business. Although you may use the email system for personal messages, you may do so during non-work hours only. If you send personal messages through the Company's email system, you must exercise discretion as to the number and type of messages you send. Any employee who abuses this privilege may be subject to discipline.

Email Is Not Private

Email messages sent using Company communications equipment are the property of the Company. We reserve the right to access, monitor, read and/or copy email messages at any time, for any reason. You should not expect that any email message you send using Company equipment—including messages you consider to be, or label as, personal—will be private.

Email Rules

All of our policies and rules of conduct apply to employee use of the email system. This means, for example, that you may not use the email system to send harassing or discriminatory messages, including messages with explicit sexual content or pornographic images; to send threatening messages; or to solicit others to purchase items for non-Company purposes.

We expect you to exercise discretion in using electronic communications equipment. When you send email using the Company's communications equipment, you are representing the Company. Make sure that your messages are professional and appropriate, in tone and content. Remember, although email may seem like a private conversation, email can be printed, saved and forwarded to unintended recipients. You should not send any email that you wouldn't want your boss, your mother or our Company's competitors to read.

Deleting Emails

Because of the large volume of emails our Company sends and receives, we discourage employees from storing large numbers of email messages. Please make a regular practice of deleting emails once you have read and/or responded to them. If you need to save a particular email, you may print out a paper copy, archive the email or save it to your hard disk. The Company will purge email messages that have not been archived after [number] days.

Violations

Any employee who violates this policy can be subject to discipline, up to and including termination.

Need advice on how to investigate? If you need information on how to investigate alleged misconduct in the workplace, including harassment complaints, *Dealing with Problem Employees*, by Amy DelPo & Lisa Guerin (Nolo), will guide you through every step of the process—from deciding who should conduct the investigation to figuring out what to do once your investigation is complete.

How to Complete This Policy

Many email policies provide that messages will be purged every 60 days (for more on the importance of purging email, see below). Some recommend that you purge your system every 30 days, to minimize your potential legal exposure. Others suggest longer time periods (90 days or more) between purges, to make sure you don't lose important business information accidentally. Select a time period that makes sense for your business, given your rate of email traffic, the capacities of your system and how quickly your employees read (and respond to) their email.

Reality Check: Don't Fight the Urge to Purge E-Mail

There are two very good reasons to purge your email system by deleting older messages regularly. First, if you don't delete messages, you will eventually have a storage problem on your hands. Many employees simply don't get around to deleting old messages, no matter what your policy asks them to do. If you have a lot of email traffic, your system's capacity to store information will be overwhelmed unless you take steps to get rid of the messages you don't need.

Second, purging emails can reduce your legal liability and your legal obligations if you are sued. In many kinds of business lawsuits, including lawsuits brought by employees, customers or other businesses, email becomes evidence. Realizing this, lawyers who sue businesses routinely ask for months, or even years, of the company's email messages in "discovery," the legal process by which parties to a lawsuit gather documents and information from each other and from third parties. Although courts often put limits on what companies have to hand over (for example, they may require only emails on a certain subject matter or emails for a limited time period to be produced), businesses that get hit with one of these requests can spend a lot of time trying to pull together the requested documents. What's worse, they may end up having to turn over an email that hurts their cause.

An email purging policy reduces your risks and your obligations if you get sued. After all, you can only hand over what you've got. If you regularly delete older emails, you won't have to wade through and, perhaps, give your opponent years' worth of messages.

Optional Modifications

To Prohibit Personal Use of Email

Some employers don't want employees to use their email systems for personal messages at all. Although this is entirely reasonable, such a policy might pose practical and legal problems. The practical problem is quite straightforward: most people send the occasional personal message using their office email system. Some might not have an Internet connection at home; others might have a message that has to be conveyed immediately ("I'll be home late" or "don't forget to pick the kids up after soccer practice"). Whatever the reason, the truth is that a policy forbidding any personal use of email will probably be violated regularly, by everyone from the CEO on down and if you don't enforce the policy, it isn't worth much (and it may undermine your credibility).

The legal problem is a bit more complicated. The National Labor Relations Board (NLRB), the federal government agency that issues decisions and makes rules relating to union workplace issues, has said that prohibiting all personal uses of email might illegally prevent workers from talking about forming a union. Although employers can prohibit workers from talking about union issues during work hours in work areas, they cannot prohibit these discussions during non-work hours in non-work areas (a locker room or lunch room, for example). The NLRB says that a ban on all personal messages deprives employees of the right to talk about union issues during non-work hours and might therefore run afoul of the law. So far, this is only the NLRB's opinion; no legal decision has settled the issue.

Our policy balances these issues and your interest in preventing a lot of personal use of your equipment by allowing personal messages only outside of work hours, and only at the company's discretion. This policy avoids the legal and practical problems discussed above, but also leaves you room to discipline an employee who taxes the system by sending files with gigantic attachments, spending hours sending instant messages or sending "chain letter" correspondence to dozens of recipients.

However, if you're intent on prohibiting any personal use of your email system, you can modify the policy by replacing the language under "Use of the Email System" as follows:

Modification

> The email system is to be used for official Company business only—not for personal reasons.

To Announce Your Plans to Monitor

Our sample policy states that you "reserve the right" to monitor email messages. However, if have monitoring software that you plan to use, or if you intend to read employee email on a regular basis, you should modify this portion of the policy to let your employees know. After all, the purpose of an email policy is not only to allow you to read those problematic messages after they've been sent, but also to deter your employees from sending them in the first place. Telling employees that you *will* read their messages will almost certainly help you accomplish this second goal.

Whether you should read employee email on a regular basis is a tough issue to sort through. Doing so will force your employees to take the email policy seriously and thereby reduce the possibility that they will send messages that are harassing, threatening or otherwise in violation of your policy. It's just human nature: We are less likely to break rules if we think we will get caught. But there are some serious downsides as well with employee dissatisfaction topping the list. Employees don't want to feel like the company doesn't trust them or plans to check up on their every keystroke. Monitoring also costs time and money: You will have to invest in monitoring software and assign someone the task of actually reading the messages. And some employers just find monitoring distasteful. They don't want to be cast in the role of Big Brother.

Ultimately, only you can decide, based on your workforce and the needs of your company, whether the benefits of monitoring outweigh the disadvantages. If you do decide to monitor regularly, you should modify our sample policy to tell your employees what you plan to do. Use one of the modifications below in place of the "Email Is Not Private" paragraph in our sample policy. Which modification you choose will depend on the monitoring software or other system you adopt.

Modification A: Monitoring Systems That Copy Every Draft

Email Is Not Private

Email messages sent using Company communications equipment are the property of the Company. The Company's monitoring software automatically creates a copy of every message you draft—even if you never send it. Company personnel will regularly read these copies to make sure that no employee violates this policy. You should not expect that any email message you draft or send using Company equipment—including messages you consider to be personal—will be private.

Modification B: Monitoring Systems that Flag Key Words

Email Is Not Private

Email messages sent using Company communications equipment are the property of the Company. The Company's software automatically searches the messages you send for questionable content —including sexual or racial comments, threats, Company trade secrets or competitive information and inappropriate language. Any message deemed questionable will be forwarded to, and read by, Company management. In addition, the Company reserves the right to read any message, whether or not the software singles it out for review. You should not expect that any email message you send using Company equipment—including messages you consider to be personal—will be private.

Modification C: Random Monitoring

Email Is Not Private

Email messages sent using Company communications equipment are the property of the Company. We reserve the right to access, monitor, read and/or copy email messages at any time, for any reason. In addition, the Company will select and read employee messages at random to ensure that employees are in compliance with this policy. You should not expect that any email message you send using Company equipment—including messages you consider to be personal—will be private.

To Add Email Rules—"Netiquette" and Other Issues

You can include as much—or as little—in your policy about appropriate use of the email system as you wish. However, you should tell employees that their email messages are subject to the same rules (no harassment, no threats and so on) that apply to their workplace behavior in general. You can make a general statement to this effect or go into more detail, listing the types of misconduct to which email is particularly susceptible.

Some employers include email-writing guidelines in their policies. Because email is often seen as an informal medium, some workers send out even work-related messages sprinkled with icons (little smiley-faces or other symbols) and exclamation points, written in all lower- or upper-case letters or filled with acronyms and usages peculiar to the online world. What's worse, some workers send out email without considering its content or style, then later regret having expressed anger too hastily or sent a message that doesn't look professional.

The standard policy, above, includes a general statement about proper email use. If you're concerned about these problems, however, you can include more explicit instructions on the proper use of email.

Modification

Guidelines for Email Writing

1. Always spell-check or proofread. Email is official Company correspondence. Spelling errors in email are all too common —and they look sloppy and unprofessional. Always take the time to check for spelling errors before you send email.

2. Use lowercase and capital letters in the same way that you would in a letter. Using all capital letters is the email equivalent of shouting at someone—and it can be hard on the eyes. Failing to use capital letters at all (to begin a sentence or a formal noun) can confuse your reader and seem overly cute. Unless you are writing poetry, use standard capitalization.

3. Remember your audience. Although email encourages informal communication, that might not be the most appropriate style to use if you are addressing the CEO of an important customer. And remember that your email can be forwarded to unintended recipients—some of whom may not appreciate joking comments or informalities.

4. Don't use email for confidential matters. Again, remember the unintended recipient—your email might be forwarded to some-one you didn't anticipate, or might be sitting on a printer for all to see. If you need to have a confidential discussion, do it in person or over the phone.

5. Send messages sparingly. There is rarely a need to copy everyone in the Company on an email. Carefully consider who really needs to see the message, and address it accordingly.

6. Always think before you send. Resist the urge to respond in anger, to "flame" your recipient or to get emotional. Although email gives you the opportunity to respond immediately, you don't have to take it.

15:2   Internet Use

If you offer your employees Internet access, you should have a policy telling them what uses of that equipment you consider appropriate. Without such a policy, you run the practical risk that your employees will spend work time surfing the Web, shopping online, exchanging instant messages with friends both near and far and perhaps unwittingly downloading viruses that will crash your company's computer system. You also run the legal risk that your employees will use your Internet access to engage in illegal behavior —such as pirating software or viewing pornographic images that create a hostile work environment (and therefore a potential sexual harassment problem).

Your Internet policy should describe proper uses of the Internet and tell employees which sites are off limits. If you use software that prevents employees from visiting certain sites and/or makes a record of sites an employee visits, you should include that information in your policy as well.

We offer you two different versions of an Internet policy. Policy A is a basic Internet policy, while Policy B is designed for employers who use blocking or screening software to prevent their employees from visiting certain websites.

Standard Policy A

Using the Internet

We may provide you with computer equipment and capabilities, including Internet access, to help you perform your job. This policy governs your use of that equipment to access the Internet.

Personal Use of the Internet

Our network and Internet access are for official Company business only. Employees may access the Internet for personal use only outside of work hours and only in accordance with the other terms of this policy. An employee who engages in excessive Internet use, even during non-work hours, or who violates any other provision of this policy, may be subject to discipline.

Prohibited Uses of the Internet

Employees may not, at any time, access the Internet using Company equipment or links for any of the following purposes:

- To visit websites that feature pornography, gambling or violent images, or are otherwise inappropriate in the workplace.
- To operate an outside business, solicit money for personal purposes or to otherwise act for personal financial gain—this includes running online auctions.
- To download software, articles or other printed materials in violation of copyright laws.
- To download any software program without the express consent of _____.
- To read, open or download any file from the Internet without first screening that file for viruses using the Company's virus detection software.

Internet Use Is Not Private

We reserve the right to monitor employee use of the Internet at any time, to ensure compliance with this policy. You should not expect that your use of the Internet—including but not limited to the sites you visit, the amount of time you spend online and the communications you have—will be private.

Standard Policy B

Using the Internet

We may provide you with computer equipment and capabilities, including Internet access, to help you perform your job. This policy governs your use of that equipment to access the Internet.

Personal Use of the Internet

Our network and Internet access are for official Company business only. Employees may access the Internet for personal use only outside of work hours and only in accordance with the other terms of this policy. An employee who engages in excessive Internet use, even during non-work hours, may be subject to discipline.

Prohibited Uses of the Internet

Employees may not, at any time, access the Internet using Company equipment or links for any of the following purposes:
- To visit websites that feature pornography, gambling or violent images, or are otherwise inappropriate in the workplace.
- To operate an outside business, solicit money for personal purposes or to otherwise act for personal financial gain—this includes running online auctions.
- To download software, articles or other printed materials in violation of copyright laws.
- To download any software program without the express consent of _____.
- To read, open or download any file from the Internet without first screening that file for viruses using the Company's virus detection software.

Internet Use Is Not Private

To assure that employees comply with this policy, we use filtering software, which will block your access to many prohibited sites. However, some inappropriate websites may escape detection by the software—the fact that you can access a particular site does not necessarily mean that site is appropriate for workplace viewing.

We also use monitoring software, which keeps track of the sites an employee visits and how much time is spent at a particular site, among other things. You should not expect that your use of the Internet—including but not limited to the sites you visit, the amount of time you spend online and the communications you have—will be private.

How to Complete This Policy

Both versions of our policy leave you a space to designate someone authorized to approve software downloads. The purpose of this provision is to keep you out of trouble for unauthorized use of copyrighted software, otherwise known as software piracy. If someone in your company has to approve downloads ahead of time, you can make sure that your employees don't unwittingly violate someone else's copyright or license.

For companies with computer specialists or dedicated technical help, simply fill in the position of the appropriate person (for example, the systems operator). For those who run smaller companies, don't worry—you don't need to have a highly-paid technical army to enforce this provision. If you have an employee who oversees your computer system, that person should be able to figure out which software can be downloaded freely (and which can't). If you use an outside consultant to provide technical support, you can simply name a company official, who can pass questions on to your consultant, then let employees know what to do. In either case, name the person to whom employees should bring their questions.

Optional Modification to Ban All Personal Uses of the Internet

Our standard policies allow personal use of the Internet outside of work hours—as long as that use is not excessive and does not violate the policy's other prohibitions. The purpose of this provision is simple: many employees do use the Internet for personal purposes (such as holiday gift shopping, keeping up with their investments or checking the news or weather). Allowing them to do so during non-work hours will make it more likely that they spend their work hours actually doing what you pay them to do.

However, some employers ban any personal use of the Internet, reasoning that a flat prohibition is clearer for employees and easier for employers to enforce. If you wish to include a ban on personal use, you can replace the "Personal Use of the Internet" provision with the following language:

Modification

Personal Use of the Internet Is Prohibited

Our network and Internet access are for official Company business only. Employees may not access the Internet for personal use at any time. Any employee who uses the Company's Internet access for personal reasons, or who violates any other provision of this policy, may be subject to discipline.

Form D: Email and Internet Policy Acknowledgment Form

If you adopt an email policy or an Internet policy that allows you to monitor, you should ask employees to sign a form acknowledging that they have read the policy and agree to abide by its terms.

Currently, at least one state (Delaware) requires employers to get a signed acknowledgment form from their employees before they engage in Internet or email monitoring. Other states are considering legislation that would impose a similar requirement. If you live in a state with this type of law, you must use this acknowledgment form.

Even if your state doesn't require an employee's signed acknowledgment, however, it's a good idea to use this form. Having to sign a form draws an employee's attention to the policy—which not only makes the employee more likely to comply with the policy, but also takes away the employee's ability to argue, later, that he was unaware of it.

Email and Internet Policy Acknowledgment

My signature on this form indicates that I have read the Company's email and Internet policies and I agree to abide by their terms. I understand that any email messages I send or receive using Company equipment are not private, and that the Company may access, monitor, read and/or copy those messages at any time, for any reason. I also understand that the Company reserves the right to monitor my Internet use, and that such monitoring may occur at any time, for any reason.

_____   _____
Signature   Date

_____
Print name

Optional Modification If You Haven't Adopted All Policies Mentioned in Form D

If you have chosen not to adopt one of the policies above, you will have to modify this form. For example, if you have adopted an email policy but have chosen not to adopt a policy that allows you to monitor Internet traffic, be sure to modify the form to delete the language referring to Internet monitoring.

15:3   Software Use

The purpose of a software policy is to prevent your employees from using company software in violation of your licensing agreements—and to make sure that employees don't download pirated software from the Internet. If your employees violate the terms of a software license agreement that the company is party to, you will be on the hook. Illegal software copying and use is very common —so much so that many employees don't even know it's illegal. An employee might think it's perfectly fine to make a copy of company software to install on a home computer, as long as that computer is used for work, for example. But software licenses typically authorize only a single user, at a single computer. Adopting a policy will let your employees know the rules.

This policy also tells your employees that you will conduct periodic audits of company computer equipment, to monitor compliance with the software policy. This language lets employees know that you are serious about enforcing the policy—and puts them on notice that you reserve the right to inspect their computers.

Standard Policy

Software Use

It is our Company's policy to use licensed software only in accordance with the terms of its license agreement. Violating a license agreement is not only unethical—it is also illegal and can subject the Company to criminal prosecution and substantial monetary penalties.

To help us adhere to this policy, employees may not do any of the following without permission from _____:

- Make a copy of any Company software program, for any reason.
- Install a Company software program on a home computer.
- Install a personal software program (that is, software owned by the employee) on any Company computer.
- Download any software program from the Internet to a Company computer.

The Company may audit Company-owned computers at any time to ensure compliance with this policy.

How to Complete This Policy

We've left you a space to designate someone authorized to approve any deviations from the policy. Choose the same person that you designated to approve software downloads in your Internet Policy, above. ■

Employee Records

If you are like most employers, you keep all of the records pertaining to an employee in one place—usually a manila folder in a file cabinet labeled "personnel files." Typically, these files contain documents such as the employee's job application and resumé, letters of reference, offer letter, IRS W-4 Form, records of performance and discipline, emergency contacts, a signed handbook acknowledgment form and so on.

Prudent employers keep these files under lock and key. After all, personnel records contain highly sensitive, personal information. Sometimes, however, it is appropriate for an employee, manager or supervisor to review some or all of the file's contents.

The records section of your handbook should inform employees that you maintain personnel files, explain that the files are confidential and indicate whether—and under what circumstances—employees and others can inspect them.

In this chapter, we include the following policies:

For a Handbook Acknowledgment Form, see Chapter 2.

16:1   Personnel Records

Your personnel file policy should start with some general information, to lay the foundation for the policies to come—in particular, the policy requiring employees to notify you of changes to personal information and the policy alerting employees to their right to inspect personnel records. After all, employees can understand their rights and obligations regarding personnel records only if they know about the records in the first place.

The following standard policy notifies employees that you maintain personnel files, and it gives employees an idea of what records you do—and do not—keep in the file.

Standard Policy

Your Personnel File

This Company maintains a personnel file on each employee. The purpose of this file is to allow us to make decisions and take actions that are personally important to you, including notifying your family in case of an emergency, calculating income tax deductions and withholdings and paying for appropriate insurance coverage.

Although we cannot list here all of the types of documents that we keep in your personnel file, examples include: _[list examples of the documents you keep in the file]_

_____.

We do not keep medical records or work eligibility forms in your personnel file. Those are kept separately. To find out more about those types of records, see Section ___ and Section ___, respectively, of this Handbook.

Your personnel file is physically kept by _____.

If you have any questions about your personnel file, contact _____.

16:2   Confidentiality

Always treat your employee personnel records as private. To do otherwise is to risk embarrassment for the employee and a lawsuit for yourself. Employees need to feel confident that their personal information won't become public knowledge just because it is in a file. Otherwise, employees might be reticent to give you personal information.

The need for confidentiality must sometimes give way to other considerations, however. For example, an employee's supervisor might want to look at the employee's resume when it becomes clear that the employee can't do the job. Or your office manager might need the employee's emergency contact information if the employee becomes incapacitated at work. You want a confidentiality policy that gives you the flexibility to reveal information in the file to people in your organization who need to know it.

The following standard policy gives the confidentiality assurance employees need while keeping things flexible for you.

Standard Policy

Confidentiality of Personnel Files

Because the information in your personnel file is by its nature personal, we keep the file as confidential as possible. We allow access to your file only on a need-to-know basis.

16:3   Changes in Personal Information

Your personnel records are only as good as the information that's in them. Take good care to keep the information up to date. Obviously, the employee is the best person to keep your records from becoming stale. As things happen in their personal lives, however, it may not occur to employees to let you know of the changes. This could have implications for work. For example, the boss may not be the first person an employee thinks to tell when the employee's spouse files for divorce. If the employee becomes sick at work, however, and the office manager calls the soon-to-be-ex spouse (who is still listed as an emergency contact) the situation could turn embarrassing at best and medically dangerous at worst.

This standard policy reminds employees of the importance of keeping you posted about certain changes in their personal information.

Standard Policy

Please Notify Us If Your Information Changes

Because we use the information in your personnel file to take actions on your behalf, it is important that the information in that file be accurate. Please notify _____ whenever any of the following changes:

- your name
- your mailing address
- your phone number
- your dependents
- the number of dependents you are designating for income tax withholding
- your marital status
- the name and phone number of the individual whom we should notify in case of an emergency
- restrictions on your driver's license.

16:4 Inspection of Personnel Records

Although many employers would rather not have employees inspecting their own personnel records, many state laws require that you give your employees access. These laws vary greatly in the details. In some states, employees may review their files only at specified hours. In other states, only past employees, not current employees, have the right to inspect.

Typically, these laws state who can inspect, when they can inspect, whether they have to give notice, whether they can photocopy their file and whether they have to pay for the copies. To find out about your state's law, refer to the "State Laws on Access to Personnel Records" chart at the end of this chapter. You can also check with your state labor department. (See Appendix C for contact details.)

Because the laws vary so much, we cannot provide a standard policy for you to use. The following is an example of what your policy might look like.

SAMPLE POLICY LANGUAGE:

Current employees who want to inspect their personnel files must make an appointment with the Human Resources Department. Appointments will typically take place Monday through Friday between 1:00 p.m. and 5:00 p.m. Although we will make every effort to give employees an appointment quickly, it may take up to 48 hours. If an employee would like a representative to view his or her file, the employee must make the request in writing.

Former employees who would like to inspect their files must make a written request to do so. Upon receiving the written request, the Human Resources Department will call the former employee to schedule an appointment.

We do not allow current or former employees to photocopy their file. If you would like a copy of a document in the file, the Human Resources Department will copy it for you at a price of $.10 per page.

If you have any questions about this policy, please contact Myrtle Means, the Human Resources Manager.

Drafting Your Own Policy

A typical inspection policy will state:

- who can inspect the file (current employees, former employees, designated representatives)
- when they can inspect the file
- where they can inspect the file
- whether they need to make a request
- whether their request must be in writing
- whether they can photocopy the file, and
- how much you will charge for photocopying.

Be sure to check on your state's law as you draft your policy so that you don't create a policy that is contrary to legal requirements.

16:5   Work Eligibility

Federal law requires you to check whether your employees can legally work in the United States. As part of this process, you have to complete a form issued by the federal Bureau of Citizenship and Immigration Services ("BCIS") called Form I-9. You should not keep Form I-9 or other work eligibility forms in your personnel files. The BCIS is entitled to inspect these forms (and often does). If you keep them in a worker's personnel file, the BCIS will be looking at all those other documents as well. Not only does this compromise your worker's privacy, but it also might open your business up to additional questions and investigation.

The following policy reassures employees that you will not keep their work status records in their personnel file.

For more information about work eligibility forms, including a policy telling employees that they must complete these forms, see Chapter 4.

Standard Policy

Work Eligibility Records

In compliance with federal law, all newly hired employees must present proof that they are legally eligible to work in the United States. We must keep records related to that proof, including a copy of the BCIS Form I-9 that each employee completes for us.

Those forms are kept as confidential as possible. We do not keep them in your personnel file.

If you would like more information about your I-9 form, see Section ___ of this Handbook or contact _____.

16:6   Medical Records

Employers come into possession of worker medical records for a variety of reasons. Perhaps a worker has requested an accommodation for a disability and has presented you with a medical evaluation verifying the disability. Or maybe a worker has requested medical leave and has given you the files to show you the extent of the medical condition.

Medical records should not go into a worker's personnel file. The federal Americans with Disabilities Act has very strict rules on how to handle records relating to an employee's disability. You must keep this medical information separate from non-medical records, and you must store the medical files in a locked cabinet. Your state might have a similar—perhaps even stricter—law.

Although the confidentiality provisions of these laws apply only to workers who are disabled, it is a good practice to keep all medical records confidential and in a separate, locked file cabinet.

The following standard policy informs employees that you will keep their medical records separate.

Standard Policy

Medical Records

We understand the particularly sensitive nature of an employee's medical records, so we do not place those records in the employee's personnel file. We keep those records in a separate and secure place.

If you have any questions about the storage of your medical records or about inspecting your medical records, contact

_____.

State Laws on Access to Personnel Records

This chart includes only those states with laws that authorize access to personnel files. Generally an employee is allowed to see evaluations, performance reviews and other documents that determine a promotion, bonus or raise; access usually does not include letters of reference, test results or records of a criminal or workplace-violation investigation. Under other state laws employees may have access to their medical records and records of exposure to hazardous substances; these laws are not included in this chart.

Alaska

Alaska Stat. § 23.10.430

Employers affected: All.

Employee access to records: Employee or former employee may view and copy personnel files.

Conditions for viewing records: Employee may view records during regular business hours under reasonable rules.

Copying records: Employee pays (if employer so requests).

California

Cal. Lab. Code §§ 1198.5; 432

Employers affected: All employers subject to wage and hour laws.

Employee access to records: Employee has right to inspect at reasonable intervals any personnel records relating to performance or to a grievance proceeding. Employee also has a right to a copy of any personnel document employee has signed.

Conditions for viewing records: Employee may view records at reasonable times, during break or non-work hours. If records are kept offsite or employer does not make them available at the workplace, then employee must be allowed to view them at the storage location without loss of pay.

Connecticut

Conn. Gen. Stat. Ann. §§ 31-128a to 31-128h

Employers affected: All.

Employee access to records: Employee has right to inspect personnel files within a reasonable time after making a request, but not more than twice a year. Employer must keep files on former employees for at least one year after termination.

Written request required: Yes.

Conditions for viewing records: Employee may view records during regular business hours in a location at or near worksite. Employer may require that files be viewed on the premises and in the presence of employer's designated official.

Copying records: Employer must provide copies within a reasonable time after receiving employee's written request; request must identify the materials employee wants copied. Employer may charge a fee that is based on the cost of supplying documents.

Employee's right to insert rebuttal: Employee may insert a written statement explaining any disagreement with information in the personnel record. Rebuttal must be maintained as part of the file.

Delaware

Del. Code Ann. tit. 19, §§ 730 to 735

Employers affected: All.

Employee access to records: Current employee, employee who is laid off with reemployment rights or employee on leave of absence may inspect personnel record; employee's agent is not entitled to have access to records. Unless there is reasonable cause, employer may limit access to once a year.

Written request required: Yes. Employer may require employee to file a form and indicate either the purpose of the review or what parts of the record employee wants to inspect.

Conditions for viewing records: Records may be viewed during employer's regular business hours. Employer may require that employees view files on their own time; may also require that files be viewed on the premises and in the presence of employer's designated official.

Copying records: Employer is not required to permit employee to copy records. Employee may take notes.

Employee's right to insert rebuttal: If employee disagrees with information in personnel file and cannot reach an agreement with employer to remove or correct it, employee may submit a written statement explaining her position. Rebuttal must be maintained as part of the personnel file.

Illinois

820 Ill. Comp. Stat. §§ 40/1 to 40/12

Employers affected: Businesses with 5 or more employees.

Employee access to records: Current employee, or former employee terminated within the past year, is permitted to inspect records twice a year at reasonable intervals, unless a collective bargaining agreement provides otherwise. An employee involved in a current grievance may designate a

State Laws on Access to Personnel Records (continued)

representative of the union or collective bargaining unit, or other agent, to inspect personnel records that may be relevant to resolving the grievance. Employer must make records available within 7 working days after employee makes request (if employer cannot meet deadline, may be allowed an additional 7 days).

Written request required: Yes. Employer may require use of a form.

Conditions for viewing records: Records may be viewed during employer's normal business hours at or near employee's worksite or, at employer's discretion, during nonworking hours at a different location. Employer may require that records be viewed on the premises.

Copying records: After reviewing records, employee may get a copy. Employer may charge only actual cost of duplication. If employee is unable to view files at worksite, employer, upon receipt of a written request, must mail employee a copy.

Employee's right to insert rebuttal: If employee disagrees with any information in the personnel file and cannot reach an agreement with employer to remove or correct it, employee may submit a written statement explaining his position. Rebuttal must remain in file with no additional comment by employer.

Iowa

Iowa Code § 91B.1

Employers affected: All employers with salaried employees or commissioned sales people.

Employee access to records: Employee may have access to personnel file at time agreed upon by employer and employee.

Conditions for viewing records: Employer's representative may be present.

Copying records: Employer may charge copying fee for each page that is equivalent to a commercial copying service fee.

Maine

Me. Rev. Stat. Ann. tit. 26, § 631

Employers affected: All.

Employee access to records: Within 10 days of submitting request, employee, former employee or authorized representative may view and copy personnel files.

Written request required: Yes.

Conditions for viewing records: Employee may view records during normal business hours at the location where the files are kept, unless employer, at own discretion, arranges a time and place more convenient for employee. If files are in electronic or any other non-print format, employer must provide equipment for viewing and copying.

Copying records: Employee pays for copies.

Massachusetts

Mass. Gen. Laws ch. 149, § 52C

Employers affected: All. (Employers with 20 or more employees must maintain personnel records for 3 years after termination.)

Employee access to records: Employee or former employee must have opportunity to review personnel files within 5 business days of submitting request. (Law does not apply to tenured or tenure-track employees in private colleges and universities.)

Written request required: Yes.

Conditions for viewing records: Employee may view records at workplace during normal business hours.

Copying records: Employee must be given a copy of record within 5 business days of submitting a written request.

Employee's right to insert rebuttal: If employee disagrees with any information in personnel record and cannot reach an agreement with employer to remove or correct it, employee may submit a written statement explaining her position. Rebuttal becomes a part of the personnel file.

Michigan

Mich. Comp. Laws §§ 423.501 to 423.505

Employers affected: Employers with 4 or more employees.

Employee access to records: Current or former employee is entitled to review personnel records at reasonable intervals, generally not more than twice a year, unless a collective bargaining agreement provides otherwise.

Written request required: Yes. Request must describe the record employee wants to review.

Conditions for viewing records: Employee may view records during normal office hours either at or reasonably near the worksite. If these hours would require employee to take time off work, employer must provide another time and place that is more convenient for the employee.

Copying records: After reviewing files, employee may get a copy; employer may charge only actual cost of duplication.

State Laws on Access to Personnel Records (continued)

If employee is unable to view files at the worksite, employer, upon receipt of a written request, must mail employee a copy.

Employee's right to insert rebuttal: If employee disagrees with any information in personnel record and cannot reach an agreement with employer to remove or correct it, employee may submit a written statement explaining his position. Statement may be no longer than five 8½" by 11" pages.

Minnesota

Minn. Stat. Ann. §§ 181.960 to 181.966

Employers affected: All.

Employee access to records: Current employee may review files once per 6-month period; former employee may have access to records once only during the first year after termination. Employer must be given 7 days advance request (14 days if personnel records kept out of state). Employer may not retaliate against an employee who asserts rights under these laws.

Written request required: Yes.

Conditions for viewing records: Current employee may view records during employer's normal business hours at worksite or a nearby location; does not have to take place during employee's working hours. Employer or employer's representative may be present.

Copying records: Employer must provide copy free of charge. Current employee must first review record and then submit written request for copies. Former employee must submit written request; providing former employee with a copy fulfills employer's obligation to allow access to records.

Employee's right to insert rebuttal: If employee disputes specific information in the personnel record, and cannot reach an agreement with employer to remove or revise it, employee may submit a written statement identifying the disputed information and explaining her position. Statement may be no longer than 5 pages and must be kept with personnel record as long as it is maintained.

Nevada

Nev. Rev. Stat. Ann. § 613.075

Employers affected: All.

Employee access to records: An employee who has worked at least 60 days and a former employee, within 60 days of termination, must be given a reasonable opportunity to inspect personnel records.

Conditions for viewing records: Employee may view records during employer's normal business hours.

Copying records: Employer may charge only actual cost of providing access and copies.

Employee's right to insert rebuttal: Employee may submit a reasonable written explanation in direct response to any entry in personnel record. Statement must be of moderate length; employer may specify the format.

New Hampshire

N.H. Rev. Stat. Ann. § 275:56

Employers affected: All.

Employee access to records: Employer must provide employees a reasonable opportunity to inspect records.

Copying records: Employer may charge a fee related to actual cost of supplying copies.

Employee's right to insert rebuttal: If employee disagrees with any of the information in personnel record and cannot reach an agreement with the employer to remove or correct it, employee may submit a written statement of her version of the information along with evidence to support her position.

Oregon

Or. Rev. Stat. § 652.750

Employers affected: All.

Employee access to records: Employer must provide employees a reasonable opportunity to inspect personnel records used to determine qualifications for employment, promotion or additional compensation, termination or other disciplinary action. Employer must keep records for 60 days after termination of employee.

Conditions for viewing records: Employee may view records at worksite or place of work assignment.

Copying records: Employer must provide a certified copy of requested record to current or to former employee (if request made within 60 days of termination). May charge only actual cost of providing copy.

Pennsylvania

43 Pa. Cons. Stat. Ann. §§ 1321 to 1324

Employers affected: All.

Employee access to records: Employer must allow employee to inspect personnel record at reasonable times. (Employee's agent, or employee who is laid off with reemployment rights or on leave of absence, must also be given access.)

State Laws on Access to Personnel Records (continued)

Unless there is reasonable cause, employer may limit review to once a year by employee and once a year by employee's agent.

Written request required: At employer's discretion. Employer may require the use of a form as well as a written indication of the parts of the record employee wants to inspect or the purpose of the inspection. For employee's agent: employee must provide signed authorization designating agent; must be for a specific date and indicate the reason for the inspection or the parts of the record the agent is authorized to inspect.

Conditions for viewing records: Employee may view records during normal business hours at the office where records are maintained, when there is enough time for employee to complete the review. Employer may require that employee or agent view records on their own time; may also require that inspection take place on the premises and in the presence of employer's designated official.

Copying records: Employer not obligated to permit copying. Employee may take notes.

Employee's right to insert rebuttal: The Bureau of Labor Standards, after a petition and hearing, may allow employee to place a counter statement in the personnel file, if employee claims that the file contains an error.

Rhode Island

R.I. Gen. Laws § 28-6.4-1

Employers affected: All.

Employee access to records: Employer must permit employee to inspect personnel files when given at least 7 days advance notice (excluding weekends and holidays). Employer may limit access to no more than 3 times a year.

Written request required: Yes.

Conditions for viewing records: Employee may view records at any reasonable time other than employee's work hours. Inspection must take place in presence of employer or employer's representative.

Copying records: Employee may not make copies or remove files from place of inspection. Employer may charge a fee reasonably related to cost of supplying copies.

Washington

Wash. Rev. Code Ann. §§ 49.12.240 to 49.12.260

Employers affected: All.

Employee access to records: Employee may have access to personnel records at least once a year within a reasonable time after making a request.

Employee's right to insert rebuttal: Employee may petition annually that employer review all information in employee's personnel file. If there is any irrelevant or incorrect information in the file, employer must remove it. If employee does not agree with employer's review, employee may request to have a statement of rebuttal or correction placed in file. Former employee has right of rebuttal for two years after termination.

Wisconsin

Wis. Stat. Ann. § 103.13

Employers affected: All employers who maintain personnel records.

Employee access to records: Employee and former employee must be allowed to inspect personnel records within 7 working days of making request. Access is permitted twice per calendar year unless a collective bargaining agreement provides otherwise. Employee involved in a current grievance may designate a representative of the union or collective bargaining unit, or other agent, to inspect records that may be relevant to resolving the grievance.

Written request required: At employer's discretion.

Conditions for viewing records: Employee may view records during normal working hours at a location reasonably near worksite. If this would require employee to take time off work, employer may provide another reasonable time and place for review that is more convenient for the employee.

Copying records: Employee's right of inspection includes the right to make or receive copies. If employer provides copies, may charge only actual cost of reproduction.

Employee's right to insert rebuttal: If employee disagrees with any information in the personnel record and cannot come to an agreement with the employer to remove or correct it, employee may submit a written statement explaining his position. Employer must attach the statement to the disputed portion of the personnel record.

Current as of March 2003.

17

Drugs and Alcohol

Employee drug and alcohol problems can take a toll on a workplace in so many ways. Employees who abuse alcohol and drugs
(including illegal drugs, prescription drugs and over-the-counter
drugs) pose significant problems for their employers, managers and
co-workers—from diminished job performance and low productivity
to excessive absenteeism and tardiness. Out-of-pocket costs include
increased workers' compensation claims, increased occupational
health claims and higher health insurance premiums.

As a result, most employers include in their handbook a policy
or set of policies designed to combat substance abuse. These policies
range from bare-bones statements prohibiting alcohol and drug use
to complicated frameworks that include rehabilitation, employee
searches and drug testing.

From a legal standpoint, the bare-bones approach is the easiest,
because the law gives employers the right to prohibit illegal drug
and alcohol use in the workplace. If you confine your policies to
conduct and activities in which you have a legitimate business
interest—for example, performance and safety—you should be on
safe legal ground.

If you decide to enter the world of employee searches and drug
testing, however, you'll have a number of legal obstacles to face.
Remember that your employees have a right to privacy. Depending
on the state in which you live, the law may be more or less aggressive in protecting this right. We address these legal issues in more
detail in the individual policy discussions below.

The set of policies you choose will depend on your values and
the type of business that you run. In this chapter, we help you
tailor your policies to your business needs by explaining the various
options you have. We include the following policies:

This chapter provides information about substance abuse policies that you can include in your handbook. It does not discuss in detail the legal issues involved in actually dealing with an employee who abuses substances. Both state and federal law have a lot to say about what employers can and cannot do when faced with such an employee, and prudent employers familiarize themselves with these laws before taking action. For more information on this issue, see Chapter 1, Section E, of *Dealing With Problem Employees: A Legal Guide*, by Amy DelPo & Lisa Guerin (Nolo).

17:1   Prohibition Against Drug and Alcohol Use at Work

Given the amount of social drinking and drug use in our culture, there's no room for ambiguity in a substance use policy; it must be clear as to when employees can and cannot partake. Although illegal drug use is always unacceptable, there are times when a drink on company time may be appropriate (see modifications, below).

Your drug and alcohol use policy should explain to employees when they can and cannot use legal drugs and alcohol, that you are prohibiting substance use for their own safety and well-being and that you can discipline or even terminate them for violating the policy.

Standard Policy

Policy Against Illegal Drug and Alcohol Use

This Company is committed to providing a safe, comfortable and productive work environment for its employees. We recognize that employees who abuse drugs or alcohol at work—or who appear at work under the influence of illegal drugs or alcohol—harm both themselves and the work environment.

As a result, we prohibit employees from doing the following:

- appearing at work under the influence of illegal drugs or alcohol
- conducting Company business while under the influence of illegal drugs or alcohol (whether or not the employee is actually on work premises at the time)
- using illegal drugs or alcohol on the worksite
- using illegal drugs or alcohol while conducting Company business (whether or not the employee is actually on work premises at the time)
- possessing, buying, selling or distributing illegal drugs or alcohol on the worksite
- possessing, buying, selling or distributing illegal drugs or alcohol while conducting Company business (whether or not the employee is actually on work premises at the time).

Illegal drug use includes more than just outlawed drugs such as marijuana, cocaine or heroin. It also includes the misuse of otherwise legal prescription and over-the-counter drugs.

This policy covers times when employees are on call but not working and times when employees are driving Company vehicles or using Company equipment.

Employees who violate this policy may face disciplinary action, up to and including termination.

Who Needs This Policy

Federal law requires federal contractors to have policies that ensure a drug-free workplace (see "The Drug-Free Workplace Act of 1988," below.) Some state laws also have this requirement. To find out if your state has such a law, contact your state labor department (see Appendix C for contact details). If you are an employer covered by these laws, then you will need some type of anti-drug/anti-alcohol policy. That policy might look like the one above or, depending on the legal requirements, be even more comprehensive.

All other employers are free to choose whether to have this type of policy. Given the negative impact of drugs and alcohol on morale, performance and productivity, we cannot imagine a reason for failing to include such a policy in a handbook. As we explained above, there are no murky legal issues involved in such a bare-bones policy, and including one gives employers more leeway in combating any drug and alcohol problems that arise in their workplace.

Don't prohibit legal drug use. When crafting any substance abuse policy, it is important to understand the difference between legal drug use and illegal drug use. You can prohibit the latter, but not the former. This is because legal drug use —for example, taking prescription or over-the-counter drugs according to a doctor's orders—is sometimes protected by state and federal disability laws. For more information on this issue, see Chapter 1, Section E, of *Dealing With Problem Employees: A Legal Guide*, by Amy DelPo & Lisa Guerin (Nolo). To learn more about the federal disability law, contact the U.S. Equal Employment Opportunity Commission. (See Appendix for contact details.) You can also read about the law in detail in *Federal Employment Laws: A Desk Reference*, by Amy DelPo & Lisa Guerin (Nolo). To learn more about your state's disability law, contact your state labor department. (See Appendix C for contact details.)

The Drug-Free Workplace Act of 1988

If you are a federal government contractor or grant recipient, then you must abide by the federal Drug-Free Workplace Act of 1988 (41 U.S.C. § 701 and following). This law requires you to do a number of things, including publishing an anti-drug-use statement (perhaps in your handbook) and establishing a drug awareness program.

The Act is beyond the scope of this book. The U.S. Department of Labor (DOL) enforces the Act and can provide you with information you need to comply with the Act's requirements. (See Appendix C for contact details.) The DOL keeps a lot of this information on its website at www.dol.gov. Click on the search index at the top right-hand portion of the home page; scroll down to "D," and then click on "Drug-free workplace."

If you'd like to read the text of the law, you can do so by using Nolo's Legal Research Center at www.nolo.com. Click on "U.S. Laws and Regulations." Then scroll up until you see a heading for "U.S. Code." Type "41" in the title field and "701" in the section field.

Be aware that many states have similar drug-free workplace laws. To find out about your state's law, see the "State Drug and Alcohol Testing Laws" chart at the end of this chapter. You can also contact your state department of labor. (See Appendix C for contact details.)

Serving alcohol? Talk to a lawyer first. There are certain legal risks involved whenever you allow employees to consume alcohol —either because you've served them the alcohol or because you've sanctioned their drinking while on the job. If the employee consumes the alcohol and then hurts himself or someone else, you might be liable for those injuries—and your workers' compensation insurance might not cover you (so check your insurance policy before serving alcohol or allowing employees to consume alcohol). If you plan to serve alcohol to your employees or sanction employee drinking on the job, consider consulting with legal counsel to learn ways to shield yourself from liability.

Optional Modifications

If You Serve Alcohol

Some companies sponsor functions, such as holiday parties or anniversary celebrations, at which the company serves alcohol. Those companies will have to modify the standard policy above to allow alcohol use *sometimes*. Otherwise, the company is sending employees contradictory and confusing messages, serving them alcohol while at the same time prohibiting it.

If you think that your company will serve alcohol, either on-site or during work hours, consider adding the following paragraph to the standard policy:

Modification

We do not prohibit employees from consuming alcohol at social or business functions that we sponsor where alcohol is served. Even at these functions, however, employees may not consume alcohol to the point of intoxication or to the point where they endanger their own safety or the safety of others. In addition, employees involved in security and employees who work with heavy or dangerous machinery or materials may not consume any alcohol at these functions if they will be returning to work that same day.

If Your Employees Entertain

Some employees must entertain clients and customers as part of their job. For example, a salesman might take a buyer to dinner to seal a deal, or an attorney might celebrate with a client after winning a big case. Often, entertainment includes sharing a drink or two.

If you'd like your employees to be able to consume alcohol while entertaining clients, consider adding the following paragraph to the standard policy:

Modification

This policy does not prohibit employees from consuming alcohol while entertaining clients or prospective clients. However, employees may not consume alcohol to the point of intoxication, nor may they consume alcohol if they are going to drive. In addition, employees must always conduct themselves professionally and appropriately while on Company business.

17:2 Inspections to Enforce Policy Against Drugs and Alcohol

Some employers choose to inspect the workplace and their employees to enforce their policy against alcohol and illegal drug use. Although most state laws allow inspections in some form, these same laws impose strict limits on how and when employers can conduct these inspections. Most often, these laws seek to balance the employer's right to keep the workplace free of drugs and alcohol against the employee's right to privacy. Exactly how to strike that balance varies from state to state.

This policy reserves your right to inspect without going into detail, thereby giving you the flexibility to use procedures that comply with your state's law.

 Legal rules regarding inspections vary from state to state. They also vary from year to year, depending on what the courts and lawmakers have had to say on the subject. Because inspection rules are complicated and ever-changing, we recommend you consult with legal counsel before conducting any employee or workplace inspection. Otherwise, you may find yourself on the unpleasant end of a lawsuit charging violation of privacy.

Standard Policy

Inspections to Enforce Drug and Alcohol Policy

This Company reserves the right to inspect employees, their possessions and their workspaces to enforce our policy against illegal drug and alcohol use.

Who Needs This Policy

Not every employer needs to inspect the workplace, but if you would like to have the option of searching your employees and their workspaces for drugs and alcohol, then you should probably include this type of policy in your handbook.

Whether you want to have this option depends in large part on your needs and values as an employer. One drawback of the policy is that it sends a message of mistrust to employees. If you are a large employer who has experienced large-scale problems with employees abusing drugs and alcohol, however, you might be willing to live with that drawback in exchange for being able to aggressively address drug and alcohol use in your workplace. On the other hand, if you are a small employer who has not had many problems with substance-abusing employees, you probably do not need to include this type of policy in your handbook.

17:3   Drug Testing

In recent years, drug tests have become cheaper and more reliable, spurring more and more employers to use drug testing as a tool for creating a drug-free workplace. Employers test for drugs in a variety of contexts—some test all prospective hires, others test only when the employee seems to be under the influence, and still others randomly test employees who are in jobs where safety or security is an issue.

Your state's laws will determine whether, when and how you can test your employees. Many states ban outright any drug testing of employees, while other states only allow it for certain occupations or in certain circumstances. In addition, state privacy laws regulate how and when an employer can conduct the test.

To learn more about your state's rules on drug testing, contact your state labor department. (See Appendix for contact details.) You can also refer to the chart "State Drug and Alcohol Testing Laws" at the end of this chapter.

Although the varied nature of state laws means that we cannot provide a standard drug testing policy, here is an example of what such a policy might look like:

SAMPLE POLICY LANGUAGE:

As part of our efforts to keep this workplace safe and free of illegal drug use, we will conduct random and intermittent drug tests of all employees in positions where the safety or security of the employee or others is an issue.

In addition, we may ask any employee, regardless of job responsibilities, to submit to a drug test in the following circumstances:

1. *when we suspect that the employee is under the influence of illegal drugs*
2. *when we suspect that the employee has been involved in the sale, purchase, use or distribution of illegal drugs on the work site or while performing job duties*
3. *when the employee has been involved in a workplace accident or incident*
4. *when the employee has been involved in an accident or incident off site but while on company business, or*
5. *when the employee has violated a safety rule.*

Who Needs This Policy

The U.S. Department of Transportation requires drug testing in certain transportation industries, including aviation, trucking, railway, maritime and mass transit. Those regulations are beyond the scope of this book. If your business uses trucks or boats or is involved in transporting goods or people, you can find out more by contacting the Department of Transportation. (See Appendix for contact details.) The department posts some excellent information on its website at www.dot.gov. From the home page, click on "Safety" in the left-hand column. Then click on "Drug and Alcohol Safety."

There are so many legal risks and practical problems involved in drug testing that employers other than those covered by DOT regulations—or similar state regulations—should think twice before taking this step. Nonetheless, if you do want to have the option of drug testing your employees, be sure to include this type of policy in your handbook.

 Ask a lawyer for help drafting a drug testing policy. Because state law in this area is so varied and mercurial, we advise you to consult with legal counsel when drafting a drug testing policy and before conducting any drug test.

17:4   Leave for Rehabilitation

Although some employers take a zero tolerance approach to employee substance abuse problems, others recognize that they can help employees who have fallen prey to alcohol and drug abuse kick their habits—and become valuable, productive and loyal workers in the process. For some employers, this means something as small and inexpensive as giving employees paid or unpaid leave to participate in a rehabilitation program.

Your rehabilitation policy should let employees know that you care about them and their well-being and that, as a result, you may allow them to take leave to deal with their substance abuse problem. It should not, however, promise such leave to anyone who requests it. You policy should also remind employees who have a substance abuse problem that they must meet the same performance, productivity and conduct standards as everyone else.

Standard Policy

Leave to Participate in Rehabilitation Program

We believe that employees who have a substance abuse problem can help themselves by enrolling in a rehabilitation program. Not only will overcoming their problem help these employees in their personal lives, it will help them to be more effective and productive workers.

Although we cannot guarantee that we will grant this leave to all employees who request it, employees who would like to participate in a rehabilitation program may, subject to approval, be able to use up to ___ weeks of [*paid or unpaid*] leave from work to attend the program.

Employees [*will or will not*] be entitled to health and other benefits while on rehabilitation leave.

Employees [*will or will not*] be allowed to accrue vacation and other benefits while on rehabilitation leave.

At the end of the rehabilitation leave, we [*will or will not*] require proof that the employee successfully completed the program.

To learn more about this type of leave, including whether you qualify for it, the circumstances under which we will grant it and the requirements that you must meet, contact _____. We will keep all conversations regarding employee substance abuse problems as confidential as possible.

Please note that even as you might be seeking assistance for your substance abuse problem, we still expect you to meet the same standards of performance, productivity and conduct that we expect of all employees. We reserve the right to discipline you—up to and including termination—for failing to meet those standards.

Who Needs This Policy

Some states require employers to allow employees to take leave to participate in a rehabilitation program. If you operate in such a state, include this policy (or one similar to it) in your handbook. To find out about your state's law, contact your state department of labor (see Appendix C for contact details).

If you don't operate in a state that requires rehabilitation leave, you can still benefit from this type of policy. The expense of the policy is quite small when compared to the potential reward of assisting problem employees in becoming valuable and productive members of the workforce.

How to Complete This Policy

As you can see from reading the standard rehabilitation leave policy, above, you will have to make a number of decisions when drafting your leave policy. You will have to decide:

- Which employees qualify for the leave. For example, will you have a length of service requirement—that is, a requirement that employees have been in your employ for a certain amount of time before they qualify? Will only full-time employees be eligible? Will you require employees to provide medical proof of the substance abuse problem?
- The amount of leave you will allow. When making this decision, you might consult with rehabilitation programs in your area to get an estimate of what is reasonable.
- Whether you will require employees to provide proof that they successfully completed the program.
- Whether the leave will be paid or unpaid.
- Whether you will allow employees to accrue benefits while on leave.

In most states, the law does not provide you with much direction on these issues. The way you answer these questions will depend on your values as an employer and what your business can afford.

In the states that require this type of leave, however, the law may also have rules about issues relating to the leave. These rules typically mandate such things as whether employees are entitled to benefits while on leave and whether the leave is paid or unpaid. If your state has such a law, you may have to modify the standard policy that we provide above.

17:5   Rehabilitation and Your EAP

Most employee assistance plans (EAPs) include drug and alcohol rehabilitation and counseling services. If you offer an EAP as a benefit to your employees, check to see whether your plan includes these things. If it does, inform employees of this fact either through the standard policy below or through a policy provided by your EAP administrator.

Standard Policy

Rehabilitation and Your EAP

Because we care about the health and welfare of our employees, your benefits package includes an Employee Assistance Program (EAP) that provides assistance to employees who suffer from substance abuse problems, personal problems or emotional problems.

If you would like assistance in dealing with your substance abuse problem, see _____ for information about our EAP program. Your request for assistance will be kept as confidential as possible.

[If you will include in your handbook a policy allowing leave to participate in a rehabilitation program, refer to that policy here.]

Please note that even as you might be seeking assistance for your substance abuse problem, we still expect you to meet the same standards of performance, productivity and conduct that we expect of all employees. We reserve the right to discipline you for failing to meet those standards.

State Drug and Alcohol Testing Laws

Note: The states of Colorado, Delaware, District of Columbia, Massachusetts, Michigan, Missouri, New Hampshire, New Jersey, New Mexico, New York, Pennsylvania, South Dakota, Washington, West Virginia, Wisconsin and Wyoming are not included in this chart because they do not have drug and alcohol testing laws governing private employers. Check with your state department of labor if you need more information (see Appendix C for contact list).

Alabama

Ala. Code §§ 25-5-330 to 25-5-340

Employers affected: Employers who establish a drug-free workplace program to qualify for a workers' compensation rate discount.

Testing applicants: Must test upon conditional offer of employment. Must test all new hires. Job ads must include notice that drug and alcohol testing required.

Testing employees: Random testing permitted. Must test after an accident that results in lost work time. Must also test upon reasonable suspicion; reasons for suspicion must be documented and made available to employee upon request.

Employee rights: Employees have 5 days to contest or explain a positive test result. Employer must have an employee assistance program or maintain a resource file of outside programs.

Notice and policy requirements: All employees must have written notice of drug policy. Must give 60 days advance notice before implementing testing program. Policy must state consequences of refusing to take test or testing positive.

Drug-free workplace program: Yes.

Alaska

Alaska Stat. §§ 23.10.600 and following

Employers affected: Voluntary for employers with one or more full-time employees. (There is no state mandated drug and alcohol testing.)

Testing employees: Employer may test:
- for any job-related purpose
- to maintain productivity and safety
- as part of an accident investigation
- upon reasonable suspicion.

Employee rights: Employer must provide written test results within 5 working days. Employee has 10 working days to request opportunity to explain positive test results; employer must grant request within 72 hours or before taking any adverse employment action.

Notice and policy requirement: Before implementing a testing program employer must distribute a written drug policy to all employees and must give 30 days' advance notice. Policy must state consequences of a positive test or refusal to submit to testing.

Arizona

Ariz. Rev. Stat. §§ 23-493 and following

Employers affected: Employers with one or more full-time employees.

Testing applicants: Employer must inform prospective hires that they will undergo drug testing as a condition of employment.

Testing employees: Employees are subject to random and scheduled tests:
- for any job-related purpose
- to maintain productivity and safety
- upon reasonable suspicion.

Employee rights: Policy must inform employees of their right to explain positive results.

Notice and policy requirement: Before conducting tests employer must give employees a copy of the written policy. Policy must state the consequences of a positive test or refusal to submit to testing.

Drug-free workplace program: Yes.

Arkansas

Ark. Code Ann. §§ 11-14-105 to 11-14-112

Employers affected: Employers who establish a drug-free workplace program to qualify for a workers' compensation rate discount.

Testing applicants: Must test upon conditional offer of employment. Job ads must include notice that drug and alcohol testing required.

Testing employees: Employer must test any employee
- on reasonable suspicion of drug use
- as part of a routine fitness-for-duty medical exam
- after an accident that results in injury
- as follow-up to a required rehabilitation program.

Employee rights: Employer may not refuse to hire applicant or take adverse personnel action against an employee on the basis of a single positive test that has not been verified by a confirmation test. An applicant or employee has 5 days after receiving test results to contest or explain them.

Notice and policy requirements: Employer must give all employees a written statement of drug policy and must give 60 days' advance notice before implementing program.

Drug-free workplace program: Yes.

California

Cal. Lab. Code §§ 1025, 1026

Employers affected: No provisions for private employer testing. An employer with 25 or more employees must reasonably accommodate an employee who wants to enter

State Drug and Alcohol Testing Laws (continued)

a treatment program. Employer is not, however, required to provide paid leave. Employer may fire or refuse to hire an employee whose drug or alcohol use interferes with job duties or workplace safety.

Employee rights: Employer must safeguard privacy of employee who enters treatment program.

Connecticut

Conn. Gen. Stat. Ann. § 31-51t

Employers affected: Any individual, corporation, partnership or unincorporated association.

Testing applicants: Employer must inform job applicants in writing that drug testing is required as a condition of employment.

Testing employees: Employer may test:
- when there is reasonable suspicion that employee is under the influence of drugs or alcohol and job performance is or could be impaired
- when authorized by federal law
- when employee's position is dangerous or safety-sensitive
- as part of a voluntary employee assistance program.

Employee rights: Employer may not take any adverse personnel action on the basis of a single positive test that has not been verified by a confirmation test.

Florida

Fla. Stat. Ann. §§ 440.101 to 440.102

Employers affected: Employers who establish a drug-free workplace program to qualify for a workers' compensation rate discount.

Testing applicants: Must inform job applicants that drug and alcohol testing is required as a condition of employment.

Testing employees: Must test any employee:
- on reasonable suspicion of drug use
- as part of a routine fitness-for-duty medical exam
- as part of a required rehabilitation program.

Employee rights: Employees who voluntarily seek treatment for substance abuse cannot be fired, disciplined or discriminated against, unless they have tested positive or have been in treatment in the past. All employees have the right to explain positive results within 5 days. Employer may not take any adverse personnel action on the basis of an initial positive result that has not been verified by a confirmation test.

Notice and policy requirements: Prior to implementing testing, employer must give 60 days' advance notice and must give employees written copy of drug policy.

Drug-free workplace program: Yes.

Georgia

Ga. Code Ann. §§ 34-9-410 to 34-9-421

Employers affected: Employers who establish a drug-free workplace program to qualify for a workers' compensation rate discount.

Testing applicants: Applicants are required to submit to a substance abuse test after they have been offered employment.

Testing employees: Must test any employee:
- on reasonable suspicion of drug use
- as part of a routine fitness-for-duty medical exam
- as part of a required rehabilitation program.

Employee rights: Employees have 5 days to explain or contest a positive result. Employer must have an employee assistance program or maintain a resource file of outside programs.

Notice and policy requirements: Employer must give applicants and employees notice of testing; must give 60 days' notice before implementing program. All employees must receive a written policy statement; policy must state the consequences of refusing to submit to a drug test or of testing positive.

Drug-free workplace program: Yes.

Hawaii

Haw. Rev. Stat. §§ 329B-1 and following

Testing applicants: Same conditions as current employees.

Testing employees: Employer may test employees only if these conditions are met:
- employer pays all costs including confirming test
- tests are performed by a licensed laboratory
- employee receives a list of the substances being tested for
- there is a form for disclosing medicines and legal drugs
- the results are kept confidential.

Idaho

Idaho Code §§ 72-1701 to 72-1714

Employers affected: Voluntary for all private employers.

Testing applicants: Employer may test as a condition of hiring.

Testing employees: May test as a condition of continued employment.

An employer who follows drug-free workplace guidelines may fire employees who refuse to submit to testing or who test positive for drugs or alcohol. Employees will be fired for misconduct and denied unemployment benefits.

Employee rights: An employee or applicant who receives notice of a positive test may request a retest within 7 working days. If the retest results are negative, the employer

State Drug and Alcohol Testing Laws (continued)

must pay for the cost; if they are positive, the employee must pay.

Drug-free workplace program: Yes (compliance is optional).

Illinois

775 Ill. Comp. Stat. § 5/2-104(C)(3)

Employers affected: Employers with 15 or more employees.

Testing employees: Employer may prohibit all employees from using or being under the influence of alcohol and illegal drugs. Employer may test employees who have been in rehabilitation. Employee may be held to the same standards as other employees, even if the unsatisfactory job performance or behavior is due to drug use or alcoholism.

Indiana

Ind. Code Ann. §§ 22-9-5-6(b), 22-9-5-24

Employers affected: Employers with 15 or more employees.

Testing employees: Employer may prohibit all employees from using or being under the influence of alcohol and illegal drugs. Employer may test employees who have been in rehabilitation. Employee may be held to the same standards as other employees, even if the unsatisfactory job performance or behavior is due to drug use or alcoholism.

Iowa

Iowa Code § 730.5

Employers affected: Employers with one or more full-time employees.

Testing applicants: Employer may test as a condition of hiring.

Testing employees: Employer may test employees:
- as a condition of continued employment
- upon reasonable suspicion
- during and after rehabilitation
- following an accident that caused a reportable injury or more than $1,000 property damage.

Employee rights: Employee has 7 days to request a retest. Employers with 50 or more employees must provide rehabilitation for any employee who has worked for at least one year and has not previously violated the substance abuse policy; no adverse action may be taken if employee successfully completes rehabilitation. Employer must have an employee assistance program or maintain a resource file of outside programs.

Drug-free workplace program: Yes (compliance is optional).

Louisiana

La. Rev. Stat. Ann. §§ 49:1001 and following

Employers affected: Employers with one or more full-time employees. (Does not apply to oil drilling, exploration or production.)

Testing applicants: Employer may require all applicants to submit to drug and alcohol test. Employer does not have to confirm a positive result of a pre-employment drug screen, but must offer the applicant the opportunity to pay for a confirmation test and a review by a medical review officer.

Employee rights: Except for a pre-employment test, employer may not take adverse personnel action on the basis of an initial screen. Employees with confirmed positive results have 7 working days to request access to all records relating to the drug test. Employer may allow employee to undergo rehabilitation without termination of employment.

Maine

Me. Rev. Stat. Ann. tit. 26, §§ 681 to 690

Employers affected: Employers with one or more full-time employees. (Law does not require or encourage employers to conduct substance abuse testing.)

Testing applicants: Employer may require applicant to take a drug test only if offered employment or placed on an eligibility list.

Testing employees: Employer may test for probable cause, but may not base belief on a single accident; must document the facts and give employee a copy. May test when:
- there could be an unreasonable threat to the health and safety of coworkers or the public
- an employee returns to work following a positive test.

Employee rights: Employee who tests positive has 3 days to explain or contest results. Employee must be given an opportunity to participate in a rehabilitation program for up to 6 months; an employer with more than 20 full-time employees must pay for half of any out-of-pocket costs. After successfully completing the program, employee is entitled to return to previous job with full pay and benefits.

Notice and policy requirements: All employers must have a written policy approved by the state Department of Labor. Policy must be distributed to each employee at least 30 days before it takes effect. Any changes to policy require 60 days advance notice. An employer with more than 20 full-time employees must have an employee assistance program certified by the Office of Substance Abuse before implementing a testing program.

Maryland

Md. Code Ann., [Health-Gen.] § 17-214

Employers affected: Law applies to all employers.

Testing applicants: May use preliminary screening to test applicant. If initial result is positive, may make job offer conditional on confirmation of test results.

Testing employees: Employer may require substance abuse testing for legitimate business purposes only.

State Drug and Alcohol Testing Laws (continued)

Employee rights: The sample must be tested by a certified laboratory; at the time of testing employee may request laboratory's name and address. An employee who tests positive must be given:

- a copy of the test results
- a copy of the employer's written drug and alcohol policy
- written notice of any adverse action employer intends to take
- statement of employee's right to an independent confirmation test at own expense.

Minnesota

Minn. Stat. Ann. §§ 181.950 to 181.957

Employers affected: Employers with one or more full-time employees. (Employers are not required to test.)

Testing applicants: Employers may require applicants to submit to a drug or alcohol test only after they have been given a job offer and have seen a written notice of testing policy. May only test if required of all applicants for same position.

Testing employees: Employers may require drug or alcohol testing only according to a written testing policy. Testing may be done if there is a reasonable suspicion that employee:

- is under the influence of drugs or alcohol
- has violated drug and alcohol policy
- has been involved in an accident
- has sustained or caused another employee to sustain a personal injury. Random tests permitted only for employees in safety-sensitive positions. With 2 weeks' notice, employers may also test as part of an annual routine physical exam.

Employee rights: If test is positive, employee has 3 days to explain the results; employee must notify employer within 5 days of intention to obtain a retest. Employer may not discharge employee for a first-time positive test without offering counseling or rehabilitation; employee who refuses or does not complete program successfully may be discharged.

Notice and policy requirements: Employees must be given a written notice of testing policy which includes consequences of refusing to take test or having a positive test result. 2 weeks' notice required before testing as part of an annual routine physical exam.

Mississippi

Miss. Code Ann. §§ 71-7-1 and following; 71-3-205 and following

Employers affected: Employers with one or more full-time employees. Employers who establish a drug-free workplace program to qualify for a workers' compensation rate discount must implement testing procedures.

Testing applicants: May test (must test, if drug-free workplace) all applicants as part of employment application process. Employer may request a signed statement that applicant has read and understands the drug and alcohol testing policy and/or notice.

Testing employees: May (must, if drug-free workplace) require drug and alcohol testing of all employees:

- on reasonable suspicion
- as part of a routinely scheduled fitness for duty medical examination
- as a follow-up to a rehabilitation program
- who have tested positive within the previous 12 months.

Employee rights: Employer must inform an employee in writing within 5 working days of receipt of a positive confirmed test result; employee may request and receive a copy of the test result report. Employee has 10 working days after receiving notice to explain the positive test results. Private employer who elects to establish a drug-free workplace program must have an employee assistance program or maintain a resource file of outside programs.

Notice and policy requirements: 30 days before implementing testing program employer must give employees written notice of drug and alcohol policy which includes consequences

- of a positive confirmed result
- of refusing to take test
- of other violations of the policy.

Drug-free workplace program: Yes.

Montana

Mont. Code Ann. §§ 39-2-205 to 39-2-211

Employers affected: Employers with one or more employees.

Testing applicants: May test as a condition of hire.

Testing employees: Employees may be tested:

- on reasonable suspicion
- after involvement in an accident that causes personal injury or more than $1,500 property damage
- as a follow-up to a previous positive test
- as a follow-up to treatment or a rehabilitation program.

Employer may conduct random tests as long as there is an established date and all personnel are subject to testing.

Employer may require an employee who tests positive to undergo treatment as a condition of continued employment.

Employee rights: After a positive result, employee may request additional confirmation by an independent laboratory; if the results are negative, employer must pay the test costs.

Notice and policy requirements: Written policy must be available for review 60 days before testing.

State Drug and Alcohol Testing Laws (continued)

Nebraska

Neb. Rev. Stat. §§ 48-1901 and following

Employers affected: Employers with 6 or more full-time and part-time employees.

Testing employees: Employer may require employees to submit to drug or alcohol testing and may discipline or discharge any employee who refuses.

Employee rights: Employer may not take adverse action on the basis of an initial positive result unless it is confirmed according to state and federal guidelines.

Nevada

Nev. Rev. Stat. Ann. § 608.156

Employers affected: All employers who offer health benefits.

Employee rights: Employee health benefits must include treatment for drug or alcohol abuse. Limits are: $1,500 per year for treatment for withdrawal; $9,000 per year for in-patient facility; $2,500 for outpatient counseling. Maximum of $39,000 per lifetime.

North Carolina

N.C. Gen. Stat. §§ 95-230 to 95-235

Employers affected: Law applies to all employers.

Testing employees: Employer must preserve samples for at least 90 days after confirmed test results are released.

Employee rights: Employee has right to retest a confirmed positive sample at own expense.

North Dakota

N.D. Cent. Code § 34-01-15

Employers affected: Any employer who requires a medical exam as a condition of hire or continued employment may include a drug or alcohol test.

Testing employees: Employer may test following an accident or injury that will result in a workers' compensation claim: if employer has a mandatory policy of testing under these circumstances, or if employer or physician has reasonable grounds to suspect injury was caused by impairment due to alcohol or drug use.

Ohio

Ohio Admin. Code §§ 4123-17-58, 4123-17-58.1

Employers affected: Employers who establish a drug-free workplace program to qualify for a workers' compensation rate discount.

Testing applicants: Must test all applicants and new hires within at least 90 days of employment.

Testing employees: Must test employees:
- on reasonable suspicion
- following a return to work after a positive test

- after an accident which results in an injury requiring offsite medical attention or property damage over limit specified in drug and alcohol policy.

Employee rights: Employer must have an employee assistance plan. Employer must offer healthcare coverage which includes chemical dependency counseling and treatment.

Notice and policy requirements: Policy must state consequences for refusing to submit to testing or for violating guidelines. Policy must include a commitment to rehabilitation.

Drug-free workplace program: Yes.

Oklahoma

Okla. Stat. Ann. tit. 40, §§ 551 to 565

Employers affected: Employers with one or more employees. (Drug or alcohol testing not required or encouraged.)

Testing applicants: Employer may test applicants as a condition of employment; may refuse to hire applicant who refuses to undergo test or has a confirmed positive result.

Testing employees: Before requiring testing employer must provide an employee assistance program. Random testing is allowed. May test employees:
- on reasonable suspicion
- after an accident resulting in injury or property damage over $500
- as part of a routine fitness-for-duty examination
- or as follow-up to a rehabilitation program.

Employee rights: Employee has right to retest a positive result at own expense; if the confirmation test is negative employer must reimburse costs.

Notice and policy requirements: Before requiring testing employer must:
- adopt a written policy
- give a copy to each employee and to any applicant offered a job
- allow 30 days' notice.

Oregon

Or. Rev. Stat. §§ 659.840; 659A.300; 438.435

Employers affected: Law applies to all employers.

Testing applicants: Unless there is reasonable suspicion that an applicant is under the influence of alcohol, no employer may require a breathalyzer test as a condition of employment. Employer is not prohibited from conducting a test if applicant consents.

Testing employees: Unless there is reasonable suspicion that an employee is under the influence of alcohol, no employer may require a breathalyzer or blood alcohol test as a condition of continuing employment. Employer is not prohibited from conducting a test if employee consents.

State Drug and Alcohol Testing Laws (continued)

Employee rights: No action may be taken based on the results of an on-site drug test without a confirming test performed according to state Health Division regulations. Upon written request test results will be reported to the employee.

Rhode Island

R.I. Gen. Laws §§ 28-6.5-1 to 28-6.5-2

Employers affected: Law applies to all employers.

Testing employees: May require employee to submit to a drug test only if there are reasonable grounds, based on specific observations, to believe employee is using controlled substances that are impairing job performance.

Employee rights: Employee who tests positive may have the sample retested at employer's expense and must be given opportunity to explain or refute results. Employee may not be terminated on the basis of a positive result, but must be referred to a licensed substance abuse professional. After referral employer may require additional testing; may terminate employee if test results are positive.

South Carolina

S.C. Code Ann. §§ 41-1-15; 38-73-500

Employers affected: Employers who establish a drug-free workplace program to qualify for a workers' compensation rate discount.

Testing employees: Must conduct random testing among all employees. Must conduct a follow-up test within 30 minutes of the first test.

Employee rights: Employee must receive positive test results in writing within 24 hours.

Notice and policy requirements: Employer must notify all employees of the drug-free workplace program at the time it is established or at the time of hiring, whichever is earlier. Program must include a policy statement that balances respect for individuals with the need to maintain a safe, drug-free environment

Drug-free workplace program: Yes.

Tennessee

Tenn. Code Ann. §§ 50-9-101 and following

Employers affected: Employers who establish a drug-free workplace program to qualify for a workers' compensation rate discount.

Testing applicants: Must test applicants upon conditional offer of employment. Job ads must include notice that drug and alcohol testing required.

Testing employees: Employer must test upon reasonable suspicion; must document behavior on which the suspicion is based within 24 hours or before test results are released,

whichever is earlier, and must give a copy to the employee upon request. Employer must test employees:
- who are in safety-sensitive positions
- as part of a routine fitness-for-duty medical exam
- after an accident that results in injury
- as a follow-up to a required rehabilitation program.

Employee rights: Employee has the right to explain or contest a positive result within 5 days. Employee may not be fired, disciplined or discriminated against for voluntarily seeking treatment unless employee has previously tested positive or been in a rehabilitation program.

Notice and policy requirements: Before implementing testing program, employer must provide 60 days' notice and must give all employees a written drug and alcohol policy statement.

Drug-free workplace program: Yes.

Texas

Tex. Lab. Code Ann. § 411.091

Employers affected: Employers with 15 or more employees who have a workers' compensation insurance policy.

Notice and policy requirements: Must adopt a drug abuse policy and provide a written copy to employees.

Utah

Utah Code Ann. §§ 34-38-1 to 34-38-15

Employers affected: Employers with one or more employees.

Testing applicants: Employer may test any applicant for drugs or alcohol as long as management also submits to periodic testing.

Testing employees: Employer may test employee for drugs or alcohol as long as management also submits to periodic testing. Employer may also require testing to:
- investigate an accident or theft
- maintain employee or public safety
- ensure productivity, quality or security.

Employee rights: Employer may suspend, discipline, discharge or require treatment on the basis of a confirmed positive test result.

Notice and policy requirements: Testing must be conducted according to a written policy that has been distributed to employees and is available for review by prospective employees.

Vermont

Vt. Stat. Ann. tit. 21, §§ 511 and following.

Employers affected: Employers with one or more employees.

Testing applicants: Employer may not test applicants for drugs or alcohol unless there is a job offer conditional on a negative test result, and a written notice of the testing procedure and a list of the drugs to be tested.

State Drug and Alcohol Testing Laws (continued)

Testing employees: Random testing not permitted unless required by federal law. Employer may not require testing unless:

- there is probable cause to believe an employee is using or is under the influence
- employer has an employee assistance program which provides rehabilitation
- employee who tests positive and agrees to enter employee assistance program is not terminated.

Employee rights: Employer must contract with a medical review officer who will review all test results and keep them confidential. Medical review officer to contact employee or applicant to explain a positive test result. Employee or applicant has right to an independent retest at own expense.

Employee who successfully completes employee assistance program may not be terminated, although employee may be suspended for up to 3 months to complete program. Employee who tests positive after completing treatment may be fired.

Virginia

Va. Code Ann. § 65.2-813.2

Employers affected: Employers who establish drug-free workplace programs to qualify for workers' compensation insurance discount.

Drug-free workplace program: State law gives insurers the authority to establish guidelines and criteria for testing.

Current as of February 2003

Trade Secrets and Conflicts of Interest

More often than not, what gives your business a competitive advantage is the specialized knowledge that it has gained through ingenuity, innovation or just plain hard work. This specialized knowledge could be something as mundane as a list of customers who have a specific need for your services or as glamorous as the top secret formula for your product, from a cookie recipe to an industrial chemical. The law of trade secrets protects this specialized knowledge from disclosure to, and use by, your competitors.

Employees pose a thorny dilemma for businesses with valuable trade secrets. After all, you have to let some of these people in on your trade secrets—either because they need the information to do their jobs or because they helped you develop the information in the first place. Yet these same people may harm your business— either accidentally or through bad intentions—by revealing your trade secrets to competitors.

Most states have laws that impose on employees a duty of loyalty to their employer, and this duty includes keeping mum about trade secrets. Nonetheless, it doesn't hurt to specifically inform employees in your handbook that you expect them to keep confidential any information they learn through their employment with you.

A similar issue arises with regard to conflicts of interest. Most employers do not want their current employees also working for competitors. Such work inherently divides an employee's loyalties and creates a risk that the employee will reveal trade secrets to the competitor. By the same token, such work creates the risk that the employee will reveal the competitor's trade secrets to you. Although having a double agent on your team might not sound so bad at first, it's illegal—and your competitor could drag you into court if it suspected you were learning its valuable trade secrets.

⚠ **If you have valuable information that you want to protect, you'll need a lot more than a few handbook policies to do the job.** You'll need policies and procedures in place to identify confidential information and to limit access to it, among other things. For basic information about trade secrets and employees, including a discussion of what trade secrets are and how you can protect them, see Chapter 10 of *Everyday Employment Law: The Basics,* by Lisa Guerin & Amy DelPo (Nolo).

One of the first steps in protecting yourself is to put your employees on notice about what you expect. We designed the following policies to do just that:

18:1   Confidentiality and Trade Secrets

Often, ensuring that your employees don't disclose your sensitive information is as simple as cluing them in to the importance of keeping quiet and alerting them to the consequences of failing to do so. This policy does just that.

Standard Policy

Confidentiality and Trade Secrets

Information is part of what makes this Company competitive. During your employment here, you will periodically learn sensitive information, either because you help to develop that information or because you need that information to do your job. It is important for the health of this business—and for the well-being of employees who depend on this business for their livelihood—that you keep information you learn through your employment confidential. Employees who improperly disclose sensitive information, confidential information, proprietary information or trade secret information to anyone outside the Company will face disciplinary action, up to and including termination. Therefore, we encourage you to contact _____ if you would like to learn more about this policy or if you have any questions.

After you leave this Company, you are still legally prohibited from disclosing sensitive, proprietary, trade secret or confidential information. If you disclose such information, we will seek legal remedies.

To learn how to create your own confidentiality agreements, see *Nondisclosure Agreements: Protect Your Trade Secrets & More,* by Richard Stim & Stephen Fishman (Nolo).

Reality Check: Use Confidentiality Agreements and Designate Confidential Information

As you read the policy, notice that it raises more questions than it answers. What information qualifies as "sensitive information, confidential information, proprietary information or trade secret information"? What does it mean to "improperly disclose" such information? Unfortunately, your handbook cannot answer these questions for your employees; only you can—through training, procedures and practices. If your business depends on trade secret information to keep a competitive advantage, it behooves you to develop confidentiality procedures to protect your valuable information from disclosure. These procedures typically include fairly simple means—such as labeling certain documents as "confidential"—of informing employees about what information is confidential and what information isn't.

In addition, it is important to remember that your handbook is not a contract. It does not bind you, and it does not bind your employees. This means that you cannot go to court to enforce the provisions in the handbook. If you have employees who will learn or develop sensitive information while working for you, consider having them sign a confidentiality agreement (also called a nondisclosure agreement). Although the duty of loyalty that we mentioned above should be technically sufficient to protect your trade secrets, nondisclosure agreements underscore the importance of confidentiality and clear up any ambiguity about what information you consider a trade secret. They can also be helpful if you ever have to haul an employee into court for revealing a trade secret, whether the employee is still working for you or not.

Optional Modification for Employers With Confidentiality Procedures in Place

If you have procedures in place to protect your confidential information, pat yourself on the back. Then modify the standard policy above to inform employees of this fact. You don't need to give exhaustive detail about the procedures. It is sufficient to alert employees to their existence and to tell employees where they can go for more information. Consider adding the following paragraph to the standard policy, above:

Modification

Because of the grave importance of keeping certain information confidential, this Company follows practices designed to alert employees to sensitive and confidential information, to limit access to that information and to inform employees about what disclosures are and are not acceptable. We expect employees to follow these procedures. Employees who fail to do so face discipline, up to and including termination. To find out more about these procedures, refer to _____. If you have any questions about these procedures, contact _____.

This policy only applies to current employees; it does not prohibit former employees from working for competitors. No handbook policy can do that. Instead, you'll need to use a contract called a noncompete agreement. To learn how to create your own noncompete agreements, see *How to Create a Noncompete Agreement,* by Shannon Miehe (Nolo).

Conflicts of interest or freedom of choice? Although you have a legal right to protect your business against conflicts of interest, your employees also have rights—to invest as they see fit and to work for whomever they want. The law balances your rights against those of your employees. If you need to discipline or terminate someone for violating this policy, consult with an attorney first to make sure that your actions don't violate laws designed to protect your employees.

18:2   Conflicts of Interest

You probably want and expect your employees to be loyal to you and not to your competitors. You're a team, after all. You and your employees work together to compete in the marketplace and to create a healthy, thriving business.

In most instances, the fact that an employee has a little job on the side isn't going to do much—if any—damage to your business. If that job is with a competitor, however, the risk arises that the job will divide your employee's loyalties.

Similarly, investments will pose little harm to your company, unless those investments make the employees act in a way that is contrary to your company's interests.

This policy tells employees that loyalty is part of their job description—and it informs them that they will face consequences if they act in ways that could harm the company.

Standard Policy

Conflicts of Interest

Our Company's success depends on the hard work, dedication and integrity of everyone who works here. In turn, our employees' livelihood depends on the success of our Company.

Because we depend so much on our employees, and because they depend so much on us, we expect all employees to devote their energies and loyalties to our Company. We do not allow employees to engage in any activities or relationships that create either an actual conflict of interest or the potential for a conflict of interest.

Although we cannot list every activity or relationship that would create either an actual or potential conflict of interest, examples of activities that violate this policy include the following:

- working for a competitor or customer or vendor as a part-time employee, full-time employee, consultant, independent contractor or in any other capacity
- owning an interest in a competitor, customer, vendor or anyone else who seeks to do business with this Company
- using the resources of this Company for personal gain
- using your position in this Company for personal gain.

Employees who violate this policy face disciplinary action, up to and including termination.

If you are unsure about whether an activity might violate this policy, or if you have any questions at all about this policy, please talk to _____.

Discrimination and Harassment

Most employers are required to follow federal anti-discrimination laws, including laws prohibiting sexual harassment. Depending on where you do business, you may also have to follow state and even local laws banning discrimination. Your obligation to comply with these laws has nothing to do with your personnel policies—whether you have an anti-discrimination policy or not, you must follow the rules.

So why have anti-discrimination and anti-harassment policies in your handbook? First, these policies educate your employees and your managers about what constitutes discrimination or harassment, what types of conduct are prohibited and what your company will do to stop it. Armed with this information, your employees and managers will know what to do if they are victims of, or witnesses to, illegal behavior. And they will know that your company believes in equal employment opportunity for everyone, a philosophy that can help you build solid relations with your workers.

Second, anti-discrimination and anti-harassment policies will encourage your workers to bring misconduct to your attention immediately. Unless you run a very small company or spend all of your time walking the shop floor, this could be the only way that you learn when a potentially troublesome situation is brewing. If your employees complain quickly, you have a chance to deal with the problems right away, before they poison the workplace environment.

Finally, a well-crafted anti-harassment policy buys you some legal protection, should you find yourself dragged into court by an employee. If you have a clear written policy prohibiting harassment, your employees must follow the procedures you outline to make complaints. If they fail to alert you to a problem, courts might not let them sue you for failing to deal with it.

We address the following policies in this chapter:

19:1   Anti-Discrimination Policy

Your anti-discrimination policy should explain your company's commitment to equal opportunity. It should describe what is prohibited, let employees know what to do if they witness or suffer discrimination and tell employees how the company will deal with discrimination in the workplace.

Standard Policy

Our Commitment to Equal Employment Opportunity

[*Company name*] is strongly committed to providing equal employment opportunity for all employees and all applicants for employment. For us, this is the only acceptable way to do business.

All employment decisions at our Company—including those relating to hiring, promotion, transfers, benefits, compensation, placement and termination—will be made without regard to [*prohibited bases for discrimination*].

Any employee or applicant who believes that he or she has been discriminated against in violation of this policy should immediately file a complaint with _____, as explained in our Complaint Policy. We encourage you to come forward if you have suffered or witnessed what you believe to be discrimination—we cannot solve the problem until you let us know about it. The Company will not retaliate, or allow retaliation, against any employee or applicant who complains of discrimination, assists in an investigation of possible discrimination or files an administrative charge or lawsuit alleging discrimination.

Managers are required to report any discriminatory conduct or incidents, as described in our Complaint Policy.

Our Company will not tolerate discrimination against any employee or applicant. We will take immediate and appropriate disciplinary action against any employee who violates this policy.

Who Needs This Policy

No law requires you to include an anti-discrimination policy in your handbook. Because of the benefits such a policy can provide, however, all employers who are subject to anti-discrimination laws should have one (you can find details on which employers have a legal obligation not to discriminate below).

How to Complete This Policy

There are two things you will have to figure out in order to fill in the blanks, above. First, you need to know what anti-discrimination laws you are required to follow—this will tell you what to put in the first blank, where you need to list prohibited bases for discrimination. Federal laws require many employers not to discriminate on the basis of race, color, national origin, religion, sex, age, disability or citizenship status. However, these laws don't apply to every employer—only to employers who have a specified minimum number of employees, as explained below.

In addition, most states and some municipalities have their own anti-discrimination laws. Some of these laws duplicate the federal protections, others apply to smaller employers or prohibit discrimination based on characteristics the feds left out—such as marital status or sexual orientation. To find out which federal laws you have to follow—and therefore, which characteristics to list in your policy—refer to "Which Federal Anti-Discrimination Laws Apply to Your Company," below. To find out whether your state imposes any additional obligations on you, consult the chart entitled "Laws Prohibiting Discrimination in Employment" at the end of this chapter. You can find out whether any local laws apply to you by getting in touch with your state fair employment department (see Appendix C for contact information) or your local Chamber of Commerce.

 For more information on federal anti-discrimination laws, see *Federal Employment Laws: A Desk Reference*, by Amy DelPo & Lisa Guerin (Nolo). This helpful resource devotes an entire chapter to each of the major federal employment laws, including the anti-discrimination laws listed above.

Which Federal Anti-Discrimination Laws Apply to Your Company

Not every anti-discrimination law applies to every employer. For the most part, whether you have to follow these laws depends on the size and location of your company. Federal anti-discrimination laws (listed below) apply only to employers with more than a minimum number of employees—and this minimum number is different for each law.

Name of Law:	Discrimination Prohibited on the Basis of:	Applies to:
Title VII	Race, national origin, religion, sex	Employers with 15 or more employees
Age Discrimination in Employment Act	Age (over 40 only)	Employers with 20 or more employees
Americans with Disabilities Act	Physical or mental disability	Employers with 15 or more employees
Equal Pay Act	Sex (applies only to wage discrimination)	All Employers
Civil Rights Act of 1866	Race	All Employers
Immigration Reform and Control Act	Citizenship status, national origin	Employers with 4 or more employees

Your handbook should refer only to those types of discrimination that are prohibited for your company. For example, if you do business in a state that outlaws discrimination based on sexual orientation, you should include sexual orientation in the list of prohibited bases for discrimination. Similarly, if your business has only 15 employees, you do not have to comply with the Age Discrimination in Employment Act—and you should not include age in your list.

The second thing you will have to decide is who should take complaints of discrimination. In this space, designate the person or persons whom you name in your complaint policy (see Chapter 20). If you have a human resources department, you can refer employees there.

Optional Modification Emphasizing Company's Commitment

You may want to include additional language explaining your commitment to equal employment opportunity. Some employers take special pride in their efforts to combat discrimination, to provide goods or services to traditionally underserved communities or to honor cultural diversity.

SAMPLE POLICY LANGUAGE:

Our Company was founded to help women achieve equal opportunity in the field of sports. This commitment to equal opportunity for everyone extends to our workplace and the way we treat each other. Discrimination of any kind is contrary to the principles our Company stands for.

SAMPLE POLICY LANGUAGE: A company that imports ethnic food products might add:

Our mission is to bring fresh, high-quality food products from around the world to customers in the United States. We take pride in the great diversity of our customers and of our employees. We treat our employees, and expect our employees to treat each other, with respect and dignity. Discrimination of any kind is against our Company philosophy and policies, and will not be tolerated.

19:2   Harassment

Legally, harassment is a form of discrimination. The same laws that prohibit discrimination also require employers to stop harassment. Therefore, every employer who is subject to the anti-discrimination laws discussed above should also have a harassment policy.

No law requires you to have a harassment policy. However, in addition to the practical benefits such a policy can provide, a harassment policy gives you one very substantial legal benefit: protection against certain harassment lawsuits. If you have a harassment policy that includes the essential elements we discuss below (and include in our sample policy), and you fully and fairly investigate complaints of harassment, an employee who fails to complain of harassment may not be allowed to sue you.

This protection applies only to certain types of harassment cases, however. If you were aware of the harassment even though the employee did not complain (for example, there were lewd posters and X-rated graffiti displayed prominently throughout the workplace), the employee's failure to complain won't get you off the hook. And if the harassment was committed by a manager or supervisor and resulted in a serious, negative job action against the employee (for example, the employee was fired or denied a promotion because she refused to have a sexual relationship with a supervisor), you will be responsible whether or not the employee complained. However, if no negative job action was taken against the employee (for example, an employee was repeatedly teased or subjected to lewd jokes and stories, but was not demoted or fired), she can sue you for harassment by a manager or supervisor only if she first complained to you, using your harassment and complaint policies.

Your harassment policy should explain what harassment is, let workers know that harassment will not be tolerated, tell workers and managers what to do if they witness or suffer harassment and assure everyone that retaliation against those who complain of harassment or participate in a harassment investigation is strictly prohibited.

Standard Policy

Harassment Will Not Be Tolerated

It is our policy and our responsibility to provide our employees with a workplace free from harassment. Harassment on the basis of [*prohibited bases for discrimination*] undermines our workplace morale and our commitment to treat each other with dignity and respect. Accordingly, harassment will not be tolerated at our Company.

Harassment can take many forms, including but not limited to touching or other unwanted physical contact, posting offensive cartoons or pictures, using slurs or other derogatory terms, telling offensive or lewd jokes and stories and sending email messages with offensive content. Unwanted sexual advances, requests for sexual favors and sexually suggestive gestures, jokes, propositions, email messages or other communications all constitute harassment.

If you experience or witness any form of harassment in the workplace, please immediately notify the company by following the steps outlined in our Complaint Policy (see Section _____ of this Handbook). We encourage you to come forward with complaints—the sooner we learn about the problem, the sooner we can take steps to resolve it. The Company will not retaliate, or allow retaliation, against anyone who complains of harassment, assists in a harassment investigation or files an administrative charge or lawsuit alleging harassment. All managers are required to immediately report any incidents of harassment, as set forth in our Complaint Policy.

Complaints will be investigated quickly. Those who are found to have violated this policy will be subject to appropriate disciplinary action, up to and including termination.

How to Complete This Policy

Because harassment is legally considered to be a type of discrimination, your obligation to prevent and remedy harassment tracks your obligation not to discriminate—for example, if the law protects your employees from discrimination on the basis of race, they are also protected from racial harassment. In the blank space, fill in the same prohibited bases for harassment that you included in your anti-discrimination policy.

Laws Prohibiting Discrimination in Employment
Private employers may not make employment decisions based on

State	Law applies to employers with	Age	Ancestry or national origin	Disability	AIDS/HIV	Gender	Marital status	Pregnancy, childbirth and related medical conditions	Race or color	Religion or creed	Sexual orientation	Genetic testing information	Additional protected categories
Alabama Ala. Code §§ 21-7-1; 25-1-20	20 or more employees	40 and older											
Alaska Alaska Stat. §§ 18.80.220; 47.30.865	One or more employees	40 and older	✓	Physical and mental	✓	✓	✓ (Includes changes in status)	Parenthood	✓	✓			Mental illness
Arizona Ariz. Rev. Stat. § 41-1461	15 or more employees	40 and older	✓	Physical	✓	✓			✓	✓		✓	
Arkansas Ark. Code Ann. §§ 16-123-101; 11-4-601; 11-5-403	9 or more employees		✓	Physical, mental and sensory		✓		✓	✓	✓		✓[1]	
California Cal. Gov't. Code §§ 12920,12941; Cal. Lab. Code § 1101	5 or more employees	40 and older	✓	Physical and mental	✓	✓	✓	✓	✓	✓	✓	✓	• Medical condition • Political activities or affiliations
Colorado Colo. Rev. Stat. §§ 24-34-301, 24-34-401; 27-10-115	Law applies to all employers.	40 to 70	✓	Physical, mental and learning	✓	✓		✓	✓	✓			• Lawful conduct outside of work • Mental illness
Connecticut Conn. Gen. Stat. Ann. §§ 46a-51, 46a-60	3 or more employees	40 and older	✓	Present or past physical, mental or learning	✓	✓	✓	✓	✓	✓		✓	Mental retardation
Delaware Del. Code Ann. tit. 19, § 710	4 or more employees	40 to 70	✓	Physical or mental	✓	✓	✓	✓	✓	✓		✓	
District of Columbia D.C. Code Ann. §§ 2-1401.01; 7-1703.03	Law applies to all employers.	18 and older	✓	Physical or mental	✓	✓	✓	✓ Parenthood	✓	✓	✓		• Enrollment in vocational or professional or college education • Family duties • Perceived race • Personal appearance • Political affiliation • Smoker
Florida Fla. Stat. Ann. §§ 760.01, 760.50; 448.075	15 or more employees	No age limit	✓	"Handicap"	✓	✓	✓		✓	✓			Sickle cell trait

[1] Employees covered by FLSA

	Laws Prohibiting Discrimination in Employment (continued)												
		Private employers may not make employment decisions based on											
State	Law applies to employers with	Age	Ancestry or national origin	Disability	AIDS/HIV	Gender	Marital status	Pregnancy, childbirth and related medical conditions	Race or color	Religion or creed	Sexual orientation	Genetic testing information	Additional protected categories
Georgia Ga. Code Ann. §§ 34-6A-1; 34-1-23; 34-5-1	15 or more employees (disability) 10 or more employees (gender)	40 to 70		Physical or mental		✓²							
Hawaii Haw. Rev. Stat. § 378-1	One or more employees	No age limit	✓	Physical or mental	✓	✓	✓	Breastfeeding	✓	✓	✓	✓	Arrest and court record (unless there is a conviction directly related to job)
Idaho Idaho Code § 67-5909	5 or more employees	40 and older	✓	Physical or mental		✓		✓	✓	✓			
Illinois 775 Ill. Comp. Stat. §§ 5/1-101, 5/2-101; Ill. Admin. Code tit. 56, § 5210.110	15 or more employees	40 and older	✓	Physical or mental	✓	✓	✓	✓	✓	✓			• Arrest record • Citizen status • Military status • Unfavorable military discharge
Indiana Ind. Code Ann. §§ 22-9-1-1, 22-9-2-1	6 or more employees	40 to 70	✓	Physical or mental		✓			✓	✓			
Iowa Iowa Code § 216.1	4 or more employees	18 or older	✓	Physical or mental	✓	✓		✓	✓	✓			
Kansas Kan. Stat. Ann. §§ 44-1001, 44-1111, 44-1125; 65-6002(e)	4 or more employees	18 or older	✓	Physical or mental	✓	✓			✓	✓		✓	Military status
Kentucky Ky. Rev. Stat. Ann. §§ 344.040; 207.130; 342.197	8 or more employees	40 or older	✓	Physical (Includes black lung disease)	✓	✓			✓	✓			Smoker or non-smoker
Louisiana La. Rev. Stat. Ann. §§ 23:301 to 23:352	20 or more employees	40 or older	✓	Physical or mental		✓		✓ (Applies to employers with 25 or more employees)	✓	✓		✓	Sickle cell trait
Maine Me. Rev. Stat. Ann. tit. 5, §§ 4551, 4571	Law applies to all employers.	No age limit	✓	Physical or mental		✓		✓	✓	✓	✓	✓	
Maryland Md. Code 1957 Art. 49B, § 15	15 or more employees	No age limit	✓	Physical or mental		✓	✓	✓	✓	✓	✓	✓	

² Wage discrimination only

Laws Prohibiting Discrimination in Employment (continued)

Private employers may not make employment decisions based on

State	Law applies to employers with	Age	Ancestry or national origin	Disability	AIDS/HIV	Gender	Marital status	Pregnancy, childbirth and related medical conditions	Race or color	Religion or creed	Sexual orientation	Genetic testing information	Additional protected categories
Massachusetts Mass. Gen. Laws ch. 151B, § 4	6 or more employees	40 or older	✓	Physical or mental	✓	✓			✓	✓	✓	✓	
Michigan Mich. Comp. Laws §§ 37.1201, 37.2201, 37.1103	One or more employees	No age limit	✓	Physical or mental	✓	✓	✓	✓	✓	✓		✓	• Height or weight • Arrest record
Minnesota Minn. Stat. Ann. §§ 363.01; 181.974	One or more employees	18 or older	✓	Physical or mental	✓	✓	✓	✓	✓	✓	✓	✓	• Member of local commission • Perceived sexual orientation • Receiving public assistance
Mississippi No state law													
Missouri Mo. Rev. Stat. §§ 213.010; 191.665; 375.1306	6 or more employees	40 to 70	✓	Physical or mental	✓	✓		✓	✓	✓		✓	
Montana Mont. Code Ann. §§ 49-2-101, 49-2-303	One or more employees	No age limit	✓	Physical or mental		✓		✓	✓	✓			
Nebraska Neb. Rev. Stat. §§ 48-1101; 48-1001; 20-168	15 or more employees	40 to 70³	✓	Physical or mental	✓	✓	✓	✓	✓	✓		✓	
Nevada Nev. Rev. Stat. Ann. § 613.310 and following	15 or more employees	40 or older	✓	Physical or mental		✓		✓	✓	✓	✓	✓	Lawful use of any product when not at work
New Hampshire N.H. Rev. Stat. Ann. §§ 354-A:2 and following; 141-H:3	6 or more employees	No age limit	✓	Physical or mental		✓	✓	✓	✓	✓	✓	✓	
New Jersey N.J. Stat. Ann. §§ 10:5-1; 34:6B-1	Law applies to all employers.	18 to 70	✓	Past or present physical or mental	✓	✓	✓	✓	✓	✓	✓	✓	• Hereditary cellular or blood trait • Military service or status • Smoker or nonsmoker
New Mexico N.M. Stat. Ann. § 28-1-1	4 or more employees	40 or older	✓	Physical or mental		✓	✓ (Applies to employers with 50 or more employees)	✓	✓	✓			Serious medical condition

³ Employers with 25 or more employees

Laws Prohibiting Discrimination in Employment (continued)

Private employers may not make employment decisions based on

State	Law applies to employers with	Age	Ancestry or national origin	Disability	AIDS/HIV	Gender	Marital status	Pregnancy, childbirth and related medical conditions	Race or color	Religion or creed	Sexual orientation	Genetic testing information	Additional protected categories
New York N.Y. Exec. Law § 296; N.Y. Lab. Law § 201-d	4 or more employees	18 and over	✓	Physical or mental	✓	✓	✓	✓	✓	✓	✓	✓	• Lawful use of any product when not at work • Observance of Sabbath • Political activities
North Carolina N.C. Gen. Stat. §§ 143-422.2; 168A-1; 95-28.1; 130A-148	15 or more employees	No age limit	✓	Physical or mental	✓	✓			✓	✓		✓	• Lawful use of any product when not at work • Sickle cell trait
North Dakota N.D. Cent. Code §§ 14-02.4-01; 34-01-17	One or more employees	40 or older	✓	Physical or mental		✓	✓	✓	✓	✓			• Lawful conduct outside of work • Receiving public assistance
Ohio Ohio Rev. Code Ann. §§ 4111.17; 4112.01	4 or more employees	40 or older	✓	Physical, mental or learning		✓		✓	✓	✓			
Oklahoma Okla. Stat. Ann. tit. 25, § 1301; tit. 36, § 3614.2; tit. 40, § 500; tit. 44, § 208	15 or more employees	40 or older	✓	Physical or mental		✓			✓	✓		✓	• Military service • Smoker or nonsmoker
Oregon Or. Rev. Stat. §§ 659A.100 and foll.; 659A.303	One or more employees	18 or older	✓	Physical or mental⁴		✓		✓	✓	✓		✓	
Pennsylvania 43 Pa. Cons. Stat. Ann. § 953, 336.3	4 or more employees	40 to 70	✓	Physical or mental		✓		✓ (Pregnancy not treated as a disability in terms of benefits)	✓	✓			• Familial status • GED rather than high school diploma
Rhode Island R.I. Gen. Laws §§ 28-6-17; 28-5-11; 2-28-10; 23-6-22; 23-20.7.1-1	4 or more employees	40 or older	✓	Physical or mental	✓	✓		✓	✓	✓	✓	✓	• Domestic abuse victim • Gender identity or expression • Smoker or nonsmoker
South Carolina S.C. Code Ann. § 1-13-20 and following	15 or more employees	40 or older	✓	Physical or mental		✓		✓	✓	✓			
South Dakota S.D. Codified Laws Ann. §§ 20-13-1; 60-12-15; 60-2-20; 62-1-17	Law applies to all employers.		✓	Physical, mental and learning		✓			✓	✓		✓	Preexisting injury

⁴ Employer

				Laws Prohibiting Discrimination in Employment (continued)										
				Private employers may not make employment decisions based on										
State	Law applies to employers with	Age	Ancestry or national origin	Disability	AIDS/HIV	Gender	Marital status	Pregnancy, childbirth and related medical conditions	Race or color	Religion or creed	Sexual orientation	Genetic testing information	Additional protected categories
Tennessee Tenn. Code Ann. §§ 4-21-102; 4-21-401 and following; 8-50-103; 50-2-202	8 or more employees	40 or older	✓	Physical or mental		✓		✓ (Full-time employee who worked the previous 12 months is entitled to 4 months maternity leave. Pay at discretion of employer.)[5]	✓	✓			
Texas Tex. Lab. Code Ann. §§ 21.002, 21.101, 21.401	15 or more employees	40 or older	✓	Physical or mental		✓		✓	✓	✓		✓	
Utah Utah Code Ann. § 34A-5-102	15 or more employees	40 or older	✓	Follows federal law	✓[6]	✓		✓	✓	✓			
Vermont Vt. Stat. Ann. tit. 21, § 495; tit. 18, § 9333	One or more employees	18 or older	✓	Physical, mental or learning	✓	✓			✓	✓	✓	✓	Place of birth
Virginia Va. Code Ann. §§ 2.2-3900; 40.1-28.6; 51.5-3	Law applies to all employers.	No age limit	✓	Physical or mental		✓	✓	✓	✓	✓			
Washington Wash. Rev. Code Ann. §§ 49.60.040, 49.60.172 and foll.; 49.12.175; 49.44.090; Wash. Admin. Code § 162-30-020	8 or more employees	40 or older	✓	Physical, mental or sensory	✓	✓	✓	✓	✓	✓			Member of state militia
West Virginia W.Va. Code §§ 5-11-3, 5-11-9; 21-5B-1	12 or more employees	40 or older	✓	Physical or mental	✓	✓[7]			✓	✓			Smoker or non-smoker
Wisconsin Wis. Stat. Ann. § 111.32	One or more employees	40 or older	✓	Physical or mental	✓	✓	✓	✓	✓	✓	✓	✓	• Arrest or conviction • Lawful use of any product when not at work • Military service or status
Wyoming Wyo. Stat. §§ 27-9-105; 19-11-104	2 or more employees	40 to 69	✓			✓			✓	✓			• Military service or status • Smoker or nonsmoker

[5] Employers with 100 or more employees
[6] Follows federal ADA statutes
[7] Employers with one or more employees

Complaint Policies

The purpose of a complaint policy is simple: to encourage employees to come forward with concerns and problems. If your employees let you know when trouble is brewing, you'll have an opportunity to resolve workplace difficulties right away, before morale suffers or workers start siding with and against each other. A complaint policy also helps your managers and supervisors, by letting them know what their responsibilities are if they observe misconduct or receive a complaint.

A complaint policy also offers you a legal bonus: some protection against harassment lawsuits brought by current or former employees. If you have a complaint policy, that fact becomes a defense if you are sued by someone who didn't make a complaint—and thereby deprived you of a chance to fix the problem.

But you'll reap these benefits only if your policy is user-friendly and genuinely encourages employees to make problems known. In this chapter, we'll show you how to put together policies that will do just that. We cover:

For more information on the legal benefits of complaint policies, see *Dealing with Problem Employees*, by Amy DelPo & Lisa Guerin (Nolo). This book includes an entire chapter on complaints, including step-by-step instructions on how to conduct an effective investigation.

20:1 Complaint Procedures

Your complaint policy should describe the conduct about which employees can complain, explain how to make a complaint and let workers know what will happen once a complaint is filed.

Standard Policy

Complaint Procedures

[*Company Name*] is committed to providing a safe and productive work environment, free of threats to the health, safety and well-being of our workers. These threats include, but are not limited to, harassment, discrimination, violations of health and safety rules and violence.

Any employee who witnesses or is subject to inappropriate conduct in the workplace may complain to _____ or to any Company officer. Any supervisor, manager or Company officer who receives a complaint about, hears of or witnesses any inappropriate conduct is required to immediately notify _____ _____. Inappropriate conduct includes any conduct prohibited by our policies about harassment, discrimination, discipline, workplace violence, health and safety, and drug and alcohol use. In addition, we encourage employees to come forward with any workplace complaint, even if the subject of the complaint is not explicitly covered by our written policies.

We encourage you to come forward with complaints immediately, so we can take whatever action is needed to handle the problem. Once a complaint has been made, _____ will determine how to handle it. For serious complaints alleging harassment, discrimination and other illegal conduct, we will immediately conduct a complete and impartial investigation. All complaints will be handled as confidentially as possible. When the investigation is complete, the Company will take corrective action, if appropriate.

We will not engage in or allow retaliation against any employee who makes a good faith complaint or participates in an investigation. If you believe that you are being subjected to any kind of negative treatment because you made or were questioned about a complaint, report the conduct immediately to _____.

Who Needs This Policy

There are really no drawbacks to having a complaint policy—and plenty of good reasons to adopt one. From a legal standpoint, a complaint policy provides a possible defense against claims of harassment, as explained above. And the practical advantages of encouraging employees to make workplace problems known are many: You will have the opportunity to correct problems before they get out of hand, you will promote communication and team-work and you will let your employees know that you care about their concerns. Because of these benefits, we recommend that every employer adopt a complaint policy.

How to Complete This Policy

Our sample policy leaves you a space to designate the person or department that will be available to take complaints. If your company has a human resource function, you can simply fill in all these blanks with "the human resources department."

If, like many smaller companies, your company doesn't have a dedicated human resources department, you will need to modify this policy to let employees know where to direct their complaints —and who will deal with them. If you ask workers to complain to their direct supervisor or manager, make sure that employees can also complain to someone outside their chain of command, such as another supervisor or officer or even the head of the company. If an employee is being harassed or mistreated by his or her own supervisor, this allows the worker to bypass that person and complain to someone who isn't part of the problem. Even if the employee's direct supervisor is not the source of the complaint, some employees feel more comfortable talking to someone who won't be responsible for evaluating their performance and making decisions on promotions, raises and assignments.

Because complaints—particularly complaints of harassment, discrimination, violence or safety concerns—are a serious matter, many companies prefer to designate someone at the top of the corporate ladder, such as the president or CEO.

Make sure that the people whom you designate to take complaints are accessible to employees. For example, if your human resources department is located in a distant office or the company president spends most work days traveling to promote the company, you should choose alternate complaint-takers who are local and available.

For more information on federal anti-discrimination laws, see *Federal Employment Laws: A Desk Reference*, by Amy DelPo & Lisa Guerin (Nolo). This helpful resource devotes an entire chapter to each of the major federal employment laws, including the anti-discrimination laws listed above.

20:2 Open-Door Promise

Many employers choose to adopt an open-door policy in addition to a more formal complaint policy. Your complaint policy will encourage employees to come forward with big problems: serious misconduct and violations of company rules. An open-door policy serves a slightly different purpose: it encourages your employees to keep in touch with their supervisors about day-to-day work issues. An employee who has a personality conflict with a client, a creative idea to boost profits or a sense that his or her work group isn't coming together successfully as a team, probably wouldn't think of filing a formal complaint. But an open-door policy will encourage employees to bring these issues to your attention—thereby giving you the chance to make improvements (by modifying work responsibilities, adopting that good idea or offering training, for example).

Standard Policy

Our Doors Are Open to You

We want to maintain a positive and pleasant environment for all of our employees. To help us meet this goal, [_Company name_] has an open-door policy, by which employees are encouraged to report work-related concerns.

If something about your job is bothering you, or if you have a question, concern, idea or problem related to your work, please discuss it with your immediate supervisor as soon as possible. If for any reason you don't feel comfortable bringing the matter to your supervisor, feel free to raise the issue with any company officer.

We encourage you to come forward and make your concerns known to the Company. We can't solve the problem if we don't know about it.

Who Needs This Policy

An open-door policy doesn't offer the legal benefit of a complaint policy. But its practical advantages are similar: It helps you learn what's going on in your workplace, encourages communication and promotes good will.

The potential disadvantage of an open-door policy is wasted time: if your workers feel compelled to keep you apprised of their every thought and feeling, you will soon be tempted to close your door—and lock it. However, you can usually deal with this problem effectively through individual counseling—telling the one or two employees who might abuse the policy that you appreciate their enthusiasm, but need for them to use more discretion in deciding which matters are important enough to bring to your attention.

In our opinion, the benefits of having an open-door policy outweigh this potential downside. However, this is a decision you'll have to make for yourself, based on the character of your workforce and the amount of time you and your managers can afford to spend listening to whoever comes through your open doors. ■

Ending Employment

Ending the employment relationship can be difficult for employer and employee alike. As an employer, your goal is to keep your operations running smoothly as employees come and go—and to make sure that any employees you have to fire or lay off don't come back to haunt you with a lawsuit.

If you adopted an at-will policy, discussed in Chapter 2, you have already gone a long way towards accomplishing this second goal. You've warned workers that their employment can be terminated at any time and for any reason. And for those workers who didn't hear it the first time, other policies throughout the handbook we're helping you create will give them fair warning that they can expect to be disciplined or fired for taking part in certain types of prohibited conduct.

Your termination policies serve a slightly different purpose: to tell employees how you will handle the practical concerns that may arise when an employee leaves, such as their severance packages, references and insurance coverage. Explaining these matters up front will help smooth the transition when employees leave: they'll know exactly what to expect and be able to plan accordingly. Termination policies can also help you make sure you've met your legal obligations—to offer health insurance continuation and cut final paychecks on time, for example. By adopting uniform policies and applying them even-handedly when employees leave, you can also avoid claims of unfairness—and the lawsuits that these feelings sometimes fuel.

In this chapter, we cover:

This book doesn't cover lay-offs. In a layoff, an employer generally terminates the employment of a group of employees for reasons related to business productivity—for example, because of economic problems or shifts in the company's direction. When you lay off workers, you are legally required to provide them with a certain amount of notice and, in a few states, severance pay. If you wish to adopt a layoff policy, you'll have to consider a number of factors, such as how you'll choose employees for layoff, what benefits (if any) you'll give laid-off workers, whether laid-off workers are eligible for rehire if circumstances turn around and what procedures you'll use to inform employees of the layoff. Because these issues can get fairly complicated, we advise you to consult with a lawyer if you plan to adopt a layoff policy.

21:1   Final Paychecks

Although no federal law requires employers to pay terminated employees by a particular date, the laws of most states impose fairly tight deadlines for final paychecks. Often, these deadlines vary depending on whether the employee quits or is fired. In some states, including California, Colorado and Nevada, employers must pay a fired employee immediately. Other states allow employers to wait until the next payday.

By adopting a final paycheck policy that includes these deadlines, you'll go a long way towards making sure that your company complies with these laws. And you'll let employees know when they can expect that check—a matter of pressing importance to those who don't have another job lined up right away.

Standard Policy

Final Paychecks

Employees who quit will receive their final paycheck _____ _____. Employees who are terminated involuntarily will receive their final paycheck _____ _____.

Final paychecks will include all compensation earned but not paid through the date of termination.

How to Complete This Policy

This policy includes two blanks for you to complete based on your state's law. The "State Laws That Control Final Paychecks" chart at the end of this chapter lists state law requirements for final paychecks. In the first blank, insert the time limit for paying an employee who is fired (for example, *within two weeks after termination*). In the second, insert the time limit for paying an employee who quits.

Optional Modification to Specify Compensation Included in Final Paycheck

As you'll see from the chart at the end of this chapter, some states require employers to include unused vacation pay in an employee's final check. However, these laws apply only to vacation pay that has already been earned or accrued. For example, if your employees accrue one day of vacation leave per month, and you fire someone who has worked at your company for a year without taking any vacation, that employee would be entitled to 12 additional days of pay in her final paycheck. But an employee who is fired after a couple of months gets only two days of vacation pay, assuming those days haven't been used.

In addition to vacation pay, some employers choose to pay out unused sick leave or personal leave, some portion of a discretionary bonus or other forms of compensation. No law requires you to do this. Employers who follow this route generally do so to maintain a good relationship with the departing employee and the workers who remain, and to create incentives for solid performance. By paying out unused sick time, for example, employers encourage their employees not to take sick leave unless it's absolutely necessary. And paying out a portion of a discretionary bonus encourages employees to do their best right up until their last day of work.

If your state requires you to pay out unused vacation time, or if you wish to pay this or other types of compensation even though it's not legally required, add the sentence below to the end of our sample policy. In the blank space, insert the type of additional compensation you'll pay out (for example, *all unused vacation time that the employee has earned as of the date of termination* or *a pro rata share of any discretionary bonus for which the employee is eligible, based on the length of the employee's employment during the bonus period and the employee's performance*).

Modification

Final paychecks will also include _____

_____ .

21:2   Severance

No law says that employers must give their employers severance pay. Unless you promise severance pay or lead your employees to believe they will receive it, by saying so in a written contract or policy, for example, you are under no obligation to pay severance to terminated employees.

That's all many employers need to know—if it isn't required, they aren't going to pay it. But before you decide to join their ranks, consider the benefits of paying severance. For starters, it helps a fired worker get by until another job comes along—which means that by paying severance, you are sending the message that you care about your workers and want to help out. This can go a long way not only towards building morale in your workforce, but also towards nipping potential lawsuits in the bud. Studies have shown that the way in which employment terminations are handled plays a big role in determining whether a fired employee will sue the employer. Against your eminently sensible desire not to pay out money unnecessarily, you will have to weigh these very tangible benefits.

Your severance policy should let employees know whether and under what circumstances you offer severance pay. If you choose to offer severance, your policy should tell employees who is eligible and how severance pay will be calculated.

We offer you several alternative policies below. Sample Policy A is a simple no-severance policy. Sample Policy B is a policy to pay severance at the employer's discretion. And Sample Policy C is a severance policy with eligibility requirements and a formula for determining severance pay.

Standard Policy A

No Severance Pay

Our Company does not pay severance to terminated employees, whether they quit, are laid off or are fired for any reason.

Standard Policy B

Severance Pay Is Discretionary

Generally, [_Company name_] does not pay severance to terminated employees, whether they quit, are laid off or are fired for any reason. However, we reserve the right to pay severance to a terminated employee. Decisions about severance pay will be made on a case-by-case basis, and are entirely within the discretion of the Company. No employee has a right to severance pay and you should not expect to receive it.

Standard Policy C

Severance Pay

Employees may be eligible for severance pay upon the termination of their employment. Employees must meet all of the following criteria to be eligible:

- You must have worked for the Company for at least one year prior to your termination
- You must not have quit or resigned, and
- Your employment must have been terminated for reasons other than misconduct or violation of company rules.

Eligible employees will receive _____ of severance pay for every full year of employment with [_Company name_].

Severance plans can be tricky. If you plan to adopt a policy to pay severance, according to a formula or other criteria, ask a lawyer to review it for you—and to let you know whether you have to follow the requirements of a federal law called ERISA (the Employees Retirement Income Savings Act, 29 U.S.C. § 1001 and following). This highly technical law imposes a number of requirements on employers who provide certain types of benefit plans to their employees. Severance plans may or may not be subject to these requirements, depending on the plan's features and the way courts in your state have interpreted the law.

How to Complete This Policy

If you adopt Sample Policy C, simply fill in the blank with the amount of severance you plan to offer—most employers offer one or two weeks of pay, at the employee's current rate, for every year of work. You can do the same by inserting _one week_ or _two weeks_ in the blank.

21:3   Insurance Continuation

If you offer your employees health insurance coverage under a group health plan, you may be required to offer them continued coverage under the circumstances outlined in the sample policy below. A federal law called the Consolidated Omnibus Budget Reconciliation Act (or COBRA for short) mandates that employees who quit, suffer a reduction in hours or are fired for reasons other than serious misconduct, are entitled to choose to continue on the employer's group health care plan for 18 months. However, the employees must pay the full premium. COBRA applies only to employers with 20 or more employees.

Many states also have their own health insurance continuation laws. These laws generally apply to smaller employers. Some echo most of COBRA's provisions; others provide for shorter periods of insurance continuation and/or place limits on the types of benefits that must be provided. You'll find a chart of these state laws ("State Health Insurance Continuation Laws") below.

Your insurance continuation policy should tell employees:

- whether, and under what circumstances, they will be able to continue their insurance coverage after termination
- how long the continued coverage will last, and
- who will pay for coverage.

Standard Policy

Continuing Your Health Insurance Coverage

___[Company name]___ offers employees group health insurance coverage as a benefit of employment. If you are no longer eligible for insurance coverage because of a reduction in hours, because you quit or because you are fired for reasons other than serious misconduct, you have the right to continue your health insurance coverage for up to _____. You will have to pay the cost of this coverage.

Others covered by your insurance (your spouse and children, for example) also have the right to continue coverage if they are no longer eligible for certain reasons. If you and your spouse divorce or legally separate, or if you die while in our employ, your spouse may continue coverage under our group health plan. And once your children lose their dependent status, they may continue their healthcare as well. In any of these situations, your family members are entitled to up to _____ of continued healthcare. They must pay the cost of this coverage.

You will receive an initial notice of your right to continued health insurance coverage when you first become eligible for health insurance under the Company's group plan. You will receive an additional notice when your hours are reduced, you quit or are fired. This second notice will tell you how to choose continuation coverage, what your obligations will be and how much the insurance will cost. You must notify us if any of your family members becomes eligible for continued coverage due to divorce, separation or reaching the age of majority.

How to Complete This Policy

In the blanks in this policy, insert the length of time for which employees and their dependents can continue their health insurance coverage. If you are covered by COBRA, employees are entitled to continue their coverage for 18 months (insert this in the first blank), and dependents for 36 months (this goes in the second blank).

Smaller employers that are not covered by COBRA may nevertheless have to comply with a state insurance continuation law. Some of these laws also provide for 18 and 36 months of coverage; others provide for shorter periods of coverage. Consult the "State Health Insurance Continuation Laws" chart, at the end of this chapter, to find out what your state requires.

Who Needs This Policy

If you are not covered by COBRA or a similar state law, or you don't offer health insurance coverage to your employees (see Chapter 8 for information on benefits policies), leave this policy out of your handbook. However, if you are covered by COBRA or a state health insurance continuation law, this policy can alleviate a lot of anxiety for your workers. One of the first questions a newly terminated employee is likely to ask is, "What about my health insurance?" As the costs of medical care skyrocket, many employees can't afford to go without insurance until they find another job—and even if they line up new work quickly, their new employer might not offer insurance coverage or there may be a waiting period before coverage begins. By adopting a health insurance continuation policy, you can let your employees know, right up front, that they won't have to worry about insurance coverage, as long as they are able to pay for it.

Optional Modification to Add Eligibility Requirements

Some states require employers to offer continued coverage only to certain employees. Most commonly, employees are eligible only if they have worked for the employer, and been covered by the employer's health insurance plan, for at least three months. If you are not covered by COBRA (which protects all employees who are covered by the employer's plan), but you are covered by a state health insurance continuation law that protects only certain employees, modify our policy by adding the following language after the first sentence. In the blank, insert your state's eligibility requirements (for example, *have been covered continuously under our insurance policy for at least three months* or *work at least 25 hours a week*.)

Modification

Only employees who _____
_____ are entitled to continue their health insurance coverage under this policy.

21:4   Exit Interviews

Exit interviews are a great way to learn valuable information about your workplace—and to defuse the tension of an involuntary termination. Your former employees can give you the lowdown on dozens of issues, from workplace morale and teamwork to how well (or poorly) your managers and supervisors are doing their jobs. An employee on the way out the door is more likely to be candid in offering opinions—maybe brutally so. Although you should certainly take these parting comments with a healthy dose of salt, you may get some helpful information about how your company is perceived by its workers—and what you can do to improve.

When you interview an employee who quits, try to find out why that employee is moving on: Did your company fail to offer opportunities to advance? Are your pay scales in line with those of other businesses in your industry? Are there problems in your company that you don't know about?

It can be equally valuable to interview fired employees, although for a slightly different reason. You'll have to expect that these employees are somewhat upset about losing their jobs—and they may have a long list of negative comments about the company as a result. But they will have a chance to air these complaints during the interview, which allows you to demonstrate that you understand and take seriously their concerns. If a fired employee feels that the company "gets it," that employee is less likely to seek a courtroom forum for his or her grievances. Adopting an exit interview policy tells these employees that there will be a time and a place when their voices can be heard.

Your exit interview policy should let employees know that you will conduct such interviews for all departing employees, what the interview will cover and procedures for returning company property.

Standard Policy

Exit Interviews

We will hold an exit interview with every employee who leaves the Company, for any reason. During the interview, you will have the opportunity to tell us about your employment experience here— what you liked, what you didn't like and where you think we can improve. We greatly value these comments.

The exit interview also gives us a chance to handle some practical matters relating to the end of your employment. You will be expected to return all Company property at the interview. You will also have an opportunity to ask any questions you might have about insurance, benefits, final paychecks, references or any other matter relating to your employment.

Optional Modification to Make Exit Interview Optional

Some employers hold exit interviews only if the departing employee wants one. Such a policy has the benefit of drastically reducing the time you spend conducting these interviews—very few employees, other than those with a large axe to grind, will bother to take the time to share their opinions with you on the way out the door. The corresponding drawback is that you won't be able to gather as much valuable information about your company, because you'll probably only be hearing from those whose employment experience was negative.

If you decide to make exit interviews optional, replace the first paragraph of the sample policy with the following paragraph, then delete the first two sentences of the second paragraph. Remember that you'll have to make other arrangements to collect company property.

Modification

We will hold an exit interview with every departing employee who requests one. We strongly encourage employees to schedule exit interviews. During the interview, you will have the opportunity to tell us about your employment experience here—what you liked, what you didn't like and where you think we can improve. We greatly value these comments.

21:5   References

Reference requests are fraught with legal and practical dangers for employers. If you criticize a former employee unduly, or unfairly prevent that employee from getting a job, you risk a lawsuit for defamation or blacklisting. If you give a reference that is too positive for an employee whom you know to be dangerous or grossly unqualified, you risk legal trouble from the new employer if the truth comes out. Given these risks, many employers choose to take a "name, rank and serial number" approach, giving prospective new employers only the ex-employees' dates of employment, titles and salary.

If you decide to go this route, Sample Policy A—a minimal reference policy to confirm dates of employment, salary and positions held—will work for you. But before you make up your mind, consider the purpose of a reference. Former employees count on them to find new work—and the sooner a fired employee finds new work, the less likely you are to face a wrongful termination claim. Employers use them to figure out whom to hire and to read between the lines of carefully prepared resumes and interview responses. Both of these tasks are made a lot tougher if you adopt a minimal reference approach.

You can give an informative reference without undue risk of legal trouble if you insist on a written release from the employee, giving you permission to talk to a prospective employer. And you can further protect yourself by insisting on written reference requests, and responding to them only in writing. This way, you have a clear record of exactly what you said if anyone accuses you later of a false statement. And you can take the time to craft a careful response. Sample Policy B adopts this approach.

Standard Policy A

Reference Policy

When we are contacted by prospective employers seeking information about former employees, we will release the following data only: the position(s) the employee held, the dates the employee worked for our Company and the employee's salary or rate of pay.

Standard Policy B

Reference Policy

When we are contacted by prospective employers seeking information about former employees, we will release the following data only: the position(s) the employee held, the dates the employee worked for our Company and the employee's salary or rate of pay.

If you would like us to give a more detailed reference, you will have to provide us with a written release—a consent form giving us your permission to respond to a reference request. We will respond only to written reference requests, and we will respond only in writing. Please direct all reference requests to _____ _____.

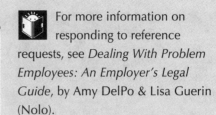 For more information on responding to reference requests, see *Dealing With Problem Employees: An Employer's Legal Guide*, by Amy DelPo & Lisa Guerin (Nolo).

State Laws That Control Final Paychecks

State	Paycheck due when employee is fired	Paycheck due when employee quits	Unused vacation pay included	Special employment situations
Note: The states of Alabama, Florida, Georgia, Mississippi and Ohio are not included in this chart because they do not have laws specifically controlling final paychecks. Contract your state department of labor for more information (see Appendix C for contact list.				
Alaska Alaska Stat. § 23.05.140(b)	Within 3 working days.	Next regular payday at least 3 days after employee gives notice.	Yes.	
Arizona Ariz. Rev. Stat. § 23-353	Next payday or within 3 working days, whichever is sooner.	Next payday.	Yes.	
Arkansas Ark. Code Ann. § 11-4-405(b)	Within 7 days from discharge date.	No provision.	No.	Railroad or railroad construction: day of discharge.
California Cal. Lab. Code §§ 201 to 202, 227.3	Immediately.	Immediately if employee has given 72 hours notice; otherwise, within 72 hours.	Yes.	Motion picture business: if fired, within 24 hours (excluding weekends & holidays); if laid off, next payday. Oil drilling industry: within 24 hours (excluding weekends & holidays) of termination. Seasonal agricultural workers: within 72 hours of termination.
Colorado Colo. Rev. Stat. § 8-4-104	Immediately. (Within 6 hours of start of next workday, if payroll unit is closed; 24 hours if unit is offsite.) Employer decides check delivery.	Next payday.	Yes.	
Connecticut Conn. Gen. Stat. Ann. § 31-71c	Next business day after discharge.	Next payday.	No.	
Delaware Del. Code Ann. tit. 19, § 1103	Next payday.	Next payday.	No.	
District of Columbia D.C. Code Ann. § 32-1303	Next business day.	Next payday or 7 days after quitting, whichever is sooner.	Yes, unless there is express contrary policy.	
Hawaii Haw. Rev. Stat. § 388-3	Immediately.	Next payday or immediately, if employee gives one pay period's notice.	No.	
Idaho Idaho Code §§ 45-606; 45-617	Next payday or within 10 days (excluding weekends & holidays), whichever is sooner. If employee makes written request for earlier payment, within 48 hours of receipt of request (excluding weekends & holidays).	Next payday or within 10 days (excluding weekends & holidays), whichever is sooner. If employee makes written request for earlier payment, within 48 hours of receipt of request (excluding weekends & holidays).	Yes.	

State Laws That Control Final Paychecks (continued)				
State	Paycheck due when employee is fired	Paycheck due when employee quits	Unused vacation pay included	Special employment situations
Illinois 820 Ill. Comp. Stat. § 115/5	At time of separation if possible, but no later than next payday.	At time of separation if possible, but no later than next payday.	Yes.	
Indiana Ind. Code Ann. §§ 22-2-5-1, 22-2-9-2	Next payday.	Next payday. (If employee has not left address, 10 days after employee demands wages or provides address where check may be mailed.)	No.	
Iowa Iowa Code §§ 91A.4, 91A.2(7.b.)	Next payday.	Next payday.	Yes.	If employee is owed commission, employer has 30 days to pay.
Kansas Kan. Stat. Ann. § 44-315	Next payday.	Next payday.	No.	
Kentucky Ky. Rev. Stat. Ann. §§ 337.010(c), 337.055	Next payday or 14 days, whichever is later.	Next payday or 14 days, whichever is later.	Yes.	
Louisiana La. Rev. Stat. Ann. § 23:631	Next payday or within 15 days, whichever is earlier.	Next payday or within 15 days, whichever is earlier.	Yes.	
Maine Me. Rev. Stat. Ann. tit. 26, § 626	Next payday or within 2 weeks of requesting final pay, whichever is sooner.	Next payday or within 2 weeks of requesting final pay, whichever is sooner.	Yes.	
Maryland Md. Code Ann., [Lab. & Empl.] § 3-505	Next scheduled payday.	Next scheduled payday.	No.	
Massachusetts Mass. Gen. Laws ch. 149, § 148	Day of discharge.	Next payday. If no scheduled payday, then following Saturday.	Yes.	
Michigan Mich. Comp. Laws §§ 408.474 to 408.475; Mich. Admin. Code R. 408.9007	Next payday.	Next payday.	Yes.	Hand-harvesters of crops: within one working day of termination.
Minnesota Minn. Stat. Ann. §§ 181.13 to 181.14	Immediately, but no later than 24 hours after employee demands wages.	Next payday. If payday is less than 5 days from last day of work, then following payday or 20 days from last day of work, whichever is earlier.	Yes.	Migrant agricultural workers who resign: within 5 days.
Missouri Mo. Rev. Stat. § 290.110	Day of discharge.	No provision.	No.	

			State Laws That Control Final Paychecks (continued)	
State	Paycheck due when employee is fired	Paycheck due when employee quits	Unused vacation pay included	Special employment situations
Montana Mont. Code Ann. § 39-3-205	Immediately if fired for cause or laid off, (unless there is a written policy extending time to earlier of next payday or 15 days).	Next payday or within 15 days, whichever comes first.	No.	
Nebraska Neb. Rev. Stat. §§ 48-1229 to 48-1230	Next payday or within 2 weeks, whichever is sooner.	No provision.	Yes.	
Nevada Nev. Rev. Stat. Ann. §§ 608.020 to 608.030	Immediately.	Next payday or 7 days, whichever is earlier.	No.	
New Hampshire N.H. Rev. Stat. Ann. §§ 275:43(III), 275:44	Within 72 hours. If laid off, next payday.	Next payday, or within 72 hours if employee gives one pay period's notice.	Yes.	
New Jersey N.J. Stat. Ann. § 34: 11-4.3	Next payday.	Next payday.	No.	
New Mexico N.M. Stat. Ann. §§ 50-4-4 to 50-4-5	Within 5 days.	Next payday.	No.	If paid by task or commission, 10 days after discharge.
New York N.Y. Lab. Law §§ 191(3), 198-c(2)	Next payday.	Next payday.	Yes.	
North Carolina N.C. Gen. Stat. §§ 95-25.7, 95-25.12	Next payday.	Next payday.	Yes.	If paid by commission or bonus, on next payday after amount calculated.
North Dakota N.D. Cent. Code § 34-14-03; N.D. Admin. Code R. 46-02-07-02(12)	Next payday. Must pay by certified mail or as agreed upon by both parties.	Next payday.	No.	
Oklahoma Okla. Stat. Ann. tit. 40, §§ 165.1(4), 165.3	Next payday.	Next payday.	Yes.	
Oregon Or. Rev. Stat. §§ 652.140, 652.145	End of first business day after termination.	Immediately, with 48 hours notice (excluding weekends & holidays). Without notice, within 5 days (excluding weekends & holidays) or next payday, whichever comes first.	No.	Seasonal farm workers: fired or quitting with 48 hours notice, immediately; quitting without notice, within 48 hours or next payday, whichever comes first.

	State Laws That Control Final Paychecks (continued)			
State	**Paycheck due when employee is fired**	**Paycheck due when employee quits**	**Unused vacation pay included**	**Special employment situations**
Pennsylvania 43 Pa. Cons. Stat. Ann. § 260.5	Next payday.	Next payday.	No.	
Rhode Island R.I. Gen. Laws § 28-14-4	Next payday.	Next payday.	Yes, if employee has worked for one full year.	
South Carolina S.C. Code Ann. §§ 41-10-10(2), 41-10-50	Within 48 hours or next payday, but not more than 30 days.	Within 48 hours or next payday, but not more than 30 days.	No.	
South Dakota S.D. Codified Laws Ann. §§ 60-11-10 to 60-11-14	Next payday (or until employee returns employer's property).	Next payday (or until employee returns employer's property).	No.	
Tennessee Tenn. Code Ann. § 50-2-103	Next payday or 21 days, whichever is later.	Next payday or 21 days, whichever is later.	Yes.	Applies to employers with 5 or more employees.
Texas Tex. Lab. Code Ann. § 61.014	Within 6 days.	Next payday.	No.	
Utah Utah Code Ann. §§ 34-28-2, 34-28-5	Within 24 hours.	Next payday.	No.	
Vermont Vt. Stat. Ann. tit. 21, § 342(c)(1)	Within 72 hours.	Next regular payday or next Friday, if there is no regular payday.	No.	
Virginia Va. Code Ann. § 40.1-29(A.1)	Next payday.	Next payday.	No.	
Washington Wash. Rev. Code Ann. § 49.48.010	Next payday.	Next payday.	No.	
West Virginia W.Va. Code §§ 21-5-1, 21-5-4	Within 72 hours.	Immediately if employee has given one pay period's notice; otherwise, next payday.	Yes.	
Wisconsin Wis. Stat. Ann. §§ 109.01(3), 109.03	Next payday. If termination is due to merger, relocation or liquidation of business, within 24 hours.	Next payday.	No.	Does not apply to sales agents working on commission basis.
Wyoming Wyo. Stat. Ann. § 27-4-104	5 working days.	5 working days.	No.	

Note: Alabama, Florida, Georgia, Mississippi and Ohio have no laws concerning final paychecks.

Current as of February 2003

State Health Insurance Continuation Laws

Note: The states of Alaska, Delaware and Idaho are not included in this chart because they do not have laws specifically controlling health insurance continuation. Check your state department of labor if you need more information (See Appendix C for contact list).

Alabama

Ala. Code § 27-55-3 (4)

No general continuation laws, but subjects of domestic abuse, who have lost coverage under abuser's plan and who do not qualify for COBRA, may have 18 months coverage (applies to all employers).

Arizona

Ariz. Rev. Stat. Ann. §§ 20-1377, 20-1408

Employers affected: All employers who offer group health and disability insurance.

Qualifying event: Death of employee; change in marital status.

Length of coverage for dependents: May convert to individual policy upon death of covered employee or divorce or legal separation. Coverage must be the same unless the insured chooses a lesser plan. (Insurer may offer group insurance as long as there is no change in coverage.)

Time employer has to notify employee of continuation rights: No provisions for employer. Insurance policy must include notice of conversion privilege. Clerk of court must provide notice to anyone filing for divorce that dependent spouse is entitled to convert health insurance coverage.

Time employee has to apply: 31 days after termination of existing coverage.

Special benefits: Applies to blanket accident and sickness insurance policies and to all disability insurance issued by hospital, medical, dental and optometric service corporations, healthcare services organizations and fraternal benefit societies.

Arkansas

Ark. Code Ann. §§ 23-86-114 to 23-86-116

Employers affected: All employers who offer group health insurance.

Eligible employees: Employees continuously insured for previous 3 months.

Qualifying event: Termination of employment; death of employee; change in marital status.

Length of coverage for employee: 120 days.

Length of coverage for dependents: 120 days.

Time employee has to apply: 10 days.

Special benefits: Excludes: dental care; prescription drugs; vision services.

California

Cal. Health & Safety Code §§ 1373.6, 1373.621; Cal. Ins. Code §§ 10128.50 to 10128.59

Employers affected: Employers with 2 to 19 employees.

Eligible employees: Employees continuously insured for previous 3 months.

Qualifying event: Termination of employment; reduction in hours.

Length of coverage for employee: 18 months; 29 months if disabled at termination or during first 60 days of continuation coverage. (Employee also has choice of converting to an individual insurance plan.)

Length of coverage for dependents: 18 months; 29 months if disabled at termination or during first 60 days of continuation coverage; 36 months upon death of employee, divorce or legal separation, loss of dependent status, employee's eligibility for Medicare. (Dependents also have choice of converting to an individual insurance plan.)

Time employer has to notify employee of continuation rights: 15 days.

Time employee has to apply: 31 days after group plan ends; 30 days after COBRA or Cal-COBRA ends (63 days if converting to an individual plan).

Special benefits: Includes vision and dental benefits (if the employer offers them).

Special situations: Employee who is 60 or older and has worked for employer for previous 5 years may continue benefits for self and spouse beyond COBRA or Cal-COBRA limits (also applies to COBRA employers). Beginning 9/1/03, any employee who began receiving COBRA coverage on or after 1/1/03 and whose coverage is for less than 36 months, is entitled to additional continuation coverage to total 36 months.

Colorado

Colo. Rev. Stat. § 10-16-108

Employers affected: All employers who offer group health insurance.

Eligible employees: Employees continuously insured for previous 3 months. (If eligible due to reduction in hours,

State Health Insurance Continuation Laws (continued)

must have been continuously insured for previous 6 months.)

Qualifying event: Termination of employment; reduction in hours; death of employee; change in marital status.

Length of coverage for employee: 18 months.

Length of coverage for dependents: 18 months.

Time employer has to notify employee of continuation rights: Within 10 days of termination of coverage.

Time employee has to apply: 31 days after termination of coverage.

Special benefits: Excludes: specific diseases; accidental injuries.

Connecticut

Conn. Gen. Stat. Ann. §§ 38a-538, 38a-554; § 31-51o

Employers affected: All employers who offer group health insurance.

Eligible employees: Employees continuously insured for previous 3 months.

Qualifying event: Layoff; reduction in hours; termination of employment; death of employee; change in marital status.

Length of coverage for employee: 18 months.

Length of coverage for dependents: 18 months; 36 months in case of employee's death or divorce.

Time employer has to notify employee of continuation rights: 14 days.

Time employee has to apply: 60 days.

Special benefits: Excludes: specific diseases; accidental injuries.

Special situations: When facility closes or relocates, employer must pay for insurance for employee and dependents for 120 days or until employee is eligible for other group coverage, whichever comes first. (Does not affect employee's right to regular continuation coverage which begins when 120-day period ends.)

District of Columbia

D.C. Code Ann. §§ 32-731 to 32-732

Employers affected: Employers with fewer than 20 employees.

Eligible employees: All insured employees are eligible.

Qualifying event: Any reason employee or dependent becomes ineligible for coverage.

Length of coverage for employee: 3 months.

Length of coverage for dependents: 3 months.

Time employer has to notify employee of continuation rights: Within 15 days of termination of coverage.

Time employee has to apply: 45 days after termination of coverage.

Special benefits: Excludes: dental or vision only insurance.

Florida

Fla. Stat. Ann. § 627.6692

Employers affected: Employers with fewer than 20 employees.

Eligible employees: Full-time (25 or more hours per week) employees covered by employer's health insurance plan.

Qualifying event: Layoff; reduction in hours; termination of employment; death of employee; change in marital status.

Length of coverage for employee: 18 months.

Length of coverage for dependents: 18 months.

Time employer has to notify employee of continuation rights: Carrier notifies employee within 14 days of learning of qualifying event (employer is responsible for notifying carrier).

Time employee has to apply: 30 days from receipt of carrier's notice.

Georgia

Ga. Code Ann. §§ 33-24-21.1 to 33-24-21.2

Employers affected: All employers who offer group health insurance.

Eligible employees: Employees continuously insured for previous 6 months.

Qualifying event: Termination of employment (except for cause).

Length of coverage for employee: 3 months plus any part of the month remaining at termination.

Length of coverage for dependents: 3 months plus any part of the month remaining at termination.

Special situations: Employee, spouse or former spouse, who is 60 or older and who has been covered for previous 6 months may continue coverage until eligible for Medicare. (Applies to companies with more than 20 employees; does not apply when employee quits for reasons other than health.)

Hawaii

Haw. Rev. Stat. § 393-15

Employers affected: All employers required to offer health insurance (those paying a regular employee a monthly

State Health Insurance Continuation Laws (continued)

wage at least 86.67 times the state hourly minimum wage—about $542).

Qualifying event: Employee is hospitalized or prevented by sickness from working.

Length of coverage for employee: Employer must pay insurance premiums for 3 months or for as long employer continues to pay employee's wages, whichever is longer.

Illinois

215 Ill. Comp. Stat. §§ 5/367e, 5/367.2

Employers affected: All employers who offer group health insurance.

Eligible employees: Employees continuously insured for previous 3 months.

Qualifying event: Termination of employment.

Length of coverage for employee: 9 months.

Length of coverage for dependents: 9 months.

Time employee has to apply: 10 days after termination or receiving notice from employer, whichever is later, but not more than 60 days from termination.

Special benefits: Excludes: dental care; prescription drugs; vision services; disability income; specified diseases.

Special situations: Upon death or divorce, 2 years coverage for spouse under 55; until eligible for Medicare or other group coverage for spouse over 55.

Indiana

Ind. Code Ann. § 27-8-15-31.1

Employers affected: Employers with 2 to 50 employees.

Eligible employees: Employed by same employer for at least one year and continuously insured for previous 90 days.

Qualifying event: Termination of employment; reduction in hours; dissolution of marriage; loss of dependent status.

Length of coverage for employee: 12 months.

Length of coverage for dependents: 12 months.

Time employer has to notify employee of continuation rights: 10 days after employee becomes eligible for continuation coverage.

Time employee has to apply: Must apply directly to insurer within 30 days after becoming eligible for continuation coverage.

Iowa

Iowa Code §§ 509B.3 to 509B.5

Employers affected: All employers who offer group health insurance.

Eligible employees: Employees continuously insured for previous 3 months.

Qualifying event: Any reason employee or dependent becomes ineligible for coverage.

Length of coverage for employee: 9 months.

Length of coverage for dependents: 9 months.

Time employer has to notify employee of continuation rights: 10 days after termination of coverage.

Time employee has to apply: 10 days after termination of coverage or receiving notice of continuation rights from employer, whichever is later, but no more than 31 days from termination of coverage.

Special benefits: Excludes: dental care; prescription drugs; vision services.

Kansas

Kan. Stat. Ann. § 40-2209(i)

Employers affected: All employers who offer group health insurance.

Eligible employees: Employees continuously insured for previous 3 months.

Qualifying event: Any reason employee or dependent becomes ineligible for coverage.

Length of coverage for employee: 6 months.

Length of coverage for dependents: 6 months.

Time employee has to apply: 31 days from termination of coverage.

Kentucky

Ky. Rev. Stat. Ann. § 304.18-110

Employers affected: All employers who offer group health insurance.

Eligible employees: Employees continuously insured for previous 3 months.

Qualifying event: Any reason employee or dependent becomes ineligible for coverage.

Length of coverage for employee: 18 months.

Length of coverage for dependents: 18 months.

Time employer has to notify employee of continuation rights: Employer must notify insurer as soon as employee's coverage ends; insurer then notifies employee.

State Health Insurance Continuation Laws (continued)

Time employee has to apply: 31 days from receipt of insurer's notice.

Special benefits: Excludes: specific diseases; accidental injury.

Louisiana

La. Rev. Stat. Ann. §§ 22:215.7, 22:215.13

Employers affected: All employers who offer group health insurance.

Eligible employees: Employees continuously insured for previous 3 months.

Qualifying event: Termination of employment.

Length of coverage for employee: 12 months.

Length of coverage for dependents: 12 months.

Time employee has to apply: Must apply and submit payment before group coverage ends.

Special benefits: Excludes: dental care; vision care; specific diseases; accidental injury.

Special situations: Surviving spouse who is 50 or older may have coverage until remarriage or eligibility for Medicare or other insurance.

Maine

Me. Rev. Stat. Ann. tit. 24-A, § 2809-A

Employers affected: All employers who offer group health insurance.

Eligible employees: Employees continuously insured for previous 3 months.

Qualifying event: Termination of employment.

Length of coverage for employee: One year (either group or individual coverage at discretion of insurer).

Length of coverage for dependents: One year (either group or individual coverage at discretion of insurer). Upon death of insured, continuation only if original plan provided for coverage.

Time employee has to apply: 90 days from termination of group coverage.

Special situations: Temporary layoff or work-related injury or disease: Employee and dependents entitled to one year group or individual continuation coverage. (Must have been continuously insured for previous 6 months; must apply within 31 days.)

Maryland

Md. Code Ann., [Ins.] §§ 15-407 to 15-410

Employers affected: All employers who offer group health insurance.

Eligible employees: Employees continuously insured for previous 3 months.

Qualifying event: Involuntary termination of employment; death of employee; change in marital status.

Length of coverage for employee: 18 months.

Length of coverage for dependents: 18 months upon death of employee; upon change in marital status, 18 months or until spouse remarries or becomes eligible for other coverage.

Time employer has to notify employee of continuation rights: Must notify insurer within 14 days of receiving employee's request.

Time employee has to apply: 45 days from termination of coverage. Employee begins application process by requesting an election of continuation notification form from employer.

Massachusetts

Mass. Gen. Laws ch. 175, §§ 110G, 110I; ch. 176J, § 9

Employers affected: All employers who offer group health insurance.; special rules for employers with Small Group Health Insurance (2 to 19 employees).

Eligible employees: All insured employees are eligible.

Qualifying event: Involuntary layoff; death of insured employee. For Small Group Health Insurance employer add: reduction in hours; divorce or legal separation; loss of dependent status; employee's eligibility for Medicare; employer's bankruptcy.

Length of coverage for employee: 39 weeks (but may not exceed time covered under original coverage).

   Small Group Health Insurance employer: 18 months. (29 months if disabled.)

Length of coverage for dependents: 39 weeks. (Divorced or separated spouse entitled to benefits only if included in judgment decree.)

   Small Group Health Insurance employer: 18 months upon termination or reduction in hours; 29 months if disabled; 36 months on divorce, death of employee, employee's eligibility for Medicare, employer's bankruptcy.

Time employer has to notify employee of continuation rights: When employee becomes eligible for continuation benefits.

Time employee has to apply: 30 days. Small Group Health Insurance employer, 60 days.

State Health Insurance Continuation Laws (continued)

Special situations: Termination due to plant closing: 90 days coverage for employee and dependents, at the same payment terms as before closing.

Michigan

Mich. Comp. Laws § 500.3612

Employers affected: All employers offering group health and disability insurance.

Eligible employees: Employees continuously insured for 3 months.

Qualifying event: Termination of group coverage for any reason except discharge for gross misconduct.

Length of coverage for employee: Eligible employee and dependents may convert to an individual policy without evidence of insurability or regard for preexisting condition.

Time employer has to notify employee of continuation rights: Within 14 days of termination of coverage.

Time employee has to apply: No later than 30 days from termination of coverage.

Minnesota

Minn. Stat. Ann. § 62A.17

Employers affected: All employers who offer group health insurance.

Eligible employees: All insured employees are eligible.

Qualifying event: Termination of employment; reduction in hours.

Length of coverage for employee: 18 months.

Length of coverage for dependents: 18 months.

Time employer has to notify employee of continuation rights: Within 10 days of termination of coverage.

Time employee has to apply: 60 days from termination of coverage or receipt of employer's notice, whichever is later.

Mississippi

Miss. Code Ann. § 83-9-51

Employers affected: All employers who offer group health insurance.

Eligible employees: Employees continuously insured for previous 3 months.

Qualifying event: Termination of employment; divorce; employee's death; employee's eligibility for Medicare; loss of dependent status.

Length of coverage for employee: 12 months.

Length of coverage for dependents: 12 months.

Time employer has to notify employee of continuation rights: Insurer must notify former or deceased employee's dependent child or divorced spouse of option to continue insurance within 14 days of their becoming ineligible for coverage on employee's policy.

Time employee has to apply: Employee must apply and submit payment before group coverage ends; dependents or former spouse must elect continuation coverage within 30 days of receiving insurer's notice.

Special benefits: Excludes: dental and vision care; any benefits other than hospital, surgical or major medical.

Missouri

Mo. Rev. Stat. § 376.428

Employers affected: All employers who offer group health insurance.

Eligible employees: Employees continuously insured for previous 3 months.

Qualifying event: Termination of employment.

Length of coverage for employee: 9 months.

Length of coverage for dependents: 9 months.

Time employer has to notify employee of continuation rights: No later than date group coverage would end.

Time employee has to apply: 31 days from date group coverage would end.

Special benefits: Excludes: dental and vision care; any benefits other than hospital, surgical or major medical. Must include: maternity benefits if they were provided under group policy.

Montana

Mont. Code Ann. §§ 33-22-506 to 33-22-510

Employers affected: All employers who offer group health insurance.

Eligible employees: Employees continuously insured for previous 3 months.

Qualifying event: Reduction in hours.

Length of coverage for employee: One year. Upon reduction in hours (with employer's consent).

Length of coverage for dependents: One year. Upon reduction in hours (with employer's consent).

Time employee has to apply: 31 days from date group coverage would end.

State Health Insurance Continuation Laws (continued)

Special situations: Insurer may not discontinue benefits to child with disabilities after child exceeds age limit for dependent status.

Nebraska

Neb. Rev. Stat. §§ 44-1640 and following, 44-7406

Employers affected: Employers not subject to federal COBRA laws.

Eligible employees: All insured employees are eligible.

Qualifying event: Involuntary termination of employment (layoff due to labor dispute not considered involuntary).

Length of coverage for employee: 6 months.

Length of coverage for dependents: One year upon death of insured employee.

Time employer has to notify employee of continuation rights: Within 10 days of termination of employment must send notice by certified mail.

Time employee has to apply: 10 days from receipt of employer's notice.

Special situations: Subjects of domestic abuse, who have lost coverage under abuser's plan and who do not qualify for COBRA, may have 18 months coverage (applies to all employers).

Nevada

Nev. Rev. Stat. Ann. §§ 689B.245 and following; 689B.0345

Employers affected: Employers with less than 20 employees.

Eligible employees: Employees continuously insured for previous 12 months.

Qualifying event: Involuntary termination of employment; involuntary reduction in hours; death of employee; divorce or legal separation; loss of dependent status; employee's eligibility for Medicare.

Length of coverage for employee: 18 months.

Length of coverage for dependents: 36 months.

Time employer has to notify employee of continuation rights: 14 days after receiving notice of employee's eligibility.

Time employee has to apply: Must notify employer within 60 days of becoming eligible for continuation coverage; must apply within 60 days after receiving employer's notice.

Special situations: Leave without pay due to disability: 12 months for employee and dependents (applies to all employers).

New Hampshire

N.H. Rev. Stat. Ann. § 415:18(VIIg), (VII-a)

Employers affected: Employers with 2 to 19 employees.

Eligible employees: All insured employees are eligible.

Qualifying event: Any reason employee or dependent becomes ineligible for coverage.

Length of coverage for employee: 18 months; 29 months if disabled at termination or during first 60 days of continuation coverage.

Length of coverage for dependents: 18 months; 29 months if disabled at termination or during first 60 days of continuation coverage; 36 months upon death of employee, divorce or legal separation, loss of dependent status, employee's eligibility for Medicare.

Time employer has to notify employee of continuation rights: Within 15 days of termination of coverage.

Time employee has to apply: Within 31 days of termination of coverage.

Special benefits: Includes dental insurance.

Special situations: Layoff or termination due to strike: 6 months coverage with option to extend for an additional 12 months. Surviving, divorced or legally separated spouse who is 55 or older may continue benefits until eligible for Medicare or other employer-based group insurance.

New Jersey

N.J. Stat. Ann. §§ 17B:27-30, 17B:27-51.12, 17B:27A-27

Employers affected: Employers with 2 to 50 employees.

Eligible employees: Employed full-time (25 or more hours).

Qualifying event: Termination of employment; reduction in hours.

Length of coverage for employee: 12 months.

Length of coverage for dependents: 180 days upon death of employee (applies to all employers).

Time employer has to notify employee of continuation rights: At time of qualifying event employer or carrier notifies employee.

Time employee has to apply: Within 30 days of qualifying event.

Special benefits: Coverage must be identical to that offered to current employees.

Special situations: Total disability: Employee who has been insured for previous 3 months and employee's dependents

State Health Insurance Continuation Laws (continued)

entitled to continuation coverage that includes all benefits offered by group policy (applies to all employers).

New Mexico

N.M. Stat. Ann. § 59A-18-16

Employers affected: All employers who offer group health insurance.

Eligible employees: All insured employees are eligible.

Qualifying event: Termination of employment.

Length of coverage for employee: 6 months.

Length of coverage for dependents: May continue group coverage or convert to individual policy upon death of employee, divorce or legal separation

Time employer has to notify employee of continuation rights: Must give written notice at time of termination.

Time employee has to apply: 30 days after receiving employer's or insurer's notice.

New York

N.Y. Ins. Law §§ 3221(f), 3221(m)

Employers affected: All employers who offer group health insurance.

Eligible employees: All insured employees are eligible.

Qualifying event: Termination of employment; death of employee; divorce or legal separation; loss of dependent status; employee's eligibility for Medicare.

Length of coverage for employee: 18 months; 29 months if disabled at termination or during first 60 days of continuation coverage.

Length of coverage for dependents: 18 months; 29 months if disabled at termination or during first 60 days of continuation coverage; 36 months upon death of employee, divorce or legal separation, loss of dependent status, employee's eligibility for Medicare.

Time employee has to apply: 60 days after termination or receipt of notice, whichever is later.

Special situations: Employee who has been insured for previous 3 months and dependents may convert to an individual plan instead of group continuation (must apply within 45 days of termination).

Employee who is 60 or older and has been continuously insured for at least 2 years is entitled to a converted policy with set maximum premium limits.

North Carolina

N.C. Gen. Stat. §§ 58-53-5 to 58-53-40

Employers affected: All employers who offer group health insurance.

Eligible employees: Employees continuously insured for previous 3 months.

Qualifying event: Termination of employment.

Length of coverage for employee: 18 months.

Length of coverage for dependents: 18 months.

Time employer has to notify employee of continuation rights: Employer has option of notifying employee as part of the exit process.

Time employee has to apply: 60 days.

Special benefits: Excludes: dental care; prescription drugs; vision care; any benefits other than hospital, surgical or major medical.

North Dakota

N.D. Cent. Code §§ 26.1-36-23, 26.1-36-23.1

Employers affected: All employers who offer group health insurance.

Eligible employees: Employees continuously insured for previous 3 months.

Qualifying event: Termination of employment.

Length of coverage for employee: 39 weeks

Length of coverage for dependents: 39 weeks. 36 months if required by divorce or annulment decree.

Time employee has to apply: Within 10 days of termination or of receiving notice of continuation rights, whichever is later, but no more than 31 days from termination.

Special benefits: Excludes: dental care; prescription drugs; vision care; any benefits other than hospital, surgical or major medical.

Ohio

Ohio Rev. Code Ann. §§ 3923.38; 1751.53

Employers affected: All employers who offer group health insurance.

Eligible employees: Employees continuously insured for previous 3 months who are entitled to unemployment benefits.

Qualifying event: Involuntary termination of employment.

Length of coverage for employee: 6 months.

Length of coverage for dependents: 6 months.

Time employer has to notify employee of continuation rights: At termination of employment.

State Health Insurance Continuation Laws (continued)

Time employee has to apply: Whichever is earlier: 31 days after coverage terminates; 10 days after coverage terminates if employer notified employee of continuation rights prior to termination; 10 days after employer notified employee of continuation rights, if notice was given after coverage terminated.

Special benefits: Excludes: dental care; prescription drugs; vision care; any benefits other than hospital, surgical or major medical.

Oklahoma

Okla. Stat. Ann. tit. 36, § 4509

Employers affected: All employers who offer group health insurance.

Eligible employees: Insured for at least 6 months. (All other employees and their dependents entitled to 30 days continuation coverage.)

Qualifying event: Any reason coverage terminates.

Length of coverage for employee: 3 months for basic coverage, 6 months for major medical at the same premium rate prior to termination of coverage.

Length of coverage for dependents: 3 months for basic coverage, 6 months for major medical at the same premium rate prior to termination of coverage.

Special benefits: Includes maternity care.

Oregon

Or. Rev. Stat. §§ 743.600 to 743.610

Employers affected: Employers not subject to federal COBRA laws.

Eligible employees: Employees continuously insured for previous 3 months.

Qualifying event: Termination of employment.

Length of coverage for employee: 6 months.

Length of coverage for dependents: 6 months.

Time employee has to apply: 10 days after termination or receiving notice of continuation rights, whichever is later, but not more than 31 days.

Special benefits: Excludes: dental care; prescription drugs; vision care; any benefits other than hospital, surgical or major medical.

Special situations: Surviving, divorced or legally separated spouse who is 55 or older and dependent children entitled to continuation benefits until spouse remarries or is eligible for other coverage. Must include dental, vision or prescrip-

tion drug benefits if they were offered in original plan (applies to employers with 20 or more employees).

Pennsylvania

40 Pa. Cons. Stat. Ann. § 756.2(d)

No laws for continuation insurance. Employees who have been continuously insured for the previous 3 months may convert to an individual policy.

Rhode Island

R.I. Gen. Laws §§ 27-19.1-1, 27-20.4-1 to 27.20.4-2

Employers affected: All employers who offer group health insurance.

Eligible employees: All insured employees are eligible.

Qualifying event: Involuntary termination of employment; death of employee; change in marital status; permanent reduction in workforce; employer's going out of business.

Length of coverage for employee: 18 months (but not longer than continuous employment).

Length of coverage for dependents: 18 months (but not longer than continuous employment).

Time employer has to notify employee of continuation rights: Employers must post a conspicuous notice of employee continuation rights.

Time employee has to apply: 30 days from termination of coverage.

Special situations: If right to receive continuing health insurance is stated in the divorce judgment, divorced spouse has right to continue coverage as long as employee remains covered or until divorced spouse remarries or becomes eligible for other group insurance. If covered employee remarries, divorced spouse must be given right to purchase an individual policy from same insurer.

South Carolina

S.C. Code Ann. § 38-71-770

Employers affected: All employers who offer group health insurance.

Eligible employees: Employees continuously insured for previous 6 months.

Qualifying event: Any reason employee or dependent becomes ineligible for coverage.

Length of coverage for employee: 6 months (in addition to part of month remaining at termination).

Length of coverage for dependents: 6 months (in addition to part of month remaining at termination).

State Health Insurance Continuation Laws (continued)

Time employer has to notify employee of continuation rights: At time of termination must clearly and meaningfully advise employee of continuation rights.

Special benefits: Excludes: accidental injury; specific diseases.

South Dakota

S.D. Codified Laws Ann. §§ 58-18-7.5, 58-18-7.12; 58-18C-1

Employers affected: All employers who offer group health insurance.

Eligible employees: Employees continuously insured for previous 6 months.

Qualifying event: Termination of employment; death of employee; divorce or legal separation; loss of dependent status; employee's eligibility for Medicare.

Length of coverage for employee: 18 months; 29 months if disabled at termination or during first 60 days of continuation coverage.

Length of coverage for dependents: 18 months; 29 months if disabled at termination or during first 60 days of continuation coverage; 36 months upon death of employee, divorce or legal separation, loss of dependent status, employee's eligibility for Medicare.

Special situations: When employer goes out of business: 12 months continuation coverage available to all employees. Employer must notify employees within 10 days of termination of benefits; employees must apply within 60 days of receipt of employer's notice or within 90 days of termination of benefits if no notice given.

Tennessee

Tenn. Code Ann. § 56-7-2312

Employers affected: All employers who offer group health insurance.

Eligible employees: Employees continuously insured for previous 3 months.

Qualifying event: Termination of employment; death of employee; change in marital status.

Length of coverage for employee: 3 months (in addition to part of month remaining at termination).

Length of coverage for dependents: 3 months (in addition to part of month remaining at termination); 15 months upon death of employee or divorce.

Special situations: Employee or dependent who is pregnant at time of termination entitled to continuation benefits for 6 months following the end of pregnancy.

Texas

Tex. Ins. Code Ann. §§ 3.51-6(d3), 3.51-8

Employers affected: All employers who offer group health insurance.

Eligible employees: Employees continuously insured for previous 3 months.

Qualifying event: Termination of employment (except for cause); employee leaves for health reasons.

Length of coverage for employee: 6 months.

Length of coverage for dependents: 6 months.

Time employee has to apply: 31 days from termination of coverage or receiving notice of continuation rights from employer or insurer, whichever is later.

Special situations: Layoff due to a labor dispute: employee entitled to continuation benefits for duration of dispute, but no longer than 6 months.

Utah

Utah Code Ann. §§ 31A-22-703, 31A-22-714

Employers affected: All employers who offer group health insurance.

Eligible employees: Employees continuously insured for previous 6 months.

Qualifying event: Termination of employment.

Length of coverage for employee: 6 months.

Length of coverage for dependents: 6 months.

Time employer has to notify employee of continuation rights: In writing within 30 days of termination of coverage.

Time employee has to apply: Within 30 days of receiving employer's notice of continuation rights.

Special benefits: Excludes: accidental injury; catastrophic benefits; dental care; specific diseases.

Vermont

Vt. Stat. Ann. tit. 8, §§ 4090a to 4090c

Employers affected: All employers who offer group health insurance.

Eligible employees: Employees continuously insured for previous 3 months.

Qualifying event: Termination of employment; death of employee; change of marital status; loss of dependent status.

Length of coverage for employee: 6 months.

Length of coverage for dependents: 6 months.

State Health Insurance Continuation Laws (continued)

Time employee has to apply: Within 60 days (upon death of employee or group member), or within 30 days (upon termination of employment, change of marital status or loss of dependent status) of the date that group coverage terminates, or the date of being notified of continuation rights, whichever is sooner.

Virginia

Va. Code Ann. §§ 38.2-3541 to 38.2-3542; 38.2-3416

Employers affected: All employers who offer group health insurance.

Eligible employees: Employees continuously insured for previous 3 months.

Qualifying event: Any reason employee or dependent becomes ineligible for coverage.

Length of coverage for employee: 90 days.

Length of coverage for dependents: 90 days.

Time employer has to notify employee of continuation rights: 15 days from termination of coverage.

Time employee has to apply: Must apply for continuation and pay entire 90-day premium before termination of coverage.

Special situations: Employee may convert to an individual policy instead of group continuation coverage (must apply within 31 days of termination of coverage).

Washington

Wash. Rev. Code Ann. §§ 48.21.250, 48.21.075

Employers affected: Optional for all employers who offer group health insurance (except during strike).

Eligible employees: All insured employees are eligible.

Qualifying event: Any reason employee or dependent becomes ineligible for coverage.

Length of coverage for employee: Term and rate of coverage agreed upon by employer and employee.

Length of coverage for dependents: Term and rate of coverage agreed upon by employer and employee.

Special situations: Layoff or termination due to strike: 6 months coverage with employee paying premiums (mandatory for all employers). In other situations: if optional continuation benefits are not offered, employee may convert to an individual policy (must apply within 31 days of termination of group coverage).

West Virginia

W.Va. Code §§ 33-16-2, 33-16-3(e)

Employers affected: Employers providing insurance for at least 10 employees.

Eligible employees: All insured employees are eligible.

Qualifying event: Involuntary layoff.

Length of coverage for employee: 18 months.

Wisconsin

Wis. Stat. Ann. § 632.897

Employers affected: All employers who offer group health insurance.

Eligible employees: Employees continuously insured for previous 3 months.

Qualifying event: Any reason employee or dependent becomes ineligible for coverage.

Length of coverage for employee: 18 months (or longer at insurer's option).

Length of coverage for dependents: 18 months (or longer at insurer's option).

Time employer has to notify employee of continuation rights: 5 days from termination of coverage.

Time employee has to apply: 30 days after receiving employer's notice.

Wyoming

Wyo. Stat. § 26-19-113

Employers affected: Employers not subject to federal COBRA laws.

Eligible employees: Employees continuously insured for previous 3 months.

Qualifying event: Termination of employment.

Length of coverage for employee: 12 months.

Length of coverage for dependents: 12 months.

Time employee has to apply: 31 days from termination of coverage.

Special benefits: If dental, vision care or any benefits other than hospital, surgical or major medical were included in the group policy, they may be continued at employee or dependent's request.

Current as of February 2003

A

How to Use the CD-ROM

The employee handbook sections discussed in this book are included on a CD-ROM in the back of the book. This CD-ROM, which can be used with Windows computers, installs files that can be opened, printed and edited using a word processor or other software. It is *not* a stand-alone software program. Please read this Appendix and the README.TXT file included on the CD-ROM for instructions on using the Employee Handbook CD.

Note to Mac users: This CD-ROM and its files should also work on Macintosh computers. Please note, however, that Nolo cannot provide technical support for non-Windows users.

How to View the README File

If you do not know how to view the file README.TXT, insert the Employee Handbook CD into your computer's CD-ROM drive and follow these instructions:

- Windows 9x, 2000, Me and XP: (1) On your PC's desktop, double-click the My Computer icon; (2) double-click the icon for the CD-ROM drive into which the Employee Handbook CD was inserted; (3) double-click the file README.TXT.
- Macintosh: (1) On your Mac desktop, double-click the icon for the CD-ROM that you inserted; (2) double-click on the file README.TXT.

While the README file is open, print it out by using the Print command in the File menu.

A. Installing the Handbook Section Files Onto Your Computer

Handbook section files that you can open, complete, print and save with your word processing program (see Section B, below) are contained on the Employee Handbook CD. Before you can do anything with the files on the CD-ROM, you need to install them onto your hard disk. In accordance with U.S. copyright laws, remember that copies of the CD-ROM and its files are for your personal use only.

Insert the Employee Handbook CD and do the following:

1. Windows 9x, 2000, Me and XP Users

Follow the instructions that appear on the screen. (If nothing happens when you insert the Employee Handbook CD, then (1) double-click the My Computer icon; (2) double-click the icon for the CD-ROM drive into which the Employee Handbook CD was inserted; and (3) double-click the file WELCOME.EXE.)

- By default, all the files are installed to the \Employee Handbook Sections folder in the \Program Files folder of your computer. A folder called "Employee Handbook Sections" is added to the "Programs" folder of the Start menu.

2. Macintosh Users

Step 1: If the "Employee Handbook CD" window is not open, open it by double-clicking the "Employee Handbook CD" icon.

Step 2: Select the "Employee Handbook Sections" folder icon.

Step 3: Drag and drop the folder icon onto the icon of your hard disk.

B. Using the Handbook Section Files to Create an Employee Handbook

This discussion concerns the files for handbook sections that can be opened and edited with your word processing program.

All word processing handbook section files come in rich text format. These files have the extension ".RTF." For example, the handbook section for At-Will Protections discussed in Chapter 2 is on the file Ch02_At-Will Protections.RTF. All handbook section files and their filenames are listed in Section C, below.

RTF files can be read by most recent word processing programs including all versions of MS Word for Windows and Macintosh, WordPad for Windows and recent versions of WordPerfect for Windows and Macintosh.

To use the handbook section files from the CD to create your employee handbook you must: (1) open a file in your word processor or text editor; (2) edit the handbook section by filling in the required information; (3) rename and save your revised handbook section file; (4) assemble your employee handbook by pasting your completed handbook sections into the Employee Handbook Outline; and (5) print it out.

The following are general instructions on how to do this. However, each word processor uses different commands to open, format, save and print documents. Please read your word processor's manual for specific instructions on performing these tasks.

Do not call Nolo's technical support if you have questions on how to use your word processor.

Step 1: Opening a File

There are three ways to open the word processing files included on the CD-ROM after you have installed them onto your computer.

- Windows users can open a file by selecting its "shortcut" as follows: (1) Click the Windows "Start" button; (2) open the "Programs" folder; (3) open the "Employee Handbook Sections" subfolder; and (4) click on the shortcut to the handbook section you want to work with.

- Both Windows and Macintosh users can open a file directly by double-clicking on it. Use My Computer or Windows Explorer (Windows 9x, 2000, Me or XP) or the Finder (Macintosh) to go to the folder you installed or copied the

CD-ROM's files to. Then, double-click on the specific file you want to open.

- You can also open a file from within your word processor. To do this, you must first start your word processor. Then, go to the File menu and choose the Open command. This opens a dialog box where you will tell the program (1) the type of file you want to open (*.rtf); and (2) the location and name of the file (you will need to navigate through the directory tree to get to the folder on your hard disk where the CD's files have been installed). If these directions are unclear you will need to look through the manual for your word processing program—Nolo's technical support department will *not* be able to help you with the use of your word processing program.

Where Are the Files Installed?

Windows Users
- RTF files are installed by default to a folder named \Employee Handbook Sections in the \Program Files folder of your computer.

Macintosh Users
- RTF files are located in the "Employee Handbook Sections" folder.

Step 2: Editing Your Employee Handbook Sections

Fill in the appropriate information according to the instructions and sample handbook sections in the book. Underlines are used to indicate where you need to enter your information, frequently with bracketed instructions embedded within them. *Be sure to delete the underlines and instructions from your edited version.* If you do not know how to use your word processor to edit a document, you will need to look through the manual for your word processing program—Nolo's technical support department will *not* be able to help you with the use of your word processing program.

Editing Handbook Sections That Have Optional or Alternative Text

Some of the handbook sections have optional or alternate text:

- With optional text, you choose whether to include or exclude the given text.
- With alternative text, you select one alternative to include and exclude the other alternatives.

When editing these handbook sections, we suggest you do the following:

Optional text

If you **don't want** to include optional text, just delete it from your document.

If you **do want** to include optional text, just leave it in your document.

In either case, delete the italicized instructions.

NOTE: if you choose not to include an optional numbered policy, be sure to renumber all the subsequent clauses after you delete it.

Alternative text

First delete all the alternatives that you do not want to include, then delete the italicized instructions.

Step 3: Saving Your Handbook Section Files

After filling in a particular handbook section, use the "Save As" command to save and rename the file. (This is an intermediate step; later we'll help you combine the handbook section files into a single document.) Because all the files are "read-only," you will not be able to use the "Save" command. This is for your protection. *If you save the file without renaming it, the underlines that indicate where you need to enter your information will be lost and you will not be able to create a new document with this file without recopying the original file from the CD-ROM.*

If you do not know how to use your word processor to save a file, you will need to look through the manual for your word processing program—Nolo's technical support department will *not* be able to help you with the use of your word processing program.

Step 4: Assembling Your Employee Handbook

When you've edited the handbook sections to your satisfaction and are ready to begin assembling your employee handbook, open the Employee Handbook Outline following the instructions in Step 1, above. You can then start opening, copying and pasting from your completed handbook section files into the Employee Handbook Outline. *Be sure to delete the bracketed instructions from the Employee Handbook Outline as you paste in your handbook sections.* If you do not know how to use your word processor to copy and paste to and from a file, you will need to look through the manual for your word processing program—Nolo's technical support department will *not* be able to help you with the use of your word processing program.

After you've finished pasting in your handbook sections, save your final document following the instructions in Step 3, above.

Step 5: Printing Out the Employee Handbook

Use your word processor's or text editor's "Print" command to print out your final document. If you do not know how to use your word processor to print a document, you will need to look through the manual for your word processing program—Nolo's technical support department will *not* be able to help you with the use of your word processing program.

 Tips for Saving Your Completed Files. As you edit and save your handbook section files, bear in mind that:

- you won't be able to access your saved files using shortcuts that opened the unedited, blank section files (Step 1, above), and
- you'll need to access these saved files later to put together your employee handbook (Step 5, below).

So, to make the task of putting your handbook together as easy as possible, remember these tips:

1. As you rename the files, use names that you will recognize.
2. Save all your handbook section files to the same location (or folder) on your computer.
3. Note the location to which you saved the files.

C. Files Included on the Employee Handbook CD

File Name	Section Name
00_Outline.rtf	Employee Handbook Outline
01_Introduction.rtf	1. Introduction
02_Employment.rtf	2. The Employment Relationship
03_Hiring.rtf	3. Hiring
04_New Employee Info.rtf	4. New Employee Information
05_Employee Class.rtf	5. Employee Classifications
06_Hours.rtf	6. Hours
07_Pay Policies.rtf	7. Pay Policies
08_Employee Benefits.rtf	8. Employee Benefits
09_Company Property.rtf	9. Use of Company Property
10_Time Off.rtf	10. Leave and Time Off
11_Performance.rtf	11. Performance
12_Work Behavior.rtf	12. Workplace Behavior
13_Health Safety.rtf	13. Health and Safety
14_Privacy.rtf	14. Employee Privacy
15_Computers.rtf	15. Computers, Email and the Internet
16_Records.rtf	16. Employee Records
17_Drugs Alcohol.rtf	17. Drugs and Alcohol
18_Trade Secrets.rtf	18. Trade Secrets and Conflicts of Interest
19_Discrimination.rtf	19. Discrimination and Harassment
20_Complaints.rtf	20. Complaint Policies
21_Ending Employment.rtf	21. Ending Employment

Model Handbook

This Appendix contains a model handbook created for a fictional company, using the policies, examples and discussions in this book. Your handbook may or may not look much like this one, depending on which policies you choose and what handbook format works best for your company. We provide this model handbook so that you can see how all our suggested policies fit together. Please do not photocopy it and use it for your company!

Section 1:   Introduction

1:1   Welcome to Our Company!

It's our pleasure to welcome you to J&J Books. We're an energetic and creative bunch, dedicated to high standards of excellence and quality. We value each one of our employees, and we hope that you find your work here rewarding and satisfying.

This section introduces you to our Company's history, purpose and goals. Please read it carefully so that you can better understand who we are and what we do. We think we are a special place—made all the more so by the hard work and dedication of our employees.

1:2   Introduction to the Company

Juanita Jones founded this company in 1978 on a very basic principle: Customers will pay for exceptional service and knowledge. Using that principle as her beacon, she took a small independent bookstore and created a chain of 300 stores serving customers throughout the Western United States.

Here at J&J Books, we continue to believe that a knowledgeable and courteous staff can sell more books than discount prices can. For this reason, we encourage our employees to read the publishing and literary magazines that you will find in the break room, to use your employee discount to buy and read as many books as possible and to take advantage of our tuition reimbursement program to take literature and writing classes at local colleges. When our customers come to you with questions, we want you to be able to answer them—with a smile.

We know that only happy and relaxed employees can give the quality and good-natured service that our customers demand. So take all of the breaks you are scheduled for, alert your manager to any problems in your work area and communicate any ideas you might have for making this a better place to work.

At J&J Books, we want our employees to put the customer first. That's why we, in management, put our employees first. We know that we are only as good as you are.

1:3   Our Company's History

The first J&J Books was opened in a one-room brick storefront in Portland, Oregon. It included a small coffee stand and café in front.

Though there wasn't room to stock huge quantities of books, Juanita Jones made sure that all the stock was high quality—and that our customer service staff knew where every book was and why it was worth reading. J&J also made sure to be ready and able to fill any special customer orders.

The first customers were just walk-ins, people browsing during their lunch hour. Before long, however, these customers were telling their friends—and Juanita's vision began to turn into a reality.

1:4 The Purpose of This Handbook

We think that employees are happier and more valuable if they know what they can expect from our Company and what our Company expects from them. In the preceding sections, we introduced you to our Company's history, values, culture and goals. We expect you to incorporate that information into your day-to-day job performance, striving to meet our Company's values in everything you do.

The remainder of this Handbook will familiarize you with the privileges, benefits and responsibilities of being an employee at J&J Books. Please understand that this Handbook can only highlight and summarize our Company's policies and practices. For detailed information, you will have to talk to your supervisor or Myrtle Means, the Human Resources manager.

In this Company, as in the rest of the world, circumstances are constantly changing. As a result, we may have to revise, rescind or supplement these policies from time to time. Nothing in this Handbook is a contract or a promise. The policies can change at any time, for any reason, without warning.

We are always looking for ways to improve communications with our employees. If you have suggestions for ways to improve this Handbook in particular or employee relations in general, please feel free to bring them to Myrtle Means.

1:5 Be Sure to Check Out Our Bulletin Board

You can find important information about this Company and your employment posted on the bulletin board located in the employee break room. This is also the place where we post important information regarding your legal rights, including information about equal employment opportunity laws and wage and hour laws. We expect all employees to periodically read the information on the bulletin board.

Because this bulletin board is our way of communicating with employees, we do not allow anyone but managers and company officials to post information there.

Section 2: Nature of Employment

2:1 Employment Is At Will

We are happy to welcome you to J&J Books. We sincerely hope that your employment here will be a positive and rewarding experience. However, we cannot make any guarantees about your continued employment at J&J Books. Your employment here is at will. This means that you are free to quit at any time, for any reason, just as we are free to terminate your employment at any time, for any reason—with or without notice, with or without cause.

No employee or company representative, other than Juanita Jones, has the authority to change the at-will employment relationship or to contract with any employee for different terms of employment. Furthermore, Juanita may change the at-will employment relationship only in a written contract, signed by herself and the employee. Nothing in this Handbook constitutes a contract or promise of continued employment.

Section 3:   Hiring Practices

3:1   Commitment to Equal Opportunity

J&J Books believes that all people are entitled to equal employment opportunity. We follow state and federal laws prohibiting discrimination in hiring and employment. We do not discriminate against employees or applicants in violation of those laws.

3:2   Recruitment

We know that we are only as good as our employees, so we search as widely as possible for talented and motivated individuals to fill vacant positions in our Company. Our recruitment methods include advertising, employment agencies and referrals.

Although these methods have served us well in the past, we know that the marketplace is ever changing and that finding high quality people is an evolving process. We encourage our employees to share with us their ideas as to what more we can do to find and recruit talented and motivated individuals.

We conduct all recruiting in a fair and nondiscriminatory manner.

3:3   Internal Application Procedures

Sometimes, the best person for a job is right under our Company's nose. As a result, we encourage current employees to apply for vacant positions that interest them.

We post all internal job openings on the main bulletin board. To apply for a position, give a cover letter, current resumé and copy of the job posting to Myrtle Means, the Human Resources manager.

3:4   Refer a New Hire; Get a Bonus!

Our employees know our needs and company culture better than anyone else and are often the best situated to find and recruit new employees to fill open positions within our ranks.

To encourage employees to act as recruiters on our behalf, and to reward employees who help make a successful match, we operate an Employee Referral Bonus Program. We will give $500 to any employee who refers an individual whom we hire.

To find out more about the program, or to refer a potential applicant for an open position, contact Myrtle Means in Human Resources.

3:5   Employment of Relatives

Usually, this Company will not refuse to hire someone simply because he or she is related to one of our current employees. If you have a relative who you think would be perfect to fill an open position in our Company, please don't hesitate to refer this person to us.

There are times, however, when employing relatives is inappropriate and has the potential to affect the morale of other employees and to create conflicts of interest for the relatives involved.

Therefore, we will not hire relatives of current employees where one relative will have to supervise the other.

If two employees become related while working for this Company, and if one of them is in a position of supervision over the other, only one of the employees will be allowed to keep his or her current position. The other will either have to transfer to another position or leave the Company.

Under this policy, the term "relatives" encompasses husbands, wives, live-in partners, parents, children, siblings, in-laws, cousins, aunts and uncles. This policy covers biological relationships, marriage relationships and step relationships.

Section 4:   Information for New Employees

4:1   New Employee Orientation

Within a day or two of starting work, you will be scheduled for a new employee orientation meeting. During this meeting, you will receive important information about our Company's policies and procedures. You will also be asked to complete paperwork and forms relating to your employment, such as tax withholding forms, emergency contact forms and benefits paperwork.

Please feel free to ask any questions you might have about the Company during the orientation meeting. If additional questions come up after the meeting, you can ask your supervisor or Myrtle Means in Human Resources.

4:2   Orientation Period

The first 90 days of your employment are an orientation period. During this time, your supervisor will work with you to help you learn how to do your job successfully and what the Company expects of you. This period also provides both you and the Company with an opportunity to decide whether you are suited for the position for which you were hired.

When your employment begins, you will meet with Myrtle Means, who will explain our benefits and payroll procedures and assist you in completing your employment paperwork. (For our Company's benefits policies, see Section 8 of this Handbook.) You will also meet with your supervisor to go over your job goals and performance requirements. During the orientation period, your supervisor will give you feedback on your performance and will be available to answer any questions you might have.

Employees are not eligible for the following benefits unless and until they complete the orientation period: Sick Leave and Vacation Leave.

Although we hope that you will be successful here, the Company may terminate your employment at any time, either during the orientation period or afterwards, with or without cause and with or without notice. You are also free to quit at any time and for any reason, either during the orientation period or afterwards, with or without notice. Successful completion of your orientation period does not guarantee you a job for any period of time or in any way change the at-will employment relationship. (For an explanation of at-will employment, see Section 2:1 of this Handbook.)

4:3   Proof of Work Eligibility

Within three business days of your first day of work, you must complete federal Form I-9 and show us documentation proving your identity and your eligibility to work in the United States. The federal government requires us to do this.

If you have worked for this Company previously, you need only provide this information if it has been more than three years since you last completed an I-9 Form for us or if your current I-9 Form is no longer valid.

Myrtle Means will give you an I-9 Form and tell you what documentation you must present to us.

4:4   Child Support Reporting Requirements

Federal and state laws require us to report basic information about new employees, including your name, address and Social Security number, to a state agency called the State Directory of New Hires. The state collects this information to enforce child support orders. If the state determines that you owe child support, it will send us an order requiring us to withhold money from your paycheck to pay your child support obligations.

Section 5: Classifications of Employees

5:1   Temporary Employees

Periodically, it becomes necessary for us to hire individuals to perform a job or to work on a project that has a limited duration. Typically, this happens in the event of a special project, special time of year, abnormal workload or emergency.

Individuals whom we hire for such work are temporary employees. They are not eligible to participate in any of our company benefit programs, nor can they earn or accrue any leave, such as vacation leave or sick leave.

Of course, we will provide to temporary employees any and all benefits mandated by law.

Temporary employees cannot change from temporary status to any other employment status by such informal means as remaining in our employ for a long period of time or through oral promises made to them by coworkers, members of management or supervisors. The only way a temporary employee's status can change is through a written notification signed by Juanita Jones.

Like all employees who work for this Company, temporary employees work on an at-will basis. This means that both they and this Company are free to terminate their employment at any time for any reason that is not illegal—even if they have not completed the temporary project for which they have been hired.

5:2   Part-Time and Full-Time Employees

Depending on the number of hours per week you are regularly scheduled to work, you are either a part-time or a full-time employee. It is necessary that you understand which of these classifications you fit into, because it will be important in determining whether you are entitled to benefits and leave. (See Section 8 of this Handbook for information about who is entitled to benefits and leave.)

Part-time employees: Employees who are regularly scheduled to work fewer than 40 hours per week are part-time employees.

Full-time employees: Employees who are regularly scheduled to work at least 40 hours per week are full-time employees.

5:3   Exempt and Non-exempt Employees

Your entitlement to earn overtime pay depends on whether you are classified as an exempt or a non-exempt employee.

Exempt employees are those who do not earn overtime because they are exempt from the overtime provisions of the federal Fair Labor Standards Act and applicable state laws.

Non-exempt employees are those who meet the criteria for being covered by the overtime provisions of the federal Fair Labor Standards Act and applicable state laws.

If you are uncertain about which category you fall into, speak to either your supervisor or Myrtle Means in Human Resources.

Section 6:   Hours

6:1   Hours of Work

Our Company's regular hours of business are from 9:30 a.m. to 7:30 p.m. Monday through Saturday, and 10 a.m. to 5 p.m. on Sunday.

Your supervisor will let you know your work schedule, including the time when you will be expected to start and finish work each day.

6:2   Flexible Scheduling

We understand that many employees have to balance the demands of their job with the needs of their families and other outside commitments. Therefore, we offer our employees the opportunity to work a flexible schedule.

If you would like to change your work schedule—for example, to come in and leave a couple of hours earlier or to work more hours on some days and fewer on others—please talk to your supervisor. The Company will try to accommodate your request, to the extent practical. Because not all jobs are suitable to flexible scheduling, and because we must ensure that our staffing needs are met, we cannot guarantee that the Company will grant your request.

6:3   Meal and Rest Breaks

Employees are allowed a 15-minute break every four hours. These breaks will be paid. In addition, all employees who work at least eight hours in a day are entitled to take a 30-minute meal break. Meal breaks are generally unpaid. However, employees who are required to work or remain at their stations during the meal break will be paid for that time.

6:4   Overtime

On occasion, we may ask employees to work beyond their regular scheduled hours. We expect employees to work a reasonable amount of overtime—this is a job requirement.

We will try to give employees advance notice when overtime work is necessary; however, it will not always be possible to notify workers in advance.

Exempt employees will not be paid extra for working beyond their regular scheduled hours. Non-exempt employees are entitled to payment for overtime, according to the rules set forth below. (For information on which employees are exempt and which are non-exempt, see Section 5 of this Handbook.)

- All overtime work must be approved in writing, in advance, by the employee's supervisor. Working overtime without permission violates company policy and may result in disciplinary action.

- For purposes of calculating how many hours an employee has worked in a day or week, our workweek begins at 12:01 a.m. on Monday and ends at midnight on Sunday. Our workday begins at 12:01 a.m. and ends at midnight each day.

- Only time actually spent working counts as hours worked. Vacation time, sick days, holidays or any other paid time during which an employee did not actually work will not count as hours worked.

- Non-exempt employees will be paid 1½ times their regularly hourly rate of pay for every hour worked in excess of 40 hours per week.

Section 7:   Pay Policies

7:1   Payday

Employees are paid twice a month. You will receive your paycheck on the 15th and the last day of each month. If payday falls on a holiday, you will receive your paycheck on the last workday immediately before payday.

7:2   No Advances

Our company does not allow employees to receive pay advances for any reason.

7:3   Tip Credit

Employees who hold certain positions in our Company receive some of their compensation in the form of tips from customers. If you receive tips, the Company will pay you an hourly wage of at least $6.50. However, if that wage plus the tips you actually earn during any pay period does not add up to at least the minimum wage for every hour you work, the Company will pay you the difference.

7:4   Tip Pooling

Employees in the following positions are required to pool tips: café counter staff and café wait staff. If you hold one of these positions, you must contribute 100% of your tips to the pool at the end of each workday. The pool will be divided equally among all employees who worked that day and hold one of the positions listed above.

7:5   Shift Premiums

Employees who work a Sunday shift will be paid a premium for each shift. This premium will be an additional 25% of their normal hourly pay.

7:6   Payroll Deductions

Your paycheck includes your total earnings for the pay period, as well as any mandatory or voluntary deductions from your paycheck. Mandatory deductions are deductions that we are legally required to take. Such deductions include federal income tax, Social Security tax

(FICA) and any applicable state taxes. Voluntary deductions are deductions that you have authorized. Such deductions might include insurance premiums and contributions to pensions, 401(k)s or other retirement accounts.

If you have any questions about your deductions, or wish to change your federal withholding form (Form W-4), contact Eleanor Po, the payroll manager.

7:7 Wage Garnishments

A wage garnishment is an order from a court or a government agency directing us to withhold a certain amount of money from an employee's paycheck and send it to a person or agency. Wages can be garnished to pay child support, spousal support or alimony, tax debts, outstanding student loans or money owed as a result of a judgment in a civil lawsuit.

If we are instructed by a court or agency to garnish an employee's wages, the employee will be notified of the garnishment at once. Please note that we are legally required to comply with these orders. If you dispute or have concerns about the amount of a garnishment, you must contact the court or agency that issued the order.

7:8 Expense Reimbursement

From time to time, employees may incur expenses on behalf of J&J Books. We will reimburse you for the actual work-related expenses you incur, as long as those expenses are reasonable. You must follow these procedures to get reimbursed:

- Get permission from your supervisor before incurring an expense.
- Spend the company's money wisely—make an effort to save money and use approved vendors if possible.
- Keep a receipt or some other proof of payment for every expense.
- Submit your receipts, along with an expense report, to your supervisor for approval within 30 days of incurring an expense.
- Your supervisor is responsible for submitting your expense report to Eleanor Po, the payroll manager. If your report is approved, you will receive your reimbursement within 14 days.

Remember that you are spending the Company's money when you pay for business-related expenses. We expect you to save money wherever possible. Your supervisor can assist you in deciding whether an expense is appropriate.

Section 8:   Employee Benefits

8:1   Employee Benefit Plans

As part of our commitment to our employees and their well-being, J&J Books provides employees with a variety of benefit plans: health insurance, retirement benefits, stock options, unemployment compensation and workers' compensation.

Although we introduce you to those plans in this section, we cannot provide the details of each plan here. At your new employee orientation, you should have received official plan documents for each of the benefit plans that we offer. Those documents (along with any updates that we give to you) should be your primary resource for information about your benefit plans. If you see any conflict between those documents and the information in this Handbook, the official plan documents are what you should rely upon.

The benefits we provide are meant to help employees maintain a high quality of life—both professionally and personally. We sincerely hope that each employee will take full advantage of these benefits. If you don't understand information in the plan documents or if you have any questions about the benefits we offer, please talk to Myrtle Means in Human Resources.

8:2   Domestic Partner Coverage

At J&J Books, we recognize that some of our employees are members of families that do not meet the traditional definition of the word— that is, a husband, wife and, perhaps, children. For those employees who are not married but who are in a committed relationship with another adult, we provide domestic partnership coverage.

To be eligible for benefits, the employee and the employee's partner must meet all of the following criteria:

1. They must have lived together in an exclusive committed relationship for at least 12 months.
2. They must be at least 18 years of age.
3. They must live together in the same residence.
4. They cannot be legally married to—or in a registered domestic partnership with—anyone else.
5. They must not be related by blood more closely than would be allowed under the marriage laws of this state.
6. They must complete and sign a Domestic Partnership Affidavit.

8:3   Healthcare Benefits

Because your health is of great importance to us, we provide you with the following healthcare benefits: medical, dental, vision and alternative (including acupuncture and massage). If you have not already received detailed plan documents about each of these benefits, contact Myrtle Means in the Human Resources Department. She can provide you with all of the information that you need to start enjoying your healthcare benefits package right away. Even if you have received plan documents, Myrtle can answer any questions you might have.

Eligibility to receive healthcare benefits depends on your employee classification. (See Section 5 of this Handbook for information about employee classifications.) If you are a regular full-time or regular part-time employee, you are eligible to receive full healthcare benefits, and we will pay 100 percent of the premium for you.

And don't worry. We haven't forgotten about your loved ones. We will pay 100 percent of the premium for eligible dependents (including domestic partners).

You and your dependents become eligible for benefits 30 days after the day you start work.

As with all of the policies in this Handbook, our healthcare coverage may change at any time. For the most up-to-date information about your healthcare benefits, refer to the plan documents or contact Myrtle.

8:4   State Disability Insurance

Sometimes, an employee suffers an illness or injury outside of the workplace that prevents the employee from working and earning income. If this happens to you, the state disability insurance may provide you with a percentage of your salary while you are unable to work. All employees are eligible for this coverage and pay for it through deductions from their paychecks.

To find out more about state disability insurance, contact Myrtle Means.

If you suffer from an illness or injury that is work-related, then you may be eligible for workers' compensation insurance instead of state disability insurance. See the Workers' Compensation policy, below, or contact Myrtle Means for more information.

8:5   Workers' Compensation Insurance

If you suffer from an illness or injury that is related to your work, you may be eligible for workers' compensation benefits. Workers' compensation will pay for medical care and lost wages resulting from job-related illnesses or injuries.

If you are injured or become ill through work, please inform your supervisor immediately regardless of how minor the injury or illness might be.

To find out more about workers' compensation coverage, contact Myrtle Means.

If you are unable to work because of an illness or injury that is not related to work, then you might be eligible for state disability insurance instead of workers' compensation. See the Disability Insurance policy, above, or contact Myrtle Means for more information.

8:6   Unemployment Insurance

If your employment with our Company ends, you may be eligible for unemployment benefits. These benefits provide you with a percentage of your wages while you are unemployed and looking for work. To find out more, contact Myrtle Means.

Section 9:   Use of Company Property

9:1   Company Property

We have invested a great deal of money in the property and equipment that you use to perform your job. It is a senseless and avoidable drain on this Company's bottom line when people abuse company property, misuse it or wear it out prematurely by using it for personal business.

We ask all employees to take care of company property and to report any problems to Raymond Del, the property manager. If a piece of equipment or property is unsafe for use, please report it immediately.

Please use property only in the manner intended and as instructed.

We do not allow personal use of company property unless specifically authorized in this Handbook.

Failure to use company property appropriately, and failure to report problems or unsafe conditions, may result in disciplinary action, up to and including termination.

For information on use of the telephone system, see Section 9:3 of this Handbook.

For information on use of computers, the Internet and software, see Section 15 of this Handbook.

9:2   Company Cars

We have invested in company vehicles so that our employees can use them on company business in place of their own vehicle. This saves wear and tear on personal vehicles and eliminates the need for keeping track of mileage.

We need your help in keeping company cars in the best condition possible. Please keep them clean, and please remove any trash or personal items when you are finished using the vehicles.

Please immediately report any accidents, mechanical problems or other problems to Raymond Del, the property manager. We will try to have company vehicles repaired or serviced as soon as possible.

Only authorized employees may use company cars, and they may do so only on company business.

You may not use company vehicles while under the influence of drugs or alcohol or while otherwise impaired.

You must have a valid driver's license to use company cars, and we expect that you will drive in a safe and courteous manner. If you receive any tickets for parking violations or moving violations, you are responsible for taking care of them.

Violating this policy in any way may result in disciplinary action, up to and including termination.

9:3   Telephone System

The company's telephone system is for business use only. Employees are expected to keep personal calls to a minimum. If you must make or receive a personal call, please keep your conversation brief. Extensive personal use of company phones is grounds for discipline.

See Section 14 of this Handbook for information on privacy and telephones.

9:4   Return of Company Property

When your employment with this Company ends, we expect you to return company property—and to return it clean and in good repair. This includes this Employee Handbook, all manuals and guides, documents, phones, computers, equipment, keys and tools.

We reserve the right to take any lawful action to recover or protect our property.

Section 10: Leave and Time Off

10:1 Vacation

Our Company recognizes that our employees need to take time off occasionally, to rest and relax, to enjoy a vacation or to attend to personal matters. That's why we offer a paid vacation program.

All full-time employees who have completed their orientation period are eligible to participate in the paid vacation program.

Eligible employees accrue vacation time according to the following schedule:

Years of Employment	Vacation Accrual
0-2	10 days per year, at the rate of $5/6$ of a day per month
2-4	15 days per year, at the rate of $1\frac{1}{4}$ days per month
4 or more	20 days per year, at the rate of $1\frac{2}{3}$ days per month

Employees must schedule their vacations in advance, with their supervisor. We will try to grant every employee's vacation request for the days off of his or her choice. However, we must have enough workers to meet our day-to-day needs—which means we might not be able to grant every vacation request, especially during holiday periods.

10:2 Holidays

Our Company observes the following holidays each year: New Year's Day, Martin Luther King Day, President's Day, Good Friday, Memorial Day, Independence Day, Labor Day, Columbus Day, Veterans' Day, Thanksgiving, the Friday following Thanksgiving, Christmas Eve, Christmas Day and New Year's Eve.

If a holiday falls on a weekend, the company will inform you when the holiday will be observed. Ordinarily, holidays falling on a Saturday will be observed the preceding Friday; holidays falling on a Sunday will be observed the following Monday.

10:3 Sick Leave

Our Company provides paid sick days to all full-time and part-time employees who have completed their orientation period. (For information on employee classifications, see Section 5 of this Handbook.) Eligible employees accrue 12 sick days per year at the rate of one day per month. The Company will not pay employees for sick days that have accrued but have not been used when employment ends.

Employees may use sick leave when they are unable to work due to illness or injury. Sick leave is not to be used as extra vacation time, personal days or "mental health" days. Any employee who abuses sick leave may be subject to discipline.

You must report to your supervisor if you will need to take sick leave. We ask that employees call in as soon as they realize that they will be unable to work, before the regular start of their workday. You must report to your supervisor by phone each day you are out on leave.

10:4 Family and Medical Leave

Employees who have worked for our Company for at least a full year, and have worked an average of at least 25 hours per week during that time, are eligible to take unpaid family and medical leave for one or more of these purposes:

- because the employee's own serious health condition makes the employee unable to work
- to care for a spouse, child or parent who has a serious health condition, or
- to care for a newborn, newly adopted child or recently placed foster child.

Leave Available

Eligible employees may take up to 12 weeks of unpaid leave per calendar year for any of the above purposes. For purposes of calculating available family and medical leave, the year starts on January 1.

A parent who takes leave to care for a newborn, newly adopted child or recently placed foster child must begin this leave within a year after the birth, adoption or placement.

Notice Requirements

Employees are required to give notice at least 30 days in advance of their need for a family and medical leave, if their need for leave is foreseeable. In emergencies and unexpected situations, employees must give as much notice as is practicable under the circumstances.

Reinstatement Rights

When you return from an approved family and medical leave, you have the right to return to your former position or an equivalent position, except:

- You have no greater right to reinstatement than you would have had if you had not been on leave. If your position is eliminated for reasons unrelated to your leave, for example, you have no right to reinstatement.
- The Company is not obligated to reinstate you if you are a key employee—that is, you are among the highest-paid 10% of our workforce and holding your job open during your leave would cause the Company substantial economic harm. If the Company classifies you as a key employee under this definition, you will be notified when you request leave.

Substitution of Paid Leave

An employee who has accrued paid time off may use these benefits to receive pay for all or a portion of family and medical leave.

Medical Certification

The Company may ask employees who take leave for their own serious health condition or to care for a spouse, parent or child with a serious health condition to provide a doctor's form certifying the need for leave. The Company is also entitled to seek a second opinion and periodic recertifications. In some cases, the Company may ask employees who take leave because of their own serious health condition to provide a fitness for duty report from their doctors before they return to work.

Intermittent Leave

If you will need to take family and medical leave on an intermittent basis—that is, a day or two at a time rather than all at once—for your own serious health condition or to take care of a family member with a serious health condition, you will be allowed to do so. However, the Company may temporarily reassign you to a different position with equivalent pay and benefits to accommodate the intermittent schedule.

The Company will consider requests for intermittent leave to care for a new child on a case-by-case basis.

10:5 Bereavement Leave

If you suffer the death of an immediate family member, you are entitled to take up to four days off work. This leave will be paid.

Immediate family members include parents, children, siblings, spouses and domestic partners.

The Company will consider, on a case-by-case basis, requests for bereavement leave for the death of someone who does not qualify as an immediate family member under this policy.

10:6 Military Leave

Our Company supports those who serve in the armed forces to protect our country. In keeping with this commitment, and in accordance with state and federal law, employees who must be absent from work for military service are entitled to take a military leave of absence. This leave will be paid for 30 days, and unpaid after that.

When an employee's military leave ends, that employee will be reinstated to the position he or she formerly held, or to a comparable position, as long as the employee meets the requirements of federal and state law.

Employees who are called to military service must tell their supervisors as soon as possible that they will need to take military leave. An employee whose military service has ended must return to work or inform the company that he or she wants to be reinstated in accordance with these guidelines:

- For a leave of 30 or fewer days, the employee must report back to work on the first regularly scheduled workday after completing military service, allowing for travel time.
- For a leave of 31 to 180 days, the employee must request reinstatement within 14 days after military service ends.
- For a leave of 181 days or more, the employee must request reinstatement within 90 days after military service ends.

10:7 Voting

Our Company encourages employees to exercise their right to vote. If your work schedule and the location of your polling place will make it difficult for you to get to the polls before they close, you are entitled to take up to two hours off work, at the beginning or end of your shift, to cast your ballot. This time will be paid.

Employees who will need to take time off work to vote must inform their supervisors at least four days in advance. Employees are expected to work with their supervisors to ensure that their absence doesn't negatively impact Company operations.

10:8 Jury Duty

If you are called for jury duty, you are entitled to take time off, as necessary, to fulfill your jury obligations. This leave will be paid. No employee will face discipline or retaliation for jury service.

You must immediately inform your supervisor when you receive your jury duty summons. If you are chosen to sit on a jury, you must inform your supervisor how long the trial is expected to last. You must also check in with your supervisor periodically during your jury service, so the Company knows when to expect you back at work.

Section 11: Employee Job Performance

11:1 Your Job Performance

Each and every employee at J&J Books contributes to the success or failure of our Company. If one employee allows his or her performance to slip, then all of us suffer. We expect everyone to perform to the highest level possible.

Poor job performance can lead to discipline, up to and including termination.

11:2 Performance Reviews

Because our employees' performance is vital to our success, we conduct periodic reviews of individual employee performance. We hope that, through these reviews, our employees will learn what we expect of them and we will learn what they expect of us.

We require all employees to participate in the review process. Failure to participate could lead to discipline, up to and including termination.

To learn more about our performance review system, contact your supervisor or Myrtle Means in Human Resources.

Section 12: Workplace Behavior

12:1 Please Act Professionally

People who work together have an impact on each other's performance, productivity and personal satisfaction in their jobs. In addition, how our employees act toward customers and vendors will influence whether those relationships are successful for our Company.

Because your conduct affects many more people than just yourself, we expect you to act in a professional manner whenever you are on company property, conducting company business or representing the Company at business or social functions.

Although it is impossible to give an exhaustive list of everything that professional conduct means, it does, at a minimum, include the following:

- following all of the rules in this Handbook that apply to you
- refraining from rude, offensive or outrageous behavior
- refraining from ridicule and hostile jokes
- treating coworkers, customers and vendors with patience, respect and consideration
- being courteous and helpful to others, and
- communicating openly with supervisors, managers and co-workers.

Individuals who act unprofessionally will face discipline, up to and including termination.

12:2 Punctuality and Attendance

You are important to the effective operation of this business. When you are not here at expected times or on expected days, someone else must do your job or delay doing his own job while he waits for you to arrive. If you work with customers or vendors, they may grow frustrated if they can't reach you during your scheduled work times.

As a result, we expect you to keep regular attendance and to be on time and ready to work at the beginning of each scheduled workday. (In Section 6 of this Handbook, you can find a description of this Company's work hours, timekeeping and scheduling policies.)

Of course, things will sometimes happen that will prevent you from showing up to work on time. For example, you may be delayed by weather, a sick child or car trouble. If you are going to be more than ten minutes late, please call your supervisor. If you cannot reach this person, please contact Lolly March at Reception. Please give this notice as far in advance as possible.

If you must miss a full day of work for reasons other than vacation, sick leave or other approved leave (such as leave to serve on a jury or for a death in a family), you must notify your supervisor as far in advance as possible. (You can find information about this Company's vacation and leave policies in Handbook Section 10.)

If you are late for work or fail to appear without calling in as required by this policy or by other policies in this Handbook, you will face disciplinary action, up to and including termination.

12:3 Employee Appearance and Dress

We ask all employees to use common sense when they dress for work. Please dress appropriately for your position and job duties, and please make sure you are neat and clean at all times.

If you have any questions about the proper attire for your position, please contact Myrtle Means in Human Resources. We will try to reasonably accommodate an employee's special dress or grooming needs that are the result of religion, ethnicity, race or disability.

12:4 Pranks and Practical Jokes

Although we want our employees to enjoy their jobs and have fun working together, we cannot allow employees to play practical jokes or pranks on each other. At best, these actions disrupt the workplace and dampen the morale of some; at worst, they lead to complaints of discrimination, harassment or assault.

If you have any questions about this policy, contact Myrtle Means in Human Resources.

Employees who play pranks or practical jokes will face disciplinary action, up to and including termination.

12:5 Threatening, Abusive or Vulgar Language

We expect our employees to treat everyone they meet through their jobs with courtesy and respect. Threatening, abusive and vulgar language has no place in our workplace. It destroys morale and relationships, and it impedes the effective and efficient operation of our business.

As a result, we will not tolerate threatening, abusive or vulgar language from employees while they are on the worksite, conducting

Company business or attending Company-related business or social functions.

If you have any questions about this policy, contact Myrtle Means in Human Resources.

Employees who violate this policy will face disciplinary action, up to and including termination.

12:6 Horseplay

Although we want our employees to have fun while they work, we don't allow employees to engage in horseplay—which is fun that has gotten loud and boisterous and out of control. Horseplay disrupts the work environment and can get out of hand, leading to fighting, hurt feelings, safety hazards or worse.

Employees who engage in horseplay will face disciplinary action, up to and including termination.

12:7 Fighting

Verbal or physical fighting among employees is absolutely prohibited. Employees shall not engage in, provoke or encourage a fight. Those who violate this policy will be disciplined, up to and including termination.

12:8 Sleeping on the Job

When our employees arrive at work, we expect them to be physically prepared to work through their day. Employees who sleep on the job dampen morale and productivity and deprive us of their work and companionship.

As a result, we do not allow any employees to sleep while at work. Employees who feel sick or unable to finish the day because of weariness should talk to their supervisor about using sick leave to take the rest of the day off. (See Section 10 of this Handbook for information about our sick leave policy.)

12:9 Insubordination

This workplace operates on a system of mutual respect between supervisors and employees. Supervisors must treat their employees with dignity and understanding, and employees must show due regard for their supervisors' authority.

Insubordination occurs when employees unreasonably refuse to obey the orders or follow the instructions of their supervisors. It also occurs when employees, through their actions or words, show disrespect toward their supervisors.

Insubordinate employees will face discipline, up to and including termination.

We understand, however, that there will be times when employees have valid reasons for refusing to do as their supervisor says. Perhaps the employee fears for his safety or the safety of others, believes that following instructions will violate the law or pose some other problem for this Company. Or maybe the employee thinks that there is a better way to accomplish a goal or perform a task. When these issues arise, we do not ask that employees blindly follow orders. Instead, we ask that employees explain the situation to their supervisor. If, after hearing the employee's side, the supervisor continues to give the same order or rule, the employee must either obey or use the complaint procedures described in Section 20 of this Handbook.

12:10 Progressive Discipline

Any employee conduct that, in the opinion of the Company, interferes with or adversely affects our business is sufficient grounds for disciplinary action.

Disciplinary action can range from oral warnings to immediate discharge. Our general policy is to take disciplinary steps in the following order:

- oral warning(s)
- written reprimand(s)
- suspension, and
- termination.

However, we reserve the right to alter the order described above, to skip disciplinary steps, to eliminate disciplinary steps or to create new and/or additional disciplinary steps.

In choosing the appropriate disciplinary action, we may consider any number of the following things:

- the seriousness of your conduct
- your history of misconduct
- your employment record
- your length of employment with this Company
- the strength of the evidence against you
- your ability to correct the conduct

- your attitude about the conduct
- actions we have taken for similar conduct by other employees
- how your conduct affects this Company, its customers and your coworkers, and
- any other circumstances related to the nature of the misconduct, to your employment with this Company and to the affect of the misconduct on the business of this Company.

We will give those considerations whatever weight we deem appropriate. Depending on the circumstances, we may give some considerations more weight than other considerations—or no weight at all.

Some conduct may result in immediate termination. Here are some examples:

- theft of company property
- excessive tardiness or absenteeism
- arguing or fighting with customers, coworkers, managers or supervisors
- brandishing a weapon at work
- threatening the physical safety of customers, coworkers, managers or supervisors
- physically or verbally assaulting someone at work
- any illegal conduct at work
- using or possessing alcohol or illegal drugs at work
- working under the influence of alcohol or illegal drugs
- failing to carry out reasonable job assignments
- insubordination
- making false statements on a job application
- violating Company rules and regulations, and
- unlawful discrimination and harassment.

Of course, it is impossible to compile an exhaustive list of the types of conduct that will result in immediate termination. The ones listed above are merely illustrations.

You should remember that your employment is at the mutual consent of you and this Company. This policy does not change this fact. This means that you or this Company can terminate our employment relationship at will, at any time, with or without cause, and with or without advance notice.

As a result, this Company reserves its right to terminate your employment at any time, for any lawful reason, including reasons not listed above. You also have the right to end your employment at any time.

Section 13: Health and Safety

13:1 Safety Policy

Our Company takes employee safety very seriously. In order to provide a safe workplace for everyone, every employee must follow our safety rules:

- Horseplay, rough-housing and other physical acts that may endanger employees or cause accidents are prohibited.
- Employees must follow their supervisors' safety instructions.
- Employees in certain positions may be required to wear protective equipment, such as hair nets, hard hats, safety glasses, work boots, ear plugs or masks. Your supervisor will let you know if your position requires protective gear.
- Employees in certain positions may be prohibited from wearing dangling jewelry or apparel, or may be required to pull back or cover their hair, for safety purposes. Your supervisor will tell you if you fall into one of these categories.
- All equipment and machinery must be used properly. This means all guards, restraints and other safety devices must be used at all times. Do not use equipment for other than its intended purpose.
- All employees must immediately report any workplace condition that they believe to be unsafe to their supervisor. The Company will look into the matter promptly.
- All employees must immediately report any workplace accident or injury to either Myrtle Means, the Human Resources Manager, or Raymond Del, the Property Manager.

13:2 Workplace Security

It is every employee's responsibility to help keep our workplace secure from unauthorized intruders. Every employee must comply with these security precautions.

When you leave work for the day, please do all of the following: turn off your computer, close and lock your windows and lock your file cabinets.

After-hours access to the workplace is limited to those employees who need to work late. If you are going to be working past our usual closing time, please let your supervisor know.

Employees are allowed to have an occasional visitor in the workplace, but workplace visits should be the exception rather than the rule. If you are anticipating a visitor, please let Lolly March at Reception know. When your visitor arrives, you will be notified.

13:3 What to Do in an Emergency

In case of an emergency, such as a fire, earthquake or accident, your first priority should be your own safety. In the event of an emergency causing serious injuries, *IMMEDIATELY DIAL 9-1-1* to alert police and rescue workers of the situation.

If you hear a fire alarm or in case of an emergency that requires evacuation, please proceed quickly and calmly to the fire exits. The company will hold periodic fire drills to familiarize everyone with the routes they should take. Remember that every second may count—don't return to the workplace to retrieve personal belongings or work-related items. Once you have exited the building, head towards the nearest corner.

(For our Company's policy on workplace violence, see Section 13:5 of this Handbook)

13:4 Smoking Is Prohibited

For the health, comfort and safety of our employees, smoking is not allowed on Company property.

13:5 Violence Is Prohibited

We will not tolerate violence in the workplace. Violence includes physical altercations, coercion, pushing or shoving, horseplay, intimidation, stalking and threats of violence. Any comments about violence will be taken seriously—and may result in your termination. Please do not joke or make offhand remarks about violence.

No Weapons

No weapons are allowed in our workplace. Weapons include firearms, knives, brass knuckles, martial arts equipment, clubs or bats and explosives. If your work requires you to use an item that might qualify as a weapon, you must receive authorization from your supervisor to bring that item to work or use it in the workplace. Any employee found with an unauthorized weapon in the workplace will be subject to discipline, up to and including termination.

What to Do in Case of Violence

If you observe an incident or threat of violence that is immediate and serious, *IMMEDIATELY DIAL 9-1-1* and report it to the police. If the incident or threat does not appear to require immediate police intervention, please contact Myrtle Means and report it as soon as possible, using the Company's complaint procedure. All complaints will be investigated and appropriate action will be taken. You will not face retaliation for making a complaint.

Section 14: Employee Privacy

14:1 Company Property Is Subject to Search

Employees do not have a right to privacy in their workspaces or in any other property belonging to the Company. The Company reserves the right to search Company property at any time, without warning, to ensure compliance with our policies on employee safety, workplace violence, harassment, theft, drug and alcohol use and possession of prohibited items. Company property includes, but is not limited to, lockers, desks, file cabinets, storage areas and workspaces. If you use a lock on any item of Company property (a locker or file cabinet, for example), you must give a copy of the key or combination to Raymond Del, the Property Manager.

14:2 Telephone Monitoring

The Company reserves the right to monitor calls made from or received on Company telephones. Therefore, no employee should expect that conversations made on Company telephones will be private.

Section 15: Computers, Email and the Internet

15:1 Email

J&J Books provides employees with computer equipment, including an Internet connection and access to an electronic communications system, to enable them to perform their jobs successfully. This policy governs your use of the Company's email system.

Use of the Email System

The email system is intended for official Company business. Although you may use the email system for personal messages, you may do so during non-work hours only. If you send personal messages through the Company's email system, you must exercise discretion as to the number and type of messages you send. Any employee who abuses this privilege may be subject to discipline.

Email Is Not Private

Email messages sent using Company communications equipment are the property of the Company. We reserve the right to access, monitor, read and/or copy email messages at any time, for any reason. You should not expect that any email message you send using Company equipment—including messages you consider to be, or label as, personal—will be private.

Email Rules

All of our policies and rules of conduct apply to employee use of the email system. This means, for example, that you may not use the email system to send harassing or discriminatory messages, including messages with explicit sexual content or pornographic images; to send threatening messages; or to solicit others to purchase items for non-company purposes.

We expect you to exercise discretion in using electronic communications equipment. When you send email using the Company's communications equipment, you are representing the Company. Make sure that your messages are professional and appropriate, in tone and content. Remember, although email may seem like a private conversation, email can be printed, saved and forwarded to unintended recipients. You should not send any email that you wouldn't want your boss, your mother or our Company's competitors to read.

Deleting Emails

Because of the large volume of emails our Company sends and receives, we discourage employees from storing large numbers of email messages. Please make a regular practice of deleting emails once you have read and/or responded to them. If you need to save a particular email, you may print out a paper copy, archive the email or save it to your hard disk. The Company will purge email messages that have not been archived after 30 days.

Violations

Any employee who violates this policy can be subject to discipline, up to and including termination.

15:2 Using the Internet

We may provide you with computer equipment and capabilities, including Internet access, to help you perform your job. This policy governs your use of that equipment to access the Internet.

Personal Use of the Internet

Our network and Internet access are for official Company business only. Employees may access the Internet for personal use only outside of work hours and only in accordance with the other terms of this policy. An employee who engages in excessive Internet use, even during non-work hours, or who violates any other provision of this policy, may be subject to discipline.

Prohibited Uses of the Internet

Employees may not, at any time, access the Internet using Company equipment or links for any of the following purposes:

- To visit websites that feature pornography, gambling or violent images, or are otherwise inappropriate in the workplace.
- To operate an outside business, solicit money for personal purposes or to otherwise act for personal financial gain—this includes running online auctions.
- To download software, articles or other printed materials in violation of copyright laws.
- To download any software program without the express consent of Nelson Utembe, the IS Manager.

- To read, open or download any file from the Internet without first screening that file for viruses using the Company's virus detection software.

Internet Use Is Not Private

We reserve the right to monitor employee use of the Internet at any time, to ensure compliance with this policy. You should not expect that your use of the Internet—including but not limited to the sites you visit, the amount of time you spend online and the communications you have—will be private.

15:3 Software Use

It is our Company's policy to use licensed software only in accordance with the terms of its license agreement. Violating a license agreement is not only unethical—it is also illegal and can subject the Company to criminal prosecution and substantial monetary penalties.

To help us adhere to this policy, employees may not do any of the following without permission from Nelson Utembe:

- Make a copy of any Company software program, for any reason.
- Install a Company software program on a home computer.
- Install a personal software program (that is, software owned by the employee) on any Company computer.
- Download any software program from the Internet to a Company computer.

The Company may audit Company-owned computers at any time to ensure compliance with this policy.

Section 16: Employee Records

16:1 Your Personnel File

This Company maintains a personnel file on each employee. The purpose of this file is to allow us to make decisions and take actions that are personally important to you, including notifying your family in case of an emergency, calculating income tax deductions and withholdings and paying for appropriate insurance coverage.

Although we cannot list here all of the types of documents that we keep in your personnel file, examples include: copies of your tax and health insurance documents, forms that you filled out on your first day of work, your employee evaluations and any written complaints lodged against you.

We do not keep medical records or work eligibility forms in your personnel file. Those are kept separately. To find out more about those types of records, see Section 16:5 and Section 16:6, respectively, of this Handbook.

Your personnel file is physically kept by Myrtle Means in the Human Resources Department.

If you have any questions about your personnel file, contact Myrtle.

16:2 Confidentiality of Personnel Files

Because the information in your personnel file is by its nature personal, we keep the file as confidential as possible. We allow access to your file only on a need-to-know basis.

16:3 Please Notify Us If Your Information Changes

Because we use the information in your personnel file to take actions on your behalf, it is important that the information in that file be accurate. Please notify Myrtle Means whenever any of the following changes:

- your name
- your mailing address
- your phone number
- your dependents
- the number of dependents you are designating for income tax withholding
- your marital status

- the name and phone number of the individual whom we should notify in case of an emergency
- restrictions on your driver's license.

16:4 Inspecting Your Personnel Records

Current employees who want to inspect their personnel files must make an appointment with the Human Resources Department. Appointments will typically take place Monday through Friday between 1:00 p.m. and 5:00 p.m. Although we will make every effort to give employees an appointment quickly, it may take up to 48 hours. If an employee would like a representative to view his or her file, the employee must make the request in writing.

Former employees who would like to inspect their files must make a written request to do so. Upon receiving the written request, the Human Resources Department will call the former employee to schedule an appointment.

We do not allow current or former employees to photocopy their file. If you would like a copy of a document in the file, the Human Resources Department will copy it for you at a price of $.10 per page.

If you have any questions about this policy, please contact Myrtle Means, the Human Resources Manager.

16:5 Work Eligibility Records

In compliance with federal law, all newly hired employees must present proof that they are legally eligible to work in the United States. We must keep records related to that proof, including a copy of the INS Form I-9 that each employee completes for us.

Those forms are kept as confidential as possible. We do not keep them in your personnel file.

If you would like more information about your I-9 form, see Section 4:3 of this Handbook or contact Myrtle Means.

16:6 Medical Records

We understand the particularly sensitive nature of an employee's medical records, so we do not place those records in the employee's personnel file. We keep those records in a separate and secure place.

If you have any questions about the storage of your medical records or about inspecting your medical records, contact Myrtle Means, Human Resources Manager.

Section 17: Drugs and Alcohol

17:1 Policy Against Illegal Drug and Alcohol Use

This Company is committed to providing a safe, comfortable and productive work environment for its employees. We recognize that employees who abuse drugs or alcohol at work—or who appear at work under the influence of illegal drugs or alcohol—harm both themselves and the work environment.

As a result, we prohibit employees from doing the following:

- appearing at work under the influence of illegal drugs or alcohol
- conducting company business while under the influence of illegal drugs or alcohol (whether or not the employee is actually on work premises at the time)
- using illegal drugs or alcohol on the worksite
- using illegal drugs or alcohol while conducting company business (whether or not the employee is actually on work premises at the time)
- possessing, buying, selling or distributing illegal drugs or alcohol on the worksite
- possessing, buying, selling or distributing illegal drugs or alcohol while conducting company business (whether or not the employee is actually on work premises at the time).

Illegal drug use includes more than just outlawed drugs such as marijuana, cocaine or heroin. It also includes the misuse of otherwise legal prescription and over-the-counter drugs.

This policy covers times when employees are on call but not working and times when employees are driving company vehicles or using company equipment.

Employees who violate this policy may face disciplinary action, up to and including termination.

17:2 Inspections to Enforce Drug and Alcohol Policy

This Company reserves the right to inspect employees, their possessions and their workspaces to enforce our policy against illegal drug and alcohol use.

17:3 Drug Testing

As part of our efforts to keep this workplace safe and free of illegal drug use, we will conduct random and intermittent drug tests of all employees in positions where the safety or security of the employee or others is an issue.

In addition, we may ask any employee, regardless of job responsibilities, to submit to a drug test in the following circumstances:

1. when we suspect that the employee is under the influence of illegal drugs
2. when we suspect that the employee has been involved in the sale, purchase, use or distribution of illegal drugs on the work site or while performing job duties
3. when the employee has been involved in a workplace accident or incident
4. when the employee has been involved in an accident or incident off site but while on company business, or
5. when the employee has violated a safety rule.

17:4 Leave to Participate in Rehabilitation Program

We believe that employees who have a substance abuse problem can help themselves by enrolling in a rehabilitation program. Not only will overcoming their problem help these employees in their personal lives, it will help them to be more effective and productive workers.

Although we cannot guarantee that we will grant this leave to all employees who request it, employees who would like to participate in a rehabilitation program may, subject to approval, be able to use up to six weeks of paid leave from work to attend the program.

Employees will be entitled to health and other benefits while on rehabilitation leave.

Employees will not be allowed to accrue vacation and other benefits while on rehabilitation leave.

At the end of the rehabilitation leave, we will require proof that the employee successfully completed the program.

To learn more about this type of leave, including whether you qualify for it, the circumstances under which we will grant it and the requirements that you must meet, contact Myrtle Means. We will keep all conversations regarding employee substance abuse problems as confidential as possible.

Please note that even as you might be seeking assistance for your substance abuse problem, we still expect you to meet the same standards of performance, productivity and conduct that we expect of all employees. We reserve the right to discipline you—up to and including termination—for failing to meet those standards.

17:5 Rehabilitation and Your EAP

Because we care about the health and welfare of our employees, your benefits package includes an Employee Assistance Program (EAP) that provides assistance to employees who suffer from substance abuse problems, personal problems or emotional problems.

If you would like assistance in dealing with your substance abuse problem, see Myrtle Means for information about our EAP program. Your request for assistance will be kept as confidential as possible.

For information on taking leave to participate in the rehabilitation program, see Section 17:4 of this Handbook.

Please note that even as you might be seeking assistance for your substance abuse problem, we still expect you to meet the same standards of performance, productivity and conduct that we expect of all employees. We reserve the right to discipline you for failing to meet those standards.

Section 18: Trade Secrets and Conflicts of Interest

18:1 Confidentiality and Trade Secrets

Information is part of what makes this Company competitive. During your employment here, you will periodically learn sensitive information, either because you help to develop that information or because you need that information to do your job. It is important for the health of this business—and for the well-being of employees who depend on this business for their livelihood—that you keep information you learn through your employment confidential. Employees who improperly disclose sensitive information, confidential information, proprietary information or trade secret information to anyone outside the Company will face disciplinary action, up to and including termination. Therefore, we encourage you to contact Myrtle Means if you would like to learn more about this policy or if you have any questions.

After you leave this Company, you are still legally prohibited from disclosing sensitive, proprietary, trade secret or confidential information. If you disclose such information, we will seek legal remedies.

18:2 Conflicts of Interest

Our Company's success depends on the hard work, dedication and integrity of everyone who works here. In turn, our employees' livelihood depends on the success of our Company.

Because we depend so much on our employees, and because they depend so much on us, we expect all employees to devote their energies and loyalties to our Company. We do not allow employees to engage in any activities or relationships that create either an actual conflict of interest or the potential for a conflict of interest.

Although we cannot list every activity or relationship that would create either an actual or potential conflict of interest, examples of activities that violate this policy include the following:

- working for a competitor or customer or vendor as a part-time employee, full-time employee, consultant, independent contractor or in any other capacity
- owning an interest in a competitor, customer, vendor or anyone else who seeks to do business with this Company
- using the resources of this Company for personal gain
- using your position in this Company for personal gain.

Employees who violate this policy face disciplinary action, up to and including termination.

If you are unsure about whether an activity might violate this policy, or if you have any questions at all about this policy, please talk to Myrtle Means.

Section 19: Discrimination and Harassment

19:1 Our Commitment to Equal Employment Opportunity

J&J Books is strongly committed to providing equal employment opportunity for all employees and all applicants for employment. For us, this is the only acceptable way to do business.

All employment decisions at our Company—including those relating to hiring, promotion, transfers, benefits, compensation, placement and termination—will be made without regard to race, color, national origin, religion, sex, age, disability or citizenship status.

Any employee or applicant who believes that he or she has been discriminated against in violation of this policy should immediately file a complaint as explained in our Complaint Policy. (See Section 20 of this Handbook for information about complaint procedures.) We encourage you to come forward if you have suffered or witnessed what you believe to be discrimination—we cannot solve the problem until you let us know about it. The Company will not retaliate, or allow retaliation, against any employee or applicant who complains of discrimination, assists in an investigation of possible discrimination or files an administrative charge or lawsuit alleging discrimination.

Managers are required to report any discriminatory conduct or incidents, as described in our Complaint Policy.

Our Company will not tolerate discrimination against any employee or applicant. We will take immediate and appropriate disciplinary action against any employee who violates this policy.

19:2 Harassment Will Not Be Tolerated

It is our policy and our responsibility to provide our employees with a workplace free from harassment. Harassment on the basis of race, color, national origin, religion, sex, age, disability or citizenship status undermines our workplace morale and our commitment to treat each other with dignity and respect. Accordingly, harassment will not be tolerated at our Company.

Harassment can take many forms, including but not limited to touching or other unwanted physical contact, posting offensive cartoons or pictures, using slurs or other derogatory terms, telling offensive or lewd jokes and stories and sending email messages with offensive content. Unwanted sexual advances, requests for sexual favors and sexually suggestive gestures, jokes, propositions, email messages or other communications all constitute harassment.

If you experience or witness any form of harassment in the workplace, please immediately notify the company by following the steps outlined in our Complaint Policy (see Section 20 of this Handbook). We encourage you to come forward with complaints—the sooner we learn about the problem, the sooner we can take steps to resolve it. The Company will not retaliate, or allow retaliation, against anyone who complains of harassment, assists in a harassment investigation or files an administrative charge or lawsuit alleging harassment. All managers are required to immediately report any incidents of harassment, as set forth in our Complaint Policy.

Complaints will be investigated quickly. Those who are found to have violated this policy will be subject to appropriate disciplinary action, up to and including termination.

Section 20: Complaint Policies

20:1 Complaint Procedures

J&J Books is committed to providing a safe and productive work environment, free of threats to the health, safety and well-being of our workers. These threats include, but are not limited to, harassment, discrimination, violations of health and safety rules and violence.

Any employee who witnesses or is subject to inappropriate conduct in the workplace may complain to any supervisor, manager or to any company officer, including Myrtle Means, the Human Resources Manager. Any supervisor, manager or company officer who receives a complaint about, hears of or witnesses any inappropriate conduct is required to immediately notify Myrtle Means. Inappropriate conduct includes any conduct prohibited by our policies about harassment, discrimination, discipline, workplace violence, health and safety, and drug and alcohol use. In addition, we encourage employees to come forward with any workplace complaint, even if the subject of the complaint is not explicitly covered by our written policies.

We encourage you to come forward with complaints immediately, so we can take whatever action is needed to handle the problem. Once a complaint has been made, Myrtle Means will determine how to handle it. For serious complaints alleging harassment, discrimination and other illegal conduct, we will immediately conduct a complete and impartial investigation. All complaints will be handled as confidentially as possible. When the investigation is complete, the Company will take corrective action, if appropriate.

We will not engage in or allow retaliation against any employee who makes a good faith complaint or participates in an investigation. If you believe that you are being subjected to any kind of negative treatment because you made or were questioned about a complaint, report the conduct immediately to any manager, supervisor or company officer, including Myrtle Means.

20:2 Our Doors Are Open to You

We want to maintain a positive and pleasant environment for all of our employees. To help us meet this goal, J&J Books has an open-door policy, by which employees are encouraged to report work-related concerns.

If something about your job is bothering you, or if you have a question, concern, idea or problem related to your work, please discuss it with your immediate supervisor as soon as possible. If for any reason you don't feel comfortable bringing the matter to your supervisor, feel free to raise the issue with any company officer, supervisor or manager, including Myrtle Means in Human Resources.

We encourage you to come forward and make your concerns known to the Company. We can't solve the problem if we don't know about it.

Section 21: Ending Employment

21:1 Final Paychecks

Employees who quit will receive their final paycheck immediately if they've given at least 48 hours notice, and within five days if they haven't. Employees who are terminated involuntarily will receive their final paycheck no later than the first business day after the termination.

Final paychecks will include all compensation earned but not paid through the date of termination.

21:2 Severance Pay Is Discretionary

Generally, J&J Books does not pay severance to terminated employees, whether they quit, are laid off or are fired for any reason. However, we reserve the right to pay severance to a terminated employee. Decisions about severance pay will be made on a case-by-case basis, and are entirely within the discretion of the Company. No employee has a right to severance pay and you should not expect to receive it.

21:3 Continuing Your Health Insurance Coverage

J&J Books offers employees group health insurance coverage as a benefit of employment. If you are no longer eligible for insurance coverage because of a reduction in hours, because you quit or because you are fired for reasons other than serious misconduct, you have the right to continue your health insurance coverage for up to six months. You will have to pay the cost of this coverage.

Others covered by your insurance (your spouse and children, for example) also have the right to continue coverage if they are no longer eligible for certain reasons. If you and your spouse divorce or legally separate, or if you die while in our employ, your spouse may continue coverage under our group health plan. And once your children lose their dependent status, they may continue their healthcare as well. In any of these situations, your family members are entitled to up to six months of continued healthcare. They must pay the cost of this coverage.

You will receive an initial notice of your right to continued health insurance coverage when you first become eligible for health insurance under the Company's group plan. You will receive an additional notice when your hours are reduced, you quit or are fired. This second notice will tell you how to choose continuation coverage, what your obligations will be and how much the insurance will cost. You must notify us if any of your family members becomes eligible for continued coverage due to divorce, separation or reaching the age of majority.

21:4 Exit Interviews

We will hold an exit interview with every employee who leaves the Company, for any reason. During the interview, you will have the opportunity to tell us about your employment experience here—what you liked, what you didn't like and where you think we can improve. We greatly value these comments.

The exit interview also gives us a chance to handle some practical matters relating to the end of your employment. You will be expected to return all company property at the interview. You will also have an opportunity to ask any questions you might have about insurance, benefits, final paychecks, references or any other matter relating to your employment.

21:5 Reference Policy

When we are contacted by prospective employers seeking information about former employees, we will release the following data only: the position(s) the employee held, the dates the employee worked for our Company and the employee's salary or rate of pay.

If you would like us to give a more detailed reference, you will have to provide us with a written release—a consent form giving us your permission to respond to a reference request. We will respond only to written reference requests, and we will respond only in writing. Please direct all reference requests to Myrtle Means.

Where to Go for Further Information

Departments of Labor

U.S. Department of Labor

Washington, DC 20210

202-693-4650

www.dol.gov

You can find a list of regional offices of the Wage and Hour Division at the Department of Labor's website at www.dol.gov/esa/contacts/whd/america2.htm and a comprehensive list of state labor resources at www.dol.gov/dol/location.htm

State Labor Departments

Note: Phone numbers are for department headquarters. Check websites for regional office locations and numbers.

Alabama

Department of Industrial Relations

Montgomery, AL

334-242-8990

www.dir.state.al.us

Alaska

Department of Labor and Workforce Development

Juneau, AK

907-465-2700

www.labor.state.ak.us

Arizona

Industrial Commission

Phoenix, AZ

602-542-4411

www.ica.state.az.us

Arkansas

Department of Labor

Little Rock, AR

501-682-4500

www.state.ar.us/labor

California

Department of Industrial Relations

San Francisco, CA

415-703-5070

www.dir.ca.gov

Colorado

Department of Labor and Employment

Denver, CO

303-318-8000

http://cdle.state.co.us

Connecticut

Department of Labor

Wethersfield, CT

860-263-6000

www.ctdol.state.ct.us

Delaware

Department of Labor

Wilmington, DE

302-761-8000

www.delawareworks.com/DeptLabor

District of Columbia

Department of Employment Services

Washington, DC

202-724-7000

http://does.dc.gov

Florida

Agency for Workforce Innovation

Tallahassee, FL

850-245-7105

www.floridajobs.org

Georgia

Department of Labor

Atlanta, GA

404-656-3045

877-709-8185

www.dol.state.ga.us

Hawaii

Department of Labor and Industrial Relations

Honolulu, HI

808-586-8865

http://dlir.state.hi.us

Departments of Labor (continued)

Idaho

Department of Labor
Boise, ID
208-332-3570
www.labor.state.id.us

Illinois

Department of Labor
Chicago, IL
312-793-2800
www.state.il.us/agency/idol

Indiana

Department of Labor
Indianapolis, IN
317-232-2655
www.in.gov/labor

Iowa

Iowa Workforce Development
Des Moines, IA
515-281-5387
800-JOB-IOWA
www.state.ia.us/government/wd/index.htm

Kansas

Department of Human Resources
Office of Employment Standards
Topeka, KS
785-296-4062
www.hr.state.ks.us

Kentucky

Labor Cabinet
Frankfort, KY
502-564-3070
www.labor.ky.gov

Louisiana

Department of Labor
Baton Rouge, LA
225-342-3111
www.ldol.state.la.us

Maine

Department of Labor
Augusta, ME
207-624-6400
www.state.me.us/labor

Maryland

Department of Labor, Licensing and Regulation
Division of Labor and Industry
Baltimore, MD
410-767-2236
www.dllr.state.md.us/labor

Massachusetts

Department of Labor and Workforce Development
Boston, MA
617-727-6573
www.state.ma.us/dlwd

Michigan

Michigan Consumer and Industry Services
Lansing, MI
517-373-1820
www.cis.state.mi.us

Minnesota

Department of Labor and Industry
St. Paul, MN
651-284-5005
800-342-5354
www.doli.state.mn.us

Mississippi

Employment Security Commission
Jackson, MS
601-354-8711
www.mesc.state.ms.us

Missouri

Department of Labor and Industrial Relations
Jefferson City, MO
573-751-4091
573-751-9691
www.dolir.state.mo.us

Departments of Labor (continued)

Montana
Department of Labor and Industry
Helena, MT
406-444-2840
http://dli.state.mt.us

Nebraska
Department of Labor
Labor and Safety Standards
Lincoln, NE
402-471-2239
Omaha, NE
402-595-3095
www.dol.state.ne.us

Nevada
Division of Industrial Relations
Carson City, NV
775-684-7260
http://dirweb.state.nv.us

New Hampshire
Department of Labor
Concord, NH
603-271-3176
www.state.nh.us/dol

New Jersey
Department of Labor
Labor Standards and Safety Enforcement
Trenton, NJ
609-292-2313
www.state.nj.us/labor

New Mexico
Labor and Industrial Division
Department of Labor
Albuquerque, NM
505-827-6875
www.dol.state.nm.us

New York
Department of Labor
Albany, NY
518-457-9000
www.labor.state.ny.us

North Carolina
Department of Labor
Raleigh, NC
919-807-2796
800-625-2267
www.dol.state.nc.us/DOL

North Dakota
Department of Labor
Bismarck, ND
701-328-2660
800-582-8032
www.state.nd.us/labor

Ohio
Labor and Worker Safety Division
Department of Commerce
Columbus, OH
614-644-2239
www.com.state.oh.us/ODOC/laws/default.htm

Oklahoma
Department of Labor
Oklahoma City, OK
405-528-1500
888-269-5353
www.oklaosf.state.ok.us/~okdol

Oregon
Bureau of Labor and Industries
Portland, OR
503-731-4200
www.boli.state.or.us

Pennsylvania
Department of Labor and Industry
Harrisburg, PA
717-787-5279
www.dli.state.pa.us

Rhode Island
Department of Labor and Training
Cranston, RI
401-462-8000
www.dlt.state.ri.us

Departments of Labor (continued)

South Carolina

Department of Labor, Licensing and Regulation
Columbia, SC
803-896-4300
www.llr.state.sc.us

South Dakota

Division of Labor and Management
Pierre, SD
605-773-3681
www.state.sd.us/dol/dlm/dlm-home.htm

Tennessee

Department of Labor and Workforce Development
Nashville, TN
615-741-6642
www.state.tn.us/labor-wfd

Texas

Texas Workforce Commission
Austin, TX
512-463-2222
www.twc.state.tx.us

Utah

Labor Commission
Salt Lake City, UT
801-530-6801
800-222-1238
www.labor.state.ut.us

Vermont

Department of Labor and Industry
Montpelier, VT
808-828-2288
www.state.vt.us/labind

Virginia

Department of Labor and Industry
Richmond, VA
804-371-2327
www.dli.state.va.us

Washington

Department of Labor and Industries
Tumwater, WA
360-902-5799
800-547-8367
www.lni.wa.gov

West Virginia

Division of Labor
Charleston, WV
877-558-5134
304-558-7890
www.state.wv.us/labor

Wisconsin

Workforce Development Department
Madison, WI
608-266-1784
www.dwd.state.wi.us

Wyoming

Department of Employment
Cheyenne, WY
307-777-6763
http://wydoe.state.wy.us

Current as of February 2003

Agencies That Enforce Laws Prohibiting Discrimination in Employment

United States Agencies

Equal Employment Opportunity Commission (EEOC)
Washington, D.C.
202-663-4900
800-669-4000
www.eeoc.gov
Field Office Locations and phone numbers
www.eeoc.gov/teledir.html

State Agencies

Alabama
EEOC Distrist Office
Birmingham, AL
205-731-0082/0083

Alaska
Commission for Human Rights
Anchorage, AK
907-274-4692
800-478-4692
www.gov.state.ak.us/aschr/aschr.htm

Arizona
Civil Rights Division
Phoenix, AZ
602-542-5263
www.attorneygeneral.state.az.us/civil_rights/index.html

Arkansas
Equal Employment Opportunity Commission
Little Rock, AR
501-324-5060
www.eeoc.gov/index.html

California
Department of Fair Employment and Housing
Sacramento District Office
Sacramento, CA
916-445-5523
800-884-1684
www.dfeh.ca.gov

Colorado
Civil Rights Division
Denver, CO
303-894-2997
800-262-4845
www.dora.state.co.us/Civil-Rights

Connecticut
Commission on Human Rights & Opportunities
Hartford, CT
860-541-3400
800-477-5737
www.state.ct.us/chro

Delaware
Office of Labor Law Enforcement
Division of Industrial Affairs
Wilmington, DE
302-761-8200
www.delawareworks.com/divisions/industaffairs/law.enforcement.htm

District of Columbia
Office of Human Rights
Washington, DC
202-727-4559
www.ohr.dc.gov/main.shtm

Florida
Commission on Human Relations
Tallahassee, FL
850-488-7082
800-342-8170
http://fchr.state.fl.us

Georgia
Atlanta District Office
U.S. Equal Employment Opportunity Commission
Atlanta, GA
404-562-6800
www.eeoc.gov

Agencies That Enforce Laws Prohibiting Discrimination in Employment (continued)

Hawaii

Hawai'i Civil Rights Commission
Honolulu, HI
808-586-8640 (Oahu only)
800-468-4644 x68640 (other islands)
www.state.hi.us/hcrc

Idaho

Idaho Human Rights Commission
Boise, ID
208-334-2873
www2.state.id.us/ihrc

Illinois

Department of Human Rights
Chicago, IL
312-814-6200
www.state.il.us/dhr

Indiana

Civil Rights Commission
Indianapolis, IN
317-232-2600
800-628-2909
www.in.gov/icrc

Iowa

Iowa Civil Rights Commission
Des Moines, IA 50309
515-281-4121
800-457-4416
www.state.ia.us/government/crc

Kansas

Human Rights Commission
Topeka, KS
785-296-3206
www.ink.org/public/khrc

Kentucky

Human Rights Commission
Louisville, KY
502-595-4024
800-292-5566
www.state.ky.us/agencies2/kchr

Louisiana

Commission on Human Rights
Baton Rouge, LA
225-342-6969
www.gov.state.la.us/depts/lchr.htm

Maine

Human Rights Commission
Augusta, ME 04333
207-624-6050
www.state.me.us/mhrc/index.shtml

Maryland

Commission on Human Relations
Baltimore, MD 21202
410-767-8600
800-637-6247
www.mchr.state.md.us

Massachusetts

Commission Against Discrimination
Boston, MA 02108
617-994-6000
www.state.ma.us/mcad

Michigan

Department of Civil Rights
Detroit, MI 48226
313-456-3700
800-482-3604
www.michigan.gov/mdcr

Minnesota

Department of Human Rights
St. Paul, MN 55101
651-296-5663
800-657-3704
www.humanrights.state.mn.us

Missisippi

Equal Opportunity Department
Employment Security Commission
Jackson, MS
601-961-7420
www.mesc.state.ms.us

Agencies That Enforce Laws Prohibiting Discrimination in Employment (continued)

Missouri

Commission on Human Rights
Jefferson City, MO 65102
573-751-3325
www.dolir.state.mo.us/hr

Montana

Human Rights Bureau
Employment Relations Division
Department of Labor & Industry
Helena, MT 59624
406-444-2884
http://erd.dli.state.mt.us/HumanRights/HRhome.htm

Nebraska

Equal Opportunity Commission
Lincoln, NE 68509
402-471-2024
800-642-6112
www.nol.org/home/NEOC

Nevada

Equal Rights Commission
Reno, NV 89509
775-688-1288
http://detr.state.nv.us/nerc

New Hampshire

Commission for Human Rights
Concord, NH 03301
603-271-2767
http://webster.state.nh.us/hrc

New Jersey

Division on Civil Rights
Newark, NJ 07102
973-648-2700
www.state.nj.us/lps/dcr

New Mexico

Human Rights Division
Santa Fe, NM 87505
505-827-6838
800-566-9471
www.dol.state.nm.us/dol_hrd.html

New York

Division of Human Rights
Bronx, NY 10458
718-741-8400
www.nysdhr.com

North Carolina

Employment Discrimination Bureau
Department of Labor
Raleigh, NC 27601
919-807-2823
www.dol.state.nc.us/edb/edb.htm

North Dakota

Human Rights Division
Department of Labor
Bismarck, ND 58505
701-328-2660
800-582-8032
www.state.nd.us/labor/services/human-rights

Ohio

Civil Rights Commission
Columbus, OH 43205
614-466-2785
888-278-7101
www.state.oh.us/crc

Oklahoma

Human Rights Commission
Oklahoma City, OK 73105
405-521-2360
www.onenet.net/~ohrc2

Oregon

Civil Rights Division
Bureau of Labor and Industries
Portland, OR 97232
503-731-4200
www.boli.state.or.us/civil/index.html

Pennsylvania

Human Relations Commission
Philadelphia, PA 19130
215-560-2496
www.phrc.state.pa.us

Agencies That Enforce Laws Prohibiting Discrimination in Employment (continued)

Rhode Island

Commission for Human Rights

Providence, RI 02903

401-222-2661

www.state.ri.us/manual/data/queries/

stdept_.idc?id=16

South Carolina

Human Affairs Commission

Columbia, SC 29204

803-737-7800

800-521-0725

www.state.sc.us/schac

South Dakota

Division of Human Rights

Pierre, SD 57501

605-773-4493

www.state.sd.us/dcr/hr/HR_HOM.htm

Tennessee

Human Rights Commission

Knoxville, TN 37902

865-594-6500

800-251-3589

www.state.tn.us/humanrights

Texas

Commission on Human Rights

Austin, TX 78711

512-437-3450

888-452-4778

http://tchr.state.tx.us

Utah

Anti-Discrimination & Labor Division

Labor Commission

Salt Lake City, UT 84111

801-530-6801

800-222-1238

http://laborcommission.utah.gov/

Utah_Antidiscrimination___Labo/

utah_antidiscrimination___labo.htm

Vermont

Attorney General's Office

Civil Rights Division

Montpelier, VT 05609

802-828-3657

888-745-9195

www.state.vt.us/atg/civil rights.htm

Virginia

Council on Human Rights

Richmond, VA 23219

804-225-2292

www.chr.state.va.us

Washington

Human Rights Commission

Seattle, WA 98101

206-464-6500

www.wa.gov/hrc

West Virginia

Human Rights Commission

Charleston, WV 25301

304-558-2616

888-676-5546

www.state.wv.us/wvhrc

Wisconsin

Department of Workforce Development

Madison, WI

608-266-6860

www.dwd.state.wi.us/er

Wyoming

Department of Employment

Cheyenne, WY

307-777-7261

http://wydoe.state.wy.us/doe.asp?ID=3

Current as of February 2003

Index